FOURTH EDITION

LINGUISTICS FOR NON-LINGUISTS

A Primer with Exercises

FRANK PARKER

Louisiana State University (Retired)

KATHRYN RILEY

Illinois Institute of Technology

PEARSON

Boston ■ New York ■ San Francisco
Mexico City ■ Montreal ■ Toronto ■ London ■ Madrid ■ Munich ■ Paris
Hong Kong ■ Singapore ■ Tokyo ■ Cape Town ■ Sydney

Executive Editor and Publisher: *Stephen D. Dragin*
Senior Editorial Assistant: *Barbara Strickland*
Production Supervisor: *Joe Sweeney*
Editorial-Production Service: *Walsh & Associates, Inc.*
Composition and Prepress Buyer: *Linda Cox*
Manufacturing Buyer: *Andrew Turso*
Cover Administrator: *Joel Gendron*
Electronic Composition: *Omegatype Composition, Inc.*

For related titles and support materials, visit our online catalog at www.ablongman.com.

Library of Congress Cataloging-in-Publication Data

Parker, Frank, 1946–
Linguistics for non-linguists : a primer with exercises / Frank Parker, Kathryn Riley—4th ed.
p. cm.
Includes bibliographical references and index.
ISBN 0-205-42118-0
1. Linguistics. I. Riley, Kathryn Louise, 1951– II. Title.

P121.P334 2004
410—dc22

2004051072

Printed in the United States of America

10 9 8 7 6 5 4 09 08 07 06 05

CONTENTS

PREFACE

In revising *Linguistics for Non-Linguists,* our goal has been to retain those features that have made it useful to readers seeking an introduction to the study of language, while at the same time updating and improving the book. Accordingly, we have kept many key elements of previous editions: a focus on English data; clearly written explanations, supplemented by numerous examples and figures; hundreds of exercises, many of them new, enabling readers to check their understanding of the material; and a "top-down" organization of the theory chapters, beginning with the less technical area of pragmatics and moving to the more technical area of phonology. (At the same time, however, the self-contained nature of the theory chapters allows readers to approach them in a different order if they wish to.)

We strongly believe that students learn best by "doing" linguistics, and, to this end, we have added dozens of new exercises. Wherever possible, we like to introduce "live" data into the exercises, since much of what makes linguistics interesting is its ability to explain everyday phenomena—the dialogue in a movie, a billboard sign, a newspaper headline, a TV advertisement, a note on an office door, and so on. As in the previous edition, most exercises are integrated into the text of each chapter, so that they appear immediately after related material. Answers are provided at the end of the book for those exercises marked with a dagger (†), to help readers check their work. In addition to the exercises within each chapter, supplementary exercises at the end of each chapter are designed to offer further practice, sometimes introducing more complex data or non-English data. Following the supplementary exercises is a new feature, exploratory exercises. In general, these require more research or analysis beyond what can be accomplished within a single classroom period. These exploratory exercises can also form the basis for short papers.

In terms of content, although the chapter topics have not changed, much of the material throughout has been revised and updated. In particular, Chapter 4, Syntax, now includes a short section on X-bar theory; Chapter 8, First-Language Acquisition, includes a more detailed discussion of acquisition stages; Chapter 10, Written Language, includes a fuller treatment of non-alphabetic writing systems; Chapter 11, Language Processing, focuses more on topics from psycholinguistics and discourse analysis; and the discussion of disorders in Chapter 12, Neurology of Language, has been revised to focus on various types of aphasia. We also updated many of the supplementary readings at the end of each chapter, while still attempting to give the reader a selection of both classic and contemporary resources.

Our thanks go to John Algeo, Jody Bailey, Matt Bauer, Lionel Bender, Kim Campbell, Robin Cosgrove, Chris Healy, D. B. Dodson, Tom Kenny, Jo Mackiewicz, Alan Manning, Chuck Meyer, Anna Schmidt, John Spartz, Dick Veit, Tom Walsh, Donna Glee Williams, and Catherine Winter, who have read and commented on various parts of this or previous editions. Special thanks to Amanda, Chex, Remington, and Roma. Thanks also to the following reviewers for their comments on the manuscript: Gary Barricklow, Rider

University; Norbert Francis, Northern Arizona University; Jeffrey P. Kaplan, San Diego State University; and Suzanne Ross, St. Cloud State University. We are especially indebted to the hundreds of students to whom we have taught linguistics over the years, many of whose questions and observations we have tried to address in this book.

Frank Parker
Kathryn Riley

CHAPTER ONE

Introduction

The title of this book, *Linguistics for Non-Linguists,* delimits both its scope and audience. Let us say something about each one. The primary audience for which this book is intended are people who are not linguists, but who feel they need some familiarity with the fundamentals of linguistic theory in order to help them practice their profession. This includes specialists in such fields as speech-language pathology, experimental phonetics, communication, education, English as a second language (ESL), composition, reading, anthropology, folklore, foreign languages, and literature.

The common thread among these disciplines is that, in one form or another and at one time or another, they all deal with language. For example, a researcher in business communication might try to characterize how different managerial styles are reflected in the way that managers give directions to their employees, noting that some managers give instructions like *Type this memo* while others say *Could you type this memo?* A kindergarten teacher might observe that students give more correct responses to questions like *Which of these girls is taller?* than to questions like *Which of these girls is shorter?* A composition instructor might encounter a student who writes *I wanted to know what could I do* rather than *I wanted to know what I could do.* An ESL teacher might have a student who writes *I will taking physics next semester,* rather than *I will take* or *I will be taking physics next semester.* A speech-language pathologist might attempt to evaluate a child who says *tay* for *stay.* In each case, these specialists have encountered phenomena that cannot be understood without some familiarity with concepts from linguistic theory.

Realistically speaking, however, there are several practical reasons that may have prevented these specialists from acquiring a background in basic linguistic theory. First, courses in linguistics are virtually nonexistent in high schools, and colleges and universities that have such courses generally do not require them of all students. Second, each university curriculum (especially a professional curriculum) quite naturally tends to focus its students' attention on the central concerns of its discipline. Of course, the more courses required of students within their discipline, the fewer they can take from fields outside of their major. Such factors often prevent students in allied areas from being exposed to linguistics. Third, once people complete their formal education, it is often difficult for them to supplement their knowledge with formal coursework, especially in an unfamiliar area. Finally, linguistics, at least at first glance, appears to be incredibly complicated. Articles and books on the subject are often filled with charts, tables, diagrams, and unfamiliar notation, and many people simply give up in frustration. In short, there are a number of practical reasons for this gap in the flow of information between linguistics and other fields that deal with language. This book is an attempt to solve this problem, at least in part. It is specifically designed to convey a basic understanding of linguistic theory to specialists in neighboring fields, whether students or practicing professionals.

The book is organized as follows. Chapters 2 through 6 cover the theoretical areas of pragmatics, semantics, syntax, morphology, and phonology, respectively. Chapters 7 through 12 cover the applied areas of language variation, first-language acquisition, second-language acquisition, written language, language processing, and the neurology of language. Each chapter contains text with exercises, supplementary readings, and supplementary exercises. The text of each chapter focuses on some of the central ideas in that area of linguistics; we have not tried to cover each subject in breadth or in detail. Also, we have made an effort to make explicit the reasoning that lies behind each area discussed. Each chapter begins with a set of observations that can be made about that subject, and the rest of the chapter constructs a partial theory to account for the original observations. Throughout the text, we have tried to emphasize the fact that linguistic theory is a set of categories and principles devised by linguists in order to explain observations about language. (More on this subject later.)

The supplementary readings at the end of each chapter consist of an annotated list of several articles and books that we have found useful in introducing others to the field. We have made no attempt to cover each field exhaustively or to restrict the readings to the latest findings, since each of the 11 areas covered here has numerous textbooks and primary works devoted to it. However, anyone interested in pursuing one of these areas can at least begin by consulting the supplementary readings.

The exercises throughout the chapter are included as a means for you to check your understanding of the text and gain practice in working with the basic concepts. In most cases, each of these exercises has a specific answer or range of answers within the framework of the chapter (for example, "Would a child exposed to English be more likely to acquire the meaning of *long* or *short* first? What principle accounts for this?"). A dagger (†) in front of an exercise means that its answer is provided at the end of the book, so that you can occasionally check your analysis as you are working through the exercises. In addition to exercises throughout the chapter, at the end of each chapter, following the supplementary readings, you will also find supplementary exercises and at least one exploratory exercise. While some of the supplementary exercises are similar to the in-chapter exercises, others introduce more complicated data or data from languages other than English. The exploratory exercises, in general, ask for analysis that would require work outside of a normal classroom period, such as additional research or analysis beyond that required by the other exercises.

Obviously, an introductory book such as this has several potential limitations. First, there are entire subdomains of linguistics that are not included—for example, animal communication and computational linguistics, to name just two. The experience of having taught linguistics for nearly 30 years convinces us that students and professionals from neighboring fields most often need a solid grounding in the core areas of pragmatics, semantics, syntax, morphology, and phonology. Once they have a basic understanding of these areas, they have little trouble mastering the applied areas that overlap with their own field of specialization. We have included chapters on language variation, first- and second-language acquisition, written language, language processing, and the neurology of language—six applied areas that seem to us to be of the most importance to the greatest number of neighboring fields.

Second, this book is written from the viewpoint of our own understanding and interpretation of the field of linguistics. No one can study an academic field without developing a particular view of that field, and certainly we are no exceptions. For example, our own views of the field are biased toward the perspective of **generative grammar,** a view of language that the linguist Noam Chomsky began developing 50 years ago and that has been especially influential on the study of syntax, phonology, and language acquisition. In short, it is wise to keep these limitations in mind as you read this book.

Having discussed the audience and scope of this book, let's now turn to its primary subject matter—linguistic theory. There are two questions central to an understanding of this field. First, what do linguists study? And second, how do they go about studying it? Let's take these questions one at a time. First, one common understanding of linguistic theory is that it is the study of the psychological system that underlies our ability to produce and interpret utterances in our native language. That is, in order to speak to one another, we need to know things about language that we're not aware of consciously. Linguistic theory is the study of this knowledge. It is not the study of how human beings actually produce speech with their vocal mechanism, nor is it the study of speech itself. Thus, we need to distinguish three different domains: (1) the psychological system of language; (2) the means of implementing this system (the vocal tract); and (3) the product (speech).

An analogy may help clarify the distinction among these three areas. In talking about computers, we can differentiate at least three domains: software, hardware, and output. The software (or program) is essentially the mind of the machine; it is the set of instructions that tells the machine what to do. The hardware is the machine itself; it is the physical mechanism that carries out the instructions contained in the software. The output is the final product that comes out of the hardware; it is the tangible result of the software having told the hardware what to do. Thus, in a very loose sense, the psychological system of language is like the software; it is essentially the mind of the system; it provides the instructions. The vocal mechanism is like the hardware; it is the physical system that implements the language. Speech is like the output; it is the final product of the vocal tract, the tangible result of the language faculty having told the vocal tract what to do. This analogy is illustrated in Figure 1.1. Thus, linguistic theory is the study of the psychological system of language. Consequently, the vocal tract and speech are of interest to linguists to the extent that they shed light on this psychological system: the internalized, unconscious knowledge that enables a speaker to produce and understand utterances in his or her native language.

Now that we have some idea of what theoretical linguists study, let's consider how they study it. At this point, our computer analogy breaks down. If a computer specialist wants to study the software of a particular computer system, he or she can access it and examine it directly (by requesting the hardware to produce the software as output) or question the person who designed it. In other words, an understanding of how the software works is part of the conscious knowledge of the person who designed it, and consequently it is directly accessible to anyone who wants to examine it. Language, on the other hand, is not so

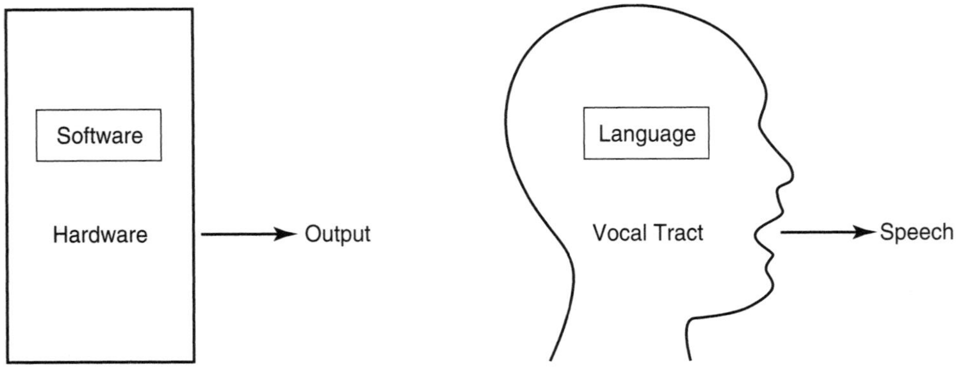

FIGURE 1.1 Analogy between computer system and linguistic system

easily accessible. First, knowledge of language is unconscious in the sense that speakers of a language cannot articulate the rules of that language. Moreover, although linguists can examine the vocal tract and the sounds it produces, they cannot examine language directly. Rather, they must approach the properties of this psychological system *indirectly.*

There are a number of methods that linguists use to infer properties of the system. Some linguists look at language change: they compare different historical stages in the development of a language and try to infer what properties of the system would account for changes. Other linguists look at language pathology: they compare normal language output to that of patients with aphasia (brain damage that has disrupted normal linguistic functioning) and try to infer what properties of the system would account for such abnormalities. Still others look at language universals—features that all human languages seem to have in common—and try to infer what properties of the system would account for these similarities. The list of approaches goes on and on.

Here, however, we will discuss in some detail another common method that theoretical linguists use to infer properties of language: investigating speakers' judgments about sentences. Under this method, the linguist asks informants (native speakers of the language under investigation) questions such as the following: Is utterance X an acceptable sentence in your language? Does utterance X have the same meaning as utterance Y? In utterance X, can word A refer to word B? And so on and so forth. Consider, for example, the following sentences.

(1) John thinks that Bill hates him.
(2) John thinks that Bill hates himself.

The linguist might present (1) and (2) to some informants and ask them to judge the two sentences for acceptability. In response, the informants would undoubtedly say that both (1) and (2) are perfectly acceptable. That is, both are completely unremarkable; people say such things day in and day out, and they go completely unnoticed. (In contrast, sentences such as *Him thinks that Bill hates John* and *John thinks that himself hates Bill* are remarkable; that is, speakers of English do not typically produce such sentences.) After having determined that both (1) and (2) are acceptable, the linguist might ask the informants the following questions. (The expected answers appear in parentheses.)

- In (1), can *him* refer to *John?* (Yes.) Can *him* refer to *Bill?* (No.)
- In (2), can *himself* refer to *John?* (No.) Can *himself* refer to *Bill?* (Yes.)
- Do sentences (1) and (2) have the same meaning? (No.)

Having gathered these data, the linguist would then try to infer the properties of the internal linguistic system of the informants that would account for these judgments. For example, the linguist might hypothesize that English contains at least two kinds of pronouns: **personal pronouns** (e.g., *him*) and **reflexive pronouns** (e.g., *himself*). Moreover, the linguist might hypothesize that a pronoun may have an **antecedent** (i.e., a preceding word or phrase to which the pronoun refers). Finally, the linguist might infer that the antecedents of these two types of pronouns behave differently; that is, the antecedent for a personal pronoun and the antecedent for a reflexive pronoun cannot occupy the same position within a sentence. In order to determine exactly where these antecedents can appear, the linguist might construct some related sentences (e.g., *John hates him, John hates himself,* and so on) and present them to informants for different types of judgments. This process would continue until the linguist had formed a picture of what the psychological system of the informants looks like, at least with respect to where the antecedents for personal and reflexive pronouns can appear.

There are several points to note about this method of inquiry. First, if the linguist is a native speaker of the language being studied, the linguist can, and often does, serve as both informant and analyst. In the previous example, any native speaker of English would be able to determine that (1) and (2) are both acceptable, but that they have entirely different meanings. Moreover, any native speaker of English would be able to trace these differences in meaning to the fact that in (1) *him* can refer to *John* but not to *Bill,* and in (2) *himself* can refer to *Bill* but not to *John.* In a clear-cut example like this, there is no need to present these sentences to thousands, hundreds, dozens, or even two speakers of English. The linguist can be reasonably certain in advance that they would all judge the sentences in the same way. Second, the linguist, in forming a picture of the internal linguistic system of the informant, is in essence constructing a **theory** of that system. That is, concepts such as personal pronoun, reflexive pronoun, and antecedent are not directly observable in the utterances themselves. Rather, the linguist *hypothesizes* such concepts to account for the observable fact that speakers of English can make such clear-cut judgments about sentences like (1) and (2). In short, the linguist uses the directly observable judgments of the informant (i.e., the data) to draw inferences about the unobservable internal system that governs such judgments (i.e., to construct a theory). This procedure can be schematized as follows.

OBSERVABLE DATA →	**LINGUIST →**	**THEORY**
Speaker's judgments of acceptability, sameness of meaning, reference, and so forth.	Makes hypotheses about internal structure of speaker's psychological linguistic system.	English has two kinds of pronouns, whose antecedents appear in different positions.

This, of course, is not a complete theory of English; it is not even a complete theory of where antecedents for personal and reflexive pronouns can occur in English. After all, the linguist in this hypothetical example has not determined where the antecedent for each type of pronoun can occur, but simply that they cannot occur in exactly the same positions within a sentence. The point of this example has been to illustrate one central goal of linguistics: constructing a theory about the unobservable, based upon observable data. And one type of data that linguists commonly use is the judgments of informants.

Having drawn a distinction between data and theory, let's pursue our example further and try to construct a more precise theory of where the antecedents for personal and reflexive pronouns can occur. The sentences in (1) and (2) are repeated in (1a-b) and (2a-b), but here we have incorporated the judgments of our hypothetical informants. (An arrow indicates the antecedent of a pronoun, and an asterisk indicates an unacceptable sentence.)

(1a) *John* thinks that Bill hates *him.*

(1b) *John thinks that *Bill* hates *him.*

(2a) **John* thinks that Bill hates *himself.*

(2b) John thinks that *Bill* hates *himself.*

Each of these structures is to be interpreted as follows.

(1a) is acceptable, if *John* is the antecedent of *him.*
(1b) is unacceptable, if *Bill* is the antecedent of *him.*
(2a) is unacceptable, if *John* is the antecedent of *himself.*
(2b) is acceptable, if *Bill* is the antecedent of *himself.*

How can we explain these observations? That is, what principle accounts for the distribution of antecedents for personal and reflexive pronouns? There is no foolproof method for knowing where to begin. We simply have to start with an educated guess and see how accurately it accounts for our observations. We can begin by noting that each of our sample sentences is complex; that is, it contains more than one clause. In fact, each of our sample sentences has exactly two clauses. Moreover, within each sentence, the dividing line between the two clauses comes precisely between *thinks* and *that.* The sentences in (1) and (2) are repeated once more, with a vertical line separating the clauses in each sentence.

(1a) *John* thinks | that Bill hates *him.*

(1b) *John thinks | that *Bill* hates *him.*

(2a) **John* thinks | that Bill hates *himself.*

(2b) John thinks | that *Bill* hates *himself.*

Now, if we consider just the examples in (1), it is clear that the personal pronoun *him* requires an antecedent *outside* of its clause. Note that in (1a), which is acceptable, the antecedent for *him* is in a different clause; but in (1b), which is unacceptable, the antecedent for *him* is in the same clause. Likewise, if we consider just the examples in (2), it is clear that the reflexive pronoun *himself* requires an antecedent *inside* of its clause. Note that in (2b), which is acceptable, the antecedent for *himself* is in the same clause; but in (2a), which is unacceptable, the antecedent for *himself* is in a different clause.

At this point, we might abstract away from the particular data in (1) and (2) and propose the following general theory governing the antecedents of personal and reflexive pronouns:

- The antecedent for a personal pronoun *cannot* be within the clause containing the pronoun.
- The antecedent for a reflexive pronoun *must* be within the clause containing the pronoun.

The next step would be to test our theory on additional examples containing personal and reflexive pronouns. If our theory predicts speakers' judgments about these other sentences, then it gains strength. If, on the other hand, it makes incorrect predictions, then we need to go back and revise the theory.

Let's consider a few other examples. The sentence *Mary lies to herself* is acceptable if *herself* refers to *Mary;* likewise, this sentence is unacceptable if *herself* refers to someone other than *Mary.* Both of these judgments are predicted by our theory: *herself* is a reflexive pronoun and thus must have an antecedent within the same clause, in this case *Mary.* Consider another example. The sentence *Mary lies to her* is acceptable only if *her* is someone other than *Mary.* Once again our theory predicts this judgment; *her* is a personal pronoun and thus cannot have an antecedent within the same clause; since *Mary* is in the same clause as *her,* it can't serve as the antecedent.

Both of these examples fit within the theory we have constructed, but what about a sentence like **John thinks that Mary hates himself?* This sentence is unacceptable regardless of whether *himself* refers to *John* or *Mary.* Our theory correctly predicts that *himself* cannot refer to *John,* since *himself* is reflexive and *John* appears in a different clause. However, our theory incorrectly predicts that *himself* should be able to refer to *Mary,* since *Mary* is in the same clause. The problem, of course, is that *himself* can refer only to words designating a male, and the word *Mary* normally designates a female. Thus, we would have to revise our rule to stipulate that pronouns and their antecedents must match in gender. This process of testing and revising the theory goes on until the theory predicts the data (in this case, speakers' judgments) exactly.

There are several points worth making about this process of theory construction. First, we have been able to account for some fairly puzzling phenomena (e.g., why can't *him* refer to *Bill* in *John thinks that Bill hates him?*) with two simple statements concerning the distribution of antecedents for personal and reflexive pronouns. Second, in the process of devising these statements (or rules), we had to try several guesses (or hypotheses) before we hit upon one that seems to provide a reasonable explanation (or theory) of the data in (1) and (2). Third, and most importantly, our theory is made up of categories (e.g., pronoun, antecedent, clause, gender) and rules (e.g., a reflexive pronoun must have an antecedent within the same clause) which are not part of the data themselves. Rather, these categories and rules are postulated to account for the fact that speakers of English interpret sentences such as (1) and (2) in a specific, limited, and uniform manner. In short, this is what linguistic theory is all about: we try to form a theory of a psychological system that we cannot observe directly, by examining the superficial manifestations of this system (i.e., speakers' judgments about utterances).

This idea of trying to model what we cannot directly observe by drawing inferences from what we can observe is not restricted to linguistic theory. In 1938, the physicists Albert Einstein and Leopold Infeld wrote a book entitled *The Evolution of Physics.* In it they had this to say:

> In our endeavor to understand reality we are somewhat like a man trying to understand the mechanism of a closed watch. He sees the face and the moving hands, even hears its ticking, but he has no way of opening the case. If he is ingenious he may form some picture of a mechanism which could be responsible for all the things he observes, but he may never be quite sure his picture is the only one which could explain his observations. He will never he able to compare his picture with the real mechanism and he cannot even imagine the possibility of the meaning of such a comparison. (1938:31)

These physicists are essentially describing the same position that theoretical linguists are in: they are trying to formulate hypotheses about the structure of what they cannot observe, based upon what they can observe. In studying language, linguists cannot observe a speaker's mind. They can, however, observe the speaker's judgments about sentences. On the basis of these observable judgments, linguists can construct a theory of the unobservable psychological system that underlies these judgments. Moreover, they will never know for sure if their theory is correct; all they can do is continue to test it against an ever-expanding range of data and revise it as necessary.

To summarize, this book is intended to provide specialists in fields neighboring linguistics with a basic introduction to the principles and methods of linguistic theory. Under one common definition, linguistic theory is the study of the psychological system of language; that is, of the unconscious knowledge that lies behind our ability to produce and interpret utterances in a language. However, since this system cannot be observed directly, it must be studied indirectly. One common method is to infer properties of the system by analyzing speakers' judgments about utterances. The goal of this enterprise is to construct a theory of the psychological system of language. This theory is composed of categories, relationships, and rules, which are not part of the directly observable physical world. We will take up the topic of theories again in the final chapter.

CHAPTER TWO

Pragmatics

Pragmatics is the study of how language is used to communicate within its situational context. Pragmatics is distinct from grammar, which is the study of the internal structure of language. (Grammar is generally divided into a number of particular areas of study: semantics, syntax, morphology, and phonology. These areas are covered in Chapters 3–6.) Keeping in mind this distinction between pragmatics (language use) and grammar (language structure), let's consider some observations that we can make about how language is used.

(1) If Jack says *Kathy's cooking dinner tonight,* and Jill replies with *Better stock up on Alka-Seltzer,* an observer might conclude that Kathy is not a good cook.

(2) The utterance *I apologize for stepping on your toe* can constitute an act of apology. The utterance *John apologized to Mary for stepping on her toe* cannot.

(3) The utterance *I now pronounce you husband and wife* can constitute an act of marriage if spoken by an appropriate authority, such as an ordained Catholic priest. If uttered by an 8-year-old child, however, it cannot.

(4) An appropriate answer to the question *Do you have the time?* might be *7:15;* an inappropriate answer would be *Yes.*

(5) When a friend says something that you agree with, you might respond by saying *You can say that again.* But it would be inappropriate for your friend to then repeat what he or she originally said.

Observation (1) illustrates the fact that sentences can imply information that is not actually stated. Observation (2) illustrates the fact that we can *do* things by uttering sentences, as well as say things. Observation (3) illustrates the fact that the nature of the participants in a verbal exchange can determine the effect of what is actually said. Observation (4) illustrates the fact that a correct answer to a question is not necessarily appropriate. Observation (5) illustrates the fact that speakers don't always mean exactly what they say.

All of these phenomena are pragmatic in nature. That is, they have to do with the way we use language to communicate in a particular context rather than the way language is structured internally. Moreover, we will assume that the phenomena in (1–5) are systematic; that is, they are governed by a system of principles. What we will now try to do is construct the system of principles that will account for these phenomena. Keep in mind that what follows is a theory designed to account for the observations in (1–5).

Implicature

In his article "Logic and Conversation," the philosopher Paul Grice pointed out that an utterance can *imply* a proposition (i.e., a statement) that is not part of the utterance and that does not follow as a necessary consequence of the utterance. Grice called such an implied statement an **implicature.** Consider the following example. John says to his wife, Mary, *Uncle Chester is coming over for dinner tonight,* and Mary responds with *I guess I'd better hide the liquor.* Someone hearing this interchange might draw the inference that Uncle Chester has a drinking problem. In Grice's terms, we might say that Mary's utterance **raises the implicature** that Uncle Chester has a drinking problem.

There are three important points to note about this example. First, the implicature (Uncle Chester has a drinking problem) is not part of Mary's utterance *(I guess I'd better hide the liquor).* Second, the implicature does not follow as a necessary consequence of Mary's utterance. (A necessary consequence of an utterance is called an **entailment** and will be covered in the chapter on semantics.) Third, it is possible for an utterance to raise more than one implicature, or to raise different implicatures if uttered in different contexts. For example, Mary's response *(I guess I'd better hide the liquor)* might raise the implicature that Uncle Chester is a teetotaler, and that the mere sight of alcohol and its consumption offends him, so Mary is hiding it from his view. Thus, implicatures are heavily dependent upon the context of an utterance, including the participants. However, we have not yet constructed any hypotheses about how these implicatures arise. We will now consider what such a theory might look like.

Conversational Maxims

Grice proposes that conversations are governed by what he calls the Cooperative Principle: the assumption that participants in a conversation are cooperating with each other. This Cooperative Principle, in turn, consists of four **conversational maxims: Quantity**—a participant's contribution should be informative; **Quality**—a participant's contribution should be true; **Relation**—a participant's contribution should be relevant; and **Manner**—a participant's contribution should be clear. Grice's claim, however, is not that we strictly adhere to these maxims when we converse; rather, he claims that we interpret what we hear *as if* it conforms to these maxims. That is, when a maxim is violated, we draw an inference (i.e., an implicature) which makes the utterance conform to these maxims. Grice used the term **flouting** to describe the *intentional* violation of a maxim for the purpose of conveying an unstated proposition. This, then, would constitute a theory of how implicatures arise. Let's now consider how this theory of conversational implicature applies in some hypothetical cases.

Maxim of Quantity. This maxim states that each participant's contribution to a conversation should be no more or less informative than required. Suppose Kenny and Tom are college roommates. Kenny walks into the living room of their apartment, where Tom is reading a book. Kenny asks Tom *What are you reading?* Tom responds with *A book,* which raises an implicature. Kenny reasons (unconsciously) as follows: I asked Tom what he was reading, and my question required him to tell me either the title of its book or at least its subject matter. Instead, he told me what I could already see for myself. He appears to be flouting the

Maxim of Quantity. There must be a reason that he gave less information than the situation requires. The inference (i.e., the implicature) that I draw is that he does not want to be disturbed, and thus is trying to end the conversation.

Maxim of Quality. This maxim states that each participant's contribution should be truthful and based on sufficient evidence. Suppose an undergraduate in a geography class says, in response to a question from the instructor, *Reno's the capital of Nevada.* The instructor, Mr. Barbados, then says *Yeah, and London's the capital of New Jersey.* The instructor's utterance raises an implicature. The student reasons (unconsciously) as follows: Mr. Barbados said that London is the capital of New Jersey; he knows that is not true. He appears to be flouting the Maxim of Quality; there must be a reason for him saying something patently false. The inference (i.e., the implicature) I draw is that my answer is false (i.e., Reno is not the capital of Nevada). (This and the next two examples are adapted from Levinson [1983].)

Maxim of Relation. This maxim states that each participant's contribution should be relevant to the subject of the conversation. Suppose a man wakes up in the morning and asks his wife *What time is it?* She responds with *Well, the paper's already come.* Her statement raises an implicature. The husband reasons (unconsciously) as follows: I asked about the time, and she mentioned something seemingly unrelated—the arrival of the newspaper. She appears to be flouting the Maxim of Relation; there must be some reason for her seemingly irrelevant comment. The inference (i.e., the implicature) I draw is that she doesn't know the exact time, but the arrival of the newspaper has something to do with the time, namely that it is now past the time of day that the newspaper usually comes (i.e., 7:00 A.M.).

Maxim of Manner. This maxim states that each participant's contribution should be expressed in a reasonably clear fashion; that is, it should not be vague, ambiguous, or excessively wordy. Suppose Mr. and Mrs. Jones are out for a Sunday drive with their two preschool children. Mr. Jones says to Mrs. Jones *Let's stop and get something to eat.* Mrs. Jones responds with *Okay, but not M-c-D-o-n-a-l-d-s.* Mrs. Jones' statement raises an implicature. Mr. Jones reasons (unconsciously) as follows: She spelled out the word *McDonald's,* which is certainly not the clearest way of saying it. She appears to be flouting the Maxim of Manner; there must be a reason for her lack of clarity. Since the kids cannot spell, the inference (i.e., the implicature) I draw is that she does not want the children to understand that part of her statement.

In summary, an implicature is a proposition implied by an utterance, but neither part of nor a logical consequence of that utterance. An implicature arises in the mind of a hearer when the speaker flouts (i.e., intentionally violates) one of the maxims of Quantity, Quality, Relation, or Manner.

Exercise A

1. In the movie *The Doctor,* an orderly is wheeling patient Jack McKee (William Hurt) down a hospital corridor on a gurney. McKee is nearly naked except for a single sheet draped over him. McKee looks up at the orderly and says, *Do you think you could get me a thinner sheet?*

(continued)

Exercise A *Continued*

I'm not sure everybody can see through this one. McKee's utterance raises an implicature—namely, that he wants more covering. Which of Grice's maxims does McKee flout?

2. Assume that you are teaching a course. A fellow instructor approaches you after you have graded a test and asks *How did Mr. Jones do?* You respond with *Well, he wrote something down for every question.*

a. Which of Grice's maxims does your response appear to flout?

b. What is the implicature raised by your response?

†3. You ask a friend *Do you know where Billy Bob is?* The friend responds with *Well, he didn't meet me for lunch like he was supposed to.*

a. Which of Grice's maxims does your friend's statement appear to flout?

b. What is the implicature raised by your friend's statement?

4. In each of the exchanges below, the italicized phrase indicates that the second speaker is trying to avoid violating a conversational maxim (i.e., Quantity, Quality, Relation, or Manner). Name the maxim.

a. WAITER: What can I get you, sir?
CUSTOMER: I'll have the roast beef. Oh, *by the way,* where's the phone?

b. JOHN: What happened during your interview today?
MARY: Well, *to make a long story short,* they didn't hire me.

5. Gretchen is married and has two children, ages 7 and 4 years. In a conversation critical of her father-in-law, held in the presence of her children, she referred to her father-in-law as *the first generation* and to her children as *the third generation.*

a. Which of Grice's maxims does Gretchen appear to flout?

b. What is the implicature raised by Gretchen's utterance?

6. For each of the following exchanges, determine (a) which of Grice's maxims the second speaker's utterance appears to flout, and (b) the implicature raised by the second speaker.

a. BOB: Do you want some dessert?
RAY: Do birds have wings?

b. DIANE: Don't you think John is a nice guy?
SUSAN: Yeah, he's about as sensitive as Attila the Hun.

c. JOHN: Who was that man I saw you with yesterday?
MARY: That was just someone.

d. SALES CLERK: Could I have your name?
CUSTOMER: It's K-A-T-H-R-Y-N R-I-L-E-Y.

7. Consider the exchange in Exercise (6d). What implicature would a customer raise by spelling his name if it were *Frank Parker?*

Speech Acts

In his book *How to Do Things with Words,* British philosopher John Austin had the fundamental insight that an utterance can be used to perform an act. That is, he was the first to point out that in uttering a sentence, we can *do* things as well as *say* things. (Before Austin, philosophers held that sentences were used simply to say things.) For example, if you say to someone who is leaving your office *Please close the door,* you are not just saying something but also making a request. Likewise, if you say to a friend after a fight *I'm sorry for the way I acted,* you are not just saying something but also apologizing. Finally, if you say to your boss *I'll come in on Saturday to finish the Katznelson Project,* you're not just saying something but you're also making a commitment.

Thus, each speech event (or **speech act**) has at least two facets to it: a **locutionary act** (i.e., the act of saying something) and an **illocutionary act** (i.e., the act of doing something). These concepts are defined in more detail as follows.

Locutionary Act. This is the act of simply uttering a sentence from a language; it is a description of what the speaker *says.* Typically, it is the act of using a referring expression (e.g., a noun phrase) and a predicating expression (e.g., a verb phrase) to express a proposition. For instance, if a doctor says to a patient *You must stop smoking,* the referring expression is *you,* and the predicating expression is *stop smoking.*

Illocutionary Act. This is what the speaker *does* in uttering a sentence. Illocutionary acts include such acts as stating, requesting, questioning, promising, apologizing, and appointing. In the preceding example *(You must stop smoking),* the illocutionary act is one of ordering. The illocutionary act is sometimes called the **illocutionary force** of the utterance.

In the rest of this section, we will examine speech acts first from the perspective of the illocutionary act involved and then from the perspective of the locutionary act.

Classification of Illocutionary Acts

The philosopher John Searle (1976), one of Austin's former students, pointed out that there is a seemingly endless number of illocutionary acts. There are statements, assertions, denials, requests, commands, warnings, promises, vows, offers, apologies, thanks, condolences, appointments, namings, resignations, and so forth. At the same time, he observed that some illocutionary acts are more closely related than others. For example, promises and vows seem to be more alike than, say, promises and requests. Thus Searle attempted to classify illocutionary acts into the following types.

- **Representative.** A representative is an utterance used to describe some state of affairs—for example, *I have five toes on my right foot.* This class includes acts of stating, asserting, denying, confessing, admitting, notifying, concluding, predicting, and so on.
- **Directive.** A directive is an utterance used to try to get the hearer to do something—for example, *Shut the door.* This class includes acts of requesting, ordering, forbidding, warning, advising, suggesting, insisting, recommending, and so on.
- **Question.** A question is an utterance used to get the hearer to provide information—for example, *Who won the 2000 presidential election?* This class includes acts of asking, inquiring, and so on. (Note: Searle treated questions as a subcategory of directives; for our purposes, however, it is more useful to treat them as a separate category.)

- **Commissive.** A commissive is an utterance used to commit the speaker to do something—for example, *I'll meet you at the library at 10:00 P.M.* This class includes acts of promising, vowing, volunteering, offering, guaranteeing, pledging, betting, and so on.
- **Expressive.** An expressive is an utterance used to express the emotional state of the speaker—for example, *I'm sorry for calling you a dweeb.* This class includes acts of apologizing, thanking, congratulating, condoling, welcoming, deploring, objecting, and so on.
- **Declaration.** A declaration is an utterance used to change the status of some entity—for example, *You're out* uttered by an umpire at a baseball game. This class includes acts of appointing, naming, resigning, baptizing, surrendering, excommunicating, arresting, and so on.

Exercise B

1. Classify each of the following utterances as a directive, commissive, representative, expressive, question, or declaration. (Take each utterance at face value; i.e., don't read anything into it.)

a. A child says to her playmate, *Happy birthday.*
b. A doctor says to a patient, *I advise you to stop smoking.*
†c. One secretary says to another, *My daughter's getting married in August.*
d. A priest says over an infant, *I baptize you in the name of . . .*
e. A mother says to her daughter, *Who washed the dishes?*
f. A passerby says to a motorist with a flat tire, *Let me help you with that.*
g. One friend says to another, *I swear I won't see Martha again.*
h. A parent says to her child, *I forbid you to leave your room.*
†i. A man says to a friend, *What time is it?*
j. A buyer says to a seller, *I agree to your terms.*

2. In the movie *The Lonely Passion of Judith Hearne,* James Madden is telling Judith how he has been wronged by his daughter. The following interchange ensues.

JUDITH: Oh, I'm sorry.
JAMES: You don't have to be sorry; you didn't do anything.

James misinterprets Judith's remark, because it is ambiguous as to what illocutionary act it performs. What are the two illocutionary acts that *I'm sorry* can perform? (Hint: They are both types of expressives.)

Felicity Conditions

Early on, Austin realized that context was an important factor in the *valid* performance of an illocutionary act. He noted, for example, that the participants and the circumstances must be appropriate. An umpire at a baseball game can cause a player to be out by uttering *You're out!* but an excited fan in the bleachers cannot. Likewise, the act must be executed completedly and correctly by all participants. If during a game of hide-and-seek, Suzie says to Billy *You're it,* and Billy responds with *I'm not playing,* then the act of naming is not valid. Finally, the participants must have the appropriate intentions. If a friend says to you *I promise I'll meet you at the movies at 8:00 P.M.,* but actually plans to be home watching television at that time, the act of promising is not valid. Austin called these conditions **felicity conditions.**

These conditions help us account for the relationship between specific illocutionary acts within the same category. Consider the difference between two different types of representatives: assertions and lies. The felicity conditions for both are the same except that in an assertion *S believes P,* and in a lie *S doesn't believe P.* This is illustrated in the following diagram (S = speaker, H = hearer, A = act, P = proposition).

REPRESENTATIVES

	ASSERTION	LIE
FELICITY CONDITIONS:	**1.** S believes H doesn't know P.	**1.** Same
	2. S wants H to know P.	**2.** Same
	3. S believes P.	**3.** S doesn't believe P.

Now consider the difference between two different types of directives: requests and orders. The felicity conditions for orders are exactly the same as those for requests except that orders have the additional condition that *S has authority over H.* This is illustrated in the following diagram.

DIRECTIVES

	REQUEST	ORDER
FELICITY CONDITIONS:	**1.** S believes H able to do A.	**1.** Same
	2. A is something H would not normally do.	**2.** Same
		3. S has authority over H.

Consider, finally, the difference between two types of commissives: promises and threats. Note that two of the felicity conditions are identical for both types of commissives. However, in a promise *S believes H wants A done,* and in a threat *S believes H doesn't want A done.* This is illustrated in the following diagram.

COMMISSIVES

	PROMISE	THREAT
FELICITY CONDITIONS:	**1.** S has power to perform A.	**1.** Same
	2. S would not normally do A.	**2.** Same
	3. S believes H wants A done.	**3.** S believes H doesn't want A done.

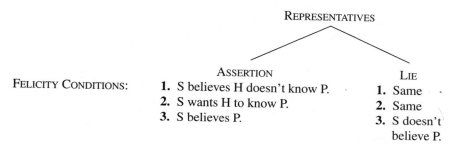

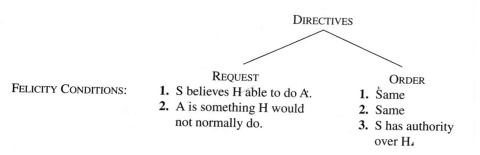

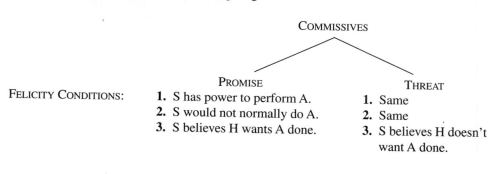

Exercise C

1. Pat and Chris are having an argument in a restaurant, and Pat throws a glass of water on Chris's shirt. Chris responds with *Thanks a lot.* What felicity condition on thanking does Chris's utterance violate?
   - **a.** The act for which one is thanked must be in the hearer's best interest.
   - **b.** The act for which one is thanked must be a past act.
   - **c.** The act for which one is thanked must be witnessed by the speaker.
   - **d.** The act for which one is thanked must be in the speaker's best interest.
   - **e.** Both (b) and (d).

†2. What felicity condition on apologies is violated by the following utterance: *I apologize for what I'm about to do.*

3. At noon a woman goes to a pharmacy to check on a prescription that is being filled. The woman is told that the prescription has to be brought from another location, but that it will arrive no later than 6:00 P.M. The woman fumes for a minute and then says, *I'm sorry, but I can't come back later this evening.* The woman's utterance appears to be an apology (i.e., *I'm sorry . . .*). However, it is not.
   - **a.** What felicity condition on apologizing does it violate?
   - **b.** If the utterance is not an apology, what is it?

4. Ordinary questions can be distinguished from exam questions—the type of question a teacher asks a student (for example, *What is the cube root of 27?*). Ordinary and exam questions differ in one of their felicity conditions. How do the felicity conditions for ordinary questions and exam questions differ?

5. A self-proclaimed "preacher" was observed at LSU's Free Speech Alley, an area of campus where speakers may publicly address passers-by. In the heat of his fervor, the preacher addressed a nearby squirrel as follows: *Repent, you squirrel; repent, you evil fornicating squirrel.* Refer to one of the felicity conditions on directives to explain why this utterance is an invalid directive.

6. It has often been noted that imperative structures, which are associated with directive speech acts, cannot be used with certain types of predicates (verb phrases); for example, **Be tall.* Use the concept of felicity conditions to explain why **Be tall* is not a valid directive, but *Stand up straight* is.

Explicit versus Nonexplicit Illocutionary Acts

One of Austin's most fundamental insights was the realization that English contains a set of verbs, each of which actually *names* the illocutionary force of that verb. Consider the following sentences:

(6) I *confess* that I stole the family jewels.

(7) I *warn* you to stop teasing your sister.

(8) May I *inquire* where you got that gun?

(9) I *promise* I'll come to your birthday party.

(10) I *apologize* for calling you a liar.

(11) I *name* this "The Good Ship Lollipop."

Note that, if said under the right circumstances, each of these sentences performs the act named by the verb: (6) constitutes a confession (a type of representative); (7) constitutes a warning (a type of directive); (8) constitutes an inquiry (a type of question); (9) constitutes a promise (a type of commissive); (10) constitutes an apology (a type of expressive); and (11) constitutes an act of naming (a type of declaration). Consequently, the verbs in each sentence are known as **performative verbs.**

In order for a performative verb to have its **performative sense** (i.e., to actually perform the illocutionary act it names), it must (i) be positive, (ii) be present tense, (iii) have a first person agent (i.e., performer of the action of the verb), and (iv) refer to a specific event. Consider, for example, the following sentences.

(12) I *promise* I'll bring the beans.
(13) I *can't promise* to bring the beans. (not positive)
(14) I *promised* I would bring the beans. (not present)
(15) *Big Bob promises* that he'll bring the beans. (not first person)
(16) I *promise* people things from time to time. (not specific)

Sentence (12) contains a performative verb *(promise)* used in its performative sense (positive, present tense, first person agent). Thus, uttering (12) can constitute a promise. On the other hand, (13–16) contain the same verb *(promise),* but in these cases it does not have its performative sense. Thus, uttering (13–16) do not constitute promises; they merely describe some state of affairs (i.e., they are all representatives).

On the other hand, not all verbs are performative verbs. Consider, for example, the verb *know,* as in the utterance *I know that the cube root of 27 is 3. Know* is not a performative verb because performative verbs must meet the following criteria: (a) a performative verb describes a *voluntary* act (you can't choose to know or not know something); (b) a performative verb describes an act that can only be performed *with words* (you can know something without saying you know it); and (c) a performative verb can be used with the performative indicator *hereby* (you can't say **I hereby know such and such*). (Recall that an asterisk before an expression means it is unacceptable.) These three tests for distinguishing performative and nonperformative verbs are summarized in the following chart.

PERFORMATIVE VERBS	**NONPERFORMATIVE VERBS**
(e.g., *deny*)	(e.g., *know*)
(a) *voluntary* act (e.g., 'denying X' is voluntary)	(a) *involuntary* act (e.g., 'knowing X' is involuntary)
(b) act can be performed *only with words* (e.g., 'denying X' requires words)	(b) act can be performed *without words* (e.g., 'knowing X' doesn't require words)
(c) can be used with *hereby* (e.g., *I hereby deny X*)	(c) can't be used with *hereby* (e.g., **I hereby know X*)

The term **explicit performative** describes an utterance that contains a performative verb used in its performative sense. Any utterance *not* containing a performative verb used in its performative sense we will call a **nonexplicit performative.** The following chart illustrates that virtually any type of illocutionary act can be achieved through either an explicit or a nonexplicit performative utterance.

	EXPLICIT PERFORMATIVE	NONEXPLICIT PERFORMATIVE
REPRESENTATIVE	I *deny* that I killed Cock Robin.	I did not kill Cock Robin.
DIRECTIVE	I *forbid* you to leave your room.	Don't leave your room.
QUESTION	I *ask* you where you were on the night of May 21.	Where were you on the night of May 21?
COMMISSIVE	I *vow* that I'll be faithful to you.	I'll be faithful to you.
EXPRESSIVE	I *thank* you for your help.	I appreciate your help.
DECLARATION	I *resign*.	I don't work here any more.

It may be necessary to expand the concept of explicit performative to include such stock utterances as *Thanks* and *Congratulations,* which serve as conventional ways of expressing *I thank you* and *I congratulate you,* respectively. Along the same lines, we might treat nouns derived from performative verbs (e.g., *advice* from *advise*) as capable of functioning as explicit performatives. Note that an utterance such as *My advice is for you to leave now* corresponds precisely to the explicit performative *I advise you to leave now.*

Exercise D

1. Explain why each of the performative verbs in the following utterances is *not* being used in its performative sense.
   - **a.** I *warned* you not to open that door.
   - **b.** *Promise* her anything, but give her Arpege. (advertisement for perfume)
   - **†c.** I *won't insist* that you leave.
   - **d.** Mr. Jones *insists* that you work late tonight.
   - **e.** *Apologize* to your Aunt Martha immediately.
2. A sign over a bar door says *Minors are forbidden to enter.*
   - **a.** What is the illocutionary force of this utterance?
   - **b.** Is the illocutionary act explicit? Explain. (Hint: Change passive voice [e.g., *Mr. X was sentenced to death*] to active [e.g., *The judge sentenced Mr. X to death*].)
3. The following announcement is made over a public address system at an airport: *Passengers are requested to proceed to gate 10.*
   - **a.** What is the illocutionary force of this utterance?
   - **b.** Is the illocutionary act explicit? Explain. (Hint: See Exercise 2.)

Direct versus Indirect Illocutionary Acts

Particular sentence types are associated with particular illocutionary acts. For example, imperative sentences *(Bring me my coat)* are uniquely designed for issuing directives. Thus, a directive delivered by means of an imperative sentence is said to constitute a **direct illocutionary act.** However, if another sentence type, for example an interrogative, is used to issue a directive *(Would you bring me my coat?),* then such an utterance is said to constitute an **indirect illocutionary act.**

Direct Illocutionary Acts. The following table gives an example of each type of illocutionary act and its associated syntactic form (i.e., sentence type).

UTTERANCE	ILLOCUTIONARY ACT	SYNTACTIC FORM
(17) Keep quiet	Directive	Imperative
(18) Do you know Mary?	*Yes-No* question	*Yes-No* interrogative
(19) What time is it?	*Wh*-question	*Wh*-interrogative
(20) How nice you are!	Expressive	Exclamatory
(21) It's raining.	Representative	Declarative
(22) I'll help you with the dishes.	Commissive	Declarative
(23) You're fired.	Declaration	Declarative

Thus, any time a directive is issued with an imperative sentence, it constitutes a direct illocutionary act; anytime a *yes-no* question is issued with a *yes-no* interrogative, it constitutes a direct illocutionary act, and so on. (The boxed material in the preceding table identifies those sentence types that are uniquely associated with a particular illocutionary act.)

Before we move on, note that direct speech acts, especially directives, can often appear abrupt or even rude *(Bring me my coat).* Thus, speakers are motivated, for reasons of politeness, to mitigate, or soften, such speech acts. One method speakers use is to phrase illocutionary acts, especially directives, indirectly.

Indirect Illocutionary Acts. In general, an illocutionary act is issued indirectly when the syntactic form of the utterance does *not* match the illocutionary force of the utterance. Consider the following examples. (For purposes of comparison, the direct phrasing is given in parentheses below each utterance.)

UTTERANCE	ILLOCUTIONARY FORCE	SYNTACTIC FORM
(24) You might give me a hand with this. (Give me a hand with this.)	Directive	Declarative
(25) And you are . . . (Who are you?)	*Wh*-Question	Declarative
(26) Could you keep quiet? (Keep quiet.)	Directive	*Yes-No* Interrogative
(27) Do you have the time? (What time is it?)	*Wh*-Question	*Yes-No* Interrogative

(28) Can I give you a hand with that? (I can give you a hand with that.)	Commissive	*Yes-No* Interrogative
(29) I'm sorry to hear about your loss. (How sorry I am to hear about your loss!)	Expressive	Declarative
(30) Why don't you be quiet? (Be quiet.)	Directive	*Wh*-Interrogative

Let's summarize this section on illocutionary acts. The illocutionary part of a speech act is what the utterance does (rather than what it says). Illocutionary acts can be grouped into six types: representatives, directives, questions, commissives, expressives, and declarations. Illocutionary acts are valid only if their felicity conditions are met. Illocutionary acts can be achieved through either an explicit or a nonexplicit performative. A nonexplicit performative is, in turn, either direct or indirect. The various means of performing illocutionary acts are illustrated in the following diagram.

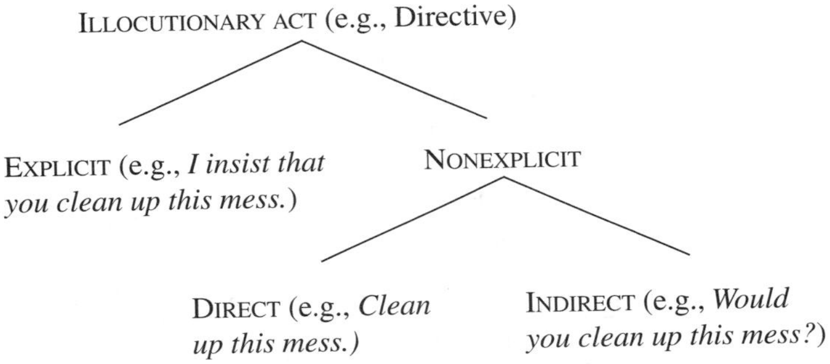

Exercise E

1. For each of the following utterances, state (i) the syntactic form, (ii) the illocutionary act it performs, and (iii) whether the illocutionary act is performed directly or indirectly.
   - **a.** A clerk says to a customer, *And your account number is . . .*
   - **b.** A sign at the entrance to a cafeteria line: *It is not impolite to pass others if there is space ahead.*
   - **†c.** An impatient husband grouses to his wife, *Shouldn't we be leaving soon?*
   - **d.** The envelope supplied for paying your credit card bill carries the following notice: *Did you remember to sign your check?*
   - **e.** A student, wheedling a teacher for an A, says *If I don't get an A in this course, I'll lose my scholarship.*
   - **f.** Smith is fixing a flat tire as Jones looks on. Smith says, *You can give me a hand with this* in order to get Jones to help him.
   - **g.** Smith is fixing a flat tire as Jones looks on. Smith says, *Why don't you give me a hand with this?* in order to get Jones to help him.

Expressed versus Implied Locutionary Acts

As we said earlier, a speech act consists of an illocutionary act (what is done) and a locutionary act (what is said). At this point, we want to turn our attention from illocutionary acts to locutionary acts. The locutionary act is concerned with the propositional content of the utterance, which is what follows the performative verb in an explicit performative and is the entire utterance in a nonexplicit performative. In the following examples, the propositional content is in italics.

(31a) EXPLICIT: I promise *I'll come to your birthday party.*
(31b) NONEXPLICIT: *I'll come to your birthday party.*

The propositional content of a locutionary act can be either expressed directly or implied via implicature. The propositional content is **expressed** if the utterance actually expresses the propositional content of the illocutionary act involved. For example, consider a warning, which is a type of directive. The propositional content of a directive must predicate a future act of the hearer. Thus a warning such as *I warn you to stop smoking* constitutes an expressed locutionary act because its propositional content predicates a future act (to stop smoking) of the hearer (you).

On the other hand, the propositional content is **implied** if the utterance does not express the propositional content of the illocutionary act involved. For example, consider the warning *I warn you that cigarette smoking is dangerous.* This utterance constitutes an implied locutionary act because it does not predicate a future act of the hearer; instead, it predicates a property of cigarettes. The hearer must infer the relevant propositional content via implicature. The hearer reasons (unconsciously) something like this. The speaker issued an explicit warning, which is a type of directive, but failed to predicate a future act of me, the hearer. Thus, since the utterance is not overtly relevant, the speaker appears to be flouting Grice's Maxim of Relation. However, the speaker knows I smoke cigarettes, and since there must be some reason for this seemingly irrelevant comment, the inference (i.e., the implicature) that I draw is that the speaker is trying to get me to stop smoking.

Some types of illocutionary acts (e.g., questions and representatives) have no restrictions on their propositional content. Thus, a common method for implying propositional content in such cases is for the speaker to express a **precondition** for the proposition he or she is trying to convey. For example, *Do you have a watch?* (as opposed to *Do you have the time?*) expresses a precondition for having the time. Likewise, *The battery's dead* (as opposed to *The car won't start*) expresses a precondition for the car starting.

Make no mistake: it's not always obvious if you're dealing with an expressed or an implied locutionary act. The same utterance may contain an implied locution on one occasion, but an expressed locution on another. For example, if an uncle asks his niece *Do you have a watch?* in order to help him decide what to get her for her birthday, then the proposition of interest is *expressed* by the utterance. However, as we saw in the preceding paragraph, if the same utterance is used to ask the time, then the proposition of interest is only *implied* by the utterance.

The following table displays a representative example of each of the six types of illocutionary act, the felicity condition governing the propositional content (if any), and examples of locutions that express and imply the proposition of interest (S = speaker, H = hearer, A = act, P = proposition).

TYPE OF ILLOCUTION (AND EXAMPLE)	PROPOSITIONAL CONTENT	UTTERANCE WITH EXPRESSED LOCUTIONARY ACT	UTTERANCE WITH IMPLIED LOCUTIONARY ACT
Representative (assertion)	any P	The car won't start.	The battery's dead.
Directive (request)	future A of H	Please do the dishes.	The dishes are piling up.
Question (*yes-no* question)	any P	Do you have the time?	Do you have a watch?
Commissive (volunteering)	future A of S	I'll help with the dishes.	You look like you could use some help with the dishes.
Expressive (condolence)	past event related to H	I am sorry to hear your mother died.	I am sorry to hear of your loss.
Declaration (firing)	H fired	You're fired.	You'll need to start entertaining job offers.

Directives in particular are prime candidates for implied locutionary acts. This is because, as we noted earlier with regard to indirect illocutionary acts, directives constitute an imposition on the hearer. Thus, it is quite often more polite to *imply* the propositional content of a directive than to express it directly. For example, suppose Amy has missed class and wants to borrow notes from Beth. The following utterances might be used.

UTTERANCE	ILLOCUTIONARY ACT	LOCUTIONARY ACT
(32) Lend me your notes from Friday.	Direct	Expressed
(33) Could you lend me your notes from Friday?	Indirect	Expressed
(34) I could sure use the notes from Friday.	Indirect	Implied

As we move from (32) to (34), the utterances become increasingly oblique, but also increasingly polite. In fact, (34), since it does not express the propositional content of a directive, could be (intentionally) misconstrued by Beth as a general comment on Amy's academic situation. The point is that implied locutionary acts serve the same function as indirect illocutionary acts. They both serve to distance the speaker from the speech act.

Consider the distancing effect of the implied locutionary act in another example. The following sign appears in the botanical gardens at Oxford: *Please make a donation to help us maintain this Historic Garden and unique collection of plants. Visiting similar gardens often costs at least two pounds.* The implied proposition in the second sentence is 'a donation is two pounds.' Moreover, this proposition is implied by an implicature which flouts Grice's Maxim of Relation. The reader of the sign reasons (unconsciously) as follows: the sign requests a donation but refers to something seemingly unrelated—the admission cost to other gardens; there must be some reason for the seemingly irrelevant comment. The inference (i.e., implicature) the reader draws is that the garden owners don't want to specify the amount of the donation directly, since a donation is voluntary and without limit. Instead, they state what other gardens charge for admission and hope the reader makes the connection.

Exercise F

1. For each of the following utterances, state whether the relevant proposition is expressed or implied.
   a. A sign on a fence reads *Parking here prohibits rubbish collection.*
   b. A warning on a can reads *Do not incinerate.*
   †c. A train conductor points to a NO SMOKING sign and says to a passenger who is smoking, *Do you see that sign?*
2. The following sign was observed on a British Rail train car: *Passengers are reminded that a valid ticket is required for each journey made.* This seems to be a roundabout way of saying *Buy a ticket.*
   a. Is the illocutionary act performed by the sign explicit or nonexplicit?
   b. Is the locutionary act performed by the sign expressed or implied?

Literal versus Nonliteral Locutionary Acts

A locutionary act can be either literal or nonliteral, depending upon whether the speaker actually means what is said or not. Consider, for example, the warning on a pack of cigarettes, which reads *Cigarette smoking is dangerous to your health.* The warning means exactly what it says; thus, it constitutes a **literal locutionary act.** On the other hand, consider an antismoking poster that depicts a bleary-eyed, disheveled man with a cigarette hanging out of his mouth; the caption reads *Smoking is glamorous.* The caption does not mean what it says (in fact, it means quite the opposite); thus, the caption constitutes a **nonliteral locutionary act.**

Nonliteral locutionary acts are those for which a literal interpretation is either impossible or absurd within the context of the utterance. For example, the famished husband who walks through the door and says to his wife, *I could eat a horse* (instead of, say, *I am very hungry*) is performing a nonliteral locutionary act. The location is nonliteral because most human beings could not (and certainly *would* not) eat an entire horse. Likewise, the college student who says to her roommate *I guess it would kill you to turn down that radio* (instead of, say, *Please turn down the radio*) is performing a nonliteral locutionary act. The locution is nonliteral because there is no known causal connection between turning down radios and death. Another example is the teacher who says to the schoolyard bully, who is picking on Little Timmy, *Pick on someone your own size* (instead of *Don't pick on Little Timmy*). The teacher is performing a nonliteral locutionary act because the teacher (presumably) does not really want the bully to pick on someone larger, but rather to stop tormenting his current victim.

Note that all of these examples have something in common. They all can be analyzed as flouting Grice's Maxim of Quality. That is, they all involve someone saying something that is blatantly false under the circumstances. Moreover, note that all cases of sarcasm essentially involve nonliteral locutionary acts (e.g., *Smoking is glamorous, I guess it would kill you to turn down the radio*), but not all nonliteral acts are sarcastic (e.g., *I could eat a horse*).

Nonliteral locutionary acts, however, can be quite complex. For example, a shop owner in England erected the following sign in front of his store: *If you want your wheel clamped, by all means park here.* (A wheel clamp is a device that keeps the car from being moved.) The literal way to word the sign would be something like *Don't park here* or *Parked cars will be clamped.* The sign as worded, however, is nonliteral because a literal interpretation would be absurd within the context of the utterance. That is, to interpret the sign literally would require the reader to assume that there are drivers who would actually like to have their wheels clamped.

Exercise G

---

1. For each of the following, state whether the locution is (i) expressed or implied, and (ii) literal or nonliteral.
   - **a.** A sign in front of a garage states, *Don't even think of parking here.*
   - **b.** A highway sign says, *Do not exceed 55.*
   - **c.** A highway sign says, *Speed Limit 55.*
2. One night you go to visit a friend in her apartment. When you walk in, your friend is sitting there with all the lights off. In an attempt to get her to turn on a light, you say, *What is this, a mausoleum?*
   - **†a.** Is the locution expressed or implied?
   - **†b.** Is the locution literal or nonliteral?

   Suppose you were in the same situation just described, but instead you said, *It's kinda dark in here.*
   - **c.** Is the locution expressed or implied?
   - **d.** Is the locution literal or nonliteral?
3. The comedians Laurel and Hardy are sitting in a jail cell commiserating about being captured in the act of robbing a bank. Laurel says *Ollie, when you said "Why don't you scream so everyone can hear?" . . . Well, I thought you really meant it.* Explain the "humor" of this routine in terms of speech act theory.

Overview of Speech Act Theory

Speech acts, as we have seen, each have two facets: an illocutionary act (i.e., what is *done*) and a locutionary act (i.e., what is *said*). The illocutionary act can be achieved either *explicitly* (i.e., by using a performative verb in its performative sense) or *nonexplicitly.* Moreover, a nonexplicit illocutionary act can be performed either *directly* (i.e., syntactic form matches illocutionary force) or *indirectly.* The locutionary act can be either *expressed* (i.e., by articulating propositional content) or *implied.* Likewise, the locutionary act can be either *literal* or *nonliteral.*

These four variables define 16 theoretically possible types of speech acts. However, since any nonexplicit illocutionary act can, at least in theory, be made explicit by prefixing a performative verb to it (e.g., *Shut up* → *I hereby order you to shut up*), we will ignore explicit performatives for present purposes. The remaining 8 types of nonexplicit illoctionary acts are illustrated in the following table. (Each utterance could be used in a particular context to get someone to refrain from smoking.)

UTTERANCE	DIRECT	EXPRESSED	LITERAL
(35) Please don't smoke.	+	+	+
(36) By all means, go right ahead and smoke. (sarcastic)	+	+	–
(37) Think about what you're doing to your lungs.	+	–	+
(38) Would you please not smoke?	–	+	+
(39) Go ahead and kill yourself, see if I care.	+	–	–
(40) I guess it would kill you to stop smoking.	–	+	–
(41) Cigarette smoking is dangerous to your health.	–	–	+
(42) Smoking is glamorous. (under picture of derelict smoking)	–	–	–

Exercise H

1. For each of the following speech acts, state whether it is (i) explicit or nonexplicit; (ii) direct or indirect (applies to nonexplicit only); (iii) expressed or implied; and (iv) literal or nonliteral.
   - **†a.** To express agreement, a friend says *How right you are!*
   - **†b.** A teacher says to his student, *I suggest you spend more time on your homework.*
   - **c.** A sign on the side of the road reads *Construction ahead.*
   - **d.** A congratulations card depicts a baby and the words *Your baby boy has arrived.*
   - **e.** In the movie *Honky Tonk Man,* Marlene Mooney tries to get Red Stovall to give her his sandwich by saying, *If you're not gonna eat this [sandwich], I can finish it for you.*
   - **f.** In the corner of an envelope, there's a printed message stating, *Post Office will not deliver mail without proper postage.*

(continued)

Exercise H *Continued*

g. John shows up for class after missing the previous session. He turns to his friend Mary and says, *Did you take notes during the last class?* He intends it as a request to borrow Mary's notes.

h. A parent, attempting to get his child to close her mouth, says, *You're so attractive when you talk with your mouth full.*

i. A sign on the interstate reads *Speed limit enforced by radar.*

j. A highway sign reads *YIELD.*

k. Count Monte Crisco has been insulted by Count Marmaduke; Monte Crisco says to Marmaduke, *I challenge you to a duel.*

Summary

The theory of pragmatics makes use of such concepts as implicature and conversational maxims (quantity, quality, relation, and manner), speech act (illocutionary and locutionary acts), a classification of illocutionary acts, felicity conditions on illocutionary acts, explicit/nonexplicit and direct/indirect illocutionary acts, and expressed/implied and literal/nonliteral locutionary acts. These theoretical constructs help explain how language users are able to use context to interpret utterances, to "do" things with words, and to "say" things without actually uttering them.

SUPPLEMENTARY READINGS

Primary

Austin, J. L. (1962). *How to do things with words.* Oxford: Clarendon Press.

Brown, P., & Levinson, S. C. (1987). *Politeness: Some universals in language use.* Cambridge, England: Cambridge University Press.

Grice, H. P. (1975). Logic and conversation. In P. Cole and J. L. Morgan (Eds.), *Syntax and semantics 3: Speech acts,* pp. 41–58. New York: Academic Press.

Searle, J. R. (1969). *Speech acts.* Cambridge, England: Cambridge University Press.

Searle, J. R. (1975). Indirect speech acts. In P. Cole and J. L. Morgan (Eds.), *Syntax and semantics 3: Speech acts,* pp. 59–82. New York: Academic Press.

Searle, J. R. (1976). The classification of illocutionary acts. *Language in Society, 5,* 1–24.

Secondary

Coulthard, M. (1977). *Discourse analysis.* London: Longman.

Grundy, P. (2000). *Doing pragmatics* (2nd ed.). New York: Oxford University Press.

Levinson, S. (1983). *Pragmatics.* Cambridge, England: Cambridge University Press.

Sperber, D., & Wilson, D. (1986). *Relevance.* Cambridge, MA: Harvard University Press.

Walsh, T. (1998). *A short introduction to formal discourse analysis.* Superior, WI: Parlay Enterprises.

Coulthard, Grundy, and Walsh provide clear introductions to pragmatics and discourse analysis. Levinson's *Pragmatics* is a comprehensive textbook; since it has a detailed index and bibliography, you can also use it as a reference tool. Brown and Levinson's work gives an extended treatment of politeness phenomena in various languages and provides the framework to which much recent work in politeness responds. The other works are more advanced and would be more accessible after you've completed additional work in linguistics.

Supplementary Exercises

1. Traugott and Pratt (1980:237) cite the following joke. Determine (i) which of Grice's maxims Sam violates in his *first* utterance, and (ii) the implicature that Farmer Brown draws from it. (Hint: Assume that Sam is telling the truth.)

   FARMER BROWN: Hey, Sam, my mule's got distemper. What'd you give yours when he had it?

   SAM: Turpentine.

   (a week later)

   FARMER BROWN: Sam, I gave my mule turpentine like you said and it killed him.

   SAM: Did mine, too.

2. Consider the following "tip" concerning conversations in Hungary:

   Don't be surprised by sudden, abrupt changes in subject. Hungarians often have an "official" opinion and also a private opinion. A subject change may mean one has said too much or has come too close to voicing an unacceptable political opinion. (Braganti and Devine 1984:127)

   Which of Grice's maxims would be violated by the Hungarians' behavior in such a circumstance?

3. Big Bob asks Muffy, *Who was that man I saw you talking to yesterday?* Muffy replies, *That was my mother's husband.* Which of Grice's maxims does Muffy's reply appears to violate? What implicature does her reply raise?

4. In an episode of *Leave it to Beaver,* Wally is trying to keep Beaver from finding out that he (Wally) plans to go to a football game with his friend Chester. Chester calls Wally on the phone; Wally talks and hangs up. The following interchange takes place:

   BEAVER: Who was that, Wally?

   WALLY: Just some guy that called up.

   Which of Grice's maxims does Wally's response violate? What is the implicature his reply raises?

5. On the TV show *Little House on the Prairie,* the preacher says to Mrs. Ingalls, *Family discipline is based on promises kept—whether punishment or reward.* The preacher here is lumping together two different types of illocutionary acts.
   - **a.** What are the two illocutionary acts the preacher is referring to?
   - **b.** What general category of illocutionary acts do they both belong to?
   - **c.** How do the two illocutionary acts differ in terms of their felicity conditions?

6. In the movie *Educating Rita,* the following interchange transpires between Frank (a professor) and Rita (a new student), who have not previously met.

   FRANK: And you are . . .

   RITA: What?

   FRANK: And you are . . . What is your name?
   - **a.** What is the illocutionary force of Frank's first utterance?
   - **b.** What is the syntactic form of Frank's first utterance?
   - **c.** Why does Rita fail to recognize the illocutionary force of Frank's first utterance?
   - **d.** How does Frank "repair" his first utterance by adding to it in his second utterance?

7. When an author signs a contract with a publisher to write a book for a sum of money, what type of illocutionary act are the parties performing?
8. A friend comes to visit you for the first time and, being positively impressed by where you live, says, What a nice house you have! The syntactic form of your friend's utterance is ________. The illocutionary act is ________. The illocutionary act is performed (directly, indirectly).
9. For each of the following utterances, state whether the locutionary act is literal or nonliteral.
   a. You go to a movie and the Warthog family comes in and sits down behind you. They crumple candy wrappers and talk for the first 20 minutes of the movie. Finally you have had enough, and you turn to them and say *I don't want to have to call the manager.*
   b. Assume the context is the same as in (a), except you say *I can still hear the movie; would you mind speaking up?*
10. One night you go to visit a friend in her apartment. When you walk in, your friend is sitting there with all the lights off. In an attempt to get her to turn on a light, you say *It's kinda dark in here.* She says *What are you talking about?* and you say *I'm asking you to turn on a light.* Answer the following regarding your *second* utterance.
    a. Is the illocution explicit or nonexplicit?
    b. If nonexplicit, is the illocution direct or indirect?
    c. Is the locution expressed or implied?
    d. Is the locution literal or nonliteral?
11. Dirty Harry, in trying to get a criminal to give up his gun, says *Go ahead—make my day.* Identify the type of speech act conveyed by this utterance, given the context.
    a. explicit, expressed, literal
    b. nonexplicit, direct, implied, nonliteral
    c. nonexplicit, indirect, implied, literal
    d. explicit, implied, literal
    e. nonexplicit, indirect, implied, nonliteral
12. Francine wants to find out from Jolene the name of Jolene's date. For each of the following utterances, state whether it is (i) explicit or nonexplicit; (ii) direct or indirect (applies to nonexplicit only); (iii) expressed or implied; and (iv) literal or nonliteral.
    a. You haven't told me your date's name, Jolene.
    b. What's your date's name, Jolene?
    c. For the last time, Jolene, I'm asking you to tell me the name of your date.
    d. Please don't bore me with the name of your date, Jolene.
13. A mother says to her child *Why don't you stop sucking your thumb?* in order to get the child to stop sucking his thumb. The child replies *Because I don't want to.*
    a. What pragmatic distinction has the child failed to learn (or is at least ignoring)?
    b. Explain how the child interprets the mother's utterance so he can respond to it as he does.
14. The medical staff at a women's clinic regularly sends out the following report:

    Dear [patient's name]:

    We have received a report of the Pap smear taken from your recent examination. The Pap smear shows no evidence of abnormal or unusual cells. Your smear is therefore normal.

    Best regards,

    [doctor's name]

The final sentence of the report may seem unnecessary to some readers. Explain why the clinic includes this sentence, using a theoretical concept from pragmatics.

15. In an episode of the *Andy Griffith Show,* Thelma Lou's plain-looking cousin Mary Alice comes to Mayberry for a visit. Thelma Lou and Helen refuse to go to the big dance with Barney and Andy unless they find a date for Mary Alice. Barney and Andy try to line up Gomer, and the following conversation ensues:

    ANDY: How would you like to take Thelma Lou's cousin to the dance?

    GOMER: Is she pretty, Andy?

    ANDY: She's nice, Gom. She's real nice.

    Explain what Andy is doing linguistically, when he says *She's nice, Gom. She's real nice.*

16. Explain why a sign that states *Thank you for not smoking* is a directive and not an expressive (i.e., an act of thanking).

17. The boss says to an employee, *You're fired.* The employee responds with, *You can't fire me; I quit.* The employee is essentially claiming that the boss's utterance violates a felicity condition on firing. Explain.

Exploratory Exercises

1. Brown and Levinson (1987) outline strategies that speakers (and writers) use to make their contributions more polite. These strategies are often used when issuing requests and other directives, which impose on the listener/reader. Some of the strategies discussed by Brown and Levinson are outlined below. In each case, the request on the left is a highly direct, imperative form. The revisions on the right show the more indirect (and presumably more polite) effect achieved by applying each strategy.

    Question the request

    Give me a vacation. → *Can* you give me a vacation?
    I wonder if I could have a vacation.

    Be pessimistic about the request

    Type this memo. → *Could/Would* you type this memo?
    Is it *possible* for you to type this memo?

    Minimize the imposition of the request

    Answer these questions. → Take *a moment* to answer *a few* questions.

    Give deference to the agent of the request

    Send me some information. → *As a novice,* I need your *expert* opinion.
    Please send me some information.

    Apologize to the agent of the request

    Turn in your key. → *I'm sorry,* but you'll have to turn in your key.

    Impersonalize the request

    Submit your report on Friday. → Reports must *be submitted* on Friday.
    It is necessary to submit reports on Friday.

    Generalize the request

    Wear your ID card. → *All* personnel must wear *their* ID cards.

Nominalize the request

Do not smoke at your desk. → *Smoking* is prohibited at your desk.

Incur a debt for the request

Speak at our next meeting. → *I would be grateful* if you could speak at our next meeting.

Now consider the following memo, which was sent to residents of an apartment building on the shore of Lake Superior from the property manager of the building. Identify any indirectness strategies used in this memo. Also speculate on why indirectness was used in this situation, taking into account the relationship between the property manager and the residents. Consider, for example, whether it would be appropriate or advisable for the property manager to use more direct language, and explain your reasoning.

> We have recently observed individuals out beyond the fence line below Lake View Apartments. We ask that you please be aware that this area is fenced off for safety reasons; like all lakeshores, the embankment is always changing and is not considered a safe area for walking.
>
> We understand that the quiet and serenity of the lakeshore draws people near, but for safety reasons, access to this one small area of the grounds cannot be allowed.
>
> We dislike imposing on the residents, but we would be grateful for your assistance in this matter.

2. Changing tables, for use when changing a baby's diaper, are common in commercial restrooms, especially those designed for women. Consider the following notices that were posted on or near the changing table in three different establishments.

A. Never leave baby unattended.

B. Just a reminder . . . always stay with your baby when using this table.

C. Do not leave your baby unattended.

Use concepts from pragmatics to write an analysis of the similarities and differences among these notices. Include some discussion of why the similarities and differences exist. For example, are there any advantages or disadvantages to these various modes of expression? Do they seem designed for the same type of readers? You may want to refer to the discussion of politeness in Exploratory Exercise 1 for further ideas.

CHAPTER THREE

Semantics

Semantics is the study of linguistic meaning: that is, the meaning of words, phrases, and sentences. Unlike pragmatics, semantics is part of grammar proper, the study of the internal structure of language. Unfortunately, because semantics is the most poorly understood component of grammar, it can be one of the most difficult areas of linguistics to study. The fact is that no one has yet developed a comprehensive, authoritative theory of linguistic meaning. Nonetheless, we can discuss some of the phenomena that have been studied within the domain of semantics and some of the theories that have been developed to explain them. It is important to keep in mind, however, that much of what follows is tentative and subject to debate.

Let's first consider some observations we can make about the meaning of words and sentences.

(1) The word *fly* has more than one meaning in English. The word *moth* does not.
(2) The word *hide* can mean the same thing as *conceal.*
(3) The meaning of the word *fear* includes the meaning of the word *emotion,* but not vice versa.
(4) The words *sister* and *niece* seem to be closer in meaning than the words *sister* and *girl.*
(5) In the sentence *Jimmy Carter was the 39th president of the United States,* the phrases *Jimmy Carter* and *the 39th president of the United States* refer to the same person. The phrases, however, don't "mean" the same thing.
(6) In the sentence *Monica believes that she is a genius, she* can refer either to *Monica* or to someone else. However, in the sentence *Monica believes herself to be a genius, herself* can refer only to *Monica.*
(7) If someone were to ask you to name a bird, you would probably think of a robin before you would think of an ostrich.
(8) The sentences *A colorless gas is blue* and *Oxygen is blue* are both false, but for different reasons.
(9) The sentence *John's wife is six feet tall* is neither true nor false, if John does not have a wife.

The observations in (1–9) are all essentially semantic in nature. That is, they have to do with the meaning of words and sentences. As is standard procedure in linguistics, we will assume that these phenomena are systematic; that is, they are rule-governed. What we will try to do now is construct a theory: a set of categories and principles that will at least partially explain the observations in (1–9).

Background

Contributions to semantics have come essentially from two sources—linguistics and philosophy. Linguists have contributed primarily to the study of the core meaning or sense of individual words. One method that they have used to characterize the sense of words is called **lexical decomposition.** This method represents the sense of a word in terms of the **semantic features** that comprise it. For example, consider the words *man, woman, boy,* and *girl.* The sense of each of these words can be partly characterized by specifying a value (+ or –) for the features [adult] and [male], as follows.

	man	*woman*	*boy*	*girl*
[adult]	+	+	–	–
[male]	+	–	+	–

Lexical decomposition, as a method for characterizing the sense of words, has several advantages. First, it explains our intuitions as speakers of English that the meanings of *man* and *boy* are more closely related than are the meanings of *man* and *girl. Man* and *boy* have the same value for one of these features [male], whereas *man* and *girl* do not have the same value for either of these features. Second, it is easy to characterize the senses of additional words by adding features. For example, we can account for part of the meanings of *stallion, mare, colt,* and *filly* simply by adding the feature [human], as follows.

	man	*woman*	*boy*	*girl*	*stallion*	*mare*	*colt*	*filly*
[adult]	+	+	–	–	+	+	–	–
[male]	+	–	+	–	+	–	+	–
[human]	+	+	+	+	–	–	–	–

Finally, this method allows us, at least in principle, to characterize the senses of a potentially infinite set of words with a finite number of semantic features. (Note that in the previous example, we were able to differentiate the senses of eight words with only three features.) In general, the fewer the number of statements required by a theory to account for a given set of observations, the more highly valued the theory.

On the other hand, lexical decomposition has several practical limitations. First, linguists have been unable to agree on exactly how many and which features constitute the universal set of semantic properties, especially once we go beyond the handful of features already mentioned. Moreover, nouns, especially concrete nouns, seem to lend themselves to lexical decomposition more readily than do other parts of speech. For example, what features could be used to characterize the sense of *carefully, belligerent,* and *assassinate,* not to mention *the, of,* and *however?* In sum, then, lexical decomposition in terms of semantic features provides a useful, if some what limited, account of the meaning of words.

Exercise A

1. What semantic feature or property differentiates the following sets of nouns? (Hint: Start by figuring out what the two subsets have in common.)
   a. *niece, daughter, sister* vs. *nun, woman, girl*
   b. *mailman, nephew, priest* vs. *gander, stag, bull*
   c. *hen, ewe, cow* vs. *rooster, ram, bull*
   d. *table, chair, pencil* vs. *love, thought, idea*
   †e. *table, chair, pencil* vs. *water, dirt, cream*
2. Consider the following riddle:

   A father and a son are riding in a car. The car hits a truck. The father dies and the son is rushed to the emergency room of a nearby hospital. The doctor comes in and says *I can't operate on this boy. He's my son.* What is the relationship between the doctor and the boy?

   Answer: The doctor is the boy's mother.

   A listener's inability to answer this riddle rests on his or her semantic representation of the word *doctor.* Explain.

Philosophers, on the other hand, have contributed primarily to the study of the meaning of sentences. However, rather than trying to characterize the core meaning or sense of sentences directly—which, as we have just seen, is a difficult undertaking—they have approached the semantics of sentences from two other directions: the study of **reference** and the study of **truth conditions.** Reference is the study of what objects are referred to by linguistic expressions (i.e., words, phrases, sentences, and so on). For example, in the sentence *Washington, DC, is the capital of the United States,* the expressions *Washington, DC,* and *the capital of the United States* refer to the same entity, namely Washington, DC. Truth-conditional semantics, on the other hand, is the study of the conditions under which a statement can be judged true or false. In actuality, much of what goes under the name of truth conditions involves truth relations that hold between sentences. For example, if the sentence *Fred is 80 years old* is true, then the sentence *Fred is over 50 years old* is necessarily true.

Both the study of reference and the study of truth conditions have advantages as well as limitations. The major advantage of both avenues of inquiry is that they have very restricted domains, which can be probed in a reasonable amount of detail. The drawback, of course, is that both of them overlook a great deal of what might fall within the domain of "meaning." For example, in the sentence *Washington, DC, is the capital of the United States,* determining the referents of *Washington, DC,* and *the capital of the United States* skirts the question of what these expressions "mean."

So far, we have considered semantics from the point of view of the contributors to the theory: linguists, who have studied meaning through lexical decomposition, and philosophers, who have studied meaning through reference and truth conditions. If we abstract away from the material we've been discussing, we can divide the study of semantics into three areas: **sense, reference,** and **truth.** Let's now consider each one in turn.

Sense

The study of sense (or meaning) can be divided into two areas: speaker-sense and linguistic-sense. **Speaker-sense** is the speaker's intention in producing some linguistic expression. For example, if someone utters the sentence *Fred is a real genius* sarcastically, then the speaker-sense of the sentence might be 'Fred is below average in intelligence.' Speaker-sense, because it has to do with nonliteral meaning, is outside the domain of semantics; rather, it is part of pragmatics (discussed in Chapter 2). Consequently, no further mention of speaker-sense will be made in this chapter. **Linguistic-sense,** on the other hand, is the meaning of a linguistic expression as part of a language. For example, if the sentence *Fred is a real genius* means literally something like 'Fred has a truly superior intellect,' then the linguistic-sense is within the domain of semantics, since it deals solely with literal meaning and is independent of speaker, hearer, and situational context. Note, however, that in this example we presently have no better way of indicating the linguistic-sense of a sentence than by simply paraphrasing it. All we have done so far is differentiate situationally dependent meaning (speaker-sense, part of pragmatics) from situationally independent meaning (linguistic-sense, part of semantics).

Now let's consider some sense properties and relations that any descriptively adequate theory of semantics should account for.

Lexical Ambiguity. A word is lexically ambiguous if it has more than one sense. For example, the English noun *fly* is ambiguous because it has more than one sense: an insect, a zipper on a pair of pants, or a baseball hit into the air with a bat. Thus, the sentence *Waldo saw a fly* is three-ways ambiguous. One way a semantic theory might account for this fact is to list the word *fly* in the **lexicon** of English (i.e., a dictionary listing of all English words) three times, once with each sense of the word. It is not clear, however, exactly what form each of these **lexical entries** should take. For the time being, we will assume that each one takes the form of a paraphrase, for example, *fly:* (i) an insect having the following characteristics . . . ; (ii) a zipper . . . ; (iii) a ball. . . .

Note, by the way, that not all cases of ambiguity are lexical. Consider the phrase *American history teacher,* which can mean either 'a teacher of American history' or 'a history teacher who is American.' The ambiguity here does not derive from the ambiguity of a particular word, as in the case of *fly.* Neither *American,* nor *history,* nor *teacher* has more than one sense. Instead, the ambiguity of *American history teacher* is syntactic, in that we can assign two different structures or bracketings to the phrase: for example [[American history] teacher] = 'a teacher of American history,' and [American [history teacher]] = 'a history teacher who is American.' Syntactic ambiguity will be discussed in Chapter 4.

Synonymy. Two words are synonymous if they have the same sense; that is, if they have the same values for all of their semantic features. For example, the pairs *conceal* and *hide, stubborn* and *obstinate,* and *big* and *large* seem to be synonymous in English. Presumably, the meaning of each pair consists of the same set of features marked for the same values. As mentioned earlier, however, note that it is not clear what the relevant features are for each of these pairs. Moreover, in all likelihood there are no absolute synonyms in any language—that is, words that mean exactly the same thing in all contexts. For example, even though *big* and *large* are (near) synonyms, the phrases *my big sister* and *my large sister* certainly do not have the same meaning.

Likewise, synonymity does not capture differences in **connotations,** or the associations that speakers have with a word. For example, *senior citizen* and *old coot* may denote the same entity (a person over 65), yet the former has a positive connotation, while the latter is pejorative. Other examples are *sanitation engineer* vs. *garbage collector,* and *administrative assistant* vs. *secretary.* Synonymous words may also differ in the **register,** or level of formality, with which they are associated. For example, an adult male may be referred to as a *guy* when the speaker is telling a joke (e.g., "A guy walks into a bar . . .") but as a *man* when the speaker is using language more formally, as in giving courtroom testimony ("A man walked into the bar . . . ").

Hyponymy. A **hyponym** is a word that contains the meaning of a more general word, known as the **superordinate.** For example, *oak* contains the meaning of *tree;* therefore, *oak* is a hyponym of the superordinate *tree.* In other words, a hyponym is a word whose meaning contains all the same feature values of another word, plus some additional feature values. For instance, the meaning of the word *sow* has exactly the same feature values as the word *pig* (e.g., [–human]) plus some additional ones (e.g., [+adult], [–male]). This relationship is represented in Figure 3.1.

In general, there are a number of hyponyms for each superordinate. For example, *boar* and *piglet* are also hyponyms of the superordinate *pig,* since the meaning of each of the three words *sow, boar,* and *piglet* "contains" the meaning of the word *pig.* (Note that in defining a word like *sow, boar,* or *piglet,* the superordinate word *pig* is often used as part of the definition: "A *sow* is an adult female *pig.*") Thus, it is not surprising that hyponymy is sometimes referred to as **inclusion.** The superordinate is the included word and the hyponym is the including one.

Exercise B

1. Provide three hyponyms for each of the following verbs.
   - **a.** *walk*
   - **b.** *talk*
2. Identify a superordinate (included term) for the following set: *aunt, grandmother, cousin, nephew.*

(continued)

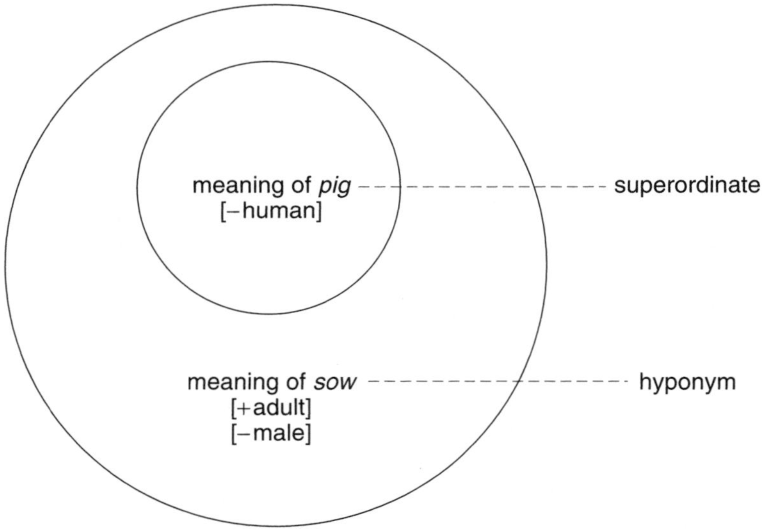

FIGURE 3.1 Representation of hyponymy

Exercise B *Continued*

3. Rearrange the following set of terms from most general (the highest superordinate) to most specific (the lowest hyponym).
   †**a.** *rectangle, quadrilateral, polygon, parallelogram, square*
   b. *animal, feline, lynx, mammal, vertebrate*
4. If a floozle is a type of schtek, then ________.
   a. The word *floozle* is a hyponym of *schtek.*
   b. The word *floozle* is a superordinate of *schtek.*
   c. The word *schtek* is a hyponym of *floozle.*
   d. The word *schtek* is a superordinate of *floozle.*
   e. both (a) and (d)

Overlap. Two words overlap in meaning if they have the same value for some (but not all) of the semantic features that constitute their meaning. For example, the words *sister, niece, aunt,* and *mother* overlap in meaning. This relationship can be captured by stating that part of the meaning of each of these words is [+human/–male/+kin]. If we were to add the words *nun* and *mistress* to the list above, then this set of words would overlap because they are all marked [+human/–male]. If we were to further add *mare* and *sow* to this list, then the meanings of this set would overlap by being marked [–male]. And so on. This relationship is displayed in the following diagram.

	sister	*niece*	*aunt*	*mother*	*nun*	*mistress*	*mare*	*sow*
[human]	+	+	+	+	+	+	–	–
[male]	–	–	–	–	–	–	–	–
[kin]	+	+	+	+	–	–	–	–

It is important to distinguish overlap from hyponymy. With hyponymy, the meaning of one word is entirely included in the meaning of another. (The meaning of *pig* is entirely included in the meaning of *sow;* i.e., all sows are pigs, but not all pigs are sows.) With overlap, on the other hand, the meanings of two words intersect, but neither one includes the other. The meanings of *sister* and *niece* intersect, but neither includes the other: not all sisters are nieces, and not all nieces are sisters. Overlap is represented in Figure 3.2.

Antonymy. Two words are antonyms if their meanings differ only in the value for a single semantic feature. The following pairs are all antonyms: *dead* and *alive, hot* and *cold,* and *above* and *below.* The meanings of the members of each pair are presumably identical, except for opposite values of some semantic feature. The meanings of *dead* and *alive,* for instance, are identical except that *dead* is marked [–living] and *alive* is marked [+living]. Once again, however, note the difficulty in determining the relevant semantic feature that distinguishes the members of each pair.

Antonyms, moreover, fall into at least three groups. **Binary antonyms** are pairs that exhaust all linguistic possibilities along some dimension. *Dead* and *alive* are examples of binary antonyms. Everything that can be dead or alive is, in fact, either dead or alive: there is no middle ground between the two. All people, for example, are either dead or alive. **Gradable antonyms,** on the other hand, are pairs that describe opposite ends of a continuous dimension. *Hot* and *cold* are examples of gradable antonyms. Not everything that can be hot or cold is, in fact, either hot or cold. A liquid, for example, may be neither hot nor cold; it can be in between, say, warm or cool. **Converse antonyms** are pairs that describe the relationship between two items from opposite perspectives. *Above* and *below* are examples of converse antonyms. If a picture, for example, is above a sofa, then the sofa is necessarily below the picture. The difference among binary, gradable, and converse antonyms is represented in Figure 3.3.

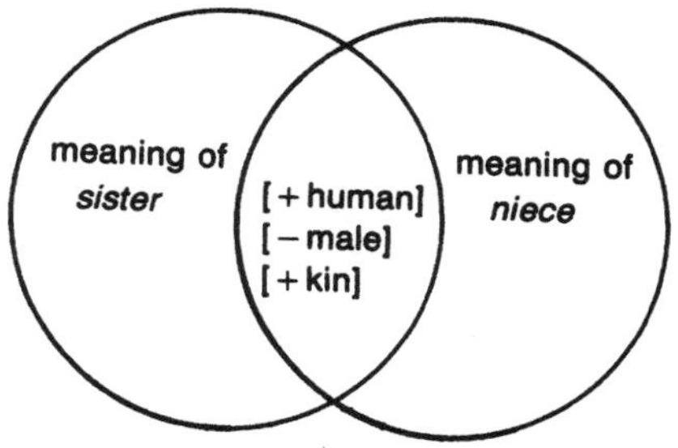

FIGURE 3.2 Illustration of overlap

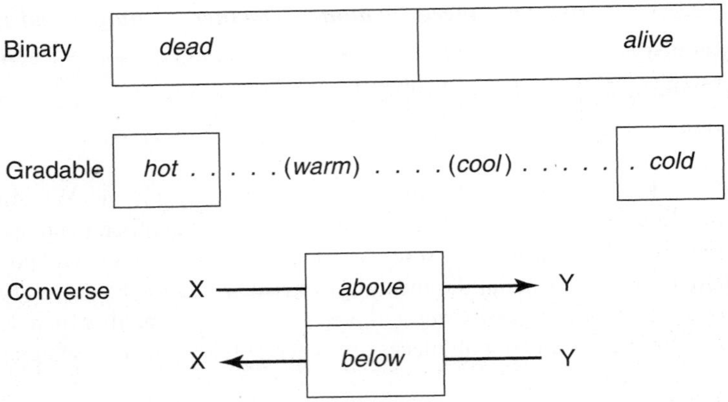

FIGURE 3.3 Illustration of binary, gradable, and converse antonyms

It is not always easy to classify a pair of antonyms as binary, gradable, or converse. There are, however, several useful tests. First, test the pair to see if they are converse antonyms. Converse antonyms that are prepositions fit into the following frame: *If X is ______ Y, then Y is ______ X.* For example, the following statement is true: *If the painting is above the sofa, then the sofa is below the painting.* Converse anytonyms that are nouns fit into the frame *If X is Y's ______, then Y is X's ______.* For example, the following statement is true: *If George is Martha's husband, then Martha is George's wife.*

If the pair does not fit the test for converse antonyms, test them to see if they are binary. This can be done by putting the pair in the following frame: *If X is not ______, then X must be ______.* For example, *If that person is not dead, then he must be alive.* If the pair fits this form, they are binary antonyms. If they don't, then test them to see if they are gradable. This can be done by putting each member of the pair in the following frame: *X is very ______.* For example, *This soup is very hot/cold.*

It is also worth pointing out that some pairs that have traditionally been treated as antonyms might be better handled as hyponyms of the same superordinate. For example, *liquid* and *solid* are not converse antonyms (**If X is liquid Y, then Y is solid X);* they are not binary antonyms (**If X is not a liquid, then it must be solid*—it could be neither; it could be a gas); and they are not gradable antonyms (**This is very liquid/solid*—neither is literally true). Instead, *liquid* and *solid* (along with *gas*) seem to be hyponyms of *matter.*

Exercise C

1. What sense relation is illustrated by the following sets of words?
   a. *chair, sofa, desk*
   b. *hate, despise*
   c. *book, magazine, pamphlet*
2. What sense property is illustrated by the word *bar* in *George passed the bar?*

Exercise C *Continued*

3. Classify the following antonyms as binary (B), gradable (G), or converse (C).
   a. B G C wide/narrow
   b. B G C smoking/nonsmoking
   †c. B G C near/far
   †d. B G C defeat/lose to
   †e. B G C innocent/guilty
   f. B G C wife/husband
   g. B G C in front of/behind
   h. B G C true/false
   i. B G C open/closed
   j. B G C debtor/creditor
   k. B G C deciduous/evergreen
   l. B G C teacher/student
   m. B G C cheap/expensive
   n. B G C man/woman

Reference

The study of reference, like the study of sense, can be divided into two areas: speaker-reference and linguistic-reference. **Speaker-reference** is what the speaker is referring to by using some linguistic expression. For example, if someone utters the sentence *Here comes Queen Elizabeth* facetiously, to refer to a snobbish acquaintance, then the speaker-reference of the expression *Queen Elizabeth* is the acquaintance. Speaker-reference, because it varies according to the speaker and context, is outside the domain of semantics; instead it is part of pragmatics. **Linguistic-reference,** on the other hand, is the systematic denotation of some linguistic expression as part of a language. For example, the linguistic expression *Queen Elizabeth* in the sentence *Here comes Queen Elizabeth* refers in fact to the public figure Queen Elizabeth. Linguistic-reference, in contrast to speaker-reference, is within the domain of semantics, since it deals with reference that is a systematic function of the language itself, rather than of the speaker and context.

Let's now consider some concepts that seem useful in thinking and talking about reference (**referent, extension, prototype,** and **stereotype**); then we will take a look at some different types of linguistic reference (**coreference, anaphora,** and **deixis**).

Referent. The entity identified by the use of a referring expression such as a noun or noun phrase is the referent of that expression. If, for example, you point to a particular robin and say *That bird looks sick,* then the referent for the referring expression *That bird* is the particular robin you are pointing at.

Extension. Extension refers to the set of all potential referents for a referring expression. For example, the extension of *bird* is the set of all entities (past, present, and future) that could systematically be referred to by the expression *bird.* In other words, the extension of *bird* is the set of all birds.

Prototype. A typical member of the extension of a referring expression is a prototype of that expression. For example, a robin or a bluebird might be a prototype of *bird;* a pelican or an ostrich, since each is somewhat atypical, would not be.

Stereotype. A list of characteristics describing a prototype is said to be a stereotype. For example, the stereotype of *bird* might be something like the following: has two legs and two wings, has feathers, is about six to eight inches from head to tail, makes a chirping noise, lays eggs, builds nests, and so on.

Exercise D

1. For each of the following words, identify a prototype, a nonprototypical member, and a stereotype. Be sure to include some features in your stereotype that would exclude the nonprototypical member.
   - **a.** *car*
   - **b.** *house*
2. Which of the following deals with a particular entity in the real world?
   - **a.** stereotype
   - **b.** prototype
   - **c.** sense
   - **d.** all of the above
   - **e.** none of the above
3. You look up the word *aardvark* in a dictionary and find a written definition accompanied by a picture of an aardvark. In this case it could be argued that this dictionary entry relies on _________.
   - **a.** sense
   - **b.** reference
   - **c.** both sense and reference
   - **d.** none of the above

†4. The men John F. Kennedy and Ronald Reagan are related to the term *President of the United States* as follows:
   - **a.** Kennedy and Reagan are hyponyms of *President of the United States.*
   - **b.** Kennedy and Reagan are part of the extension of *President of the United States.*
   - **c.** Kennedy and Reagan are stereotypes of *President of the United States.*
   - **d.** Kennedy and Reagan are superordinates of *President of the United States.*
   - **e.** none of the above

5. The word *robin* and the word *bird* are related as follows:
   - **a.** *Robin* is a prototype of *bird.*
   - **b.** *Robin* is a stereotype of *bird.*
   - **c.** *Robin* is a hyponym of *bird.*
   - **d.** *Robin* and *bird* overlap.
   - **e.** none of the above

Exercise D *Continued*

6. Consider the following description: chases cars, barks, is about two feet long, is covered with fur, wags its tail when happy. This is a ________.
   a. prototype of *dog*
   b. stereotype of *dog*
   c. referent of *dog*
   d. extension of *dog*

Coreference. Two linguistic expressions that refer to the same real-world entity are said to be coreferential. Consider, for example, the sentence *Jay Leno is the host of the Tonight Show.* The expressions *Jay Leno* and *The host of the Tonight Show* are coreferential because they both refer to the same entity, namely the person Jay Leno. Note, however, the coreferential expressions do not "mean" the same thing; that is, they are not synonymous. For example, before Jay Leno hosted the *Tonight Show,* Johnny Carson held that position; thus, there was a period of time when *Johnny Carson* was coreferential with *host of the Tonight Show.* However, we cannot describe *Johnny Carson* and *Jay Leno* as "meaning" the same thing. The fact that they are not synonymous is illustrated by the unacceptability of the sentence **Jay Leno used to be Johnny Carson.*

Anaphora. A linguistic expression that refers to another linguistic expression is said to be anaphoric or an anaphor. Consider the sentence *Mary wants to play whoever thinks himself capable of beating her.* In this sentence the linguistic expression *himself* necessarily refers to *whoever;* thus *himself* is being used anaphorically in this case. Note, moreover, that it would be inaccurate to claim that *whoever* and *himself* are coreferential (i.e., that they have the same extralinguistic referent). This is because there may in fact not be anyone who thinks himself capable of beating Mary; that is, there may not be any extralinguistic referent for *whoever* and *himself.*

It is common, however, for coreference and anaphora to coincide. Consider, for example, the sentence *The media reported that Congress voted themselves a raise.* The expressions *Congress* and *themselves* are coreferential since they refer to the same real-world entity, namely the legislative branch of the federal government. At the same time, *themselves* is an anaphor since it necessarily refers to the expression *Congress.* Note that there is no reading of this sentence such that *themselves* can be construed as referring to the expression *the media.* In sum, coreference deals with the relation of a linguistic expression to some entity in the real world, past, present, or future; anaphora deals with the relation between two linguistic expressions.

Exercise E

1. What reference relation holds between the italicized expressions in each of the following sentences?
   a. *George* won't give *himself* an injection.
   †b. *Maxine* has been named *secretary of the Student Government Association.*

(continued)

Exercise E Continued

2. In the sentence *Mary gave me all his money, his* can be interpreted ______.
   - a. anaphorically
   - b. prototypically
   - c. coreferentially
   - d. none of the above
   - e. (a) and (b) only
3. What reference relation holds between *who* and *anyone* in the following sentence: *Anyone who parks illegally will be towed.*

Deixis (pronounced DIKE-sis). A deictic expression has one meaning but can refer to different entities depending on the speaker and his or her spatial and temporal orientation. Obvious examples are expressions such as *you* and *I, here* and *there,* and *right* and *left.* Assume, for instance, that Jack and Jill are speaking to each other face to face. When Jack is speaking, *I* refers to Jack, and *you* refers to Jill. When Jill is speaking, the referents for these expressions reverse. Likewise, when Jack is speaking, *here* refers to a position near Jack, and *there* refers to a position near Jill. When Jill speaks, the referents for these expressions reverse. Similarly, *right* and *left* can refer to the same location, depending upon whether Jack or Jill is speaking; his left is her right, and vice versa. Likewise, expressions such as *yesterday, today,* and *tomorrow* are deitic. Jack may say to Jill, *Yesterday I told you I would pay you tomorrow, which is today.*

Note, moreover, that deixis can intersect with anaphora. Consider, for example, the sentence *Members of Congress believe they deserve a raise.* The expression *they* can refer either to the expression *members of Congress* or to some other plural entity in the context of the utterance. When, as in the first case, a pronoun refers to another linguistic expression, it is used anaphorically; when, as in the second case, it refers to some entity in the extralinguistic context, it is used deictically.

Exercise F

1. Consider the following interchange:

   FRED: It's the one on the right.

   ETHEL: My right or yours?

   The area of semantics that accounts for Ethel's confusion is ______.
   - a. overlap
   - b. entailment
   - c. synonymy
   - d. deixis
   - e. none of the above
2. Consider the following data.
   - A. *Come* to me.
   - B. *Go* to him.

Exercise F *Continued*

C. *Come* to him.

D. *Go* to me.

a. Which of these sentences is absolutely unacceptable?

b. *Come* and *go* both have a deictic component to their meaning. That is, they both depend on the speaker's point of reference. What is the deictic component of each?

c. Explain the deviance of the absolutely unacceptable sentence.

†3. Which of the verbs in the following set of sentences does not have a deictic component? Explain.

A. Fred *went* to New York last night.

B. Fred *came* to New York last night.

C. Fred *arrived* in New York last night.

4. In the sentence *John gave me all his money, me* can be interpreted (either deictically or anaphorically, anaphorically only, deictically only).

5. In the sentence *Mary shot herself in the toe, herself* can be interpreted (either deictically or anaphorically, anaphorically only, deictically only).

Truth

The study of truth or truth conditions in semantics falls into two basic categories: the study of different types of truth embodied in individual sentences (**analytic, contradictory,** and **synthetic**) and the study of different types of truth relations that hold between sentences (**entailment** and **presupposition**).

Analytic Sentences. An analytic sentence is one that is necessarily true simply by virtue of the words in it. For example, the sentence *A bachelor is an unmarried man* is true not because the world is the way it is, but because the English language is the way it is. Part of our knowledge of ordinary English is that *bachelor* "means" *an unmarried man,* thus to say that one is the other must necessarily be true. We do not need to check on the outside world to verify the truth of this sentence. We might say that analytic sentences are "true by definition." Analytic sentences are sometimes referred to as **linguistic truths,** because they are true by virtue of the language itself.

Contradictory Sentences. Contradictory sentences are just the opposite of analytic sentences. While analytic sentences are necessarily true as a result of the words in them, contradictory sentences are necessarily false for the same reason. The following sentences are all contradictory: *A bachelor is a married man, A blue gas is colorless, A square has five equal sides.* In each case, we know the sentence is false because we know the meaning of the words in it: part of the meaning of *bachelor* is 'unmarried'; part of the meaning of *blue* is 'has color'; part of the meaning of *square* is 'four-sided.' It is not necessary to refer to the outside world in order to judge each of these sentences false. Consequently, contradictory sentences are sometimes referred to as **linguistic falsities,** because they are false by virtue of the language itself.

Synthetic Sentences. Synthetic sentences may be true or false depending upon how the world is. In contrast to analytic and contradictory sentences, synthetic sentences are not true or false because of the words that comprise them, but rather because they do or do not accurately describe some state of affairs in the world. For example, the sentence *My next door neighbor, Bud Brown, is married* is a synthetic sentence. Note that you cannot judge its truth or falsity by inspecting the words in the sentence. Rather, you must verify the truth or falsity of this sentence empirically, for example by checking the marriage records at the courthouse. Other examples of synthetic sentences include *Nitrous oxide is blue, Nitrous oxide is not blue, Bud Brown's house has five sides,* and *Bud Brown's house does not have five sides.* In each case, the truth or falsity of the sentence can be verified only by consulting the state of affairs that holds in the world. Thus, synthetic sentences are sometimes referred to as **empirical truths** or **falsities,** because they are true or false by virtue of the state of the extralinguistic world.

The examples that we have considered so far seem fairly straightforward. Analytic and contradictory sentences are true and false, respectively, by definition. Synthetic sentences, however, are not—they must be verified or falsified empirically. Nevertheless, some sentences do not seem to fall neatly into one of these two groups. Consider, for example, the sentence *Oxygen is not blue.* It is true. But is it analytic—true by virtue of the words that make it up (i.e., part of the meaning of *oxygen* is 'without color')? Or is it synthetic—true because it coincides with the state of the world (i.e., because it just so happens that oxygen has no color)? This can get to be a thorny issue, and the experts don't always have a uniform answer to such questions. However, it would probably be reasonable to treat such cases as synthetic truths rather than analytic truths. This is because it is easy to imagine conditions under which the sentence *Oxygen is not blue* would be false. For example, suppose scientists froze oxygen and found that solid oxygen is in fact blue. Such a finding would not cause a change in the meaning of the word *oxygen,* but rather a change in our understanding of the substance oxygen. In contrast, consider the sentence *A colorless gas is not blue.* It is impossible, at least for us, to imagine a situation in which this sentence would be false. If a gas is colorless, it cannot be blue; if it is blue, it cannot be colorless. Thus it seems reasonable, at least until more light can be shed on the subject, to consider sentences like *Oxygen is not blue* as synthetically true.

Exercise G

1. What kind of truth is illustrated by each of the following sentences?
   - **a.** Waldo's living room has four right angles.
   - **b.** A square has four right angles.
2. The sentence *Siblings are not relatives* is ________.
   - **a.** analytic
   - **b.** contradictory
   - **c.** synthetic
   - **d.** both (a) and (b)
   - **e.** none of the above

†3. *Boys will be boys* is an example of a(n) ________ sentence or linguistic truth.

Exercise G *Continued*

4. *A widow is a man whose wife has died* is an example of a(n) ________ sentence or linguistic falsity.
5. *My mother is a widow* is an example of a(n) ________ sentence or empirical truth/falsity.
6. Identify each sentence as analytic (A), synthetic (S), or contradictory (C).
   - **a.** A S C This pentagon is six-sided.
   - **b.** A S C A horse is a horse.
   - **c.** A S C A triangle is a three-sided figure.
   - **d.** A S C My cat is not a mammal.
   - **e.** A S C Mia's pet is not a mammal.
   - **f.** A S C That animal is not a pet.

Entailment. An entailment is a proposition (expressed in a sentence) that follows *necessarily* from another sentence. For example, *Martina aced chemistry* entails *Martina passed chemistry,* because one cannot ace chemistry without passing chemistry. The test for entailment is as follows: sentence (a) entails sentence (b) if the truth of sentence (a) ensures the truth of sentence (b) and if the falsity of sentence (b) ensures the falsity of sentence (a). Our example sentences pass both tests. First, the truth of sentence (a) ensures the truth of sentence (b). Note that if Martina aced chemistry, she necessarily passed chemistry. Second, the falsity of sentence (b) ensures the falsity of sentence (a). If Martina didn't pass chemistry, she necessarily didn't ace chemistry.

Note, however, that the relation of entailment is unidirectional. For instance, consider our example sentences again, but in the opposite order: (b) *Martina passed chemistry* and (a) *Martina aced chemistry.* In this case, sentence (b) does not entail (a) (if Martina passed chemistry, she did not necessarily ace chemistry—she may have made a C); and the falsity of (a) does not ensure the falsity of (b) (if Martina did not ace chemistry, it is not necessarily the case that she did not pass chemistry—she may, once again, have made a C). In short, then, it should be clear that the relation of entailment is unidirectional.

This is not to say, however, that there cannot be a pair of sentences such that each entails the other. Rather, when such a relation holds, it is called **paraphrase.** For example, the sentences *Martina passed chemistry* and *What Martina passed was chemistry* are paraphrases of each other. Note, incidentally, that entailment describes the same relationship between sentences that hyponymy describes between words. Likewise, paraphrase describes the same relationship between sentences that synonymy describes between words. These relations are illustrated in Figure 3.4.

Presupposition. A presupposition is a proposition (expressed in a sentence) that must be *assumed* to be true in order to judge the truth or falsity of another sentence. For example, *Martina aced chemistry* presupposes *Martina took chemistry,* because acing chemistry assumes the person in question actually took chemistry. The simplest test for presupposition depends upon the fact that a sentence and its denial (i.e., the negative version of the sentence) have the same set of presuppositions. This test is known as **constancy under negation.**

FIGURE 3.4 Inclusion analogues between sentences and words

	SENTENCES	WORDS
unidirectional	entailment (*Martina aced chemistry* →*Martina passed chemistry*)	hyponymy (*hate*→*dislike*)
bidirectional	paraphrase (*Martina passed chemistry*↔*What Martina passed was chemistry*)	synonymy (*hate*↔*despise*)

Thus, if sentence (a) *Martina aced chemistry* presupposes sentence (b) *Martina took chemistry,* then the denial of sentence (a) *Martina did not ace chemistry* also presupposes sentence (b) *Martina took chemistry.* If Martina did not take chemistry, then *Martina did not ace chemistry* cannot be judged true or false.

The relationship between entailment and presupposition is illustrated in Figure 3.5. Figure 3.5 should be read as follows: *Martina aced chemistry* entails *Martina passed chemistry.* Both of those sentences, in turn, presuppose *Martina took chemistry.*

A further point to note is that in order to falsify or negate a sentence, you must negate the verb in the main clause of the sentence. For example, suppose we want to determine whether sentence (a) *Martina managed to pass chemistry* presupposes sentence (b) *Martina took chemistry.* To arrive at the negative or false version of sentence (a), we would negate the verb in the main clause of the sentence: *Martina didn't manage to pass chemistry.* This false version of (a) still presupposes sentence (b) *Martina took chemistry.* Since the presupposition holds for both the true and false versions of (a), we would be correct in saying that (a) presupposes (b).

A final point to note is that it is possible to start with the negative version of a sentence and test for presupposition. For example, suppose we want to determine whether sentence (a) *Martina didn't pass chemistry* presupposes (b) *Martina took chemistry.* Since sentence (a) is a negative sentence, we would falsify it by making it positive: *Martina passed*

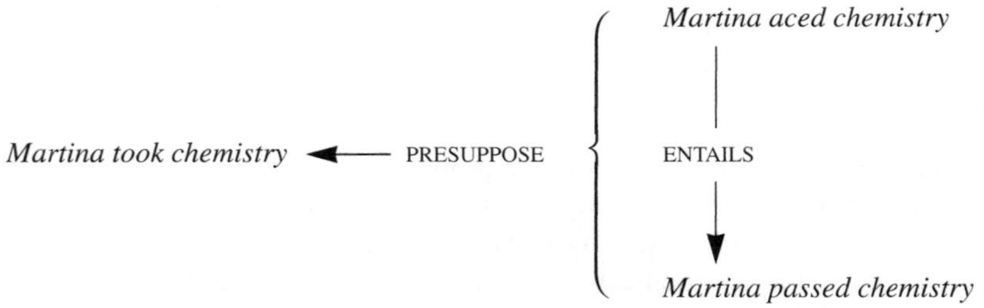

FIGURE 3.5 Relationship between entailment and presupposition

chemistry. The main point is that this procedure gives us both a true and false version of the same sentence; and both versions presuppose that *Martina took chemistry.* Hence our original test for presupposition—constancy under negation—still applies.

Exercise H

1. What truth relation holds between each pair of sentences? How can it be demonstrated?

†A.1. Fred is mortal
A.2. Fred is a man.

†B.1. Fred's wife is six feet tall.
B.2. Fred is married.

C.1. Ralph likes anchovy pizza.
C.2. Ralph has tasted anchovy pizza.

D.1. George Washington did not chop down a tree.
D.2. George Washington did not chop down a cherry tree.

E.1. Wally gave Beaver a dog biscuit.
E.2. Wally gave a dog biscuit to Beaver.

F.1. Fester has children.
F.2. Fester's middle child is a dentist.

G.1. I regret having my hair dyed green.
G.2. I had my hair dyed green.

H.1. Ana knew that the window was open.
H.2. The window was open.

I.1. Biff likes Muffy's new car.
I.2. Biff likes Muffy's new Mercedes-Benz.

J.1. Fred got wet.
J.2. Fred took a shower.

Presupposition Triggers. Presupposition plays a large role in the impression that speakers make on others. One way that people make an impression (good or bad) is by the use (or avoidance) of **presupposition triggers.** These triggers are either structures or words that assume, or presuppose, the truth of the proposition expressed in a sentence or the speaker's attitude about it. One structure that serves as a presupposition trigger is a ***wh*-question.** Consider, for example, sentences (10a–c).

(10a) When will you take out that trash?
(10b) Will you take out that trash?
(10c) If you take out that trash, put it by the curb.

Sentence (10a) is a *wh*-question and presupposes the truth of the proposition it expresses, 'You will take out that trash.' On the other hand, (10b) is a *yes-no* question and does not presuppose the truth of the proposition. Sentence (10c), containing an *if*-clause, likewise does not presuppose the truth of the proposition 'You will take out that trash.'

There are also entire classes of words that serve as presupposition triggers. One such class includes **factive verbs** (and verb phrases) Consider, for example, (11a) and (11b).

(11a) Brown's presentation *demonstrates* that the new system is superior.
(11b) Brown's presentation *suggests* that the new system is superior.

Sentence (11a) contains the factive verb *demonstrates* and presupposes the truth of the proposition in the subordinate clause, 'the new system is superior.' On the other hand, (11b) contains the nonfactive verb *suggests* and does not presuppose the truth of the proposition in the subordinate clause; it does not assume that 'the new system is superior.' Here is a partial list of factive and nonfactive verbs.

FACTIVE: acknowledge, be aware, bear in mind, demonstrate, grasp, make clear, note, prove, regret, resent, show, take into consideration, take into account

NONFACTIVE: allege, assert, assume, believe, charge, claim, conclude, conjecture, fancy, figure, maintain, suggest, suppose, think

Finally, there is a another class of verbs that serve as presupposition triggers termed **implicative verbs.** Consider examples (12a–c).

(12a) You *failed* to enclose your check.
(12b) You *forgot* to enclose your check.
(12c) You *did not* enclose your check.

All three of these express the proposition 'You did not enclose your check.' However, the implicative verbs *fail* and *forget* in (12a) and (12b) further imply an unmet obligation: 'You were supposed to enclose a check but you didn't.' Moreover, although both (12a) and (12b) presuppose some unmet obligation, they differ in their other presuppositions. Sentence (12a), with *fail,* implies a greater degree of culpability than does (12b), with *forget.* That is, *You forgot to enclose your check* presupposes that the act was unintentional, whereas *You failed to enclose your check* carries no such presupposition. Here is a partial list of implicative verbs and their presuppositions.

avoid: negative act
forget: unmet obligation, but unintentional
remember: obligation
bother: no obligation
neglect: unmet obligation
fail: unmet obligation
refrain: negative act

manage: difficult and intentional act
happen: accidental act

Exercise I

1. Ted Baxter, a well-known tightwad on the *Mary Tyler Moore Show,* is looking for a new apartment. After touring a rather expensive one, he says *I've decided not to afford this.* Explain the "humor" of his statement, using concepts from truth-conditional semantics.
2. Explain why a listener would interpret the following sentence as sarcastic: *I managed to step on some chewing gum as I was walking to my car.*

Summary

Contributions to the theory of semantics have come from two main sources: from linguists, who have traditionally been interested in the core meaning or sense of linguistic expressions (especially words), and from philosophers, who have traditionally been concerned with the reference of linguistic expressions and the truth of sentences. The study of sense makes use of such concepts as lexical decomposition, semantic features, lexical ambiguity, synonymy, hyponymy, overlap, and antonymy. The study of reference utilizes concepts such as referent, extension, prototype, stereotype, coreference, anaphora, and deixis. Finally, the study of truth conditions relies on the notions of analytic, contradictory, and synthetic sentences, as well as entailment and presupposition.

SUPPLEMENTARY READINGS

Allan, K. (2001). *Natural language semantics.* Oxford: Blackwell.
Allwood, J., Andersson, L.-G., & Dahl, Ö. (1977). *Logic in linguistics.* Cambridge, England: Cambridge University Press.
Chierchia, G., & McConnell-Ginet, S. (1991). *Meaning and grammar: An introduction to semantics.* Cambridge, MA: MIT Press.
Cruse, A. (2000). *Meaning in language.* New York: Oxford University Press.
Hurford, J. R., & Heasley, B. (1983). *Semantics: A coursebook.* New York: Cambridge University Press.
Kempson, R. (1977). *Semantic theory.* Cambridge, England: Cambridge University Press.
Kreidler, C. (1998). *Introducing English semantics.* London: Routledge.
Lyons, J. (1977). *Semantics,* 2 vols. New York: Cambridge University Press.
Riley, K., & Parker, F. (1988). Tone as a function of presupposition in technical and business writing. *Journal of Technical Writing and Communication, 18,* 325–343.
Salmon, W. C. (1973). *Logic* (2nd ed.). Englewood Cliffs, NJ: Prentice-Hall.

All of the books in this list are, or can be used as, textbooks. However, they differ in the amount of preparation you will need in order to benefit from them. You are ready to read Cruse, Hurford and Heasley, Kreidler, and Salmon right now. The other books require a minimum background of an introductory course in linguistics. We suggest you begin with Hurford and Heasley, which is a combination text and workbook. Lyons, which is a classic comprehensive treatment of semantics, is invaluable as a reference tool. Riley and Parker is an easy-to-read application.

Supplementary Exercises

1. Mark the following statements true or false.
   - **a.** T F Philosophers' most important contributions to the study of semantics have been in the area of sense.
   - **b.** T F *Fat* and *skinny* are binary antonyms.
   - **c.** T F The meaning relation illustrated by *hen, cow, mare,* and *vixen* is overlap.
   - **d.** T F The phrase *French literature teacher* constitutes a case of lexical ambiguity.
   - **e.** T F The sentence *John killed Bill* presupposes the sentence *Bill died.*
   - **f.** T F The following sentence is analytic: *If George killed the deer, then the deer died.*
   - **g.** T F Two words overlap in meaning if they share the same specifications for at least one semantic feature.
   - **h.** T F The pronoun in the following sentence is deictic: *Sam is extremely pleased with himself.*
   - **i.** T F The sentence *Buckaroo Bonzai loves his wife* entails the sentence *Buckaroo Bonzai is married.*
   - **j.** T F The pronouns in the following sentence are anaphoric: *I like you a lot.*
   - **k.** T F *Smart* and *stupid* are gradable antonyms.
   - **l.** T F The sense relation illustrated by *rooster, bull, stallion,* and *buck* is hyponymy.
2. You go to see one of your professors and find a note on the office door that says, in its entirety, *Back in 20 minutes.* You are not sure when the professor will return. Explain the confusing nature of this note. What area of semantics is most relevant to this type of phenomenon?
3. A man calls up an auto supply store on Florida Boulevard and asks if the store is located east or west of Airline Highway. The clerk who answers the phone says *It depends on where you are.* Using the relevant concept from semantics, explain why the clerk's response is nonsense.
4. On *The Match Game* on TV, Rip Taylor, a male comedian, said, *I love kids, but I can't bear them.* What concept from sense semantics can be used to explain the humor in this joke?
5. The following conversation was reported in Ann Landers's column (4/12/91):

   MAN NO. 1: My wife had amnio last week, and we know the gender of our unborn child.

   MAN NO. 2: Well, what will it be?

   MAN NO. 1: A baby woman.

   MAN NO. 2: That's really wonderful. Baby women are awfully nice. You are a very lucky guy.

   - **a.** What word are the men trying to avoid using?
   - **b.** For these men, the word *woman* is missing one semantic property that it has for most speakers of English. What is that property? (Express your answer as a semantic feature specification.)
6. A vet tells a cat owner to put medicine into the left ear of her cat. The owner appears confused and asks the vet to show her which ear he means. What concept from semantics accounts for the owner's confusion? Explain.
7. The sentence *We saw three stars tonight* is _______.
   - **a.** lexically ambiguous
   - **b.** structurally ambiguous

c. a synthetic sentence
d. both (a) and (c)
e. both (b) and (c)

8. **Ostention** deals with defining linguistic expressions by pointing. For example, if a speaker says to someone who does not know English *That is a TV* while pointing at a TV, then this constitutes a definition by ostention. Ostention is most closely related to which of the following theoretical constructs:
   a. sense
   b. stereotype
   c. presupposition
   d. truth
   e. prototype
   f. none of the above
9. The following sign was hanging on the front of a pub in Birmingham, England: *Music of the 60s and 70s every other Tuesday night.* The reader was unsure when to show up to hear the music. The area of semantics that most likely accounts for the reader's confusion is ________.
   a. overlap
   b. entailment
   c. antonymy
   d. presupposition
   e. none of the above
10. Consider the following interchange between a father and son.

    SON: Bob Feller pitched two no-hitters. True or false?

    FATHER: True.

    SON: False. He pitched three.

    Actually, the son is wrong. If Bob Feller pitched three no-hitters, it is also true that he pitched two no-hitters. What concept from semantics explains why this is so?
11. Consider the following question: *When may I come in for an interview?* What concept from truth-conditional semantics can be used to explain why this is a "loaded" question? (Hint: Compare the question *May I come in for an interview?*)
12. O'Barr (1981) describes a study similar to the following: An experimenter shows a film of a car crash to two groups of students. The first group is asked *Did you see a broken headlight?* Thirty percent say *Yes.* The second group is asked *Did you see the broken headlight?* Seventy percent say *Yes.* What area of truth-conditional semantics can be used to explain these different results? Explain.
13. Consider the following question: *Have you stopped beating your wife?* What truth relation can be used to explain why this is a "loaded" question? Explain. (Hint: Consider the meaning of either a *yes* or *no* response.)
14. Consider the following joke: *One million people in this country aren't working. But thank God they've got jobs.* What concept from semantics can be used to explain the source of humor in this joke? Explain.
15. A caption under a TV news item read *Mom chains sons to bed.* Explain the discordant nature of this caption in terms of semantic theory.

16. On the *Mary Tyler Moore Show,* Ted Baxter asks Mary an embarrassing question. Mary responds, *That is extremely none of your business!* Explain the "humor" of her response in terms of semantic theory.
17. In 2003, a college humor website ran a picture of Osama Bin Laden with the caption *Experts Agree: Al Qaeda Leader Is Dead or Alive.* Explain the source of the "humor" in terms of semantic theory.
18. On the *Tonight Show* many years ago, then-host Johnny Carson started to introduce his first guest by saying *My next guest is . . .* Someone off-camera whispered *My first guest!* Explain what's wrong with what Johnny Carson said, using truth-conditional semantics.

Exploratory Exercises

1. Visit a store or website that sells makeup and make a list of color terms used to describe shades of lipstick, eye shadow, or nail polish. What sorts of connotations do the labels seem designed to evoke? Do any different themes emerge, depending on what target group the makeup is designed to appeal to?
2. See Chapter 4, Exploratory Exercise 1, which also deals with semantic ambiguity.

CHAPTER FOUR

Syntax

Syntax is the study of phrases, clauses, and sentences. In contrast to semantics, syntax is one of the better understood areas within linguistics. In fact, during the past 40 years, more has probably been written about syntax than about any other area within linguistics. This interest in syntax has stemmed largely from the pioneering work of Noam Chomsky, who in 1957 first set out his ideas in a short book (117 pages) entitled *Syntactic Structures.* Since then, Chomsky's name has become almost synonymous with the study of generative grammar in general. However, the fact that syntactic theory has undergone such rapid and detailed development over the past several decades raises a problem for us here. What points can we discuss in just a few pages that will provide a basic grasp of the core elements of the theory of syntax? As usual, we will begin by considering some observations that we can make about the structure of phrases, clauses, and sentences.

(1) The phrase *the biggest house* is acceptable English; *theest big house* is not.
(2) The phrase *the big house* is acceptable English; the phrase *big the house* is not.
(3) The phrase *American history teacher* has two possible interpretations.
(4) The interrogative *What will Tiny Abner put on his head?* is acceptable in English; *What will Tiny Abner put a hat on his head?* is not.
(5) The sentence *Katznelson is expected to run* is acceptable in English; *Katznelson is expected will run* is not.

Observation (1) illustrates the fact that the words in a language are organized into different **categories** or, in traditional terms, parts of speech. Observation (2) illustrates the fact that words in phrases must have a particular **left-to-right ordering.** Observation (3) illustrates the fact that words in sentences are arranged not only in left-to-right order, but also in **hierarchical structure.** Observation (4) illustrates the fact that sentence structures are related by **transformations:** operations that move a category from one location to another within a structure. Observation (5) can be used to argue that transformations are subject to various **constraints** that limit their application.

All of these phenomena are essentially syntactic in nature. That is, they all have to do with the internal architecture of phrases, clauses, and sentences. Moreover, we will make the now familiar assumption that the phenomena in (1–5) are systematic; that is, they are governed by a system of principles stated in terms of theoretical constructs. What we will do now is investigate five of these constructs (categories, left-to-right ordering, constituent structure, transformations, and constraints), without which we cannot even begin to account for the observations in (1–5). It is important to bear in mind that what follows is part of an (unobservable) theory designed to account for the (observable) data in (1–5).

Categories

The classification of words into categories or parts of speech goes back at least as far as Plato, who first mentioned the categories **noun, verb,** and **sentence.** (He, of course, used the Greek terms *noma, rhema,* and *logos,* respectively.) Even today, school children learn that there are eight parts of speech in English. However, because categories have been with us so long, it is easy to be misled into thinking that they are part of the *observable* aspect of language. Nothing could be farther from the truth: categories are theoretical constructs, part of the *unobservable* theory of syntax. Linguists have historically classified words into categories solely because postulating such categories helps them explain phenomena that they otherwise could not explain.

For example, some words can be made plural *(table-tables, boy-boys, idea-ideas),* whereas others cannot *(quick-*quicks, of-*ofs, the-*thes).* (An asterisk in front of a form means that it is not acceptable in the language in question; it is ungrammatical or ill-formed.) One way to account for this phenomenon is to categorize English words into two groups: nouns (which can be made plural) and others (which cannot). Now we can make a general statement about English: nouns can be made plural; other words can't. Note that if we did not postulate a category such as noun, we would have to state as an idiosyncratic fact about each word in English whether or not it can be made plural. Before leaving this example it is worth pointing out that there is nothing sacred about the term *noun* itself. If we wanted to, we could call this group of words that can be made plural *category one,* or make up some other term, such as *dook.* The point is that words in human languages can be categorized in terms of their behavior; what we choose to call these categories is immaterial.

Consider another example. Children are taught in school that articles are a type of adjective. Is this, however, a legitimate claim? The answer, unfortunately, is no. The reason is that adjectives and articles behave differently; that is, they have different properties. First, adjectives can be made comparative and superlative *(tall-taller-tallest),* whereas articles can't *(the-*theer-*theest, a-*aer-*aest).* Second, if both an adjective and an article modify a noun, then the article must precede the adjective *(the tall man, *tall the man).* Finally, a noun can be modified by more than one adjective, but not by more than one article *(a short, fat man, *a the fat man).*

Let's go back and take a look at what we've done here. First, we have justified postulating a category **adjective** by virtue of the fact that some words can be made comparative and superlative *(short-shorter-shortest)* whereas others can't *(boy-*boyer-*boyest).* Second, we have provided three different pieces of evidence that articles are not a type of adjective simply because they do not behave like adjectives. There is in fact reason to believe that articles are members of another category **determiner,** which includes demonstratives *(this,* *that, these, those)* as well as perhaps possessive personal pronouns *(my, your, his, her, its, our, their)*. Try the tests we've discussed on these words, and see what you think.

The point of this section on categories is straightforward. First, we cannot make even the most commonplace statement about the observations in (1) without reference to the concept **category.** Second, we can group words in a language into categories based on their behavior (e.g., the types of endings they allow and their position in phrases and sentences).

Linguists have grouped words into two corresponding types of categories: **lexical** (or **word**) **categories,** which include items such as nouns, verbs, adjectives, and adverbs; and **phrasal categories,** which include items such as noun phrases, verb phrases, adjective phrases, and adverb phrases. The theory is that every phrasal category contains at least one lexical category of the same basic type. For example, every noun phrase (NP) contains at least a noun (N), every verb phrase (VP) contains at least a verb (V), and so on. For instance, the sentence *The fat man ate* contains an NP *the fat man,* which in turn contains the N *man.* Conversely, every lexical category belongs to a phrasal category of the same basic type: every N belongs to an NP, and so on.

Exercise A

†1. In the phrase *the brick house,* the word *brick* appears to be an adjective as is *old* in *the old house.* Cite one piece of evidence that *brick* is in fact not an adjective. (Hint: Consider the suffixes that can be attached to adjectives.)

2. What generalization about English is violated by the following sentence: **Some those books were on the table.*

3. Consider the following English words. Some can be made past tense; others can't. Some can be made superlative; others can't. Some can be made plural; others can't. What concept from syntactic theory will enable you to account for this? Explain.
   - **a.** walk—walked
   - **b.** wok—*woked
   - **c.** weak—weakest
   - **d.** week—*weekest
   - **e.** beast—beasts
   - **f.** best—*bests

4. Consider the claim that possessive pronouns (as in *my book, your book, their books*) constitute a type of adjective. Cite two pieces of evidence that possessive pronouns are in fact not adjectives at all.

Left-to-Right Ordering

Words in English cannot appear in any random order; for example, the phrase *the red car* is acceptable, but not **red the car.* The left-to-right sequence of items within a phrase is governed by principles that are codified in **phrase structure (PS) rules.** PS rules specify three types of information.

- which elements are permitted in a particular type of phrase
- the left-to-right ordering of those elements
- whether any of the elements are optional

Let's look at some examples of specific PS rules for English, starting with the following rules.

SENTENCE:	S→NP–VP	A sentence consists of a noun phrase followed by a verb phrase.
NOUN PHRASE:	NP→(Det)–(AP)–N–(PP)	A noun phrase must contain a noun. The noun may be preceded by a determiner, an adjective phrase, or both, and it may be followed by a prepositional phrase.
VERB PHRASE:	$VP \rightarrow V\text{–}(\left\{\begin{matrix}NP\\AP\end{matrix}\right\})\text{–}(PP)$	A verb phrase must contain a verb. The verb may be followed by a noun phrase, an adjective phrase, or neither. The verb phrase may end in a prepositional phrase, but need not.
ADJECTIVE PHRASE:	AP→(I)–Adj	An adjective phrase must contain an adjective. The adjective may be preceded by an intensifier (e.g., *very*).
PREPOSITIONAL PHRASE:	PP→Prep–NP	A prepositional phrase consists of a preposition followed by a noun phrase.

Note that each PS rule consists of two basic parts. The material to the left of the arrow specifies the phrasal category being described. The material to the right of the arrow describes the items that comprise the phrasal category. Parentheses, as shown around (Det) in the Noun Phrase rule, indicate an optional item; if the item appears, it must appear in that position. Braces, as shown in the Verb Phrase rule, indicate that exactly one of the items in the braces must appear in that position. Thus, for example, the Verb Phrase rule allows a VP to expand in one of the following ways.

- V — *The battery <u>died</u>*
- V–NP — *Chris <u>hit the ball</u>*
- V–NP–PP — *He <u>drove the car into a tree</u>*
- V–PP — *They <u>are in the kitchen</u>*

- V–AP *The teacher is angry*
- V–AP–PP *My boss was very happy with her decision*

These relatively simple rules make it possible to **generate,** or describe, an extremely large number of English phrases.

Exercise B

1. Below are some English phrases. For each one, identify the type of phrase it is (S, NP, VP, AP, PP) and determine whether it (and any phrases it contains) can be generated by the PS rules just presented. If not, what element in the phrase is not described by the rules?
   a. Ice floats.
   †b. the red car
   c. John
   d. in a bad mood
   e. in a very bad mood
   f. gave a party for Mary
   g. was a fool
   h. was extremely silly
   i. ran
   j. Those people hit that man on the head.
   k. ran with difficulty
   l. ran extremely quickly

Constructing a complete PS grammar of English is beyond our scope here. For example, our rules do not describe sentences with auxiliary verbs; nor do they describe complex sentences (those with more than one clause). However, as Exercise B demonstrates, our preliminary PS rules describe a very large number of English phrases.

Tree Diagrams. PS rules form the basis for **tree diagrams,** which allow us to visualize how the components in a phrase are related. For example, consider the following tree diagram of the sentence *A student in my class works at the mall,* shown in Figure 4.1. (Parts of the tree have been numbered for easier reference.)

This diagram allows us to see interrelationships, such as the fact that *a student in my class* is, on the one hand, ultimately part of one unit (NP_1) and, on the other hand, composed of several smaller units.

The diagram in Figure 4.1 can be used to illustrate a number of useful structural relationships among the **nodes** (branching points) in a tree diagram. Among the observations we can make are as follows:

- Node S **dominates** all of the other nodes.
- Node S **directly dominates** NP_1 and VP_1.
- Nodes NP_1 and VP_1 are **daughters** of S.
- Nodes Det_1, N_1, and PP_1 are **sisters.**

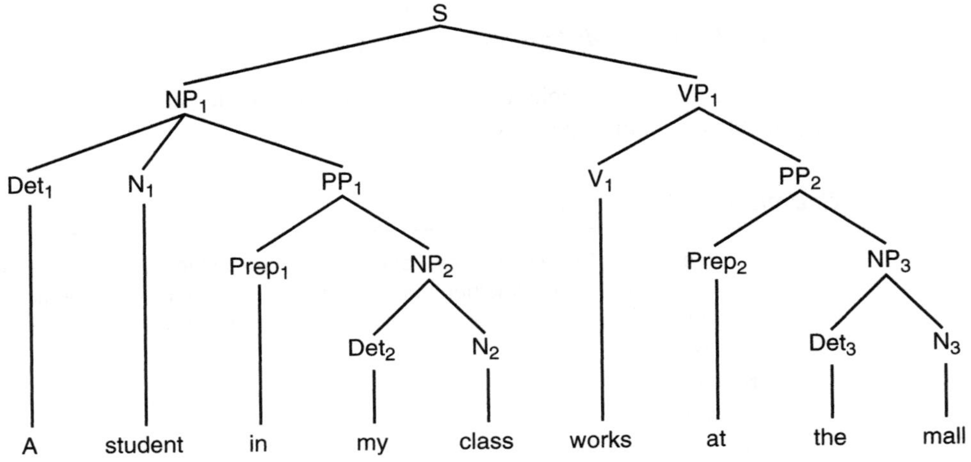

FIGURE 4.1 Diagram of *A student in my class works at the mall*

Exercise C

1. Based on the examples just given, complete the following questions about Figure 4.1.
   - **a.** What is the relationship between V_1 and PP_2?
   - **b.** What is the relationship between PP_2 and $Prep_2$-NP_3?
   - **c.** What is the relationship between VP_1 and the nodes beneath it?
   - **d.** Is there any relationship between PP_1 and PP_2?
2. Using the PS rules given earlier, draw tree diagrams for the following sentences.
   - **a.** The children laughed at the clown.
   - **b.** Haste makes waste.
   - **c.** A very small package arrived.
   - **d.** A meteor hit that red car.

Recursion. PS rules also allow us to represent an important property of human language called **recursion.** Recursion refers to the ability to repeat two types of phrases by **embedding** them in each other—that is, by allowing each type to directly dominate the other type. Consider the PS rules for NP and PP, repeated here.

NP→(Det)–(AP)–N–(PP)
PP→Prep–NP

Recursion between these two rules is possible because an NP can expand into a PP, which in turn can (in fact, must) expand into another NP. This situation allows speakers of English to produce phrases that are, at least in theory, infinitely long. For example, there is no upper limit on the number of recursions a speaker could perform on a phrase like (6).

(6) the cat in the hat on the table by the chair in the corner of the kitchen in the house under the tree . . .

A partial tree diagram of this phrase is shown in Figure 4.2.

Exercise D

1. Complete the tree diagram in Figure 4.2, showing the rest of the phrase in (6).

Constituent Structure

Phrases, clauses, and sentences are more than just a set of words or, as we have just discussed, categories arranged in left-to-right order. Rather, they are sets of categories organized into a *hierarchical* structure. As was the case with categories, linguists have postulated hierarchical structures for sentences solely in order to account for phenomena that they otherwise could not explain. For example, consider the phrase *American history teacher,* which was mentioned briefly in the chapter on semantics. As any native speaker of English can verify, this phrase is ambiguous: it can mean either 'a teacher of American history' or 'a history teacher

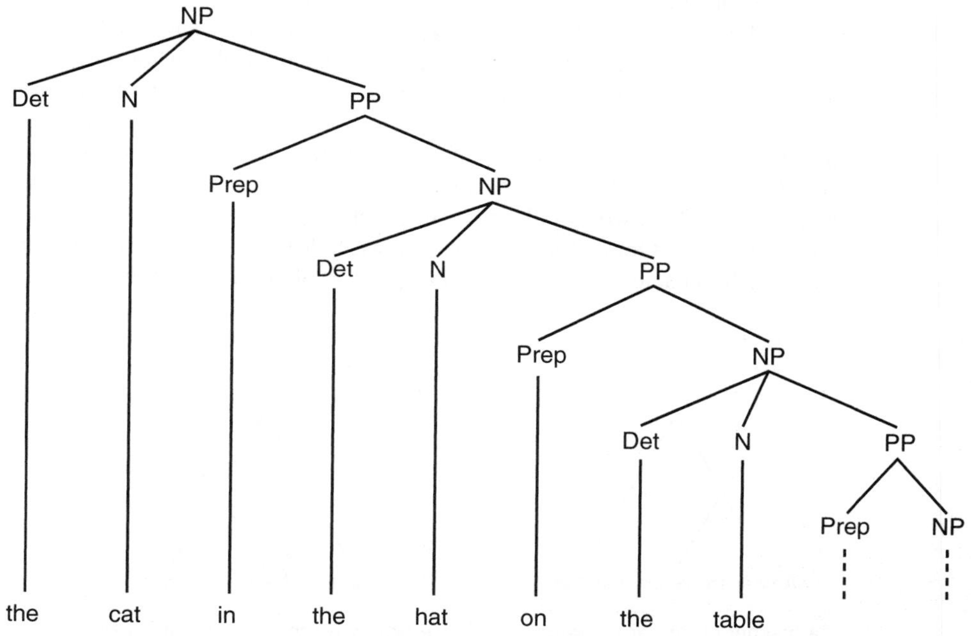

FIGURE 4.2 Partial tree diagram of the phrase in (6)

who is American.' However, we saw earlier that this ambiguity is not lexical; none of the words *(American, history,* or *teacher)* has more than one sense. If this is the case, how then are we to account for the ambiguity of *American history teacher?*

One way to explain this phenomenon is to assume that phrases are organized into hierarchical structures and that there are cases where more than one such structure can be assigned to a particular phrase. Such cases are said to exhibit **structural ambiguity.** Under this hypothesis, *American history teacher* can be assigned two different structures and, therefore, is structurally ambiguous. The two structures are given in Figure 4.3. An informal explanation of how these structures account for the ambiguity of *American history teacher* is as follows. In (i), *American* modifies *history.* In alternative terms, we might say that *American history* is a **constituent.** Two or more words form a constituent if there is a node in their associated tree structure that dominates all and only these words. In structure (i), there is a node Y that dominates all and only the words *American history.* Note also that there is no such node in (i) that dominates all and only the words *history teacher.* Thus, in (i) *history* does not modify *teacher* or, in alternative terms, *history teacher* is not a constituent. Moreover, note that structure (i), in which *American history* is a constituent, corresponds exactly to the interpretation of (i), namely that *American* describes *history.*

Now consider structure (ii). Here *history teacher* is a constituent, whereas *American history* is not. There is a node X in (ii) that dominates all and only *history teacher;* there is not a node which dominates all and only *American history.* Structure (ii), in turn, corresponds exactly to the interpretation of (ii), namely that *history* describes *teacher.*

Before moving on, it is worth mentioning several points about these two structures. First, they are theoretical constructs (i.e., part of a theory) postulated by linguists in order to account for the fact that the phrase *American history teacher* has two different senses or interpretations. Second, without postulating these hierarchical structures, there is no transparent explanation for the ambiguity of *American history teacher.* (As we saw earlier, this is not a case of lexical ambiguity.) Third, the justification for these two hierarchical structures is independent of the justification for categories. Note that, in these two structures, the words *American, history,* and *teacher* are not labeled for categories. In fact, it is immaterial what category each of these words falls into. The point is that the structures are motivated independently of the need for categories. Note, likewise, that the argument for categories discussed earlier in this chapter was completely independent of the argument for hierarchical structure.

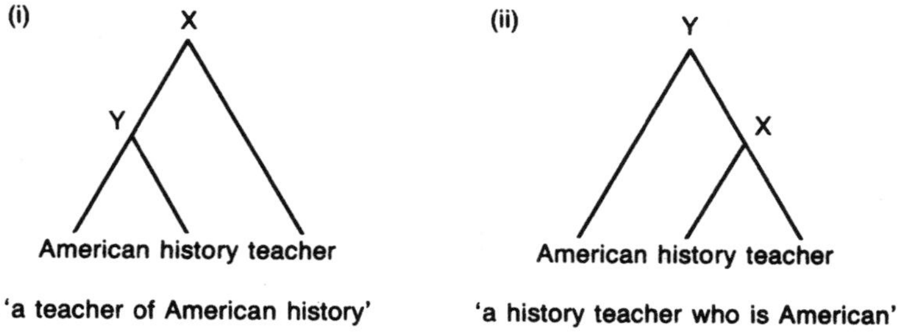

FIGURE 4.3 Structural ambiguity

Exercise E

1. Each of the following phrases is structurally ambiguous—that is, it can be assigned two different constituent structures. For each phrase, use unlabeled tree diagrams to show the two different structures. Also, provide a paraphrase which indicates the meaning associated with each tree structure.
   - †**a.** abnormal psychology professor
   - **b.** foreign student organization
   - **c.** second language teacher
   - **d.** big truck driver
2. Identify any structurally ambiguous sentences in the following group. For those that are structurally ambiguous, give two paraphrases.
   - **a.** Meet me at the bank.
   - **b.** Dr. Smith is a European history professor.
   - **c.** The men examined the plant.
   - **d.** Jane hid the letter from Dan.
   - **e.** Muffy saw some old men and women.
   - **f.** Visiting relatives are sometimes a nuisance.
   - **g.** Visiting relatives can sometimes be a nuisance.

However, the concepts of categories and constituent structure do interact in many syntactic phenomena. Consider the following sentences.

(7a) The police arrested the suspect at home.
(7b) The suspect was arrested at home by the police.
(7c) *The suspect at home was arrested by the police.
(8a) The police examined a photograph of the accident.
(8b) *A photograph was examined of the accident by the police.
(8c) A photograph of the accident was examined by the police.

What observations can we make about these sentences? First, (7a) and (8a) are active sentences, whereas (7b–c) and (8b–c) are their respective **passive** counterparts. (Active and passive sentences are paraphrases of each other in which the object of the active verb corresponds to the subject of the passive verb. Thus, *X saw Y* is active and *Y was seen by X* is the corresponding passive.) Second, (7a) and (8a) seem to contain the same categories arranged in the same order, as illustrated here.

	NP	**V**	**NP**	**PP**
(7a)	The police	arrested	the suspect	at home
(8a)	The police	examined	a photograph	of the accident

Third, in (7b) the NP *the suspect* is the subject; in (7c) the NP-PP sequence *the suspect at home* is the subject. In (8b) the NP *a photograph* is the subject; in (8c) the NP-PP sequence *a photograph of the accident* is the subject. Fourth, (7b) is an acceptable passive version of (7a), but (7c) is not. On the other hand, (8c) is an acceptable passive version of (8a), but (8b) is not. It is this last observation that seems to have no ready explanation. That is, why should the acceptable passive version of (7a) have only an NP *(the suspect)* as its subject, while the acceptable passive version of (8a) has an NP-PP sequence *(a photograph of the accident)* as its subject?

This state of affairs can be explained if we make three assumptions. First, a passive sentence will have the direct object of its active version as subject. That is, the direct object of the active corresponds to the subject of the passive. Second, the direct object of an active sentence is the NP directly under VP (or, in more technical terms, the NP directly dominated by VP). Third, (7a) and (8a) have different constituent structures, as shown in Figure 4.4. These structures provide a simple account of the problem we noted earlier, namely that in the acceptable passive of (7a), the NP *the suspect* is the subject, but in the acceptable passive of (8a), the NP-PP sequence *a photograph of the accident* is the subject. Note that in diagram (7a), *the suspect* is the direct object (the NP directly under VP) and thus corresponds to the subject of the passive version (7b). On the other hand, in diagram (8a), *a photograph of the accident* is the direct object (i.e., *a photograph of the accident* is all part of the NP directly under VP) and thus corresponds to the subject of the passive version (8c).

(As an informal exercise, try to explain how the diagram for (7a) rules out the unacceptable passive in (7c) and how the diagram for (8a) rules out the unacceptable passive in (8b).)

The main point of this example is that our explanation of the data in (7a–c) and (8a–c) depends crucially on the concepts of categories and constituent structure. Note our reference to categories (e.g., the object is the NP directly under VP) and to constituent structure (e.g., the PP in (8a) is part of the direct object NP, whereas the PP in (7a) is not). As this example shows, it is difficult, if not impossible, to make even the most commonplace observations about syntactic phenomena without using notions such as categories and constituent structure.

Exercise F

1. Consider the following sentences:
   A. Ralph put the note on the door.
   B. Ralph found the key to the door.
   Provide evidence that (A) and (B) have different structures with respect to their direct objects and their prepositional phrases. (Hint: Your evidence should consist of one grammatical and one ungrammatical sentence. For ideas on how to prove that these two sentences have different structures, review the material on p. 61.)
2. Consider the following sentences (adapted from Akmajian and Heny [1975:72–73]):
   A. John ran up the hill.
   B. John ran up the bill.
   Which pair below does *not* provide evidence that these two sentences have different syntactic structures?
   a. *John ran the hill up.
   John ran the bill up.

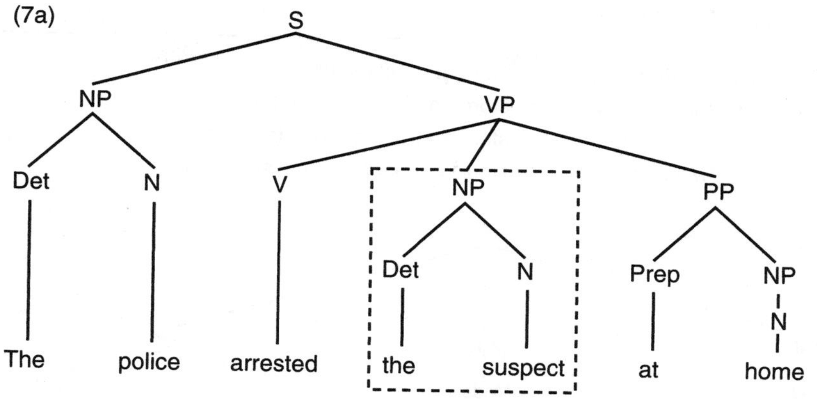

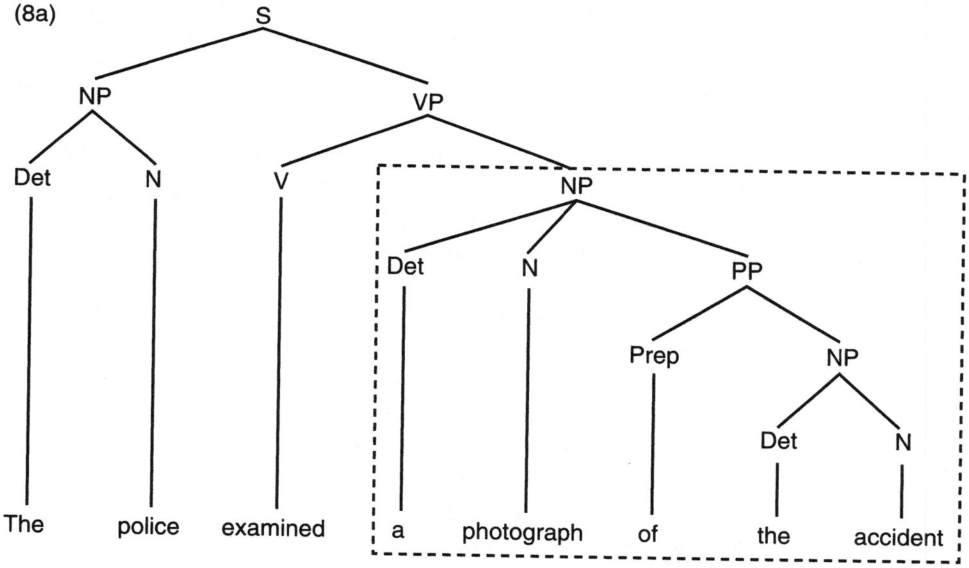

FIGURE 4.4 Constituent structures of (7a) and (8a), indicating their direct objects

Exercise F *Continued*

b. Up the hill John ran.
   *Up the bill John ran.

c. John was running up the hill.
   John was running up the bill.

3. Consider the following data and tree structure:

   A. *Muffy might rob the store and Biff might rob the, too.

   B. *Muffy might rob the store and Biff might rob, too.

(continued)

Exercise F Continued

C. Muffy might rob the store and Biff might too.
D. *Muffy might rob the store and Biff the store too.
E. *Muffy might rob the store and Biff rob the store too.
F. *Muffy might rob the store and Biff might the store too.

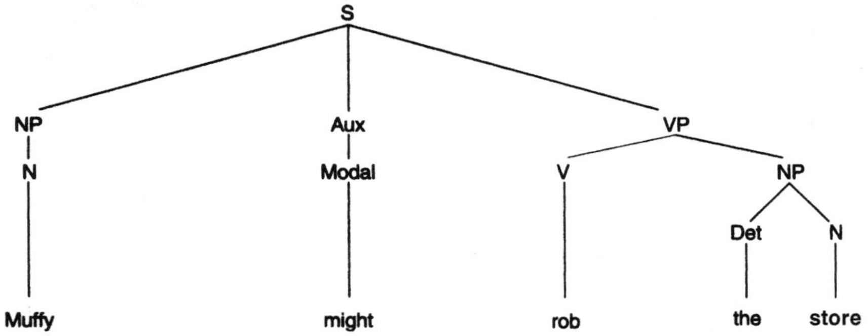

Based on these data, which of the following generalizations correctly completes the following sentence: Rather than being repeated, . . .

a. Any phrasal category can be omitted.
b. Any lexical category can be omitted.
c. Only NP can be omitted.
d. Only VP can be omitted
e. Only V can be omitted.
f. An auxiliary or a main verb can be omitted.

4. Consider the following data:

A. I wrote a letter and a postcard.
B. *I wrote a letter and to Fred.
C. I wrote to Fred and to Ricky.
D. I wrote to Fred and Ricky.
E. I wrote carefully and slowly.
F. *I wrote carefully and a letter.

The analysis that best explains these data is that:

a. Only items belonging to identical categories can be conjoined by *and.*
b. Only items belonging to different categories can be conjoined by *and.*
c. Only NPs can be conjoined by *and.*
d. Only PPs can be conjoined by *and.*
e. none of the above.

5. Consider the following data and its associated structure.

A. Fred should get a haircut, and so should Ricky.
B. *Fred should get a haircut, and so Ricky.
C. *Fred should get a haircut, and so should Ricky a haircut.

Exercise F *Continued*

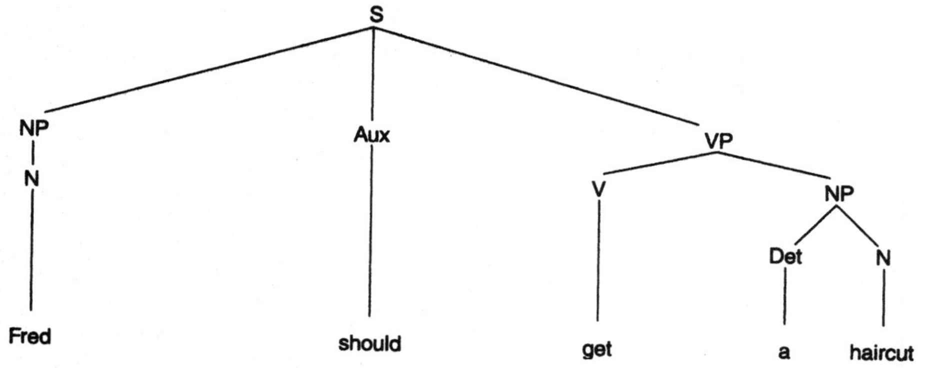

The analysis that best explains these data is that

a. The word *so* substitutes for the material dominated by AUX and VP.

b. The word *so* substitutes for the material dominated by VP.

c. The word *so* substitutes for the material dominated by NP.

d. The word *so* substitutes for the material dominated by AUX.

Before leaving the topic of constituent structure, we want to cover two concepts that deal with the relationships between constituents. **Subcategorization restrictions** are syntactic constraints on the kinds of complements (e.g., direct object, prepositional phrase) that lexical categories (e.g., verbs) can take. For example, *conceal* requires a direct object *(He concealed the bed); sleep* cannot have a direct object *(*He slept the bed).* On the other hand, **sectional restrictions** are semantic constraints on the arguments (e.g., subject and object) that lexical categories (e.g., verbs) can take. For example, *admire* requires a human subject *(My neighbor/*My dog admires my begonias); frighten* requires an animate object *(Franklin frightened his dog/*his chainsaw).*

Exercise G

1. Based on the following data, state the selectional restrictions on the object of *kill.*

A. kill a man

B. kill a dog

C. kill a tree

D. *kill a rock

†2. Based on the following data, state the selectional restrictions on the object of *murder.*

A. murder a man

B. *murder a dog

C. *murder a tree

D. *murder a rock

(continued)

Exercise G *Continued*

3. Consider the following sentences containing *frimble,* a hypothetical verb:

   A. Martha is frimbling her parakeet with a garden hose.

   B. Martha frimbled her husband in the dining room.

   C. Little Freddy might frimble the parakeet.

   D. *Little Freddy frimbled with a garden hose.

   E. *Martha is frimbling the bed with a garden hose.

   F. *Little Freddy shouldn't frimble.

   Based on these data, what is the best statement of the subcategorization restrictions on *frimble?*

   a. must be followed by both NP and PP

   b. can be followed by NP, must be followed by PP

   c. does not have to be followed by either NP or PP

   d. must be followed by NP, can be followed by PP

4. Based on the data in Exercise (3), what is the best statement of the selectional restrictions on *frimble?*

   a. must be followed by a [–human] NP

   b. must be followed by a [+human] NP

   c. must be followed by a [+animate] NP

   d. can be followed by any type of NP

5. Based on the following data, what are the selectional restrictions on the relative pronouns *who* and *which?* That is, what are the restrictions on the type of noun that each one can follow?

   A. I saw the man who lives down the street.

   B. *I saw the man which lives down the street.

   C. *I called the dog who was chasing the cat.

   D. I called the dog which was chasing the cat.

   E. *I found the hammer who I lost last week.

   F. I found the hammer which I lost last week.

X-Bar Syntax

Linguists have refined traditional PS grammars (i.e., those for constructing tree diagrams) by developing a theory of constituent structure known as **X-bar syntax.** This theory extends PS grammars in two ways. First, it recognizes a structural unit intermediate in size between a phrasal category (e.g., NP) and a lexical category (e.g., N). This intermediate category is called a "bar" category (e.g., N-bar) and is symbolized by the category with a bar over it (e.g., $\bar{N}$) or with a prime mark following it (e.g., N'). Second, X-bar syntax makes the claim that all phrase types (e.g., NP, VP, AP, etc.) have essentially the same internal structure. Thus, this system of representation (e.g., N, N', NP) can be generalized to any phrase type (e.g., X, X', XP), where X stands for any category (e.g., N, V, A, etc.). Hence the term *X-bar syntax.*

Previously, linguists assumed that phrases such as *the redheaded student* have the internal structure shown here.

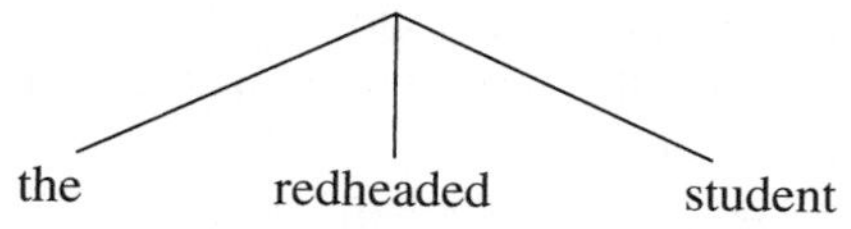

That is, *the redheaded student* can be interpreted as an NP; and *student* can be interpreted as an N; but *redheaded student* is not a constituent (i.e., a structural unit) of any sort. (This would be a good point to review your understanding of the structural definition of "constituent." If you understand this concept, you should be able to explain why *redheaded student* is not a constituent in the diagram above.)

However, one piece of evidence for the internal structure of phrases is **pro-form substitution.** A pro-form is a word which can substitute for a phrase that forms a constituent. With this in mind, consider the following data.

i. I know this [*redheaded student*] better than that [*one*].
ii. *I know [*this redheaded student*] better than [*one*].

In (i), the pro-form *one* substitutes for *redheaded student,* which means that *redheaded student* is a constituent of some sort. This constituent is intermediate in size between the NP *this redheaded student* and the N *student.* Moreover, (ii) illustrates that *one*-substitution is a good test for picking out such intermediate categories, since *one* will not substitute for the entire NP *this redheaded student.*

Linguists concluded from such facts that the internal structure of a phrase such as *the redheaded student* must be something like the following:

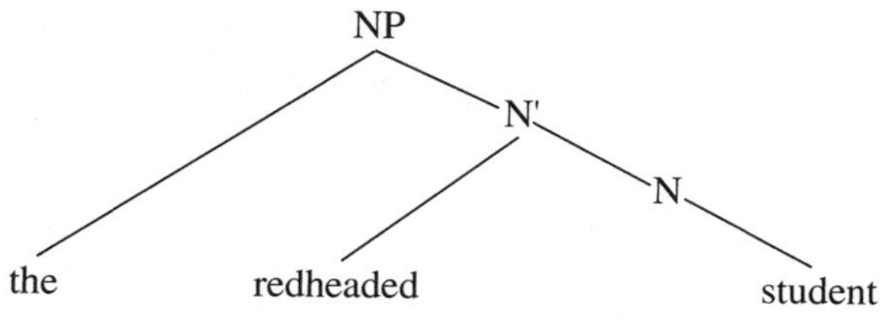

In this diagram, *the redheaded student* is an NP; *redheaded student* is an N'; and *student* is an N. In short, this diagram reflects one important basic inference that X-bar theorists have drawn about phrases such as *redheaded student: redheaded student* is a separate structural unit—a constituent.

From this insight, linguists began investigating more complex NPs such as the following.

(9a) *the redheaded music student*
(9b) *the student of music with red hair*

You'll note that both of these NPs have two modifiers each: two modifiers before the head N in (9a), *redheaded* and *music,* and two modifiers following the head N in (9b), *of music* and *with red hair.* Moreover, these two modifiers must occur in a particular order (i.e., they cannot be reversed), as shown here.

(9c) **the music redheaded student*
(9d) **the student with red hair of music*

Likewise, they cannot be coordinated, as shown here.

(9e) **the music and redheaded student*
(9f) **the student of music and with red hair*

Note that this restriction on coordination is not general; for example, the following items are grammatical.

(9g) *the music and drama student*
(9h) *the student of music and of drama*
(9i) *the redheaded and bearded student*
(9j) *the student with red hair and with a beard*

From these facts, it was concluded that NPs have three types of modifiers: **specifiers** (e.g., *the*), **adjuncts** (e.g., *redheaded/with red hair*), and **complements** (e.g., *music/of music*). Complements always occur closest to the head N (whether they precede or follow it), then adjuncts occur farther from the head (whether they precede or follow it), and specifiers occur farthest from the head (they precede it only).

Figure 4.5 summarizes what X-bar theorists have inferred about the internal structure of NPs. These X-bar diagrams account for a number of properties that were overlooked in earlier models of PS grammar:

- NPs contain constituents intermediate in size between N and NP. For example, we have *student* (N), *music student* (N'), *redheaded music student* (another N'), and *the redheaded music student* (NP).
- Adjuncts and complements can occur before or after the head of an NP (e.g., *music student* or *student of music*).
- NP modifiers are of three different types: specifier (daughter of NP), adjunct (sister of N'), and complement (sister of N).
- Complements are always closer to the head of the phrase than are adjuncts.

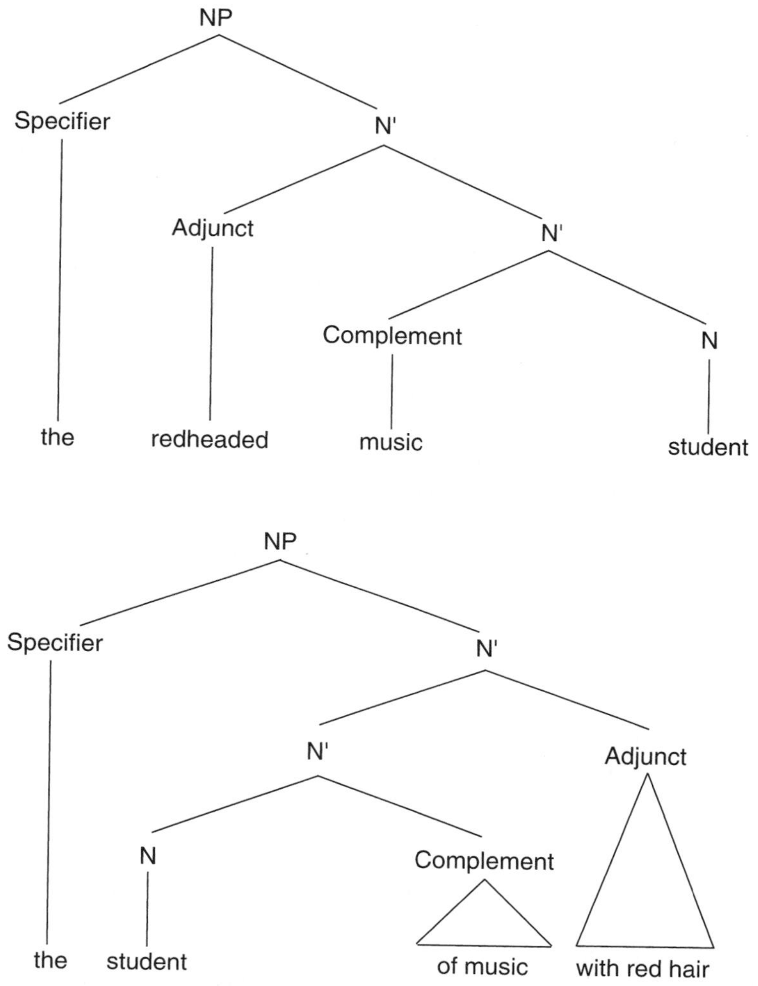

FIGURE 4.5 Internal structure of (9a) and (9b)

Exercise H

1. Consider the phrase *the French English professors.* Which of the following glosses best captures its meaning?
   - **a.** 'the professors of English and of French'
   - **b.** 'the professors from England and from France'
   - **c.** 'the professors of English from France'
   - **d.** 'the professors of French from England'

   Explain how the theory of X-bar syntax predicts your answer to the preceding question.

Transformations

In addition to postulating categories, left-to-right ordering, and constituent structure, many linguists have proposed that a complete account of the syntactic structure of sentences must include the concept of **transformation.** A transformation is an operation that moves a lexical or phrasal category (e.g., N, NP, V, VP) from one location to another within a structure. As with categories and constituent structure, linguists have postulated transformations in order to account for phenomena that they otherwise could not explain.

Let's consider a concrete example. In English, the verb *conceal* is subcategorized for one direct object NP. That is, *conceal* requires one and only one direct object NP. This property is illustrated in (10a–d).

(10a) Tiny Abner has concealed the document.
(10b) Tiny Abner has concealed Mary.
(10c) *Tiny Abner has concealed.
(10d) *Tiny Abner has concealed the document Mary.

Sentences (10a–b) are acceptable because *conceal* in each case has one and only one direct object (*the document* in (10a) and *Mary* in (10b)). Sentence (10c) is unacceptable because *conceal* has no direct object, and (10d) is unacceptable because *conceal* has more than one direct object *(the document* and *Mary).* We can account for these facts very simply with the following generalization: any sentence containing the verb *conceal* will be acceptable if it contains one and only one direct object NP; conversely, any sentence containing the verb *conceal* will be unacceptable if it contains no direct object or more than one direct object.

In passing, it is worth mentioning that sentences such as *Tiny Abner has concealed the document and the microfilm* appear to violate this generalization, since there seem to be two direct objects, *the document* and *the microfilm.* Note, however, that compound NPs (e.g., *the document and the microfilm*) behave just like single NPs for the purpose of our generalization. For example, the entire compound NP is moved to subject position when the sentence is made passive (e.g., *The document and the microfilm have been concealed by Tiny Abner*). Thus, compound NPs behave exactly like single NPs.

Now let's look at some *wh*-interrogatives containing the verb *conceal.* (A *wh*-interrogative is one introduced by a *wh*-word: *who, what, when, where, why,* or *how.*) Examples are given in (11a–d).

(11a) What has Tiny Abner concealed?
(11b) Who has Tiny Abner concealed?
(11c) *What has Tiny Abner concealed Mary?
(11d) *Who has Tiny Abner concealed the document?

These sentences seem to present a problem. Note that our generalization about the declarative sentences in (10a–d) makes exactly the *wrong* predictions about (11a–d). The generalization predicts that (11a–b) should be unacceptable, since neither of these sentences apparently has a direct object, and that (11c–d) should be acceptable, since each of these sentences apparently has one and only one direct object. (Recall our definition of direct object as an NP directly under VP.) Actually, the facts are just the reverse: (11a–b) are perfectly acceptable, and (11c–d) are absolutely unacceptable.

One way out of this predicament would be to say that sentences containing the verb *conceal* are subject to two different generalizations, depending upon whether they are declaratives or interrogatives. We can state these generalizations as follows:

GENERALIZATION 1:	A declarative sentence containing the verb *conceal* is acceptable if it contains one and only one direct object.
GENERALIZATION 2:	An interrogative sentence containing the verb *conceal* is acceptable if it contains no direct object.

Although this solution seems to work, it raises three additional problems. First, it requires us to double our number of generalizations concerning sentences containing *conceal.* This problem is not insurmountable, but it does make our analysis suspect, since it opens the door to proliferating the number of generalizations we need to cover various types of sentences. Second, there are acceptable interrogative sentences such as *Where has Tiny Abner concealed the document?* that contain the verb *conceal* and do have a direct object. Third, there are other interrogative sentences (*yes-no* interrogatives) that conform to Generalization 1 (the one for declaratives) rather than to Generalization 2 (the one for interrogatives). Consider the *yes-no* interrogatives in (12a–d). (They are called *yes-no* interrogatives because they can be answered with *yes* or *no,* unlike *wh*-interrogatives: *Has John arrived? Yes.* vs. *Who arrived? *Yes.*)

(12a) Has Tiny Abner concealed the document?
(12b) Has Tiny Abner concealed Mary?
(12c) *Has Tiny Abner concealed?
(12d) *Has Tiny Abner concealed the document Mary?

Note that these interrogative sentences do not behave like the interrogatives in (11a–d), but instead like the declaratives in (10a–d). That is, Generalization 2, the one concerning interrogatives, *incorrectly* predicts that (12a–b) are unacceptable, since they contain a direct object; and that (12c) is acceptable, because it contains no direct object. On the other hand, Generalization 1, the one concerning declaratives, *correctly* predicts that (12a–b) are acceptable, since they contain one and only one direct object; that (12c) is unacceptable, because it contains no direct object; and that (12d) is unacceptable, because it contains more than one direct object. How can we avoid these problems?

We could, of course, state that (for some unknown reason) declaratives and non-*wh*-interrogatives behave one way with respect to *conceal* and that *wh*-interrogatives behave another way. This solution would describe some of the facts, but it doesn't really explain them. That is, it doesn't give us any insight into why the facts are the way they are.

Movement. Let's consider another, completely different way of analyzing the *wh*-interrogatives in (11a–d). Let's assume that our original generalization about *conceal* was correct, namely that *conceal* requires one and only one direct object. Let's further assume that *wh*-words do not originate in clause-initial position, but instead originate elsewhere in the structure and are moved into clause-initial position by a transformation that is stated something like this: move the *wh*-phrase into clause-initial position. We will call this transformation ***wh*-Movement.**

A second transformation is involved in the derivation of interrogatives. This transformation moves the tensed verb (which is always the first verb) to the left of the subject NP. This transformation is called **Inflection Movement,** or **I-Movement,** for short. We will further identify the structure that exists before any transformations have applied as the **underlying structure** and that which exists after any transformations have applied as the **surface structure.** Finally, we will stipulate that our original generalization—that the verb *conceal* requires one and only one direct object—applies only to underlying structures.

Now we are in a position to provide a straightforward account of *wh*-interrogatives containing the verb *conceal.* The underlying structure of (11a) *What has Tiny Abner concealed?* is given in Figure 4.6. Note that this underlying structure is consistent with our original generalization, namely that *conceal* requires one and only one direct object NP (the direct object here is the NP *what*). The *wh*-Movement transformation applies to the underlying structure in Figure 4.6, transforming it into the surface structure in Figure 4.7.

The *wh*-Movement transformation accounts for the fact that even though *what* originated as the direct object in the underlying structure, it ends up in clause-initial position in the surface structure. The main point is that this analysis provides a unified treatment of sentences (10a), (11a), and (12a), repeated here.

(10a) Tiny Abner has concealed the document.
(11a) What has Tiny Abner concealed?
(12a) Has Tiny Abner concealed the document?

The underlying structure of all three sentences contains one and only one direct object, and thus meets the criterion for acceptability set out in our original generalization, namely that *conceal* requires one and only one direct object. The direct object in (11a) *(what)* is moved to clause-initial position by the *wh*-Movement transformation. The direct object in both (10a) and (12a) *(the document)* remains in its original position since it is not a *wh*-word and thus is not subject to *wh*-Movement.

Note, too, that our transformational analysis provides a straightforward account of the unaccceptability of (11c) **What has Tiny Abner concealed Mary?* The underlying structure

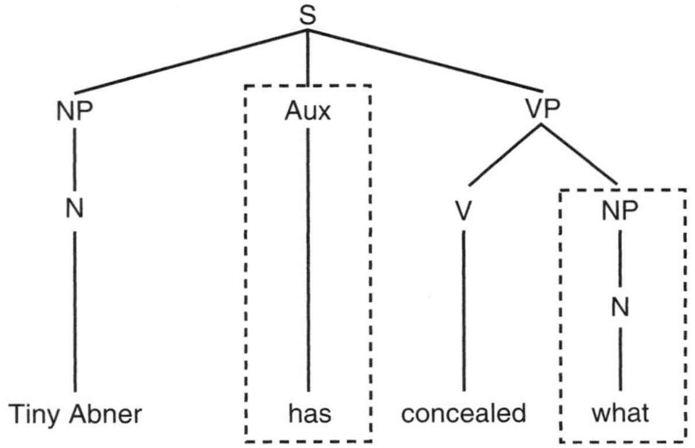

FIGURE 4.6 Underlying structure of sentence (11a)

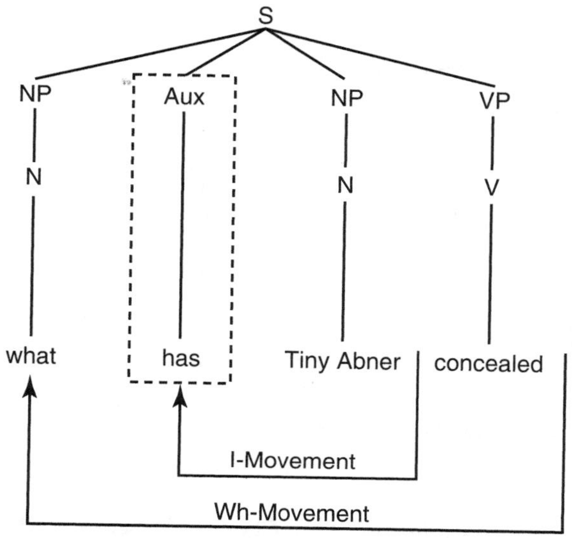

FIGURE 4.7 Surface structure of sentence (11a)

of this sentence is given in Figure 4.8. This structure violates our generalization that *conceal* requires one and only one direct object NP in the underlying structure. Even though *wh*-Movement would move *what* to clause-initial position, leaving only one direct object (i.e., *Mary*) in the surface structure, the "damage" is already done. Our generalization applies to underlying structures, not to surface structures.

Exercise I

1. The two rules of *wh*-Movement and I-Movement essentially define the four basic sentence structures in English: declaratives, *yes-no* interrogatives, exclamations, and *wh*-interrogatives. Examine each sentence type and tell which rule(s), if any, have applied in each sentence type.
   - **A.** DECLARATIVE: You are being a good boy.
   - **B.** YES-NO INTERROGATIVE: Are you being a good boy?
   - **C.** EXCLAMATION: What a good boy you are being!
   - **D.** WH-INTERROGATIVE: What kind of boy are you being?
2. "Tensed verb" plays a role not only in I-Movement (move the tensed verb to the left of the subject), but also in negative and emphatic structures. Examine the following structures and form a generalization that mentions "tensed verb" and that describes negative and emphatic sentences.
   - **A.** DECLARATIVE: She will go with you.
   - **B.** YES-NO INTERROGATIVE: Will she go with you?
   - **C.** NEGATIVE: She will *not* go with you.
   - **D.** EMPHATIC: She will *so/too* go with you.

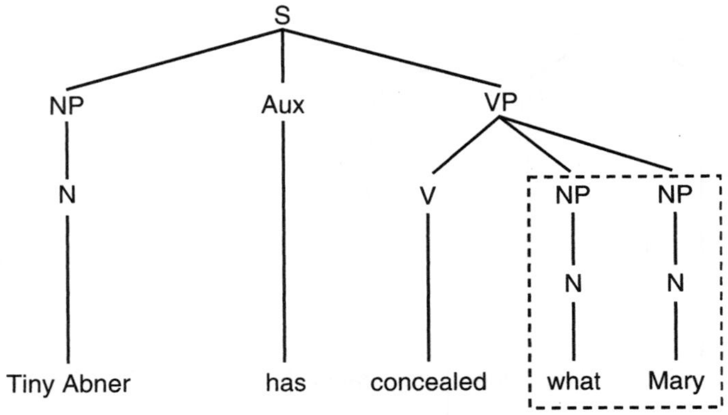

FIGURE 4.8 Underlying structure of sentence (11c)

Another transformation that plays a major role in Chomsky's theory is **NP-Movement:** move any NP to any empty NP position. This rule moves the object of a passive verb into subject position to create a passive sentence, as shown in (13).

(13) *Muffy* was being pursued _______ by the police.
NP-Movement

The arguments for NP-Movement here are exactly the same as those for *wh*-Movement in the case of *conceal. Pursue* is subcategorized for a direct object; therefore, *pursue* must have a direct object in the underlying structure of any sentence containing it. Thus, in the passive sentence *Muffy was being pursued by the police, Muffy* must originate as the direct object of *pursue.*

Exercise J

The rule of NP-Movement moves (among other things) the subject of a dependent infinitive clause to subject position of the adjacent main clause, as in (A).

A. *Franklin* seems to me [$_S$_______ to have contradicted *himself*]
NP-Movement

What argument can you construct for having the NP *Franklin* originate within the bracketed clause? (Hint: You may need to review Chapter 1.)

These two uses of NP-Movement (move the object of a passive verb to subject position, and move the subject of an infinitive clause to subject position of the main clause) interact so as to account for some seemingly complex structures. For example, sentence (14a) is derived as in (14b).

(14a) The child seemed to have been abandoned.
(14b) *The child* seemed [_____ to have been abandoned _____]

To conclude this section, we have looked at the motivation for positing transformations as part of a theory of syntax. Like the concepts of categories, left-to-right ordering, and constituent structure, the concept of transformations is postulated in order to account for phenomena that otherwise could not be explained, at least in any systematic, principled way. Before leaving the subject of transformations, let us again emphasize that transformations are part of an (unobservable) theory of syntax—that is, part of a method for describing and analyzing the structure of sentences. It would be a mistake to assume that transformations are involved in the actual production and perception of sentences by speakers and listeners. In other words, the fact that sentences can be described in terms of their underlying and surface structures should not be interpreted as meaning that a speaker "starts out" with an underlying structure and "transforms" it into a surface structure during the act of producing a sentence. A theory that includes the notions of transformations, underlying structures, and surface structures does not make any direct claims about how speakers go about producing sentences, but instead about how sentences themselves can be analyzed.

Exercise K

†1. Consider the following sentence: *Where has John put the car?* How can the following data be used to argue that *where* originated to the right of *the car* in the underlying structure (i.e., *John put the car where*) and was moved to clause-initial position in the surface structure? (Hint: Both *where* and *in the garage* indicate location.)

A. John has put the car in the garage.

B. *John has put.

C. *John has put the car.

2. The following two sentences appear to have the same structure:

A. John threw away the magazine.

B. John walked down the street.

However, certain tests can be used as evidence that one of these sentences contains a one-word verb followed by a prepositional phrase, while the other sentence contains a two-word verb followed by an object noun phrase. Try each of the following tests on these two sentences. What conclusions can you draw about which sentence has which structure?

A. A prepositional phrase can appear in both sentence-final and sentence-initial position.

i. He went *up the chimney.*

ii. *Up the chimney* he went.

B. A two-word verb can be separated by a direct object.

i. John *picked up* the garbage.

ii. John *picked* the garbage *up.*

(continued)

Exercise K *Continued*

3. Consider the following sentences:

A. John didn't notice a mistake.

B. What didn't John notice?

C. *John didn't notice.

D. *What didn't John notice a mistake?

These data can be explained by assuming that _____.

a. The word *what* is moved to clause-initial position by means of the *wh*-Movement transformation.

b. The word *notice* requires exactly one direct object NP in the underlying structure.

c. The word *notice* requires exactly one direct object NP in the surface structure.

d. both (a) and (b)

e. both (b) and (c)

Constraints on Movement

During the last 30 years, Chomsky has extended the theory of transformational grammar to include **constraints** on transformations. Each constraint is not part of a particular rule, but rather a restriction on what transformations can do in general. Consider the following constraints (adapted from Radford, 1981:212–248) and an example of how each one serves to block transformational movement in a derivation. (Movement is indicated by an arrow.)

Coordinate Structure Constraint. This constraint states that no element can be moved out of a coordinate structure.

(15) Do you put [$_{NP}$*salt and pepper*] on steak?

(16) *What* do you put [$_{NP}$———] on steak?

(17) **What* do you put [$_{NP}$*salt and* ———] on steak?

Salt and pepper is a coordinate structure, as illustrated in (15). The whole structure can be questioned (replaced by a *wh*-word) and then moved to clause-initial position, as in (16). However, one member of the coordinate structure cannot be questioned and moved, as in (17).

Unit Movement Constraint. This constraint states that no string of elements which do not form a constituent can be moved together in a single application of a movement rule.

(18a) Did he climb [$_{PP}$*up the ladder*]?

(18b) *Where* did he climb $[_{PP}$ ——]?

(19a) Did he $[_{V}$fold *up*] $[_{NP}$ *the ladder*]?

(19b) **Where* did he $[_{V}$fold ——] $[_{NP}$ ——]?

Up the ladder is a constituent (i.e., a PP) in (18a), and thus can be questioned and subsequently moved, as illustrated in (18b). However, *up the ladder* is not a constituent in (19a), and thus cannot be questioned and moved, as in (19b).

Subjacency Constraint. This constraint prohibits an element from being moved across more than one S or NP boundary in a single application of a movement rule. (The rule in this example is called **Extraposition,** which moves a relative clause or prepositional phrase away from the NP that contains it to clause-final position.)

(20a) The fact that $[_{S}[_{NP}$an article *about Trump*$_{NP}$] was just published$_{S}$] was unexpected.

(20b) The fact that $[_{S}[_{NP}$an article ——$_{NP}$] was just published *about Trump*$_{S}$] was unexpected.

(20c) *The fact that $[_{S}[_{NP}$an article ——$_{NP}$] was just published$_{S}$] was unexpected *about Trump.*

About Trump is a PP contained in the NP *an article about Trump,* as illustrated in (20a). Thus, *about Trump* can be moved via Extraposition to the end of the interior clause as in (20b), since it crosses only one NP boundary. However, it cannot be moved to the end of the exterior clause as in (20c), since it would have to cross both an NP and an S boundary.

Tensed S Constraint. This constraint prohibits an element from being moved outside of a tensed clause.

(21a) *All hell* is expected $[_{S}$—— to break loose]

(21b) **All hell* is expected $[_{S}$—— might break loose]

All hell is the subject of an untensed (infinitive) verb *(to break)* in (21a) and thus can be moved outside of that clause. However, *all hell* is the subject of a tensed verb *(might break)* in (21b) and thus cannot be so moved.

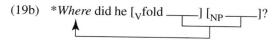

These constraints on movement represent a major step in the evolution of Chomsky's thought on syntax and the nature of language in general. In the late 1950s and 1960s Chomsky viewed each language as a set of complicated idiosyncratic rules. Twenty years later, he had begun to see the syntax of all languages as a set of very simple rules (e.g., NP-Movement and *wh*-Movement) plus the interaction of a number of very simple constraints. It is the *interaction* of the constraints (rather than the rules or constraints themselves) that Chomsky began to see as accounting for the differences among languages.

Exercise L

1. Identify the constraint violated by each of the following derivations.

   †a. *I remember the man *whom* you mentioned $[_{NP}$ ______ and the woman]

   b. **Big Ed* seems $[_{S}$ ______ will be incompetent]

   c. **The car into the garage* was put ______ by Muffy.

   d. **What* are you dating $[_{NP}$ a man $[_{S}$ that believes in ______]

   e. **John* appears $[_{S}$ ______ and Karen to be looking for Mr. Goodbar]

   f. **The commissioner* is expected $[_{S}$the police to want $[_{S}$ ______ to die]]

   g. **What* do you regret $[_{NP}$the fact $[_{S}$that you said ______]]

Summary

The theory of syntax makes use of five crucial concepts: category, left-to-right ordering, constituent structure, transformation, and constraints on transformations. These theoretical constructs are postulated to help us account for phenomena that otherwise would go unexplained.

Since the study of syntax has received more attention than any other area of linguistics during the past 45 years, it is especially important to understand that there is much more to the study of syntax than we have been able to cover here. In addition, some of the details surrounding these concepts may turn out to need revision; however, they enable us to account for syntactic phenomena better than any competing theory that has been proposed so far.

SUPPLEMENTARY READINGS

Culicover, P. (1997). *Principles and parameters: An introduction to syntactic theory.* New York: Oxford University Press.
Lyons, J. (1977). *Noam Chomsky.* New York: Penguin.
Newmeyer, F. J. (1986). *Linguistic theory in America* (2nd ed.). Orlando: Academic Press.
Parker, F., & Riley, K. (2005). *A short introduction to generative grammar.* Superior, WI: Parlay Press.
Radford, A. (1997). *Syntax: A minimalist introduction.* Cambridge, England: Cambridge University Press.
Riley, K., & Parker, F. (2005). *A short introduction to descriptive grammar.* Superior, WI: Parlay Press.
Walsh, T. (2000). *A short introduction to x-bar syntax and transformations* (2nd ed.). Superior, WI: Parlay Press.

You are now ready to read Parker and Riley, which places the generative approach within the larger context of other approaches to grammar. Riley and Parker provides an introduction to traditional descriptive grammar. Within the generative framework, so much has been written that it is a difficult area to break into on your own. Our best advice is to take an elementary course in syntax, where you will read Radford, Walsh, or something like them. Then read Lyons and Newmeyer for background. If you are in a position where you cannot take a course, read these books in the following order. Lyons provides an introduction to Chomsky's thought; Walsh is an excellent introduction to the bare essentials of generative syntax; Culicover and Radford are standard texts; and Newmeyer discusses the social and intellectual context surrounding the development of syntactic theory from the mid-1950s up to 1980.

Supplementary Exercises

1. In the movie *Funny Farm,* a couple moves from the city to a farm and ends up spending the first night on the floor. The next morning the wife says to the husband, *What they really mean when they say "hardwood floors" is "hard, wood floors."* What concept from syntax accounts for the humor of this line? Explain, using tree diagrams and paraphrases.
2. In traditional grammar, forms such as *he, she,* and *it* are called **pronouns** because they are said to substitute for nouns. Now consider the phrase *the man from the CIA,* its associated structure, and some relevant data.

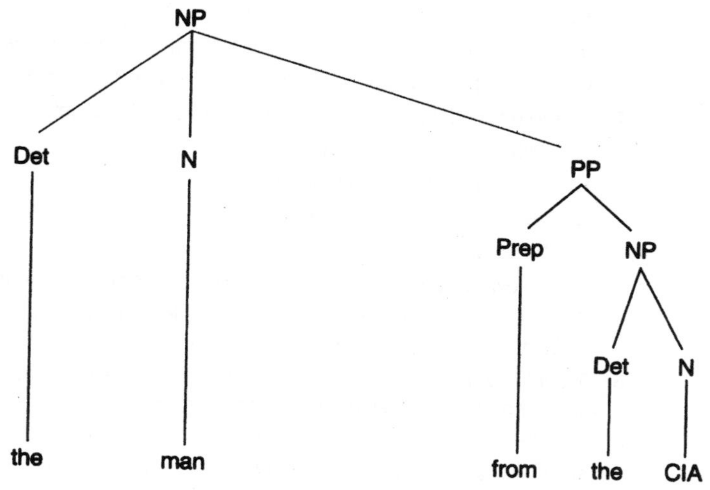

A. *The man from the CIA* came in and then *he* left.

B. *The *man* from the CIA came in and then the *he* from the CIA left.

C. **The man* from the CIA came in and then *he* from the CIA left.

D. *The *man from the CIA* came in and then the *he* left.

E. *The man *from the CIA* came in and then the man *he* left.

Based on these data, what category do pronouns substitute for?

3. The insertion of parenthetical material (e.g., *in my opinion*) into a sentence is sensitive to syntactic structure. Given the following structure and data, complete the following rule governing the insertion of parenthetical material into a sentence: Parenthetical material can be inserted into a structure only under the ________ node(s).

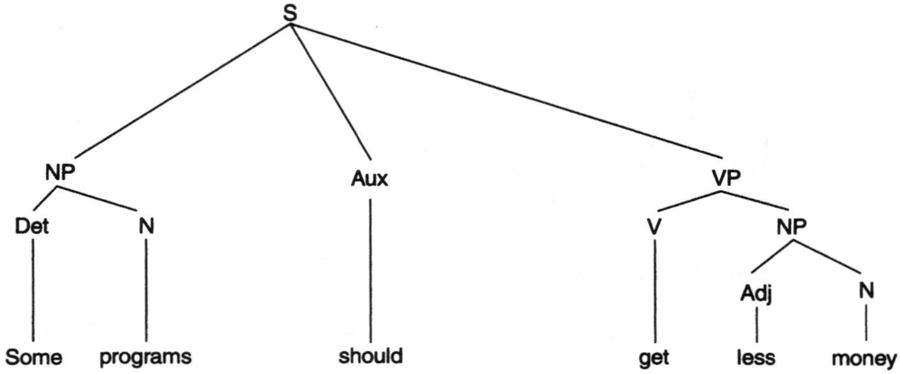

A. *In my opinion,* some programs should get less money.

B. *Some, *in my opinion,* programs should get less money.

C. Some programs, *in my opinion,* should get less money.

D. Some programs should, *in my opinion,* get less money.

E. *Some programs should get, *in my opinion,* less money.

F. *Some programs should get less, *in my opinion,* money.

G. Some programs should get less money, *in my opinion.*

4. Based on the following data, state the selection restriction on the object of *whack.*

A. Who whacked that guy?

B. *Who whacked that chipmunk?

C. *Who whacked that rose?

D. *Who whacked that pebble?

5. The following joke depends upon a concept from syntactic theory. What is that concept?

GROUCHO MARX: One morning I shot an elephant in my pajamas. How he got into my pajamas I don't know.

6. Provide evidence that (A) and (B) have different structures with respect to their direct objects and their prepositional phrases. (Hint: Your evidence should consist of one grammatical and one ungrammatical sentence. Review the material on page 61 for ideas.)

A. Ralph put the car in the garage.

B. Ralph provided the answer to the question.

7. Negative sentences in English follow a predictable pattern in terms of where *not* can occur within the sentence. Based on the following data, state a generalization about where *not* can occur.

   A.1. John has put the car in the garage.
   A.2. *John *not* has put the car in the garage.
   A.3. John has *not* put the car in the garage.
   A.4. *John has put *not* the car in the garage.
   B.1. John must have put the car in the garage.
   B.2. *John *not* must have put the car in the garage.
   B.3. John must *not* have put the car in the garage.
   B.4. *John must have *not* put the car in the garage.
   B.5. *John must have put *not* the car in the garage.

8. English contains a structure called a ***yes-no* question** that, as its name implies, asks for a *yes* or *no* response from the addressee. *Yes-no* questions can be described as systematic deviations from their declarative counterparts. Consider the following data:

   A.1. Ed has gone home.
   A.2. Has Ed gone home?
   B.1. The incumbent will win the primary.
   B.2. Will the incumbent win the primary?
   C.1. Bubba can do better than this.
   C.2. Can Bubba do better than this?

   As these data illustrate, forming a *yes-no* question involves moving a verb. (This is the transformation of Inflection-Movement discussed briefly in the chapter.) However, these data are insufficient for making a conclusive statement about exactly where the verb is moved.

   a. Based on the data above, formulate two hypotheses about where the verb is moved during the formation of a *yes-no* question.

   b. Use the following data to decide between the two hypotheses stated in your answer to question (a). That is, complete the following statement: To form a *yes-no* question from the corresponding declarative, move the verb to ________.

   A.1. In 1492, Columbus was sailing to America.
   A.2. In 1492, was Columbus sailing to America?
   A.3. *Was in 1492 Columbus sailing to America?
   B.1. After Joan is fired, I can have her office.
   B.2. After Joan is fired, can I have her office?
   B.3. *Can after Joan is fired I have her office?

   c. Use the following data to specify more precisely which verb is moved. (Note that each sentence has two auxiliary verbs and a main verb.)

   A.1. You should have taken the last left turn.
   A.2. Should you have taken the last left turn?
   A.3. *Should have you taken the last left turn?
   A.4. *Have you should taken the last left turn?
   B.1. The cat has been eating this fish.
   B.2. Has the cat been eating this fish?

B.3. *Has been the cat eating this fish?

B.4. *Been the cat has eating this fish?

d. Formulate the *yes-no* question that corresponds to each of the following declaratives. You will find that two general patterns emerge, one similar to the *yes-no* questions examined so far and one different from them. (Hint: You should find three sentences that differ from the *yes-no* questions examined so far.) What do the declarative structures associated with the new pattern have in common?

A. Ralph parked the car next to a fire hydrant.

B. I should have sent this letter by certified mail.

C. Toby would like to ride on the merry-go-round.

D. Wonder Bread builds strong bodies.

E. The dentist removed two of her wisdom teeth.

F. You can use your credit card at this store.

9. As illustrated in Exercise (8), it appears that *yes-no* questions exhibit one of two patterns, depending on what verbs are present in the corresponding declarative. If the declarative contains an auxiliary verb, then the first auxiliary verb is moved to the left of the subject NP. If the declarative contains only a main verb (i.e., no auxiliary verb), then a form of *do* is added to the *yes-no* question where an auxiliary verb would otherwise occur. Now consider the following data in light of these generalizations.

A.1. Someone is in the yard.

A.2. Is someone in the yard?

A.3. *Does someone be in the yard?

B.1. Someone is knocking at the door.

B.2. Is someone knocking at the door?

B.3. *Does someone be knocking at the door?

C.1. John has the keys.

C.2. *Has John the keys?

C.3. Does John have the keys?

D.1. Mino has eaten my blueberry muffin.

D.2. Has Mino eaten my blueberry muffin?

D.3. *Does Mino have eaten my blueberry muffin?

a. Which set of sentences contains auxiliary *be?* main verb *be?* auxiliary *have?* main verb *have?*

b. Which set of sentences illustrates an exception to the following generalization: If the declarative contains only a main verb, then a form of *do* is added in forming a *yes-no* question.

c. Based on these data, do sentences containing main verb *be* pattern more like sentences containing auxiliary verbs or like those containing only main verbs?

d. Based on these data, do sentences containing main verb *have* pattern more like sentences containing auxiliary verbs or like those containing only main verbs?

10. *Yes-no* questions provide an **operational definition** of "subject": The subject of a sentence is the NP that the first auxiliary verb moves to the left of when a *yes-no* question is formed. Use this test to identify the subject of each of the following sentences.

A. The resident manager has been given a raise.

B. Wally and Beaver could have gone to the movies.

- **C.** Kim and Kevin sent us a postcard from the French Quarter.
- **D.** Some of the people at the garage sale paid by check.
- **E.** There should have been someone at that counter.
- **F.** It will be necessary for the applicants to submit three letters of recommendation.
- **G.** It will be necessary to submit three letters of recommendation.

11. What generalization about *yes-no* questions in English is violated by each of the following structures?

- **a.** **Does John can take the babysitter home?*
- **b.** **Had he some cake?*

12. English contains a type of structure called a **tag question,** which consists of a declarative sentence with a *yes-no* question "tagged" onto the end of it. Tag questions are illustrated by the following:

- **A.** Fred hasn't been drinking, has he?
- **B.** Ralph should do his homework, shouldn't he?
- **C.** Mary is driving to Utah, isn't she?
- **D.** Betsy won't miss the meeting, will she?

Now consider the following data:

- **E.** Fred hasn't been drinking, has he?
- **F.** *Fred hasn't been drinking, is he?
- **G.** *Fred hasn't been drinking, had he?
- **H.** Ralph should do his homework, shouldn't he?
- **I.** *Ralph should do his homework, hasn't he?
- **a.** Use the data in (A–I) to construct a generalization about the verb form that appears in the tag. That is, given a declarative structure, what predictions can be made about the verb that will appear in the tag?

  Now consider some additional data.

- **J.** Ralph should do his homework, shouldn't he?
- **K.** *Ralph should do his homework, shouldn't she?
- **L.** *Ralph should do his homework, shouldn't I?
- **M.** *Ralph should do his homework, shouldn't they?
- **N.** *Ralph should do his homework, shouldn't him?

Use the data in (J–N) to construct a generalization about the pronoun that appears in the tag. That is, given a declarative structure, what predictions can be made about the pronoun that will appear in the tag?

13. Referring to Exercise (12), form tag questions based on each of the following sentences:

- **A.** The phone is ringing.
- **B.** The phone rang.
- **C.** Ralph took a shower.
- **D.** Dinner will be ready in a minute.
- **E.** Helen walked three miles this morning.
- **F.** The boys have been playing in the mud again.
- **G.** Martha and George couldn't make it to dinner.
- **H.** Ralph and Ed bought Trixie some flowers.

- **a.** In some of the examples, what auxiliary appears in the tag but never appears in the main clause?
- **b.** In what other structure in English does this auxiliary occur?
- **c.** State a generalization concerning the appearance of this auxiliary that covers both tag questions and the structure you named in question (b).

14. Examine the following data:

A.1. Alan is a Republican, isn't he?
A.2. *Alan is a Republican, doesn't he?
B.1. Those books are going back to the library, aren't they?
B.2. *Those books are going back to the library, don't they?
C.1. Mino has been eating steadily, hasn't he?
C.2. *Mino has been eating steadily, doesn't he?
D.1. *This TV has remote control, hasn't it?
D.2. This TV has remote control, doesn't it?

- **a.** Which set of tag questions contains main verb *be?* Auxiliary *be?* Main verb *have?* Auxiliary *have?*
- **b.** Does main verb *be* pattern like other main verbs in a tag question?
- **c.** Does auxiliary *be* pattern like other auxiliary verbs in a tag question?
- **d.** Does main verb *have* pattern like other main verbs in a tag question?
- **e.** Does auxiliary *have* pattern like other auxiliary verbs in a tag question?

15. Chomsky's constraints were originally formulated as restrictions on movement. Some of these constraints, however, had to be reformulated to block not only movement, but also anaphoric relations between two NPs (i.e., where one NP refers to another NP). Consider the following derivation involving anaphora (indicated by an arrow).

**Pasquale Bubba* considers [$_S$*himself* is a sensitive humanitarian]

Which of Chomsky's constraints on movement is similar to the violation in this derivation?

16. Consider the following derivation:

Who did he say [$_S$ ________ might fail]

This sentence is perfectly acceptable even though it appears to violate one of Chomsky's constraints on transformations.

- **a.** What constraint does it violate?
- **b.** The fact that this sentence is acceptable can be used to argue that the transformational rule of ________ is not subject to this constraint.

Exploratory Exercise

1. Go to your local bookstore and buy a popular book of jokes or riddles (especially those designed for younger children). Analyze the jokes or riddles with particular attention to any that rely on syntactic or semantic ambiguity for their humor or punch line. You may also be able to find some data at the following site maintained by Beatrice Santorini: www.ling.upenn.edu/~beatrice/humor/index.htm

CHAPTER FIVE

Morphology

Morphology is the study of word formation. (The word *morphology* itself comes from the Greek word *morphē,* which means 'form.') Morphology is to words what syntax is to sentences. That is, morphology is concerned with the structure of words, just as syntax is concerned with the structure of sentences. Let's begin by considering some of the observations we can make about the structure of words in English.

(1) *Boldest* can be divided into two parts (i.e., *bold* + *est*), each of which has a meaning; *bold* cannot.

(2) The word *boy* has a meaning in and of itself, the word *at* does not. Rather, *at* indicates a relationship between two meaningful expressions (e.g., *The boy at the door*).

(3) The form *serve* can stand alone as a word; the form *pre-* (as in *preserve*) cannot.

(4) *Friendliest* is a word; *friendestly* is not.

(5) *TV* and *telly* are both formed from *television.*

Observation (1) illustrates the fact that words are made up of meaningful units **(morphemes).** Observation (2) illustrates the fact that some morphemes, called **lexical morphemes,** have meaning in and of themselves; others, called **grammatical morphemes,** specify the relationship between one lexical morpheme and another. Observation (3) illustrates the fact that some morphemes, called **free morphemes,** can stand alone as words; others, called **bound morphemes,** cannot. Observation (4) can be used to argue that bound morphemes can be divided into two types, **inflectional** and **derivational.** Observation (5) illustrates the fact that languages create new words systematically.

All of these phenomena are essentially morphological in nature. That is, they have to do with the internal structure of words. Moreover, we will make our standard assumption that the phenomena in (1–5) are governed by a system of rules. What we will do now is attempt to construct a set of concepts and principles that will help us account for the phenomena in (1–5). As usual, keep in mind that what follows is a theory designed to account for the data in (1–5).

Morphemes

A **morpheme** can be loosely defined as a minimal unit having more or less *constant meaning* associated with more or less *constant form.* Consider a simple example: the word *buyers* is made up of three morphemes {buy} + {er} + {s}. (Braces are sometimes used to indicate morphemes.) Each of these morphemes has a unique meaning: {buy} = verb 'buy' (however it might be represented semantically); {er} = 'one who performs an action'; {s} = 'more than one.' Together they mean something like 'more than one person who buys things.' The strongest evidence that each of these word parts is a morpheme is the fact that each one can occur with other morphemes without changing its core meaning. For example, {buy} occurs in *buy, buying,* and *buys,* as well as in *buyers.* {er} occurs in *farmer, driver,* and *mover,* as well as in *buyers.* {s} occurs in *boys, girls,* and *dogs,* as well as in *buyers.* The more combinations a morpheme can occur in, the more **productive** it is said to be; the more productive a morpheme is, the stronger the evidence that it is a separate morpheme.

Exercise A

1. What is the meaning of the morpheme {Mc} as in *McMuffin, McNuggets,* and *McDLT?*
2. What is the meaning of the morpheme {oholic} as in *workoholic, chocoholic,* and *foodoholic?*
3. What kind of evidence could be used to argue that *action* and *package* each contain two morphemes: {act} + {ion} and {pack} + {age}? (Hint: A morpheme can appear independently in other words.)

There are four points to note about morphemes. First, they are distinct from syllables. The word *alligator,* for example, consists of one morpheme but has four syllables; *cats,* on the other hand, consists of two morphemes but has only one syllable.

Exercise B

1. Mark the following statements true or false.
   - **a.** T F Every English word ending in *-ly* is an adverb.
   - **b.** T F Any one-syllable English word will also be a one-morpheme word.
   - **c.** T F Any English word with more than one syllable will contain more than one morpheme.

Second, identical spellings do not necessarily indicate identical morphemes. For example, consider *buyer* and *shorter,* each of which ends in *-er.* Note that the *-er* in *buyer* means something like 'one who,' while the *-er* in *shorter* means something like 'to a greater degree than.' Note, moreover, that the *-er* that means 'one who' always attaches to a verb (e.g., *buy*) and the *-er* that means 'to a greater degree than' always attaches to an adjective (e.g., *short*). Thus, even though the two *-er*'s have the same form or spelling, they have different meanings, and we therefore have to treat them as different morphemes. The former is sometimes called the agentive morpheme (abbreviated {AG}), since it indicates one who performs an action, and the latter is termed the comparative morpheme ({COMP}), since it indicates the comparative degree of an adjective.

Third, the definition of a morpheme as a minimal unit with *more or less* constant meaning associated with *more or less* constant form should be taken as a general rule rather than a hard and fast criterion. The words *boys* and *girls* conform to this definition rather closely. That is, *boys* can be divided into {boy} + {s} and *girls* can be divided into {girl} + {s}, where the *-s* in each word represents the same plural morpheme. (The plural morpheme is often symbolized {PLU} rather than {s} to distinguish it from other morphemes spelled with *-s,* such as the possessive morpheme in *boy's.*) The word *men,* however, does not seem to be as easily divisible into morphemes, since plurality is marked not by the addition of an *-s* but rather by a change in vowel (from *man*). Do we want to say, then, that *men* has nothing in common with *boys* and *girls,* simply because there is no consistency in form (i.e., spelling)? Probably not. This solution would overlook the obvious generalization that the meaning relationship between *man* and *men* is identical to that between *boy* and *boys, girl* and *girls,* and so on, even though the form (or spelling) relationship between such pairs is not identical. In order to capture such obvious meaning relationships, some linguists have opted to represent the morphology of *men* as {man} + {PLU}. Note, moreover, that we will have ample opportunity to make further use of this type of abstraction. For example, *went* is to *go* as *walked* is to *walk.* Thus, *went* might be represented morphologically as {go} + {PAST}, just as *walked* would be characterized as {walk} + {PAST}. In short, all exceptional cases (e.g., *men* and *went*) can be treated on analogy with regular cases (e.g., *boys* and *walked*).

Exercise C

1. State the number of morphemes in each of the following words.
   - †**a.** actor
   - †**b.** winter
   - **c.** forthrightness
   - **d.** mother-in-law
   - **e.** undo
   - **f.** aspirin
   - **g.** best

Fourth, the goal of morphological analysis is to determine the rules that speakers actually follow for forming words in a particular language. However, it is often difficult for the linguist to distinguish between the etymology (i.e., history) of a word and its structure in the minds of present-day speakers. Consider, for example, the word *hamburger.* Historically, the word is derived from {Hamburg} = 'a city in Germany' + {er} = 'originating from' (as in *Southerner* or *New Englander*). Nowadays, speakers analyze *hamburger* (unconsciously, of course) as something like {ham} = 'ham' + {burger} = 'hot patty served on a round bun.' This is evidenced by the fact that {burger} can combine with virtually any substance that could conceivably be eaten (e.g., *cheeseburger, shrimpburger, veggieburger,* etc.) and can even occur alone, as in *a burger and fries.* Thus, over time, not only has the morpheme boundary shifted in this word, but the meanings of the morphemes themselves have changed. The fact is that the {ham} + {burger} analysis is undoubtedly "psychologically real" for most present-day speakers of American English. Nonetheless, the {Hamburg} + {er} analysis is just as real for a small subset of these same speakers. In short, it is a recurring source of frustration in morphology to decide just how much of the history of a word modern-day speakers are able to infer from the samples of the language available to them.

Let's summarize the main point of this section. A morpheme is a linguistic unit that is defined by a (more or less) constant core meaning associated with a (more or less) constant form.

Lexical and Grammatical Morphemes

The distinction between lexical and grammatical morphemes is not well defined, although many linguists seem to agree that it is a useful division to make. **Lexical morphemes** have a sense (i.e., meaning) in and of themselves. Nouns, verbs, and adjectives (e.g., {boy}, {buy}, and {big}) are typical of lexical morphemes. **Grammatical morphemes,** on the other hand, don't really have a sense in and of themselves; instead, they express some sort of relationship *between* lexical morphemes. Prepositions, articles, and conjunctions (e.g., {of}, {the}, and {but}) are typical of grammatical morphemes.

Exercise D

1. Divide the following words into morphemes. For each morpheme, state whether it is lexical or grammatical.
   - †**a.** restating
   - **b.** strongest
   - **c.** actively
   - **d.** precede
   - **e.** disentangled
   - **f.** ran
   - **g.** women

Free and Bound Morphemes

In contrast to the division between lexical and grammatical morphemes, the distinction between free and bound morphemes is straightforward. **Free morphemes** are those that can stand alone as words. They may be lexical (e.g., {serve}, {press}) or they may be grammatical (e.g., {at}, {and}). **Bound morphemes,** on the other hand, cannot stand alone as words. Likewise, they may be lexical (e.g., {clude} as in *exclude, include,* and *preclude*) or they may be grammatical (e.g., {PLU} = plural as in *boys, girls,* and *cats*).

Exercise E

1. Analyze the following morphemes as lexical or grammatical and as free or bound.
   - †**a.** The morpheme {er}, as in *teachers*
   - **b.** The morpheme {cur}, as in *recur, incur,* and *occur*

Exercise E Continued

   c. {at}, {to}, and other prepositions
   d. The morpheme {pel}, as in *repel, compel, impel*
2. List at least five different words that contain the bound, lexical morpheme {mit} 'send, go.' (Consult a dictionary if needed.) What structural pattern is shared by all the words?
3. Is *mitten* a possible answer to Exercise (2)? Why or why not?
4. Consider the morphemes {bio-} and {tele-}.
   a. Analyze these morphemes as lexical or grammatical and as free or bound.
   b. List at least five different words containing each of these morphemes.
   c. What is the meaning of each of these morphemes?

Inflectional and Derivational Morphemes

This distinction applies only to the class of bound, grammatical morphemes. (See the right-hand branch of Figure 5.1.) The more familiar term for the class of bound grammatical morphemes is **affix.** Affixes, in turn, can be subdivided into **prefixes** and **suffixes,** depending upon whether they are attached to the beginning of a lexical morpheme, as in *depress* (where {de} is a prefix), or to the end of the lexical morpheme, as in *helpful* (where {ful} is a suffix). Note that this division of affixes into prefixes and suffixes appears to present a bit of a problem in cases such as *men* = {man} + {PLU}, which technically has neither a prefix nor a suffix. What we are forced to say here is that the plural morpheme in English *generally* appears as a suffix, never as a prefix. A summary of these divisions is presented schematically in Figure 5.1.

Inflectional Affixes

Let's now return to the distinction between inflectional and derivational affixes (i.e., bound, grammatical morphemes). English has eight inflectional affixes; all other affixes are derivational. The eight inflectional affixes are listed in the following table, along with the type of root (i.e., lexical morpheme) that each one attaches to, and a representative example.

INFLECTIONAL AFFIX	ROOT	EXAMPLE
{PLU} = plural	Noun	boy*s*
{POSS} = possessive	Noun	boy*'s*
{COMP} = comparative	Adjective	old*er*
{SUP} = superlative	Adjective	old*est*
{PRES} = present	Verb	walk*s*
{PAST} = past	Verb	walk*ed*
{PAST PART} = past participle	Verb	dri*ven*
{PRES PART} = present participle	Verb	driv*ing*

Each one of these requires some comment.

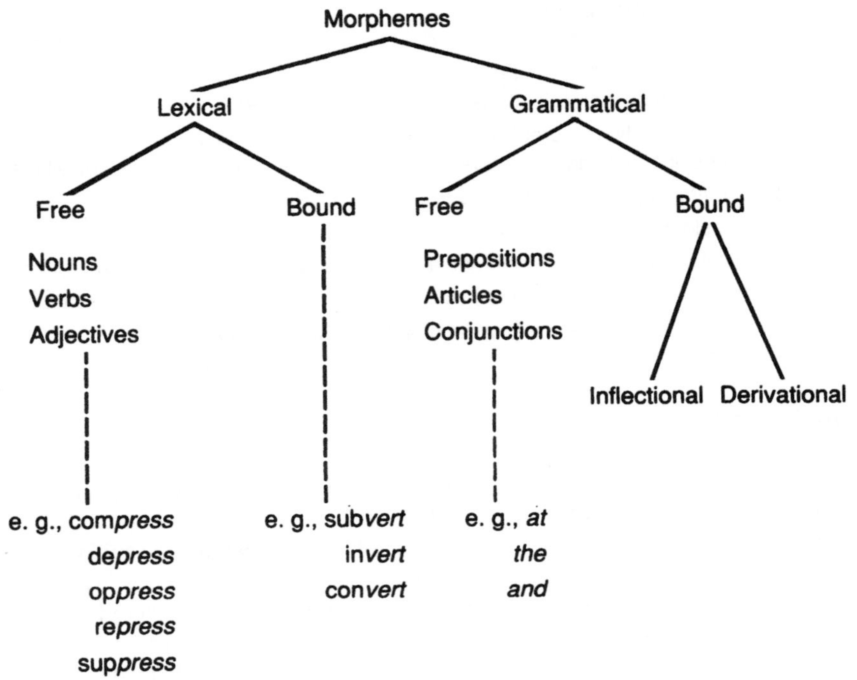

FIGURE 5.1 Division of morphemes into various types

- **{PLU}.** All plural nouns in English can be represented morphologically as a root + {PLU}, regardless of how the plural morpheme is actually spelled or pronounced. For example, *boys* = {boy} + {PLU}, *men* = {man} + {PLU}, and even the plural of *sheep* (as in *Those sheep have big noses*) = {sheep} + {PLU}.
- **{POSS}.** All possessive nouns in English can be represented morphologically as a root + {POSS}. For example, *boy's* = {boy} + {POSS}, and *man's* = {man} + {POSS}. (The reason that {PLU} and {POSS} are both generally spelled with *-s* in Modern English is the result of historical accident. The plural *-s* comes from the Old English masculine nominative-objective plural suffix *-as,* while the possessive *-s* comes from the Old English masculine possessive singular suffix *-es.*)
- **{COMP} and {SUP}.** All comparative and superlative adjectives in English can be represented morphologically as a root + {COMP} or {SUP}. For example, *happier* = {happy} + {COMP}, and *happiest* = {happy} + [SUP}. Note, even *good, better,* and *best* can be represented in this fashion: *good* = {good}, *better* = {good} + {COMP}, and *best* = {good} + {SUP}. On the other hand, it isn't clear how best to handle forms like *most beautiful.* Under some circumstances it might be reasonable to treat them as a root plus an affix (e.g., *most beautiful* = {beautiful} + {SUP}), on analogy with regular cases such as *prettiest* = {pretty} + {SUP}. However, *most* in *most beautiful* is clearly not an affix, as is *-est* in *prettiest;* rather, it's a free grammatical morpheme.

Since linguists do not always agree on how to handle forms such as *most beautiful,* we will simply leave this as an open question.

- **{PRES}.** All present tense verbs in English can be represented morphologically as a root + {PRES}. For example, *loves* (as in *John loves Mary*) = {love} + {PRES}. Note, however, that the only time this affix is spelled out is when there is a third person singular subject (i.e., *he, she, it,* or an NP for which one of these can substitute—for example, *John, Mary, the dog*).With all other subjects (e.g., *I, you, we, they, John and Mary,* and so on), the present tense verb has no surface affix. Nonetheless, the verb *love* (as in *John and Mary love each other*) can be represented as {love} + {PRES}.
- **{PAST}.** All past tense verbs in English can be represented morphologically as a root + {PAST}. For example, *walked* (as in *John walked on hot coals*) = {walk} + {PAST}. Thus, any past tense verb, regardless of its spelling, can be represented in this fashion. For example, *drove* = {drive} + {PAST}. Note, moreover, that in English (as in all Germanic languages), the first and only the first verb form in a simple sentence is inflected for tense (i.e., {PRES} or {PAST}); no verb following the first is ever inflected for tense. Thus, for example, in the sentence *I think, think* is inflected for tense ({think} + {PRES}); in *I have thought, have* is inflected for tense ({have} + {PRES}); in *I am thinking, am* is inflected for tense ({be} + {PRES}); and so on.
- **{PAST PART}.** All past participles in English can be represented morphologically as a root + {PAST PART}. For example, *driven* (as in *John has driven his mother crazy*) = {drive} + {PAST PART}. One potential problem in identifying past participles results from the fact that there is so much variation in their spelling. For example, *gone* = {go} + {PAST PART}, *come* (as in *They've come home*) = {come} + {PAST PART}, *hit* (as in *He's hit three home runs*) = {hit} + {PAST PART}, and *walked* (as in *He's walked three miles*) = {walk} + {PAST PART}. Nonetheless, there is a very simple method for identifying a past participle in a simple active sentence: a past participle always follows a form of the auxiliary verb *have.* Thus, in the sentence *They have walked home, walked* is a past participle since it immediately follows a form of *have.* However, in the sentence *They walked home, walked* is not a past participle since it does not follow a form of *have.* In fact, it is a tensed form (here past), since it is the first verb form in the sentence.
- **{PRES PART}.** All present participles in English can be represented morphologically as a root + {PRES PART}. For example, *drinking* = {drink} + {PRES PART}. Unlike other verb forms in English, present participles always appear in a constant form (i.e., with an *-ing* suffix). In addition, the present participle in a simple active sentence can be identified as the verb form following a form of the auxiliary verb *to be,* as in *They were laughing.*

Verb Forms. We should add a footnote at this point concerning verb forms in English. In simple, *active* sentences there are five different types of verbs that can occur: main verbs and four different auxiliary verbs (modal verbs, forms of *have,* forms of *be,* and forms of *do*). We will take these up one at a time.

The **main verb** is always the right-most verb in a simple sentence. Thus, in the sentence *John should have gone, gone* is the main verb; in *John might have a cold, have* is the main verb; and so on. Note that forms of *have, be,* and *do* in English can function as both main verbs and auxiliaries. If they are farthest to the right, they are main verbs; if not, they are auxiliaries.

The primary **modal verbs** are *can/could, shall/should, will/would, may/might,* and *must.* Modals are characterized by the absence of the third person singular *-s* that occurs on all other types of verbs in the present tense. For example, in the sentence *John has seen Mary,* note the *-s* on *has.* However, in the sentence *John may see Mary,* note that there is no *-s* on *may* (cf. **John mays see Mary*). Furthermore, when a modal occurs in a sentence, it is always the first verb form and it is always followed by an uninflected verb form; for example, in *John will be going,* the modal *will* is first in the series, and the following verb *be* is uninflected (cf. **John is will go* and **John will been going*).

If the **auxiliary *have*** occurs in a simple active sentence, it is always followed by a past participle. For example, in the sentence *John has eaten, eaten* follows *have* and thus is a past participle; in the sentence *John has been eating, been* follows *have* and thus is a past participle; and so on. Moreover, if both a modal and the auxiliary *have* occur in the same sentence, *have* follows the modal; for example, in *We may have gone, have* follows the modal *may* (cf. **We have may gone*).

If the **auxiliary *be*** occurs in a simple active sentence, it is always followed by a present participle. For example, in the sentence *John is eating, eating* follows a form of *be* (i.e., *is*) and thus is a present participle; in the sentence *John will be eating, eating* follows *be* and thus is a present participle; and so on. Furthermore, if both the auxiliary *have* and the auxiliary *be* occur in the same sentence, the form of *be* always follows the form of *have;* for example, in *We have been eating,* the form of *be* (i.e., *been*) follows the form of *have* (cf. **We are have eating*).

The **auxiliary *do*** never occurs with any of the other auxiliary verbs in a simple active sentence. When two items (e.g., *do* and other auxiliaries) never occur in the same environment (e.g., in a simple active sentence), the two items are said to be in **complementary distribution.** In other words, auxiliary *do* occurs only with a main verb, never with another auxiliary verb. For example, in the sentence *I do eat corn, do* is an auxiliary and *eat* is a main verb (cf. **I do may eat corn,* **I do have eaten corn,* **I do am eating corn*). Moreover, the main verb that appears with *do* is always uninflected. For example, in the sentence *We did see that movie, see* is the main verb and thus is uninflected (cf. **We did saw that movie,* **We did seen that movie,* **We did seeing that movie*).

In short, then, verbs in English are perfectly systematic. For example, using the sentence *Someone may have been knocking at the door,* we can make several observations based on this system. First, *knocking* is the main verb, because it is the right-most verb. Moreover, it is a present participle, because it immediately follows a form of *be.* Second, *been* is an auxiliary verb, because it is not the right-most verb. Furthermore, it is a past participle, because it immediately follows a form of *have.* Third, *have* is an auxiliary verb, because it is not the right-most verb. Also, it is uninflected, because it immediately follows a modal *(may).* Fourth, *may* is a modal, because it lacks the third person singular *-s.* Moreover, it is inflected for present tense (*might* would be past), since the first and only the first verb in a simple sentence in English is inflected for tense.

You will have noticed that in this discussion of verb forms, we have restricted our generalizations to *active* sentences. This is because there is another auxiliary *be* in English that shows up in all and only passive sentences. Predictably, this auxiliary is called **passive *be*,** and it has two interesting properties. It always immediately precedes the main verb (i.e., there are never any intervening verbs between it and the main verb), and it is always followed by a past participle (i.e., the main verb which follows it is always a past participle). These properties are illustrated in the following pairs:

ACTIVE: Kathy rode my horse.
PASSIVE: My horse *was ridden* by Kathy.

ACTIVE: Kathy might have been riding my horse.
PASSIVE: My horse might have been *being ridden* by Kathy.

Exercise F

†1. Consider the claim that *may* in the sentence *John may have been lying* is a modal. Which of the following facts supports this view?
   - **a.** Main verbs are obligatory in English.
   - **b.** The right-most verb in a simple sentence is the main verb.
   - **c.** Auxiliary verbs are optional in English.
   - **d.** Modal verbs lack the third person, singular *-s.*
   - **e.** none of the above

2. For the following sentence, choose the generalization that explains why the sentence is ungrammatical: **Carla has ate my dessert.*
   - **a.** The verb following a form of auxiliary *have* should be inflected for {PRES PART}.
   - **b.** The verb following a form of auxiliary *have* should be inflected for {PAST PART}.
   - **c.** The verb following a form of auxiliary *have* should be inflected for {PRES}.
   - **d.** The verb following a form of auxiliary *have* should be uninflected.
   - **e.** The verb following a form of auxiliary *have* should be inflected for {PAST}.

3. State the general principle that accounts for the deviance of the following sentence: **She is make a lot of money at her new job.*

4. Consider this overheard sentence: *Last week, he give $500 for that old car.* What are two pieces of evidence that *give* in this sentence is past tense rather than present tense? (Hint: What property would the verb exhibit if it were present tense?)

5. For each of the italicized verbs, state the form (e.g., uninflected, past participle, etc.) and explain your answer (e.g., right-most verb is main verb):
   - **a.** He *might have gone* home early.
   - **b.** She *has done* her work.
   - **c.** They *have been* in the kitchen.
   - **d.** *Did* he *walk* home?

Before ending this section on inflectional affixes, we should say something about **tense.** As we have been using the term, it refers to a particular *form* of a verb. All Germanic languages (including English) have two inflected tenses: present and past. Furthermore, a past tense verb in English is generally characterized by a *-t* or *-d* suffix. Thus, *may* is present and *might* is past; *can* is present and *could* is past; and so on. The main point to note, however, is that inflected tense does not correlate perfectly with time reference. For example, the sentence *I might go with you tonight* contains a past tense verb form *(might)* but the sentence refers to future time. Likewise, the sentence *Yesterday this guy comes up to me on the street* contains a present tense verb form *(comes)* but the sentence refers to past time.

Exercise G

1. For each of the following sentences, state the tense of the verb and the time reference of the sentence. (Hint: Remember that tense appears on the first verb form.)
   - **†a.** John leaves for Chicago tomorrow.
   - **b.** He won't go with us tonight.
   - **c.** They should be watching that child.

Derivational Affixes

After this rather long detour into inflectional affixes, let's return to their counterparts, the derivational affixes. Unlike the inflectional affixes, which number only eight in English, the set of derivational affixes is open-ended; that is, there are a potentially infinite number of them (although the number is finite at any one time for a particular speaker). Since it would be impossible to enumerate them exhaustively, let us look at a few representative examples. The suffix {ize} attaches to a noun and turns it into the corresponding verb, as in *criticize, rubberize, vulcanize, pasteurize, mesmerize,* and so on. (This suffix can also be added to adjectives, as in *normalize, realize, finalize, vitalize, equalize,* and so on.) The suffix {ful} attaches to a noun and changes it into the corresponding adjective, as in *helpful, playful, thoughtful, careful,* and so on. The suffix {ly} attaches to an adjective and turns it into the corresponding adverb, as in *quickly, carefully, swiftly, mightily,* and so on. Note that there is another separate derivational affix, also spelled *-ly,* which attaches to a noun and changes it into the corresponding adjective, as *friendly, manly, neighborly,* and so on. Obviously, we would need to come up with two different morphological symbols for these two derivational affixes spelled *-ly,* just as we came up with {AG} and {COMP} for the two affixes generally spelled *-er.*

In addition to these derivational affixes, English also has derivational prefixes. The following all exhibit some variation on the meaning 'not.' The prefix {un} appears in forms like *unhappy, unwary, unassuming,* and *unforgettable.* The prefix {dis} occurs in words such as *displeasure, disproportionate, dislike,* and *distrust.* The prefix {a} appears in forms such as *asymmetrical, asexual, atheist,* and *atypical.* And the prefix {anti} occurs in words like *anti-American, anti-Castro,* and *anti-aircraft.*

Differences between Types of Affixes

So far, we have simply assumed that there are two classes of bound grammatical morphemes: inflectional and derivational. Let's now consider some evidence for this division. Remember that one of our fundamental assumptions is that if two items exhibit different behavior under the same conditions, they must belong to different categories.

Historical Development. All inflectional affixes are native to English (i.e., they have been part of English since Old English was spoken—around A.D. 500–1000). On the other hand, many (but not all) derivational affixes are borrowings from other languages, in particular Latin and Greek. For example, {ize} is borrowed from Greek; {dis}, {de}, and {re} are borrowed from Latin; and {a} and {anti} are borrowed from Greek through Latin. Moreover, while derivational prefixes tend to show a high percentage of borrowings, there are still a number of derivational affixes (especially suffixes) that are native to English. For example, {ful}, {ly} (both varieties), {like}, and {AG} all derive ultimately from Old English. Thus we can make the generalization that if an affix is borrowed, it is derivational (i.e., all borrowed affixes are derivational).

Distribution. All inflectional affixes are suffixes; derivational affixes may be either suffixes or prefixes. That is, {PLU}, {POSS}, {COMP}, {SUP}, and the four verbal inflectional affixes all appear as suffixes, at least in the unexceptional cases. (Recall that the exceptional cases are analyzed on analogy with the regular cases; for example, *sang* = {sing} + {PAST}, since *walked* = {walk} + {PAST}.) On the other hand, it should be clear by now that derivational affixes may be either prefixes or suffixes. For example, *unfriendly* consists of the free lexical morpheme {friend} plus the derivational prefix {un} and the derivational suffix {ly}. In sum, we can say that if an affix is a prefix, then it is derivational (i.e., all prefixes are derivational).

Range of Application. Inflectional affixes have a relatively wide range of application, while derivational affixes have a wide to narrow range of application. Wide application means that an affix joins with (almost) all members of a particular category. For example, the inflectional affix {PLU} adjoins to (almost) all members of the category noun. (Note that noncount nouns are, by definition, exceptions: e.g., **dirts.*) Even proper names can be made plural (for example, *There are two Marthas in my syntax class*). Derivational affixes, on the other hand, have a varying range of applications. Many of them (especially prefixes) have a fairly narrow range of application. For example, the derivational prefix {a} can be prefixed to a very limited number of lexical morphemes: *asexual, atypical, asymmetrical, atheist, agnostic, amoral, apolitical, aseptic, aphasia.* The derivational prefix {un} seems to have a somewhat wider range of application. It is prefixed to adjectives (among other things) to form the negative: *unhappy, unreliable, unpatriotic, unpopular, unbearable, unimportant, unremarkable,* and so on. Note, however, that not all adjectives will take this prefix: **unshort, *unsad, *untall, *ungullible,* and so forth. Other derivational affixes, especially the suffixes, tend to have a wider range of application. For example, the {AG} affix can be suffixed to a wide range of verbs: *doer, achiever, thinker, builder, baker, pusher,* and so on. On the other hand, some derivational suffixes have a very limited range of application. For example, {hood} appears in the kinship terms *motherhood, fatherhood, sisterhood,* and *brotherhood,* but not **aunthood, *unclehood, *niecehood,* or **nephewhood.* In short, we can make the following generalization: if an affix has a narrow range of application, it is derivational.

Order of Appearance. Inflectional suffixes generally follow derivational suffixes. That is, if a word contains both a derivational and an inflectional suffix, then the inflectional suffix typically comes last. For example, the word *friendships* can be broken down as follows (R = root, D = derivational, and I = inflectional).

{friend} + {ship} + {PLU}
R D I

Note that reversing the suffixes results in the unacceptable form **friendsship.* Consider another example. The word *universities* consists of the following morphemes.

{universe} + {-ity} + {PLU}
R D I

As in the previous case, reversing the suffixes results in the unacceptable form **universesity.* This ordering principle follows from the tendency for inflectional affixes to halt further derivation; that is, once an inflectional affix is added to a form, no further derivational suffixes can be added. For example, the noun root {man} readily accepts the derivational suffix {-ly}, changing it into the adjective *manly.* However, once {man} is inflected with {PLU}, it can no longer accept the derivational suffix {-ly} (**menly*). Likewise, compare {create} + {-ive} = *creative,* but {create} + {PRES} + {ive} = **createsive.* Similarly, {happy} + {-ness} = *happiness,* but {happy} + {COMP} + {ness} = **happierness.*

This tendency of inflectional suffixes to follow derivational suffixes, in turn, accounts for some apparently problematic cases. Consider, for example, the forms *spoonsful* and *spoonfuls.* Proponents of prescriptive or "school" grammar would claim that *spoonsful* is "correct" and *spoonfuls* is "incorrect." On the other hand, many (if not most) speakers of English would unselfconsciously say *spoonfuls* rather than *spoonsful.* The ordering of derivational and inflectional affixes helps explain what is going on here. Historically, *spoon* and *ful* (from *full*) were two separate lexical morphemes, as in *a spoon full of castor oil.* Thus, since *spoon* was a noun and nouns take the {PLU} affix, an *-s* was added to *spoon* to make the phrase plural, as in *two spoons full of castor oil.* However, over time *spoon full* (two lexical morphemes) was reanalyzed as *spoonful* (a lexical morpheme plus a derivational suffix). Note that if you were to hear *spoon full* or *spoonful* spoken, you wouldn't be able to tell if it were one word or two. Once *full* was reanalyzed as a derivational suffix attached to the noun *spoon,* then our principle would predict that the plural morpheme would be attached to the right of the derivational affix *ful,* yielding *spoonfuls* as follows.

{spoon} + {ful} + {PLU}
R D I

Note that *spoonsful* is a violation of the generalization governing the order of suffixes.

*{spoon} + {PLU} + {ful}
R I D

In short, the morphological rules of English dictate that *spoonfuls* will eventually supplant *spoonsful.* An identical argument could be used to explain the preference for *cupfuls* over *cupsful* and *mother-in-laws* over *mothers-in-law.*

Let's now consider some apparent counterexamples to our ordering generalization. Words such as *lovingly* and *markedly* appear to violate the tendency of inflectional suffixes to follow derivational suffixes, as follows. (Our thanks to Deborah Griffin for these examples.)

{love} + {PRES PART} + {-ly}
{mark} + {PAST PART} + {-ly}

Note that {love} and {mark} appear to be verbs that have been inflected as participles and then have undergone a derivational process changing them into adverbs. Note, however, that there is an inconsistency in this analysis: {-ly} is a derivational suffix that attaches to an *adjective,* thereby turning it into an *adverb. Loving* and *marked,* however, by this analysis are not adjectives, but verbs. (One earmark of inflectional affixes is that they do not change the syntactic category of the word to which they are attached; thus, if *love* and *mark* are verbs, then *loving* and *marked* are also verbs.) There are two possible ways to solve this dilemma. (1) Either *-ing* and *-ed* do not actually represent inflectional affixes in these words (note that there are an {-ing} and an {-ed} morpheme in English that are not inflectional, but derivational, as in *carpeting* and *aged*); or (2) once *loving* and *marked* are formed as inflected verbs, they undergo what's termed a **category shift** (see the word-formation processes at the end of this chapter), which enables them to enter into a new derivational paradigm, as follows.

$[\{\text{love}\} + \{\text{PRES PART}\}]_V \rightarrow [\{\text{loving}\}]_{Adj} + \{\text{-ly}\}$
$[\{\text{mark}\} + \{\text{PAST PART}\}]_V \rightarrow [\{\text{marked}\}]_{Adj} + \{\text{-ly}\}$

In either case, *lovingly* and *markedly* do not appear to be true counterexamples to the ordering generalization presented here.

Effect on Syntactic Category. Inflectional affixes do not change the syntactic category (i.e., part of speech) of the root they are attached to; derivational affixes, however, may. First, let's consider some inflectional suffixes. *Boy* is a noun and *boys* ({boy} + {PLU}) is also a noun. *Short* is an adjective and *shorter* ({short} + {COMP}) is likewise an adjective. *Drive* is a verb and *driven* ({drive} + {PAST PART}) is also a verb. Now consider some derivational suffixes. *Critic* is a noun, but *criticize* ({critic} + {ize}) is a verb. *Quick* is an adjective, but *quickly* ({quick} + {ly}) is an adverb. *Read* is a verb, but *readable* ({read} + {able}) is an adjective. It is important to realize, however, that some derivational suffixes do not change the category of the root. For example, *brother* is a noun and so is *brotherhood* ({brother} + {hood}). Now consider derivational prefixes. Some change the category of the root: *freeze* is a verb, but *antifreeze* ({anti} + {freeze}) is a noun. Others don't: *do* is a verb and so are *undo* ({un} + {do}) and *redo* ({re} + {do}). Therefore, we can make the following generalization: if an affix changes the syntactic category of the lexical morpheme to which it is attached, it is derivational.

Number of Allowable Affixes. No more than one inflectional morpheme can be affixed to a particular syntactic category; however, there is no limit to the number of derivational morphemes that can be affixed to one category. Let's first consider the inflectional affixes.

In nontechnical terms, this principle essentially says that no noun, adjective, or verb can have more than one inflectional affix at any one time. Thus, for example, **happierest* ({happy} + {COMP} + {SUP}) is correctly predicted by this principle to be unacceptable, since the adjective {happy} has been inflected with two inflectional affixes: {COMP} and {SUP}. Likewise, the verb form **droven* ({drive} + {PAST} + {PAST PART}) is ungrammatical for the same reason.

However, what about a form like *men's,* which appears to violate this principle? That is, it looks like the form *men's* is constructed from a noun plus *two* inflectional affixes: {man} + {PLU} + {POSS}. Actually, neither this example nor plural possessives in general violate our principle. It turns out that {PLU} and {POSS} do not affix to the same category at all. In fact, {PLU} affixes to Ns (nouns), while {POSS} affixes to NPs (noun phrases). To see this, consider the NP *the man on the moon,* which contains the head N *man.* If we want to make this phrase plural, we inflect the N *man* for plurality: *the men on the moon;* we do not add a plural suffix to the end of the NP: **the man on the moons.* The significant point is that {PLU} attaches to the N *man,* not to the whole NP *the man on the moon.* On the other hand, if we want to make the phrase possessive, we inflect the entire NP: *the man on the moon's wife;* we do not inflect the N *man* for {POSS}: **the man's on the moon wife.* In short, then, *men's* does not violate our principle that there can be no more than one inflectional affix per syntactic category. Rather, the morphological structure of *men's* is represented as follows.

$$[_{NP}[_{N}\ \{\text{man}\}] + \{\text{PLU}\}] + \{\text{POSS}\}$$

Thus, the N *man* is inflected for {PLU} and the NP *man* is inflected for {POSS}.

Derivational affixes, on the other hand, are subject to no such constraint; a given syntactic category can take an infinite number of derivational affixes, at least in theory. For example, {cover} is a verb and from it we can build, by way of derivational affixes, the following forms: *coverable, recover, recoverable, uncover, unrecoverable, recoverability, unrecoverability,* and so on. Thus, we can make the following generalization: a syntactic category can take a (theoretically) infinite number of derivational affixes, but no more than one inflectional affix.

Exercise H

1. State the morphological principle that each of the following forms violates.
   - **a.** **mouthsful* for *mouthfuls*
   - **†b.** **loveding* for *loved* or *loving*
   - **c.** **roden* for *rode* or *ridden*
   - **d.** **photographser* for *photographers*
   - **e.** **two coffee blacks* for *two coffees black*
   - **f.** **The last six Queen of Englands* had sons.
   - **g.** **The girl's down the street* bike was stolen.

Exercise H *Continued*

2. Consider the following forms from Ganda, a language spoken in Uganda.

omuzaki	'woman'	abakazi	'women'
omusawo	'doctor'	abasawo	'doctors'
omusika	'heir'	abasika	'heirs'
omuwala	'girl'	abawala	'girls'
omulenzi	'boy'	abalenzi	'boys'

   a. What type of affixes are shown in this data?
   b. What is the form and meaning of each of the affixes?
   c. Assume that *abalongo* means 'twins.' What form would you predict to mean 'twin'?

3. Consider the following forms from Kanuri, a language spoken in Nigeria.

gana	'small'	numgana	'smallness'
kura	'big'	numkura	'bigness'
kuruga	'long'	numkuruga	'longness'
karite	'excellent'	numkarite	'excellence'
dibi	'bad'	numdibi	'badness'

   a. What type of affix is illustrated in this data?
   b. What is the form of the affix?
   c. What is the function of the affix?
   d. Assume that *numgula* means 'goodness.' What is a likely form for 'good'?

Word-Formation Processes

Another area of interest to linguists is the formation of new words in a language. The following are common word-formation processes.

- **Derivation.** This involves the addition of a derivational affix, changing the syntactic category of the item to which it is attached (e.g., *orient* (V) → *orientation* (N)).
- **Category Extension.** This involves the extension of a morpheme from one syntactic category to another (e.g., *chair* (N) → *chair* (V)).
- **Compound.** This involves creating a new word by combining two free morphemes (e.g., *put-down*).
- **Root Creation.** A root creation is a brand new word based on no pre-existing morphemes (e.g., *Kodak*).
- **Clipped Form.** A clipped form is a shortened form of a pre-existing morpheme (e.g., *bra* < *brassiere*).
- **Blend.** A blend is a combination of parts of two pre-existing forms (e.g., *smog* < *smoke* + *fog*).
- **Acronym.** An acronym is a word formed from the first letter(s) of each word in a phrase (e.g., *NASA* < *National Aeronautics and Space Administration*).

- **Abbreviation.** An abbreviation is a word formed from the *names* of the first letters of the prominent syllables of a word (e.g., *TV* < *television*) or of words in a phrase (e.g., *FBI* < *Federal Bureau of Investigation*).
- **Proper Name.** This process forms a word from a proper name (e.g., *hamburger* < *Hamburg*).
- **Folk Etymology.** This process forms a word by substituting a common native form for an exotic (often foreign) form with a similar pronunciation (e.g., *cockroach* < Spanish *cucuracha* 'wood louse').
- **Back Formation.** A back formation is a word formed by removing what is mistaken for an affix (e.g., *burgle* < *burglar*).

Exercise I

1. State the word-formation process involved in the creation of each of the following words.

- **†a.** *fan < fanatic*
- **b.** *Fortran < formula translation*
- **c.** *COBOL < common business oriented language*
- **d.** *narc < narcotics agent*
- **†e.** *nosebleed < nose + bleed*
- **f.** *pea < pease*
- **g.** *chaise lounge* < French *chaise longue*
- **h.** *brunch < breakfast + lunch*
- **i.** *TB < tuberculosis*
- **j.** *camcorder < camera + video recorder*
- **k.** *rhinestone < Rhine + stone*
- **l.** *ASAP < as soon as possible*

2. Determine the word-formation process responsible for each of the following words. (If you are not sure, try consulting a good dictionary.)

- **a.** *AIDS*
- **b.** *surveil*
- **c.** *Dacron*
- **d.** *bowdlerize*
- **e.** *fender*
- **f.** *fax*

3. What word-formation process accounts for all of the following?

- **A.** You hear a speaker use the term *French eyes* for *franchise.*
- **B.** Frederic Cassidy, editor of the *Dictionary of American Regional English,* states that the form *eaceworm* has been replaced by *East worm* in some parts of Rhode Island.
- **C.** Newspaper columnist Jack Smith describes a woman who says *token pole* for *totem pole,* and a man who says *Mount Sinus Hospital* for *Mount Sinai Hospital.*

Summary

Central to this theory of morphology is the concept of morpheme, as well as the distinctions between lexical and grammatical morphemes, bound and free morphemes, and inflectional and derivational morphemes. Within inflectional morphology, regularities within the English auxiliary verb system allow us to predict which inflected forms will follow which auxiliary verbs. Finally, word-formation processes provide an account of how new words are introduced into the lexicon.

SUPPLEMENTARY READINGS

Primary

Aronoff, M. (1976). *Word formation in generative grammar.* Cambridge, MA: MIT Press.

Marchand, H. (1969). *The categories and types of present-day English word-formation* (2nd ed.). Munich: Beck.

Secondary

Adams, V. (1973). *An introduction to modern English word formation.* London: Longman.

Bauer, L. (1983). *English word-formation.* Cambridge, England: Cambridge University Press.

Haspelmath, M. (2002). *Understanding morphology.* New York: Arnold and Oxford University Press.

Katamba, F. (1993). *Morphology.* New York: St. Martin's Press.

You are now prepared to tackle Adams, Bauer, and Haspelmath, which are general introductions to the field of morphology and are restricted to English. Katamba and the primary readings are more advanced and require at least an introductory course in linguistics. (A course each in phonology and syntax would enable you to get more out of these works.) Aronoff is a revised and expanded version of his MIT doctoral dissertation and deals primarily with derivational morphology. Marchand is probably the most comprehensive work on English morphology.

Supplementary Exercises

1. List the morphemes that make up the following Spanish words, and assign a meaning to each one. (For example, the meaning of {re} in *rewrite* and *reenter* might be 'perform an action again.')

tío	'uncle'	hermano	'brother'
muchacha	'girl'	abuelo	'grandfather'
abuela	'grandmother'	nieta	'granddaughter'
nieto	'grandson'	tía	'aunt'
hermana	'sister'	muchacho	'boy'

2. Consider the word *chocoholic.*
   - **a.** What word-formation process is involved in the creation of *chocoholic?*
   - **b.** Where is the morpheme boundary in *chocoholic?* (Ignore the *-ic* suffix.)
   - **c.** Which of the following words could serve as evidence for your answer to (b): *alcoholic, workoholic, foodoholic?*
3. Provide two pieces of evidence that {rupt} as in *rupture* is a separate morpheme in English.
4. English contains a group of words called **reflexive pronouns.** These pronouns are formed by adding the suffix *-self* or *-selves* to a personal pronoun. Personal pronouns, in turn, have three forms: **nominative** (the form that appears in subject position, e.g., *I*), **objective** (the

form that appears in object position, e.g., *me*), and **possessive** (the form that appears in determiner position, e.g., *my*).

a. Based on the following data, which form of the personal pronoun is *-self* or *-selves* added to in order to form a reflexive pronoun?

myself	*ourselves*
yourself	*yourselves*

b. Based on your answer to question (a), try to explain why some nonstandard dialects of English use the reflexive pronouns *hisself* (instead of *himself*) and *theirselves* (instead of *themselves*). (Hint: Compare the standard dialect reflexive pronouns *himself* and *themselves.* In what way are the nonstandard forms more consistent?)

5. What kind of evidence could be used to argue that {age} in *package* is a derivational morpheme?

6. Consider the following data:

A. Ralph drives.
Ralph drove.

B. Ralph has driven.
Ralph had driven.

C. Ralph is driving.
Ralph was driving.

D. Ralph will drive.
Ralph would drive.

E. Ralph has been driving.
Ralph had been driving.

F. Ralph will have driven.
Ralph would have driven.

G. Ralph will be driving.
Ralph would be driving.

H. Ralph will have been driving.
Ralph would have been driving.

a. Which verb form is inflected for tense?

b. Where does the main verb occur with respect to the other verbs?

c. Where do auxiliaries occur with respect to the main verb?

d. If there is a modal, where does it occur?

e. If there is a form of auxiliary *be,* where does it occur?

f. If there is a form of auxiliary *have,* where does it occur?

g. What form of the verb follows a modal? auxiliary *be?* auxiliary *have?*

7. Give an example (other than the one in this chapter) which illustrates the principle that in English the plural inflection attaches to nouns and the possessive inflection attaches to noun phrases. (Hint: You will need an NP containing a head N such that the boundaries of the NP and the N are not the same—e.g., *the man on the moon.*)

8. A *ne'er-do-well* is someone whose accomplishments are undistinguished. Which of the following best explains why *ne'ers-do-well* is not a possible plural form? (Hint: *Ne'er* is a contracted form of *never.*)

a. Only NPs can be inflected for {PLU}.

b. Only NPs can be inflected for {POSS}.

c. Only Ns can be inflected for {POSS}.

d. Only Ns can be inflected for {PLU}.

e. Both (b) and (c)

9. Identify the word-formation process that accounts for each of the following.

a. The word *DINK* was created from *double income, no kids.*

b. A woman describing clothing that was both grimy and crummy said, *These pants are getting kinda grummy.*

c. A college professor was overheard saying, incorrectly, *Most AIDS are transmitted by . . .* rather than *Most AIDS is transmitted by . . .*

d. A flight instructor told a student to check that all the *Carter pins* were in place. (A *cotter pin* is a small metal rod that holds a nut to a bolt.)

e. A person arranging a meeting says, *We'll liaise at 11:00.*

f. *Deluvy* 'flood' is a late 19th-century word from Latin *diluvium.*

g. In the mid-19th century, a *swartout* was an embezzler. The word comes from Samuel Swartout, a member of President Andrew Johnson's administration, who misappropriated more than a million dollars in public funds.

10. There are two correct answers to the following question: What word-formation process accounts for the word *ROTC < Reserve Officer Training Corps*? Explain.

11. The English word *brangle* is an 18th-century blend meaning 'to quarrel or squabble.' Speculate on its source words. What word-formation process might account for its origin?

12. So-called "pharmazooticals" are drugs derived from animal sources (e.g., a blood pressure medicine derived from snake venom).

a. What word-formation process is illustrated by the word *pharmazootical*?

b. Compare other forms that use this process, as discussed elsewhere in this chapter. How does *pharmazootical* differ from them?

13. Consider the following forms from Kurdish, a language spoken in parts of both Iraq and Turkey. (Data has been regularized.)

aaqil	'wise'	aaqilii	'forethought'
diz	'robber'	dizii	'robbery'
draiž	'long'	draižii	'length'
zaanaa	'wise'	zaanaaii	'erudition'
garm	'warm'	garmii	'warmth'

a. What type of affix is illustrated in this data?

b. What is the form of the affix?

c. What is the function of the affix?

d. Identify an affix in English that serves the same function (choose an affix not already illustrated in the glosses given here).

e. Assume that *raas* means 'true.' What is a likely meaning for *raasii*?

f. Two of the forms have the same gloss. What distinction might account for this?

Exploratory Exercises

1. Consider the following attested forms:

"I *weedeated* the yard yesterday."

"There's the place we *sightsaw* yesterday."

Headline and news excerpt: "Man insists *Bigfoots* still roam the north woods . . . Murphy, 54, said he first encountered two aging *Bigfoots* while searching for a fishing spot 30 years ago."

a. What do the italicized words have in common, in terms of the word-formation process involved?

b. What type of morpheme in each word is treated variably by the persons who produced these forms?

c. What are the two different strategies used by these persons to modify this type of root morpheme?

d. Assume that you wanted to do a study of which strategy most people use. Identify some additional forms that would cause people to have to make a choice of strategies.

2. According to http://www.askoxford.com, English place names typically reflect groups of people who inhabited the place, types of buildings or settlements, or topographical features.

   a. Do some research about the origins of the following English place names:

Chiswick	Sussex
Niton	Norfolk
Oxford	Woodbridge
Ashford	Spalding

   b. Identify three of the suffixes that were, historically, productive sources for English place names, and discuss the meaning of each.

   c. Identify the names of ten towns or cities within a 100-mile radius of your hometown. What patterns can you identify for sources of place names?

3. We have seen that proper names can be the basis for other nouns (such as *sandwich* from the Earl of Sandwich). However, the opposite process has also occurred over time. Many common surnames have their basis in the names of occupations. For example, the surname *Thatcher* reflects the common noun for someone who thatches roofs (thatch is a plant-based material used for roofs).

   Identify the occupation historically associated with each of the following last names. You may have to consult a dictionary or look for a word similar in sound.

Carter	Shaefer
Clark	Wagner
Cooper	Wasserman
Fletcher	Wright

CHAPTER SIX

Phonology

Phonology is the study of the sound system of language: the rules that govern pronunciation. (The word *phonology* itself comes from the Greek word *phōnē,* which means 'voice.') The study of *phonology* in the Western tradition goes back almost 200 years, to the early 1800s, when European linguists began studying sound change by comparing the speech sounds in a variety of related languages. However, the emphasis in modern phonology, as it has developed over the last 45 years, has been primarily on the *psychological system* that underlies production, and only secondarily on the actual physical articulation of speech.

In order to see how phonology works, let's begin by considering some observations we can make about the sound system of English.

(1) The first sound in the word *fight* is produced by bringing together the top teeth and the bottom lip, and then blowing air between them.

(2) The word *war* is produced with one continuous motion of the lungs, tongue, lips, and so on, yet we interpret this motion as a series of three separate speech sounds, *w-a-r.*

(3) The words *pea, see, me,* and *key* all have the same vowel, even though the vowel in each word is spelled differently.

(4) *p* and *b* are alike in that they are both pronounced with the lips; *p* and *k* are different in that *k* is not pronounced with the lips.

(5) The vowels in the words *cab* and *cad* are longer than the same vowels in *cap* and *cat.*

Observation (1) illustrates the fact that we use our **vocal tract** to produce speech. Observation (2) illustrates the fact that words are physically one continuous motion but are psychologically a series of discrete units called **segments.** Observation (3) illustrates that a single segment can be represented by a variety of spellings. Observations (2) and (3) can, in turn, be used to justify a **phonemic alphabet,** a system of transcription in which one symbol uniquely represents one segment. Observation (4) illustrates the fact that segments are composed of smaller units called **distinctive features.** Thus "labial" (referring to the lips) is a distinctive feature shared by *p* and *b,* but not by *p* and *k.* Observation (5) illustrates that two segments can be the same on one **level of representation** but different on another. Thus, the vowels in *cab, cad, cap,* and *cat* are the same on one level (the vowel *a*), but different on another level (long *a* in *cab* and *cad;* short *a* in *cap* and *cat*). (Note that the terms *long* and *short* are not used here in the same way as they are in phonics. In phonology, they indicate differences in duration.) These systematic variations between levels of representation can, in turn, be stated in terms of **phonological rules** (e.g., vowels are lengthened in a particular context).

All of the phenomena in (1–5) are essentially phonological in nature, in that they have to do with the system underlying the pronunciation of words. We will make the familiar assumption that these phenomena are governed by a system of rules. What we will do now is attempt to develop a set of concepts and principles to help us explain the observations in (1–5). Bear in mind that what follows is an (unobservable) theory designed to account for the (observable) data in (1–5).

Vocal Tract

The vocal tract consists of the passageway between the lips and nostrils on one end and the larynx, which contains the vocal cords, on the other. The vocal tract is important to the study of phonology for two reasons. First, human beings use the vocal tract to produce speech. Second, and more importantly, terms which refer to physical properties of the vocal tract are used to describe the psychological units of phonology. A cross-section of the vocal tract is given in Figure 6.1.

Let's go over the landmarks in this figure one by one: (1) **lips;** (2) **teeth;** (3) **tongue;** (4) **alveolar ridge,** the bony ridge right behind the upper teeth; (5) **palate,** the bony dome

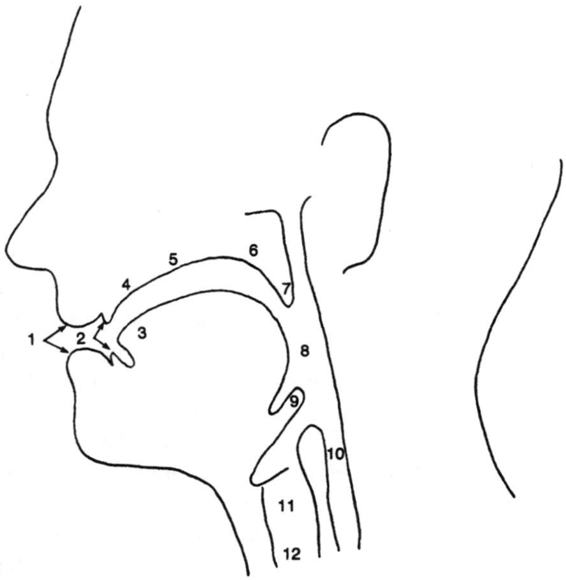

FIGURE 6.1 Cross-section of the vocal tract

constituting the roof of the mouth; (6) **velum,** the soft tissue immediately behind the palate; (7) **uvula,** the soft appendage hanging off the velum (you can see it if you open your mouth wide and look in a mirror); (8) **pharynx,** the back wall of the throat behind the tongue; (9) **epiglottis,** the soft tissue which covers the vocal cords during eating, thus protecting the passageway to the lungs; (10) **esophagus,** the tube going to the stomach; (11) **larynx,** containing the vocal cords; and (12) **trachea,** the tube going to the lungs.

Speech is produced by pushing air from the lungs up through the vocal tract and manipulating several variables at the same time. These variables include whether or not the vocal cords are vibrating; whether the velum is raised (forcing all of the air through the mouth) or lowered (allowing some of the air to escape through the nose); and whether or not the air flow is stopped or impeded at some point between the lips and the larynx. In short, the vocal tract is a tube which produces sound when air from the lungs is pumped through it. Different speech sounds are produced by manipulating the lips, tongue, teeth, velum, pharynx, and vocal cords, thus changing the shape of this tube. For our purposes, however, the primary importance of the vocal tract is the fact that phonological units and rules are described in terms of these physical properties of the vocal mechanism.

Segments

When we listen to someone talk, we *hear* speech but we *perceive* segments, psychological units which correspond more or less to "speech sounds." It is necessary to make this distinction because the sound waves produced by the vocal tract are *continuous* (not divided neatly into individual sounds); however, our interpretation of these sound waves is *discrete* (we perceive distinct sounds, one following the other). For example, if someone utters the word *war* within our hearing, what we actually hear is a sound that gradually changes shape through time. What we perceive, however, is a series of three discrete segments: *w-a-r.* This distinction between hearing and perceiving is fundamental to an appreciation of phonology, although it is not an easy concept to grasp. In particular, it is not immediately evident that speech is a gradually changing sound. In order to grasp this concept, you might try a simple experiment: take some recorded speech (e.g., an audio tape) and play it at half speed. You'll notice that the "speech sounds" blur one into the other. An experiment such as this illustrates quite dramatically that what we perceive as discrete segments is actually a continuous, gradually changing, physical signal.

Thus, the main point to keep in mind is that when we talk, we are actually producing a continuous set of movements within the vocal tract, which result in a continuous set of sound waves; what we think we are doing (unconsciously, of course) is producing a series of discrete segments. Likewise, when we listen to someone talk, we hear a continuously changing set of sound waves; what we perceive are segments. **Speech** refers to what we are actually doing when we talk and listen; **phonology** refers to the segments and rules in terms of which we organize our interpretation of speech. Put another way, speech refers to physical or physiological phenomena, and phonology refers to mental or psychological phenomena.

Phonemic Alphabet

One type of segment that we perceive when we hear speech is termed the **phoneme.** As we have already seen, however, conventional orthography (i.e., spelling) does not provide an adequate means of representing the phonological structure of words. For example, *pea* and *key* both contain the same vowel, but in *pea* the vowel is spelled *ea* and in *key* it is spelled *ey.* In order to get around this problem, linguists have developed a phonemic alphabet, in which one symbol always corresponds to a single phoneme. So, for example, in our phonemic alphabet we might choose to represent the vowel in *pea, see, me,* and *key* as /i/. (Phonemic transcription is always enclosed in slashes to distinguish it from conventional orthography.) Thus, we can capture the fact that we perceive all of these words as having the same vowel by transcribing them as follows: *pea* /pi/, *see* /si/, *me* /mi/, and *key* /ki/.

Now that we've established this principle, let's consider the entire phonemic alphabet of English.

Vowels

PHONEMIC SYMBOL	EXAMPLE
/i/	s*ea*t
/ɪ/	s*i*t
/e/	s*ay*
/ɛ/	s*ai*d
/æ/	s*a*d
/ʌ/ (unstressed = /ə/)	s*u*ds (sod*a*)
/a/	s*o*d
/u/	s*ui*t
/ʊ/	s*oo*t
/o/	s*ew*ed
/ɔ/	s*ough*t
/aɪ/	s*igh*t
/aʊ/	s*ou*th
/ɔɪ/	s*oy*

These vowel phonemes (which, remember, are percepts—psychological units) are described in terms of the following physical dimensions.

- **Tongue Height.** For any articulation corresponding to one of these vowel phonemes, the tongue is either relatively *high* in the mouth (/i, ɪ, u, ʊ/), *mid* (/e, ɛ, ʌ (ə), o/), or *low* (/æ, a, ɔ/). Compare *see* /si/ (high) and *say* /se/ (mid).
- **Frontness.** For any articulation corresponding to one of these vowel phonemes, the tongue is either relatively *front* (/i, ɪ, e, ɛ, æ/) or *back* (/ʌ (ə), a, u, ʊ, o, ɔ/). Compare *see* /si/ (front) and *sue* /su/ (back).

- **Lip Rounding.** For any articulation corresponding to one of these vowel phonemes, the lips are either relatively *round* (/u, ʊ, o, ɔ/) or *spread* (/i, ɪ, e, ɛ, æ, ʌ (ə), a/). Compare *so* /so/ (round) and *say* /se/ (spread).
- **Tenseness.** For any articulation corresponding to one of these vowel phonemes, the vocal musculature is either relatively *tense* (/i, e, u, o, ɔ/) or *lax* (/ɪ, ɛ, æ, ʌ (ə), a, ʊ/). Compare *aid* /ed/ (tense) and *Ed* /ɛd/ (lax).

Figure 6.2 charts the vowel phonemes of English in terms of these four physical dimensions. Thus, for example, /i/ in the upper left-hand corner is high, front, tense, and spread. On the other hand, /ɔ/ in the lower right-hand corner is low, back, tense, and round. And so on.

Viewed from this perspective, it becomes apparent that each of these vowel phonemes is not really an indivisible unit, but rather a composite of values (+ or –) along several dimensions. Each such dimension constitutes a **distinctive feature.** The vowel chart in Figure 6.2 can be broken down into the following distinctive features: [±high], [±low], [±back], [±tense], and [±round]. Thus, for example, /i/ and /ɔ/ are not really units in themselves, but rather each is a bundle of features as follows.

$$/i/ \quad = \quad \begin{bmatrix} \text{+high} \\ \text{–low} \\ \text{–back} \\ \text{+tense} \\ \text{–round} \end{bmatrix} \qquad /ɔ/ \quad = \quad \begin{bmatrix} \text{–high} \\ \text{+low} \\ \text{+back} \\ \text{+tense} \\ \text{+round} \end{bmatrix}$$

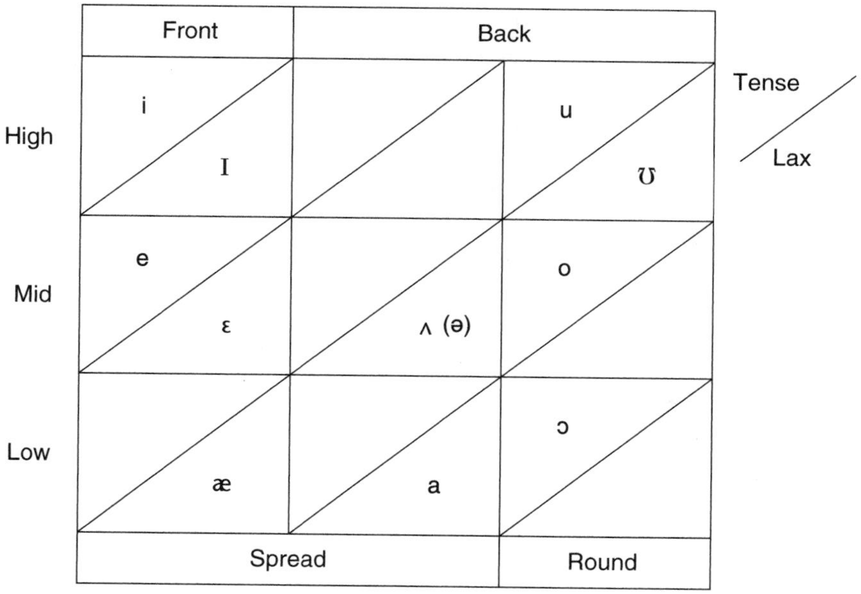

FIGURE 6.2 Vowel phonemes of English

If you have tried to articulate words containing these vowels while you were reading the chart, you may have noticed that it is hard to determine the exact configuration of your vocal tract during any particular articulation. For example, is /i/ really tense and is /ɪ/ really lax? Actually, this is of no great importance. Keep in mind that phonemes and distinctive features are theoretical constructs within a theory of phonology. Phonemes are abstract entities postulated to account for the fact that speakers of English perceive the vowels in *seat* and *sit,* for example, as different. Likewise, distinctive features are postulated to account for the fact that these segments are different along a particular dimension, here what we have somewhat arbitrarily decided to call [±tense]. The fact that phonemes and distinctive features are described in physical terms is of no real consequence. It results from the fact that modern phonology developed from the study of sound change, which in turn was thought to be a direct function of the vocal tract. In short, even though phonemes and distinctive features are described in physical terms, they are actually psychological entities: *no one has ever uttered a phoneme or a distinctive feature.* Rather, when we talk, we utter a physical speech signal which we *interpret* as containing phonemes, which in turn consist of distinctive features.

Exercise A

1. Describe each of the following vowel phonemes of English in terms of tongue height, frontness, lip rounding, and tenseness.

- **†a.** /æ/
- **†b.** /o/
- **c.** /e/
- **d.** /ʌ/
- **e.** /a/
- **f.** /ɔ/
- **g.** /ʊ/
- **h.** /i/

2. The symbol /ʌ/ represents the vowel in

- **a.** pat
- **b.** pet
- **c.** pot
- **d.** put
- **e.** putt

3. Which symbol represents the vowel in *look:*

- **a.** /ʌ/
- **b.** /u/
- **c.** /ʊ/
- **d.** /o/
- **e.** /a/

4. Match each of the following words with its phonemic vowel.

- **a.** sues ___ /ɔ/
- **b.** sews ___ /aʊ/
- **c.** sows ___ /i/
- **d.** sighs ___ /u/
- **e.** sees ___ /ɪ/
- **f.** says ___ /ɛ/
- **g.** Sis ___ /aɪ/
- **h.** sauce ___ /o/

Consonants

For each consonant phoneme in the following list, there are three examples: one each for the occurrence of the phoneme in word-initial, word-medial, and word-final position. A blank indicates that the phoneme does not occur in that position in English.

PHONEMIC SYMBOL	EXAMPLE
/p/	*p*at, zi*pp*er, ca*p*
/b/	*b*at, fi*bb*er, ca*b*
/t/	*t*ab, ca*tt*y, ca*t*
/d/	*d*ab, ca*dd*y, ca*d*
/k/	*c*ap, di*ck*er, ta*ck*
/g/	*g*ap, di*gg*er, ta*g*
/f/	*f*at, sa*f*er, belie*f*
/v/	*v*at, sa*v*er, belie*ve*
/θ/	*th*in, e*th*er, brea*th*
/ð/	*th*en, ei*th*er, brea*the*
/s/	*s*ue, la*c*y, pea*c*e
/z/	*z*oo, la*z*y, pea*s*
/š/	*sh*oe, thre*sh*er, ru*sh*
/ž/	—, trea*s*ure, rou*g*e
/h/	*h*am, a*h*ead, —
/č/	*c*hain, ske*tc*hy, besee*ch*
/ǰ/	*J*ane, e*dg*y, besie*g*e
/m/	*m*itt, si*mm*er, see*m*
/n/	*kn*it, si*nn*er, see*n*
/ŋ/	—, si*ng*er, si*ng*
/l/	*l*ight, te*ll*er, coa*l*
/r/	*r*ight, te*rr*or, co*r*e
/w/	*w*et, lo*w*er, —
/y/	*y*et, la*y*er, —

(Note: English words which appear to end in /w/ and /y/ are analyzed as ending in vowels in this system. For example, *cow* = /kaʊ/ and *sky* = /skaɪ/.)

As was the case with vowels, these consonant phonemes (which, once again, are percepts—psychological units) are described in terms of physical dimensions, as follows.

Place of Articulation. For any articulation corresponding to one of these consonant phonemes, the vocal tract is constricted at one of the following points.

- **Bilabial** (from *bi* 'two' + *labial* 'lips'). The primary constriction is at the lips (/p, b, m, w/). Compare *pea* /pi/ (bilabial) and *tea* /ti/ (non-bilabial).
- **Labiodental** (from *labio* 'lip' + *dental* 'teeth'). The primary constriction is between the lower lip and upper teeth (/f,v/). Compare *fee* /fi/ (labiodental) and *see* /si/ (non-labiodental).
- **Interdental** (from *inter* 'between' + *dental* 'teeth'). The primary constriction is between the tongue and the upper teeth (/θ, ð/). Compare *thigh* /θaɪ/ (interdental) and *shy* /šaɪ/ (non-interdental).
- **Alveolar** (from *alveolar ridge*). The primary constriction is between the tongue and the alveolar ridge (/t, d, s, z, n, l/). Compare *tea* /ti/ (alveolar) and *key* /ki/ (non-alveolar).
- **Palatal** (from *palate*). The primary constriction is between the tongue and the palate (/š, ž, č, ǰ, r, y/). Compare *shoe* /šu/ (palatal) and *sue* /su/ (non-palatal).
- **Velar** (from *velum*). The primary constriction is between the tongue and the velum (/k, g, ŋ/). Compare *coo* /ku/ (velar) and *two* /tu/ (non-velar).
- **Glottal** (from *glottis,* which refers to the space between the vocal cords). The primary constriction is at the glottis (/h/). Compare *hoe* /ho/ (glottal) and *so* /so/ (non-glottal).

Manner of Articulation. For any articulation corresponding to one of these consonant phonemes, the vocal tract is constricted in one of the following ways.

- **Stops.** Two articulators (lips, tongue, teeth, etc.) are brought together such that the flow of air through the vocal tract is completely blocked (/p, b, t, d, k, g/). Compare *tea* /ti/ (stop) and *see* /si/ (non-stop).
- **Fricatives.** Two articulators are brought near each other such that the flow of air is impeded but not completely blocked. The flow of air through the narrow opening creates friction, hence the term *fricative* (/f, v, θ, ð, s, z, š, ž, h/). Compare *zoo* /zu/ (fricative) and *do* /du/ (non-fricative).
- **Affricates.** Articulations corresponding to affricates are those that begin like stops (with a complete closure in the vocal tract) and end like fricatives (with a narrow opening in the vocal tract) (/č, ǰ/). Compare *chew* /ču/ (affricate) and *shoe* /šu/ (non-affricate). Because affricates can be described as a stop plus a fricative, some phonemic alphabets transcribe /č/ as /tš/ and /ǰ/ as /dž/.
- **Nasals.** A nasal articulation is one in which the airflow through the mouth is completely blocked but the velum is lowered, forcing the air through the nose (/m, n, ŋ/). Compare *no* /no/ (nasal) and *doe* /do/ (non-nasal).
- **Liquids and Glides.** Both of these terms describe articulations that are mid-way between true consonants (i.e., stops, fricatives, affricates, and nasals) and vowels, although they are both generally classified as consonants. *Liquid* is a cover term for all *l*-like and *r*-like articulations (/l, r/). Compare *low* /lo/ (liquid) and *doe* /do/ (non-liquid). The term *glide* refers to an articulation in which the vocal tract is constricted, but not enough to block or impede the airflow (/w, y/). Compare *way* /we/ (glide) and *bay* /be/ (non-glide).

Consonants can be divided into **obstruents** (stops, fricatives, and affricates) and **sonorants** (nasals, liquids, and glides).

Voicing. For any articulation corresponding to one of these consonant phonemes, the vocal cords are either vibrating (/b, d, g, v, ð, z, ž, ǰ, m, n, ŋ, r, l, w, y/) or not (/p, t, k, f, θ, s, š, č, h/). Compare *zoo* /zu/ (voiced) and *sue* /su/ (voiceless). Stops, fricatives, and affricates come in voiced and voiceless pairs (except for /h/); nasals, liquids, and glides are all voiced, as are vowels.

Figure 6.3 plots the consonant phonemes of English in terms of these three physical dimensions: place of articulation, manner of articulation, and voicing. Thus, for example, /p/ is a voiceless bilabial stop; /v/ is a voiced labiodental fricative; /č/ is a voiceless palatal affricate; /ŋ/ is a voiced velar nasal; and so on.

As was the case with vowels, each consonant phoneme is not really an indivisible unit, but rather a composite of values along these three dimensions. Once again, each such dimension constitutes a **distinctive feature.** For example, from one perspective /p/ and /ŋ/ are not really units in themselves, but rather each is a bundle of feature values, as follows.

$$/\text{p}/ \quad = \quad \begin{bmatrix} \text{+bilabial} \\ \text{+stop} \\ \text{−voice} \end{bmatrix} \qquad\qquad /\text{ŋ}/ \quad = \quad \begin{bmatrix} \text{+velar} \\ \text{+nasal} \\ \text{+voice} \end{bmatrix}$$

		Bilabial	Labiodental	Interdental	Alveolar	Palatal	Velar	Glottal
Stops	voiceless	p			t		k	
	voiced	b			d		g	
Fricatives	voiceless		f	θ	s	š		h
	voiced		v	ð	z	ž		
Affricates	voiceless					č		
	voiced					ǰ		
Nasals	voiceless							
	voiced	m			n		ŋ	
Liquids	voiceless							
	voiced				l	r		
Glides	voiceless							
	voiced	w				y		

FIGURE 6.3 Consonant phonemes of English

Once again, it is important to keep in mind that phonemes and distinctive features are theoretical constructs within a theory of phonology. Phonemes are postulated to account for the fact that the consonants in *pea* and *bee,* for example, are perceived as different. Likewise, distinctive features are postulated to account for the fact that they differ along a particular dimension, namely [±voice].

Before leaving this section, it may be useful to clear up several points of potential confusion. First, the specific symbols used in a phonemic alphabet are of no particular theoretical importance. For example, the symbols /p/ and /b/ in English could, in theory, be replaced by /1/ and /2/. All that is necessary is that one symbol be used to represent each segment that is perceived as unique by speakers of the language in question.

Second, a number of phonemic alphabets for English are currently in use. Thus, for example, you will see the initial phoneme in *yes* sometimes transcribed as /y/ and other times transcribed as /j/. Likewise, you will see the vowel phoneme in *pea* sometimes transcribed as /i/ and other times transcribed as /iy/. Similarly, you will see the second syllable in *mother* sometimes transcribed /ðər/ and other times transcribed as /ðɚ/. This is simply a fact of life that anyone who deals with phonology has to get used to. (Actually, with a little practice, it is quite easy to go from one transcription system to another.) Similarly, there are several different distinctive feature systems in current use. The one we have discussed for vowels ([±high], [±low], [±back], [±round], and [±tense]) is fairly standard. The one for consonants ([place], [manner], and [±voice]) is somewhat oversimplified, but is adequate for our purposes here. The "best" set of distinctive features for describing segments found in human languages is a matter of debate and need not concern us here.

Third, you will see some of the phonemes of English charted slightly differently (recall the vowel and consonant charts discussed earlier), depending upon who you read. Thus, the phoneme /h/, which we have characterized as a fricative, is sometimes classified as a glide. Likewise, the phoneme /ɔ/, which we have characterized as a low vowel, is sometimes classified as a mid vowel. And so on. Again, for our purposes these differences are of no great theoretical consequence. What is important is that each phoneme be given a *unique* representation in terms of distinctive features. After all, by calling something a phoneme, we are saying that it is different from any other segment in the language in question.

Fourth, the phonemic representation of the words in a language is not identical for every speaker of that language. For example, the vowels in *cot* and *caught* are different for some speakers of English (*cot* has /a/ and *caught* has /ɔ/) but the same for others (both *cot* and *caught* have /a/). Likewise, some speakers of English perceive the final consonant in *garage* as /ž/, while others perceive it as /ǰ/. Such differences between speakers, however, are more noticeable among the vowels. For example, in the word *think,* some speakers have /ɪ/, others have /i/, and still others have /e/! When such differences are found, they typically involve phonemes that are near each other in articulatory terms. Note, for instance, that /i/, /ɪ/, and /e/ are adjacent on the vowel chart.

Fifth, different languages have different sets of phonemes. English contains phonemes not found in some other languages; and, conversely, English lacks phonemes that are found in other languages. For example, English contains the interdental fricatives /θ/ and /ð/, which are relatively rare among the world's languages. Modern Greek has them, but French, German, Italian, Persian, and Russian (among others) do not. On the other hand, English entirely lacks front rounded vowels. French, however, has three: /ü/ (high) as in *sucre* 'sugar,' /ö/

(mid) as in *jeu* 'game,' and /œ/ (low) as in *oeuf* 'egg.' (To pronounce the vowel in *sucre,* for example, try to say the vowel in *see* while rounding your lips.)

Exercise B

1. Give the English phonemic symbol that corresponds to each of the following articulatory descriptions.
   - **a.** low front spread lax vowel
   - **†b.** voiced velar nasal
   - **c.** voiced interdental fricative
   - **d.** high back round lax vowel
   - **e.** voiced palatal glide
2. Give the English phonemes that correspond to the following feature specifications.
   - **†a.** $\begin{bmatrix}-\text{back}\\+\text{tense}\end{bmatrix}$
   - **b.** $\begin{bmatrix}+\text{fricative}\\-\text{voice}\end{bmatrix}$
   - **c.** $\begin{bmatrix}+\text{bilabial}\\+\text{voice}\end{bmatrix}$
   - **d.** $[+\text{glide}]$
   - **e.** $\begin{bmatrix}+\text{back}\\+\text{round}\end{bmatrix}$
3. For each group, identify the segment that differs in manner of articulation from the other three.
   - **a.** /n/, /f/, /s/, /z/
   - **b.** /v/, /ð/, /g/, /ž/
   - **c.** /l/, /r/, /d/
4. For each group, identify the segment that differs in place of articulation from the other three.
   - **a.** /s/, /č/, /t/, /n/
   - **b.** /k/, /n/, /g/, /ŋ/
   - **c.** /θ/, /p/, /b/, /m/
5. For each group, identify the segment that differs in voicing from the other three.
   - **a.** /m/, /g/, /ǰ/, /s/
   - **b.** /n/, /f/, /θ/, /p/
   - **c.** /b/, /p/, /r/, /v/
6. Describe each of the following consonant phonemes of English in terms of voicing and place and manner of articulation.
   - **a.** /ð/
   - **b.** /h/
   - **c.** /l/
   - **d.** /f/
   - **e.** /d/
   - **f.** /ž/

(continued)

Exercise B *Continued*

7. The transcription /taɪp/ represents the word
   - a. tap
   - b. tape
   - c. tip
   - d. type
8. The transcription /rɪč/ represents the word
   - a. reach
   - b. rich
   - c. ridge
   - d. reich
9. The transcription /ðiz/ represents the word
   - a. thighs
   - b. these
   - c. this
   - d. tease
10. Match each of the following words with its phonemic transcription.

a. cough	___ /koč/
b. cuff	___ /kag/
c. cog	___ /kɔf/
d. couch	___ /kaʊ/
e. coach	___ /kʌf/
f. cow	___ /kaʊč/

11. Write the following English words in phonemic transcription.
   - a. thrush
   - b. breathe
   - c. they
   - d. fox
   - e. choose
   - f. flies

Levels of Representation

At the beginning of this chapter, we discussed the idea that two segments might, at the same time, be both the same and different. In order to reconcile this apparent paradox, linguists have developed the notion of **level of representation.** By recognizing more than one such level, we are able to say that two segments are identical on one level of representation, yet different on another. As an illustration of this concept, let's take the fact that specific properties of a phoneme vary according to its position in a word. This variation is sometimes referred to as **allophonic variation.** Consider, for example, the following English words and phrases, each of which contains an instance of the phoneme /t/: *Tim, stem, hit, hit me,* and *Betty.* Each of these instances of /t/ differs systematically from the others. These systematic variations of /t/ are called **allophones** of /t/ and are transcribed in square brackets ([ ]).

The /t/ in *Tim* is aspirated; that is, there is a puff of air following the release of the /t/. (You can test this by holding the palm of your hand about three inches from your lips and saying *Tim.* Feel the rush of air as you release the /t/?) Aspirated /t/ is transcribed [t^h].

The /t/ in *stem* is released, but not aspirated; that is, there is no puff of air following the release of the /t/. (You can test this by using the "palm" test just described; say *Tim* and *stem* alternately. Note that there is no rush of air with the /t/ in *stem.*) Released /t/ is transcribed [t].

The /t/ in *hit* can be released or unreleased. If it is unreleased, the tip of the tongue stops at the alveolar ridge. (You can test this by saying *hit* and leaving your tongue at the alveolar ridge after the word is pronounced.) Unreleased /t/ is transcribed [t˺].

The /t/ in *hit me* may be unreleased or it may be a glottal stop. If it is a glottal stop, there is no contact between the tip of the tongue and the alveolar ridge; instead, the vocal cords are brought together and the airflow is stopped momentarily. (You can test this by saying *hit me* without ever raising your tongue to the alveolar ridge. The /t/ you perceive is actually a stop formed with the vocal cords.) A glottal stop is transcribed [ʔ].

The /t/ in *Betty* is an alveolar flap; that is, it is formed by raising the tip of the tongue to the alveolar ridge very rapidly and releasing it. An alveolar flap is more rapid than either [t] or [d]. (You can test this by saying *Betty* with an alveolar flap, which sounds like the normal pronunciation; then with a [t], which sounds British, like Cary Grant; and then with a [d], which sounds like *beddy.*) An alveolar flap is transcribed [ɾ].

Each of these allophones of /t/ is predictable, in that it typically occurs in a particular position within a word or phrase. For example, [tʰ] as in *Tim* occurs when /t/ begins a syllable and is followed by a stressed vowel. [t] as in *stem* occurs when /t/ is followed by a vowel, but does not begin a syllable. [t˺] as in *hit* occurs when /t/ occurs at the end of an utterance. [ʔ] as in *hit me* occurs when /t/ follows a vowel and precedes a consonant. [ɾ] as in *Betty* occurs when /t/ follows a stressed vowel and precedes an unstressed vowel.

Notice the consequences of what we have done. We have essentially justified two levels of phonological representation: the **phonemic,** where phonemes are described, and the **phonetic,** where allophones (i.e., systematic variants) of phonemes are described. This situation is summarized in Figure 6.4, which illustrates the fact that speakers of English perceive the words *Tim, stem, hit, hit me,* and *Betty* as containing instances of the same phoneme, /t/. Yet each instance of /t/ differs on the phonetic level, depending on the context in which /t/ occurs. Thus, by using the concept **level of representation,** we are able to capture the fact that two segments can be both the same (i.e., phonemically) and different (i.e., phonetically).

This discussion raises the issue of how to tell whether two segments are allophones of different phonemes or allophones of the same phoneme. The basic test is to substitute one phone for another. If the substitution changes one word into another, then the two phones

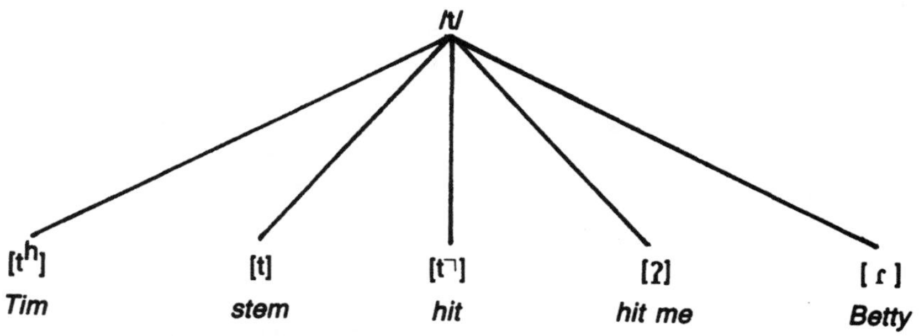

FIGURE 6.4 Phonemic and phonetic levels of representation

contrast and are allophones of different phonemes. If they do not, then they are in **free variation** and are allophones of the same phoneme. Consider, for example, *hit* [hɪt̚]. If we substitute [d̚] for [t̚], we get a different word, *hid.* Thus, [t̚] and [d̚] contrast, and therefore are allophones of different phonemes, namely /t/ and /d/, respectively. On the other hand, if we substitute [t] for the [t̚] in [hɪt̚], we are left with the same word, *hit.* Thus, [t̚] and [t] are in free variation, and therefore are allophones of the same phoneme, namely /t/.

There is one other possibility: namely, one in which two phones are not interchangeable because they never occur in the same environment (i.e., position within a word). Consider, for example, the phones [t^h] and [ɾ]. These never occur in the same context; [t^h] always occurs before a stressed vowel and [ɾ] always occurs before an unstressed vowel. Thus, in the word *tatter* /tǽtər/ (an accent mark indicates stress), the first /t/ is always [t^h] and the second /t/ is always [ɾ]. Note that if we try to substitute one phone for the other, we get something that is not even pronounceable in English, namely *[ɾǽt^hər]. Two such phones that never occur in the same context are said to be in **complementary distribution** and are allophones of the same phoneme. In this case, [t^h] and [ɾ] are allophones of /t/.

Let's summarize the main points made in this section. Linguists have posited the phonemic and phonetic levels of representation to account for the fact that two segments may be both alike (i.e., the same phoneme, e.g., /t/) and unalike (i.e., different allophones, e.g., [t^h] and [ɾ]) at the same time. If two phones contrast (i.e., substituting one for the other causes a change in meaning), they are allophones of different phonemes. On the other hand, if two phones are either in free variation (i.e., if substituting one for the other does not cause a change in meaning) or in complementary distribution, they are allophones of the same phoneme. The main point to keep in mind is that both the phonemic and phonetic levels and the segments that comprise them are psychological in nature and should not be confused with the speech production mechanism or the speech signal.

Exercise C

1. In English, the phoneme /g/ has two allophones: the voiced velar stop [g] and the voiced palatal stop [ɟ]. Examine the data below and decide whether [g] and [ɟ] are in complementary distribution, or in free variation. Explain the reasoning behind your choice.

god	[ga:d]	gone	[gɔ̃:n]
geese	[ɟis]	gain	[ɟẽ:n]
ghoul	[gu:l]	good	[gʊ:d]
gab	[ɟæ:b]	gear	[ɟɪ:r]

2. Like /g/, the phoneme /k/ in English exhibits exactly the same sort of allophonic variation between [k] (velar) and [c] (palatal): [c] occurs before /i, ɪ, e,ɛ, æ/, and [k] occurs before other vowels. State the environment for the allophones of both /k/ and /g/.

Phonological Rules

Because levels of phonological representation are not always identical to one another, part of phonology consists of rules that essentially translate segments on one level into segments on another level. We will now look at some common phonological rules or processes in English, working from the data to the rules themselves.

Aspiration

Let's begin with a phonological process that we have already discussed informally, namely aspiration. Consider the following English words, each of which is accompanied by its phonemic and phonetic representations.

sip	/síp/	[síp]
appear	/əpír/	[əp^{h}ír]
pepper	/pɛ́pər/	[p^{h}ɛ́pər]
space	/spés/	[spés]
papaya	/pəpáɪyə/	[pəp^{h}áɪyə]

In these data, /p/ has two allophones, [p^{h}] and [p]. Our task is to determine under what conditions (i.e., in what environments) /p/ becomes [p^{h}]. We might begin by trying to determine what all of the occurrences of [p^{h}] have in common. One thing we observe is that all instances of [p^{h}] occur immediately before a stressed vowel. Thus we can hypothesize the following rule: /p/ becomes [p^{h}] when it occurs before a stressed vowel. This rule, however, will not account for the fact that the [p] in *space* [spés] is not aspirated, even though the following /é/ is stressed. Since our rule is not 100 percent accurate, we will have to revise it. We might ask how the [p] in *space* is different from the [p^{h}]'s in *appear* [əp^{h}ír], *pepper* [p^{h}ɛ́pər], and *papaya* [pəp^{h}áɪyə]. Note that the [p^{h}]'s in *appear, pepper,* and *papaya,* in addition to preceding a stressed vowel, also begin a syllable, whereas the [p] in *space* does not. Now we are in a position to hypothesize a revised version of our rule: /p/ becomes [p^{h}] when it both begins a syllable and is followed by a stressed vowel. This rule accurately predicts those cases where /p/ becomes [p^{h}]; and, by exclusion, it also predicts where /p/ remains unchanged.

We might leave our Aspiration Rule as it stands, in a simple prose statement: /p/ becomes aspirated when it begins a syllable and is followed by a stressed vowel. However, since informal prose statements can often be (unintentionally) vague or ambiguous, phonologists have adopted the practice of stating rules in formal notation. The standard notation for writing phonological rules is as follows.

$$W \rightarrow X \,/\, Y \underline{\qquad} Z$$

This rule states that segment W becomes segment X when it follows Y and precedes Z. (Read the arrow as "becomes" and the slash as "in the following environment.")

The next step is to formalize our Aspiration Rule using this format. Before doing so, however, we need some way of indicating a syllable boundary. One symbol that is often used for this purpose is \$. Now we can formalize our rule as follows.

$$\text{/p/} \rightarrow [\text{+aspirated}] \,/\, \$ \underline{\qquad} \underset{[\text{+stress}]}{\text{V}}$$

This rule states that the phoneme /p/ becomes aspirated when it begins a syllable (i.e., when there is a syllable boundary to its left) and is followed by a stressed vowel (V). There are several variations on this notation; for example, you might also see this rule written as follows.

$$/p/ \rightarrow [p^h] \,/\, \$ \_\_\_\_ \acute{V}$$

The two notations mean exactly the same thing.

Before leaving this example, it is worthwhile to point out that if we were to go beyond the data on which this rule is based and include examples containing the allophones of /t/ and /k/ as well as those of /p/, we would see that /p/, /t/, and /k/ all become aspirated under identical conditions, namely when they begin a syllable and are followed by a stressed vowel. Since /p/, /t/, and /k/ constitute the set of voiceless stops in English, we could state the Aspiration Rule for them all as follows.

$$\begin{bmatrix} +\text{stop} \\ -\text{voice} \end{bmatrix} \rightarrow [+\text{aspirated}] \,/\, \$ \_\_\_\_ \underset{[+\text{stress}]}{V}$$

Note the advantage of stating the rule in terms of distinctive features rather than segments. If we were to use segments, then we would miss the generalization that this rule applies not to /p/, /t/, and /k/ individually, but rather to the intersection of their common properties: [+stop] and [–voice].

Exercise D

1. Choose the formal statement that is equivalent to the following informal statement: A vowel is lengthened when it occurs at the end of a word. (The symbol # indicates a word boundary.)

a. V→[V:] / # ___ **c.** V→[V:] / ___ C #

b. V→[V:] / # ___ C **d.** V→[V:] / ___ #

†2. Identify the formal statement that is equivalent to the following informal statement: A voiceless consonant becomes voiced when it occurs between two vowels.

a. C→[–voice] / V ___ V **c.** C→[+voice] / V ___ V

b. C→[+voice] / VV ___ **d.** C→[+voice] / ___ VV

3. Which informal statement is equivalent to the following formal statement (N indicates any nasal consonant): V→Ṽ / ___ N

a. A vowel becomes nasalized when it occurs after a nasal consonant.

b. A vowel becomes stressed when it occurs after a nasal consonant.

c. A vowel becomes nasalized when it occurs before a nasal consonant.

d. A nasal consonant is replaced by a nasalized vowel when it occurs before another nasal consonant.

e. A nasalized vowel is inserted before a nasal consonant.

†4. Correct the rule below so that it corresponds to the following informal statement: A voiced stop becomes voiceless when it occurs word-finally.

C→[–vce] / # ___
[+stop]

Exercise D *Continued*

5. Correct the rule below so that it corresponds to the following informal statement: A nasal segment is deleted when it occurs before a voiceless stop. (Hint: Ø = null set.)

$$\underset{[+\text{nas}]}{\emptyset \rightarrow \text{C}} \; / \; \_\_ \; \underset{\begin{bmatrix}+\text{stop}\\ -\text{vce}\end{bmatrix}}{\text{C}}$$

Vowel Lengthening

Consider the following English words, each of which is accompanied by its phonemic and phonetic representations.

heat	/hit/	[hit]
seize	/siz/	[si:z]
keel	/kil/	[k^hi:l]
leaf	/lif/	[lif]
heed	/hid/	[hi:d]
cease	/sis/	[sis]
leave	/liv/	[li:v]

In these data, /i/ has two allophones, [i] and [i:] (a colon after a vowel indicates that it is lengthened). Once again, our task is to determine under what conditions /i/ becomes [i:]. We might begin by hypothesizing that some property of the consonant to the *left* of the vowel causes it to lengthen. This hypothesis, however, must clearly be wrong. Consider, for example, *seize* [si:z] and *cease* [sis]. The former has a long vowel and the latter has a short vowel, yet in both cases the vowel is preceded by [s]. Thus, the consonant to the left of the vowel obviously has no effect upon the length of the vowel, since here the same consonant precedes both a long vowel and a short vowel.

Alternatively, we might hypothesize that some property of the consonant to the *right* of the vowel causes it to lengthen. Here we have more luck. Note that the vowels in *heat, leaf,* and *cease* are short, and each one is followed by a voiceless consonant ([t], [f], and [s] are [–voice]). In contrast, the vowels in *heed, leave, seize,* and *keel* are long and each one is followed by a voiced consonant ([d], [v], [z], and [l] are [+voice]). Now we are in a position to propose a rule: /i/ becomes [i:] when it precedes a voiced consonant. This rule accurately accounts for our data. It predicts exactly those cases where /i/ becomes [i:] and, by exclusion, it also predicts where /i/ remains unchanged.

Let's go one step further and formalize our rule as follows.

$$/\text{i}/ \rightarrow [+\text{long}] \; \_\_\_\_ \; \underset{[+\text{voice}]}{\text{C}}$$

This rule states that the phoneme /i/ becomes lengthened when it precedes a voiced consonant (C). As in our Aspiration Rule discussed earlier, there are variations on this notation. You might also see this rule written as follows.

$$/\text{i}/ \rightarrow [\text{i:}] \;\underline{\quad}\; \underset{[+\text{voice}]}{\text{C}}$$

In addition, if we were to go beyond the data on which we have based this rule and include examples containing allophones of the other vowels in English, we would see that *all* vowels become lengthened under the same conditions, namely when they precede a voiced consonant. Thus, we can state the Vowel Lengthening Rule as follows.

$$\text{V} \rightarrow [+\text{long}] \,/\; \underline{\quad}\; \underset{[+\text{voice}]}{\text{C}}$$

Once again, we can see that phonological rules apply to *classes* of segments (e.g., vowels) rather than to individual segments (e.g., /i/, /e/, /æ/, and so on).

Exercise E

1. Return to the data for /g/ given in Exercise C.
   - **a.** Under what conditions does /g/ occur as [ɟ]? State the rule informally (i.e., in a written statement).
   - **b.** Write a formal version of the rule that you constructed for (a).

Vowel Nasalization

Consider the following English words, each of which is accompanied by its phonemic and phonetic representations.

map	/mæp/	[mæp]
pan	/pæn/	[pæ̃n]
pad	/pæd/	[pæd]
Pam	/pæm/	[pæ̃m]
gnat	/næt/	[næt]
pang	/pæŋ/	[pæ̃ŋ]

In these data, /æ/ has two allophones, [æ] and [æ̃]. (A tilde over a vowel indicates that it is nasalized. A nasalized vowel is perceived as being pronounced with the velum lowered.) As before, our task is to determine under what conditions /æ/ becomes [æ̃]. Before getting started, however, note that the vowels in *pan, pad, Pam,* and *pang* should be long (i.e., [æ:]), since they each precede a voiced consonant; yet the phonetic transcription does not indicate this. Pay this no mind; it is common practice in phonology to ignore phonetic details irrelevant to the particular task at hand. In this case, vowel lengthening has nothing to do with vowel nasalization, so it has been ignored. Likewise, the aspiration notation in this data has been omitted, since aspiration has nothing to do with vowel nasalization.

Let's now return to the problem of determining under what conditions /æ/ becomes [æ̃]. First of all, we might assume, naturally enough, that since English has no nasalized vowel phonemes, a phonetically nasalized vowel is the result of being adjacent to a nasal consonant, /m/, /n/, or /ŋ/. Thus, our task is simplified. Is it the preceding or the following nasal consonant that is causing the vowel to become nasalized? The answer is straightforward. Since *map* [mæp] and *gnat* [næt] both contain a preceding nasal consonant but no nasalized vowel, vowel nasalization must not be caused by a preceding nasal consonant. On the other hand, since *pan* [pæ̃n], *Pam* [pæ̃m], and *pang* [pæ̃ŋ] each contain a nasalized vowel followed by a nasal consonant, it must be the following nasal consonant that is causing the vowel nasalization. We are now in a position to propose a rule: /æ/ becomes [æ̃] when it is followed by a nasal consonant. This rule accurately predicts exactly the cases where /æ/ becomes [æ̃]; and, by exclusion, it also predicts where /æ/ remains unchanged.

We can formalize this rule as follows.

$$/\text{æ}/ \rightarrow [+\text{nasal}] \;/\; \underline{\quad\quad} \begin{matrix}\text{C}\\ [+\text{nasal}]\end{matrix}$$

Or, alternatively, as follows.

$$/\text{æ}/ \rightarrow [\tilde{\text{æ}}] \;/\; \underline{\quad\quad} \begin{matrix}\text{C}\\ [+\text{nasal}]\end{matrix}$$

Once again, if we were to go beyond the data on which our rule is based, we would see that *all* vowels in English become nasalized when they precede a nasal consonant. Thus, we could state the Vowel Nasalization Rule for English as follows.

$$\text{V} \rightarrow [+\text{nasal}] \;/\; \underline{\quad\quad} \begin{matrix}\text{C}\\ [+\text{nasal}]\end{matrix}$$

Again, we see that phonological rules apply to classes of segments, rather than to individual segments. It is also worth mentioning that this type of rule, in which a segment becomes more like a neighboring segment in some way, is called an **assimilation** rule. In this case, a vowel becomes more like an adjacent nasal consonant by becoming nasalized itself.

Exercise F

1. Consider the following forms:

cloth	/klɔθ/	clothing	/kloðɪŋ/
north	/nɔrθ/	northern	/nɔrðərn/
south	/saʊθ/	southern	/sʌðərn/
bath	/bæθ/	bathing	/beðɪŋ/

a. In what environment does /θ/ show up as /ð/?

b. What type of phonological process accounts for this change? (Hint: All vowel phonemes in English are [+voice].)

c. Is there any reason to state this rule as one in which /θ/ becomes [ð], rather than a rule in which /ð/ becomes [θ]? Explain.

Flapping

Consider the following English words, each of which is accompanied by its phonemic and phonetic representations.

ride	/ráɪd/	[ráɪd]
dire	/dáɪr/	[dáɪr]
rider	/ráɪdər/	[ráɪɾər]
write	/ráɪt/	[ráɪt]
tire	/táɪr/	[táɪr]
writer	/ráɪtər/	[ráɪɾər]
lender	/lɛ́ndər/	[lɛ́ndər]
Easter	/ístər/	[ístər]
attack	/ətǽk/	[ətǽk]
adobe	/ədóbi/	[ədóbi]

In these data, both /t/ and /d/ become [ɾ] (an alveolar flap) under certain circumstances. Our task is to determine under what conditions /t/ and /d/ become [ɾ]. We might begin by noting that /t/ and /d/ never become [ɾ] when they begin or end a word. Thus, the relevant alveolar stops (/t/ and /d/) must be those that occur somewhere in the middle of the word. This narrows the field to *rider, writer, lender, Easter, attack,* and *adobe.* Of these, only the alveolar stops in *rider* and *writer* become [ɾ]. What is different about the environment of /t/ and /d/ in these words? First of all, they occur between vowels. (Compare *lender* and *Easter,* where the stop occurs between a consonant and a vowel.) Second, the vowel to the left is stressed and that to the right is unstressed. (Compare *attack* and *adobe,* where the vowel to the left of the stop is unstressed and that to the right is stressed.) Now we are in a position to propose a rule: /t/ and /d/ become [ɾ] when they occur between two vowels, the first of which is stressed and the second of which is unstressed. This rule accurately accounts for all of the [ɾ]'s in our data. That is, it predicts exactly those cases where /t/ and /d/ become [ɾ]; and, by exclusion, it also predicts where they remain unchanged.

The Flapping Rule, in turn, can be formalized as follows.

$$\begin{bmatrix}+\text{stop}\\+\text{alveolar}\end{bmatrix} \rightarrow [\text{ɾ}] \;/\; \underset{[+\text{stress}]}{\text{V}} \;\_\_\_\_\; \underset{[-\text{stress}]}{\text{V}}$$

As usual, there are variations on this notation. You might also see this rule written as follows.

$$\begin{Bmatrix}/\text{t}/\\/\text{d}/\end{Bmatrix} \rightarrow [\text{ɾ}] \;/\; \acute{\text{V}}\_\_\_\_\breve{\text{V}}$$

A breve (˘) above a vowel indicates that it is unstressed.

Flapping is a special case of **neutralization,** a process that obliterates the contrast between two segments in a particular environment.

Rule Ordering

So far we have dealt with the application of single phonological rules to particular forms. However, it is quite common for one form to reflect the application of more than one phonological rule. For example, consider a form like *potato* /pətéto/, whose phonetic form we can represent as [pətʰéɾo]. This phonetic form shows the effect of two phonological rules, as outlined below:

Phonemic form:	/pətéto/
Aspiration:	pətʰéto
Flapping:	pətʰéɾo
Phonetic form:	[pətʰéɾo]

Note that we would arrive at the same phonetic form if we were to apply the Aspiration and Flapping rules in the opposite order:

Phonemic form:	/pətéto/
Flapping:	pətéɾo
Aspiration:	pətʰéɾo
Phonetic form:	[pətʰéɾo]

In this example, the two rules of Flapping and Aspiration apply to different segments (Aspiration to the first /t/, Flapping to the second). Their order of application will therefore not make any difference, since neither rule affects the conditions needed for the other rule to operate.

In other situations, however, the order in which two rules apply does make a difference. That is, some forms are derivable only if we assume that phonological rules applied in a particular order. Consider the following phonetic forms that appear in some dialects of English (data from Katamba 1989: 132).

	PHONEMIC	**PHONETIC**
handball	/hændbɔl/	[hæmbɔl]
handbag	/hændbæg/	[hæmbæg]
handmade	/hændmed/	[hæmmed]

Each of these phonetic forms shows two changes when compared with its phonemic counterpart. This fact indicates that two phonological rules have applied in each form. First of all, a segment was deleted. Notice that the phonetic forms all have one less segment than the corresponding phonetic forms. Thus, some sort of consonant deletion rule has applied. This rule will be examined in more detail in Chapter 7; for now, we will simply refer to the rule as **Consonant Cluster Reduction** and assume that it deletes a stop consonant from a cluster, or series, of consonants.

Second, a segment was changed. Note that the nasal segment in each phonetic form differs from the nasal segment in the corresponding phonemic form. Looking more closely, it becomes apparent that the nasal segment in each case has changed from /n/ to [m]. Since these two segments differ only in their place feature—/n/ is an alveolar nasal, while [m] is a bilabial nasal—we might look for something in the environment that would explain this particular change. When we look at the phonetic forms, we find that in each case the [m] is followed by a bilabial segment—either [b] or another [m]. Thus it appears that the nasal segments have undergone place assimilation to the following bilabial segments. We will call this rule **Nasal Assimilation** to reflect the fact that a nasal segment is assimilating in place to an adjacent consonant segment.

What is crucial in these examples, however, is the fact that Consonant Cluster Reduction must apply first in order to create the environment for Nasal Assimilation. In other words, until Consonant Cluster reduction applies, the nasal segment that changes is not adjacent to the consonant segment to which it assimilates. Examine the following derivation carefully to see how Consonant Cluster Reduction creates the environment needed for Nasal Assimilation.

Phonemic form	/hændbɔl/
CCR	hænbɔl
Nasal Assimilation	hæmbɔl
Phonetic form	[hæmbɔl]

If we apply the rules in the opposite sequence, Nasal Assimilation cannot change /n/ to [m]:

Phonemic form	/hændbɔl/
Nasal Assimilation	[n] will not assimilate to [b], since they are not adjacent
CCR	hænbɔl
Phonetic form	[hænbɔl]

In short, using the order of Nasal Assimilation followed by Consonant Cluster Reduction blocks our derivation of [hambɔl].

The generalization that we can make is as follows: When two phonological rules affect, or are sensitive to, the same part of a form, the possibility arises that the two rules will have to apply in a particular order to derive the target surface form.

Exercise G

1. Assume that you are trying to describe a variety of English in which the following forms occur.

	Phonemic	**Phonetic**
pumpkin	/pʌmpkɪn/	[pʌŋkɪn]
handcrafted	/hændkræftɪd/	[hæŋkræftɪd]

What rules have applied? Would they have to apply in any particular order? Why or why not?

Exercise G *Continued*

2. In most varieties of American English, the forms *ladder* and *latter* occur phonemically as /lǽdər/ and /lǽtər/ but phonetically as [lǽːɾər] and [lǽɾər], respectively. Assume that the flap [ɾ] is a voiced segment. If so, do the rules of Flapping and Vowel Lengthening have to apply in any particular order? Why or why not? Demonstrate your reasoning by trying to derive [lǽːɾər] and [lǽɾər] using both orderings.
3. Correct the error in each of the following phonological rules of English.

   †**a.** $V \rightarrow [-\text{nas}]\ /\ \underline{\quad}\ \begin{matrix}C\\ [+\text{nas}]\end{matrix}$

   b. $\begin{matrix}C\\ \begin{bmatrix}+\text{alv}\\ +\text{fric}\end{bmatrix}\end{matrix} \rightarrow [ɾ]\ /\ \acute{V}\ \underline{\quad}\ V$

   c. $V \rightarrow [+\text{long}]\ /\ \underline{\quad}\ \begin{matrix}C\\ [-\text{vce}]\end{matrix}$

   d. $\begin{matrix}C\\ \begin{bmatrix}+\text{vce}\\ +\text{stop}\end{bmatrix}\end{matrix} \rightarrow [+\text{asp}]\ /\ \$\ \underline{\quad}\ \acute{V}$

4. A few years ago in the Baton Rouge *Morning Advocate,* a headline appeared stating *Nurses Demand More Imput* (instead of *Input*).
   a. What feature change occurs when *input* becomes *imput?*
   b. What phonological property of the /p/ in *input* might cause this change?
   c. Why would this change ordinarily not occur in forms like *input,* even though it regularly occurs in forms like *impossible?*

Summary

The theory of phonology is based (indirectly) upon the physiology of the vocal tract, and makes use of such concepts as segment, distinctive feature, allophonic variation, levels of representation, and phonological rules. Using a phonemic alphabet allows us to represent segments so that one symbol always corresponds to one phoneme; this alphabet can be supplemented by diacritics that allow us to represent allophones. All of these concepts help us to represent the systematic psychological patterns that underlie the production of speech sounds.

SUPPLEMENTARY READINGS

Primary

Anderson, S. R. (1985). *Phonology in the twentieth century.* Chicago: University of Chicago Press.
Chomsky, N., & Halle, M. (1968). *The sound pattern of English.* New York: Harper & Row.
Jakobson, R., Fant, G., & Halle, M. (1963). *Preliminaries to speech analysis.* Cambridge, MA: MIT Press.

Secondary

Carr, P. (1993). *Phonology.* New York: St. Martin's Press.

Davenport, M., & Hannahs, S. (1998). *Introducing phonetics and phonology.* London: Arnold.

Hogg, R., & McCully, C. B. (1987). *Metrical phonology: A coursebook.* Cambridge, England: Cambridge University Press.

Katamba, F. (1989). *An introduction to phonology.* Essex, England: Longman.

Schane, S. (1973). *Generative phonology.* Englewood Cliffs, NJ: Prentice-Hall.

Schane, S., & Bendixen, B. (1978). *Workbook in generative phonology.* Englewood Cliffs, NJ: Prentice-Hall.

It may be best to approach these works in the following order. Davenport and Hannahs is an introductory text dealing largely with varieties of English. Schane and the accompanying workbook provide an excellent introduction to "doing" phonology; they deal primarily with non-English data. Carr and Katamba are textbooks that deal both with standard generative theory and more recent developments such as CV and autosegmental phonology. Hogg and McCully is a textbook dealing with word stress in English. It represents the "multitiered" approach to phonology, which treats the syllable as hierarchically structured rather than as simply a string of linear segments.

Anderson is an excellent reference book dealing with the development of phonology as a field and its key figures. Chomsky and Halle is the classic statement of linear generative phonology (the theory discussed in this chapter), and Jakobson, Fant, and Halle is one of the earliest comprehensive treatments of distinctive feature theory. These last two works, however, are difficult going and are now mainly of historical interest.

Supplementary Exercises

1. Match each of the following words with its phonemic transcription.

a. thigh	___ /ðaʊ/
b. thou	___ /θaɪ/
c. thee	___ /ðe/
d. they	___ /ði/
e. though	___ /θɔ/
f. thaw	___ /ðo/

2. Match each of the following words with its phonemic transcription.

a. course	___ /karz/
b. cures	___ /kʌrs/
c. cars	___ /kyurz/
d. cares	___ /kɛrz/
e. curse	___ /kʊrz/
f. Coors	___ /kors/

3. Identify the error (omission, wrong segment, or extra segment) in the following transcriptions; then correct each transcription.

a.	mother	/mʌðhər/	**f.**	fine	/faɪne/
b.	speed	/sped/	**g.**	took	/tuk/
c.	receipt	/rəsípt/	**h.**	correct	/kərrɛ́kt/
d.	ankle	/æŋəl/	**i.**	finger	/fíŋər/
e.	crate	/cret/	**j.**	sigh	/saɪh/

4. Identify the following English words.

a. [æ̃nt]

†**b.** [sǽɾərn]

c. [ǰɔ:z]

d. [ətʰɛ̃́:nčə̃:n]

†e. [óʔmi:l]

5. Identify the phoneme that would result if each of the following features were changed.

a. Given the phoneme /o/, change [–high] to [+high].

b. Given the phoneme /ð/, change [+interdental] to [+labiodental].

6. Consider the following phonological rule: Ø⟶[ə] / C ____ [+liquid]

a. State the rule informally (i.e., in words).

b. What would be the phonetic output if the rule were applied to please?

c. What would be the phonetic output if the rule were applied to *pills*?

7. German contains both a palatal fricative [ç] and a velar fricative [x]. Consider the following forms (from Hyman [1975:63]):

siech	[zi:ç]	'sickly'	hoch	[ho:x]	'high'
mich	[mɪç]	'me'	noch	[nɔx]	'still'
Pech	[pɛç]	'pitch'	Bach	[bax]	'brook'
Buch	[bu:x]	'book'			

Based on these data, what vowel feature determines whether the following fricative is palatal or velar? (Hint: Place the vowels in these data into two groups: those that occur before /ç/ and those that occur before /x/. Examine the feature chart for vowels on page 109 to determine what feature the vowels in the first group have in common, and what other feature the vowels in the second group have in common.)

8. Spanish contains both voiced stops [b, d, g] and the corresponding voiced fricatives [β, ð, ɣ]. Consider the following forms (from Hyman [1975:62] and Halle [1985:241]):

[baŋka]	'bench'	[la βaŋka]	'the bench'
[baho]	'low'	[a βaho]	'below'
[demora]	'delay'	[la ðemora]	'the delay'
[donde]	'where'	[a ðonde]	'where to'
[gana]	'desire'	[la ɣana]	'the desire'
[gwardar]	'to watch'	[a ɣwardar]	'to wait for'

Based on these data, write a phonological rule for Spanish stating when a voiced stop becomes the corresponding voiced fricative.

9. Consider the following Swahili data (from Schane and Bendixen [1978:50]). In each form, the initial segment represents a prefix indicating singular number.

[ubao]	'a plank'	[ukuni]	'a stick'
[wayo]	'a footprint'	[ugwe]	'a string'
[wimbo]	'a song'	[wembe]	'a razor'

a. What phonological property do [u] and [w] have in common? (Hint: Try pronouncing each one.)

b. How do [u] and [w] differ phonologically? That is, to what different categories do they belong?

c. What phonological property of the root determines whether the singular prefix shows up as [u] or [w]?

10. Consider the following two sets of correspondences between non-Germanic and Germanic languages.

	NON-GERMANIC	GERMANIC
A.	*p*ater (Latin)	*f*ather
	*t*res (Spanish)	*th*ree
	*c*ardiac (Greek)	*h*eart
B.	kanni*b*is (Greek)	hem*p*
	*d*os (Spanish)	*t*wo
	*g*ynecologist	*q*ueen

These data indicate that Germanic languages have undergone two phonological changes that non-Germanic languages have not experienced.

a. For each set, transcribe the phonemic change from non-Germanic to Germanic.

b. How can the change in set A be characterized in terms of classes of segments? (Hint: Assume /h/ is a velar fricative.)

c. How can the change in set B be characterized in terms of classes of segments?

d. Which change (i.e., that in set A or set B) had to occur first? Why?

11. Consider the following data:

inaccurate	[ɪnækyərət]	indirect	[ɪndərɛkt]
impossible	[ɪmpasəbəl]	imbalance	[ɪmbæləns]
incomplete	[ɪŋkəmplit]	ingrate	[ɪŋgret]
intolerable	[ɪntalərəbel]	inept	[ɪnɛpt]

a. What three phonetic forms does the prefix take in these words?

b. What determines the phonetic form of the prefix?

c. Which of the three forms of the prefix appears to be the most basic? Which words serve as evidence for your answer?

d. What type of phonological process is illustrated by the forms that deviate from the most basic form?

12. **Phonotactics** is the study of the permissible sequences of segments allowed in a language. For example, English has phonotactic restrictions on the sequence of consonants that can begin a word. State the phonotactic restriction that rules out the ungrammatical sequences in the following data.

step	/stɛp/	*sdep	*/sdɛp/
skip	/skɪp/	*sgip	*/sgip/
spot	/spat/	*sbot	*/sbat/

13. Consider the following Yoruba data (adapted from Schane and Bendixen [1978:49]). Assume that [ŋ, n, m] are variants of /n/.

	STEM	PRESENT PROGRESSIVE
'stop'	[kuro]	[ŋkuro]
'press sand'	[tɛyɔnrin]	[ntɛyɔnrin]
'spoil'	[bajɛ]	[mbajɛ]

a. State the morphological rule for forming the present progressive form of the verb.

b. State the phonological rule for determining the shape of the present progressive affix.

Now consider the following Yoruba data:

'say'	[wi]	[ŋwi]
		*[mwi]

c. What is the most accurate way of describing the place of articulation of [w] in Yoruba?

14. Consonants are often subdivided into **obstruents** (stops, fricatives, and affricates) and **sonorants** (nasals, liquids, and glides). Now consider the following English data.

/fɔlt/	/its/	/paɪnt/	/ist/
*/nɪds/	/old/	*/isd/	/izd/
/lænd/	/nidz/	*/izt/	*/itz/

a. What English word does each non-starred form represent?

b. What phonotactic generalization can be stated using the category "obstruent" that cannot be stated using the category "consonant"?

15. English contains numerous singular/plural pairs such as *goose/geese, foot/feet, mouse/mice.* These plurals were formed historically by a process known as **umlaut,** whereby the vowel in a plural suffix had an effect on the vowel in the root. Then the suffix was lost. The vowel in the root was subsequently changed by the Great Vowel Shift (discussed more in Chapter 10). For example, the form *geese* developed as follows:

Root		Plural Suffix	Process Involved
/gos/	+	/i/	
/ges/	+	/i/	Umlaut
/ges/	+	Ø	Loss of suffix
/gis/	+	Ø	Great Vowel Shift

a. What feature changes are required to turn /o/ in English into /e/?

b. How might the vowel suffix /i/ have caused the change from /o/ to /e/?

16. When two morphemes are combined into a compound, they tend to undergo changes in stress which trigger segmental changes. Originally, both morphemes have primary stress (´); then the second morpheme reduces first to secondary stress (`) and then to zero stress; finally, the unstressed vowel reduces to schwa. Thus, for example, *cupboard* /kʌ́pbòrd/ becomes /kʌ́pbord/ and finally /kʌ́bərd/. Which of the following compounds has been in the language longer: *mailman* or *fireman?* Explain.

Exploratory Exercises

1. Assume that you encounter a variety of English in which the forms *ladder* and *latter* occur phonemically as /lǽdər/ and /lǽtər/ but that both forms occur phonetically as [lǽ:ɾer]. Explain how you could use rule ordering to account for this phenomenon. Refer to your analysis in Exercise G, problem (2), as a starting point, and explain exactly how and why you would have to adjust that analysis to account for this variety of English.

2. Assume the following division among all English vowels.

[+long]	[-long]
/i/	/ɪ/
/e/	/ɛ/
/u/	/æ/
/o/	/ʌ,ə/
/aɪ/	/a/
/aʊ/	
/ɔɪ/	

Now consider the following data, adapted from Hogg and McCully (1987:11):

a. Indicate the primary stress in each word in (i) by placing an acute accent (´) over the appropriate vowel.

b. State in words the rule assigning primary stress to the correct vowel in these words.

(i) design /dəzaɪn/ cocaine /koken/
balloon /bəlun/ domain /domen/

c. Indicate the primary stress in each word in (ii) by placing an acute accent (´) over the appropriate vowel.

d. State in words the rule assigning primary stress to the correct vowel in these words.

(ii) museum /myuziəm/ fluid /fluɪd/
aroma /əromə/ stupid /stupɪd/

e. Indicate the primary stress in each word in (iii) by placing an acute accent (´) over the appropriate vowel.

f. State in words the rule assigning primary stress to the correct vowel in these words.

(iii) polygamy /pəlɪgəmɪ/ precipice /prɛsɪpɪs/
elephant /ɛləfənt/ leviathan /ləvaɪəθən/

g. Indicate the primary stress in each word in (iv) by placing an acute accent (´) over the appropriate vowel.

h. State a rule that will assign the correct primary stress to each of these words. (Hint: Assume stress is assigned from the right.)

(iv) design /dəzaɪn/
museum /myuziəm/
elephant /ɛləfənt/

i. Indicate the primary stress in each word in (v) by placing an acute accent (´) over the appropriate vowel.

j. Is the stress pattern in these words most like that in *design, museum,* or *elephant?*

k. Assume that stress is assigned in terms of a [+long] syllable. A [+long] syllable can be defined as one containing a [+long] vowel or one containing a ________ vowel followed by ________ consonants.

(v) ellipsis /əlɪpsɪs/ republic /rəpʌblɪk/
inspector /ɪnspɛktər/ propaganda /prapəgændə/

3. Visit the Archive of Misheard Lyrics at http://www.kissthisguy.com. Many of the misperceptions can be explained as resulting from phonological processes or reanalysis of syllable and word boundaries. Write an analysis that classifies some of the data on this site into several categories, depending on what may have caused the misperception.
4. See also Chapter 11, Exploratory Exercise 3, which also deals with phonology.

CHAPTER SEVEN

Language Variation

Language variation is the study of those features of a language that differ systematically as we compare different groups of speakers or the same speaker in different situations. Rather than comparing features of two different languages (say, English and French), language variation studies **regional** varieties of the same language (e.g., English as spoken by natives of Mississippi and by natives of Massachusetts); **social, ethnic,** and **gender-related** varieties of the same language (e.g., the English of upper-middle-class New Yorkers and that of lower-working-class New Yorkers); and **stylistic** varieties of the same language (e.g., how a speaker uses language during a job interview and during a casual conversation with a close friend). This chapter looks at some examples of these types of variation.

Within each of these categories, we can further note several sources of linguistic variation. Consider the following observations.

(1) In some regions of the United States, a large container used to carry water is called a *pail;* in others, the same item is called a *bucket.*

(2) In some regions of the United States, the word *greasy* is pronounced with medial [s]; in others, it is pronounced with a [z].

(3) Among some groups in the United States, words such as *this, that, these,* and *those* are pronounced with initial [ð]; among others, they are pronounced with initial [d].

(4) For some groups of speakers in the United States, a sentence such as *He walks home every day* would be phrased as *He walk home every day.*

(5) For some groups of speakers in the United States, the question *What is it?* would be phrased as *What it is?*

(6) Men are more likely than women to use *ain't.*

(7) A person being interviewed for a job might say *In which department will I be working?* The same speaker, in a more informal situation, might say *Which department will I be working in?*

Observations (1) and (2) illustrate the fact that particular lexical (i.e., vocabulary) items and phonological forms are associated with specific geographical areas of the United States. Observations (3), (4), and (5) illustrate the fact that particular phonological, morphological, and syntactic forms are associated with specific social and ethinic groups. Observation (6) illustrates the fact that men and women use language differently. Observation (7) illustrates the fact that any one speaker commands a variety of styles appropriate for a variety of situations.

All of these phenomena involve language variation: the way language reflects regional, social, and stylistic influences. Moreover, we will assume that the phenomena in observations (1–7) are governed by a system of principles. What we will do now is try to elucidate these principles.

Language Universals, Languages, Dialects, and Idiolects

In Chapters 3 through 6, we have looked at language from the perspective of its different components—semantics, syntax, morphology, and phonology. From another perspective, the study of linguistics can be divided into other domains, depending on what group of speakers we are looking at. One such domain is **language universals,** those categories and rules that all human languages, past and present, have in common. For example, all known languages use the categories noun and verb; in languages where adjectives and nouns show agreement, it is always the adjective that changes to agree with the noun (not vice versa); if a language has a color system, it distinguishes at least black and white; if it has three colors, the third will be red; all languages have rules that depend upon structural relationships among words, not just on the order of words; and so on.

Another domain concerns the properties of a particular **language** (e.g., Classical Latin, Russian, Modern English, and so forth). Still another domain is a **dialect,** a systematic variety of a language specific to a particular group (e.g., speakers of American English, British English, Appalachian English, African American English, and so on). A final domain is the **idiolect,** the linguistic system of a particular speaker (e.g., the linguistic system of Oprah Winfrey, Jay Leno, or Katie Couric).

All but the last of these domains are of interest to linguists, although different linguists tend to focus on different domains. The reason that most linguists are not especially interested in idiolects is that individual variations from speaker to speaker are thought to be idiosyncratic rather than systematic. Figure 7.1 summarizes the relationship among these different domains.

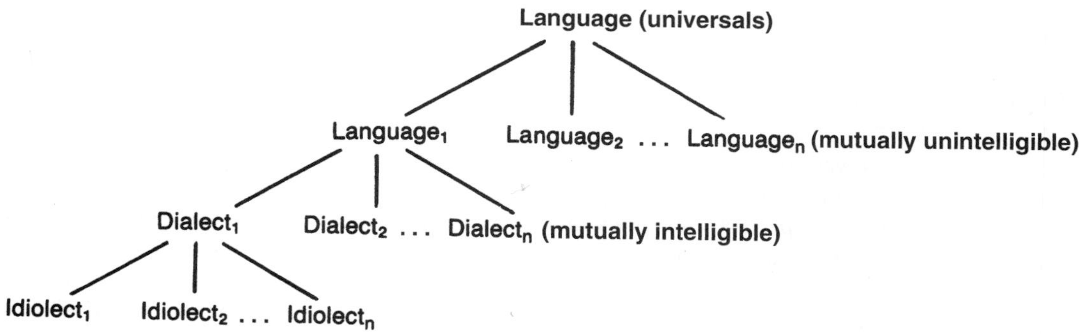

FIGURE 7.1 Domains of language study, by groups of speakers

One useful guideline for differentiating a dialect from a language is that different languages are not **mutually intelligible,** whereas different dialects generally are. For example, if you are a monolingual speaker of English and you encounter a monolingual speaker of Norwegian, the two of you will have a great deal of difficulty communicating through language alone, since English and Norwegian are two different languages. On the other hand, if you are a native Texan and you encounter a native Bostonian, the similarities between your linguistic systems will far outweigh any differences; you will have (relatively) little trouble communicating with each other, since Texan and Bostonian represent two different dialects of the same language. These different properties of languages and dialects are represented in Figure 7.1.

One point that must be made at the outset of our discussion is that a dialect is an abstraction, a theoretical construct hypothesized by linguists to account for subsystems of regularities within a particular language. Informally, we might say that each subsystem is a dialect. Keep in mind, however, that in reality every native speaker of a language speaks his or her own idiolect, one shading into another. When a significant number of idiolects share a common set of features not shared by other idiolects, then we might say that this group of idiolects forms a dialect.

Let's now take a look at three types of variation within a language: **regional variation** (or regional dialects), **social variation** (or social dialects—typically referred to as standard or nonstandard dialects), and **stylistic variation.**

Exercise A

1. The term *idiolect* refers to ________.
   - **a.** relic areas in which older forms of a language are still used
   - **b.** mutually unintelligible language variations
   - **c.** variations by individual speakers of the same dialect
   - **d.** Chomsky's innate constraints on language
2. From time to time, cases are reported in the news of twins who have invented their own "dialect," which no one else can understand. Is such a case properly termed a language, dialect, or idiolect? Explain.

Regional Variation

Regional varieties of a language result from a number of political, geographical, and cultural factors. First, the early population of an area leaves its linguistic heritage. For example, a paper napkin is sometimes called a *serviette* in modern Canadian English, because of the early French settlement of Quebec. Second, migration routes tend to demarcate dialect boundaries. For example, the United States has traditionally been thought to have three major dialect areas running horizontally from the East Coast to the Mississippi River: Northern, Midland, and Southern. This pattern resulted because the East Coast was colonized by settlers from different parts of England, who then migrated west rather than north or south. Third, political and ecclesiastical divisions contribute to regional dialect differences. For example, the equivalent of a county in Louisiana is called a *parish,* reflecting the early influence of the Catholic Church. Fourth, physical geographical boundaries can contribute to regional dialects by segregating groups of speakers. For example, the language variety known as Gullah or Sea Island Creole has not been absorbed into mainstream American English because its speakers live on islands off the coast of South Carolina. In short, regional varieties of a language often reflect settlement history and physical geography.

Regional variation in the United States has been documented largely through **dialect atlases.** A dialect atlas is essentially a series of maps, each of which plots the geographical distribution of a particular linguistic feature (e.g., Figure 7.2). During the 20th century, dialect atlases were undertaken for New England, the Middle Atlantic states, North Central states, Gulf states, Upper Midwest, Rocky Mountain states, Pacific West, and Pacific Northwest; however, not all of these have been published in their entireties. A project based on more recent data, the Atlas of North American English, is awaiting publication at the time of this writing.

A traditional feature of a dialect atlas is an **isogloss,** a line that demarcates the area in which some phonological, lexical, morphological, or syntactic feature can be found. For example, the isoglass in Figure 7.3 demarcates the southern limit, within the Upper Midwest states, of *(Devil's) darning needle* as a variant for *dragonfly.* Below this boundary, *snake feeder* is more common as a variant.

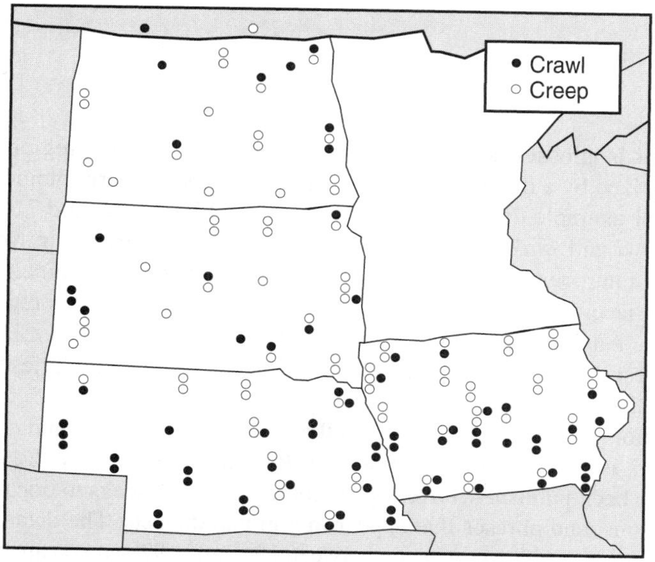

FIGURE 7.2 Geographical distribution of *creep* and *crawl*

Source: From *Linguistic Atlas of the Upper Midwest,* Volumes 1 & 2, by Harold B. Allen, Gale Group, © 1982, Gale Group. Reprinted by permission of The Gale Group.

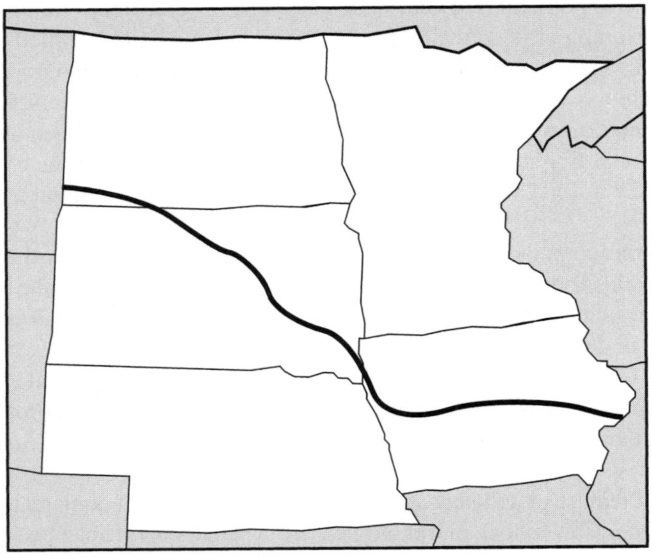

FIGURE 7.3 Isogloss for *(Devil's) darning needle* in the Upper Midwest

Source: From *Linguistic Atlas of the Upper Midwest,* Volumes 1 & 2, by Harold B. Allen, Gale Group, © 1982, Gale Group. Reprinted by permission of The Gale Group.

A **bundle of isoglosses** delineates a dialect area: a geographic region whose language is characterized by a distinct set of phonological, lexical, morphological, and syntactic features. For example, if you were to superimpose Figures 7.2 and 7.3, you would find that both *crawl* and *snake feeder* predominate over other variants in Nebraska and southern Iowa. If a number of other linguistic features were found to coincide in this region, but not in adjacent ones, then we would be justified in treating this region as a distinct dialect area. And, in fact, such a bundle of isoglosses does exist, as shown in Figure 7.4. As a result, this area has been identified as one of the boundaries between the Northern and Midland dialects.

Another major project, begun in 1965 by the late Frederic Cassidy and now edited by Joan Houston Hall, is the *Dictionary of American Regional English (DARE).* At this time, four volumes have been published, covering letters A-Sk. *DARE* seeks to document vocabulary, pronunciations, and phrases that appear in regional dialects. The data in *DARE* are based on face-to-face interviews conducted between 1965 and 1970 and on an extensive collection of written materials produced over several centuries.

Figure 7.5 shows a map of the major dialect regions in the United States, developed by Carver (1987). Whereas earlier dialect maps divided the United States into three regional

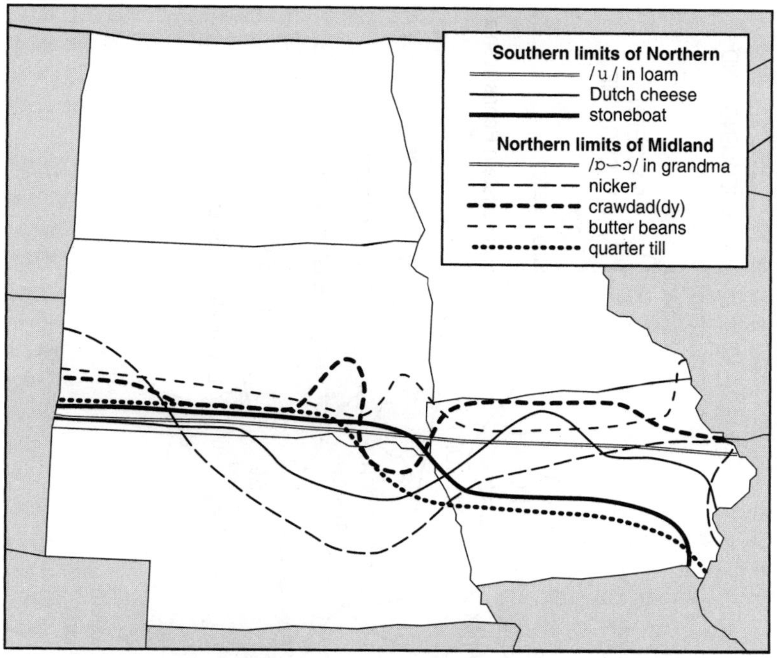

FIGURE 7.4 Bundle of isoglosses, reflecting one boundary between the Northern and Midland dialect regions

Source: From *Linguistic Atlas of the Upper Midwest,* Volumes 1 & 2, by Harold B. Allen, Gale Group, © 1982, Gale Group. Reprinted by permission of The Gale Group.

dialect areas—Northern, Midland, and Southern—Carver's map realigns these divisions into four areas: Upper North, Lower North, Upper South, and Lower South.

Exercise B

1. Identify three regions of the United States where neighboring or immigrating ethnic groups have influenced the local vocabulary, and give examples of words that have been introduced by each group.
†2. True or False: Figure 7.2 indicates that *crawl* becomes more widespread as one moves north.
3. True or False: Figures 7.3 and 7.4 both illustrate dialect boundaries. Explain.
4. Figure 7.5 illustrates that dialect areas of the United States are most clear-cut on the East Coast. Why is that the case?

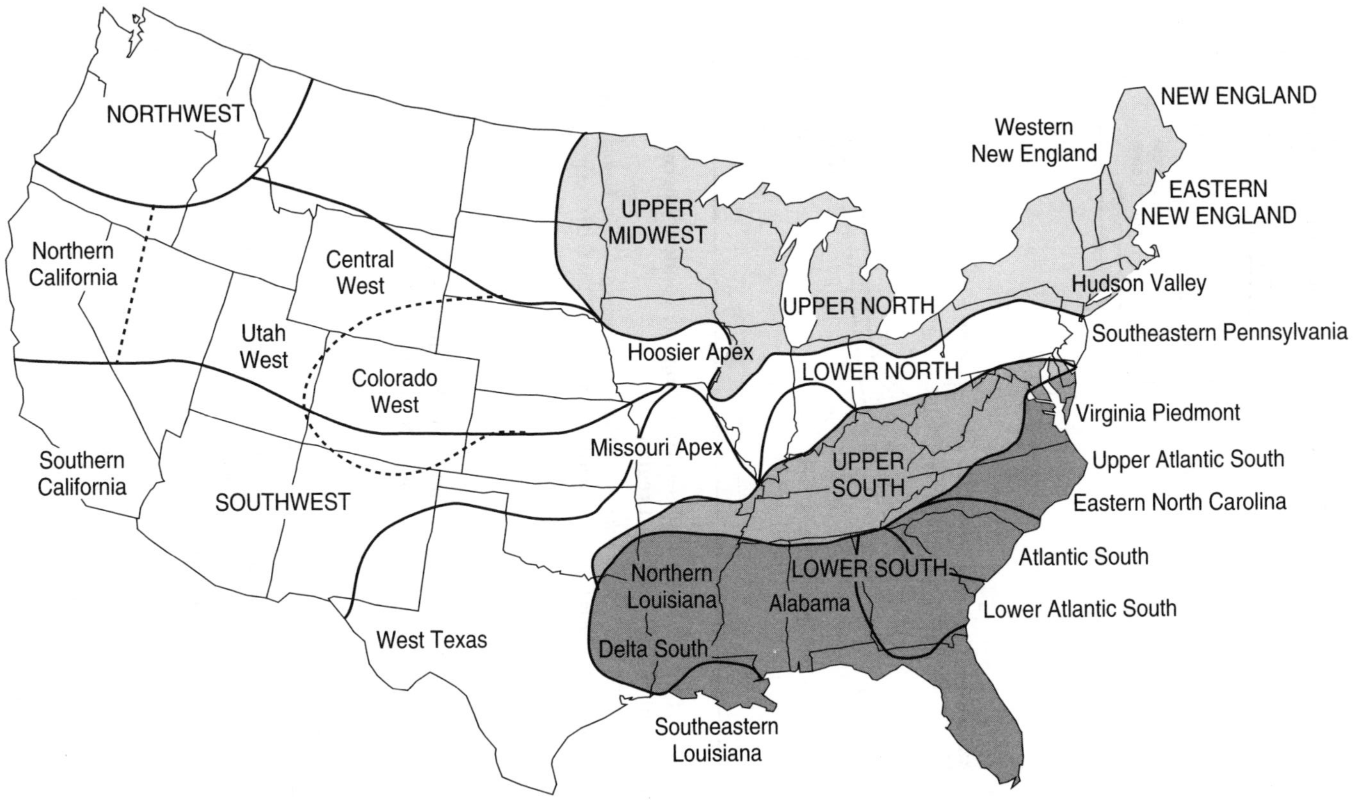

FIGURE 7.5 Dialect areas of the United States, according to Carver (1987:248)

Source: From *American Regional Dialects: A Word Geography,* by Craig M. Carver. Copyright © 1987 by University of Michigan Press. Reproduced by permission of the publisher.

Regional Lexical Variation

As mentioned earlier, Northern and Southern varieties constitute two of the main regional dialects in the United States. Following are some of the characteristic lexical (i.e., vocabulary) differences traditionally associated with each one.

NORTHERN U.S.	SOUTHERN U.S.
pail	bucket
bag	sack
faucet	spigot
quarter of four	quarter till four
sick to my stomach	sick at my stomach
(cherry) pit	(cherry) seed

Cassidy, in his research for *DARE,* found thousands of examples of more exotic regionalisms: for example, *eaceworm* 'earthworm' (Rhode Island), *democrat bug* 'box-elder bug' (Kansas and Iowa, Republican strongholds!), *snoose* 'snuff' (Wisconsin and Minnesota), *hooftie* 'hippie' (Pennsylvania; from *hooft* 'hip' in Pennsylvania German), *black Christmas* 'Christmas without snow' (Alaska), and *peach-limb tea* 'a whipping administered to a child' (Arkansas).

Lexical differences also exist between U.S. and Canadian English. The following are representative.

UNITED STATES	CANADA
electoral district	riding
faucet	tap
napkin	serviette
sofa	chesterfield
you know? right?	eh?
zee (name of letter Z)	zed

U.S. and Canadian English also spell some shared lexical items differently, with Canadian spelling sometimes patterning like British spelling: for example, U.S. *center*/Canadian *centre,* U.S. *check* (banking item)/Canadian *cheque,* U.S. *color*/Canadian *colour,* U.S. *theater*/Canadian *theatre.* However, in other cases, Canadian spelling patterns like American spelling rather than like British spelling: for example, U.S./Canadian *aluminum*/British *aluminium* (which is also pronounced differently), U.S./Canadian *tire*/British *tyre.* In fact, the phrase *tire centre* is uniquely Canadian. In the United States the phrase would be *tire center;* in England, it would be *tyre centre.*

Lexical differences between U.S. and British English are far more numerous than those between U.S. and Canadian English, so we can cover only a few examples here. Some everyday British terms, with their U.S. equivalents, include the following.

U.S. ENGLISH	BRITISH ENGLISH
lawyer	solicitor, barrister (the latter can practice as a client's advocate in higher courts)
photo	snap
pedestrian underpass	subway
line (n) (as for a bus), line up (v)	queue
7-Up (or other lemon-lime drink)	lemonade
mobile home	caravan
stove	cooker
public housing project	council estate
plan (n)	scheme (can be used without a negative connotation)
traffic circle	roundabout
costume/masquerade	fancy dress
appetizer	starter
private school	public school
public school	state school
soccer	football (the U.S. version is called *American football*)
elevator	lift
sweater	jumper
apartment	flat
ball-point	biro
trash bag	bin bag
two-week period	fortnight
trunk (of a car)	boot
washcloth	flannel
eraser	rubber
tennis shoes/sneakers	trainers
gasoline	petrol
flashlight	torch
pharmacist, pharmacy	chemist

Exercise C

1. Look up the terms *bluenose, choppies,* and *chopique* in *DARE.* What does each term mean? Where is each term most common in the United States?

Exercise C *Continued*

2. The food terms on the left are used in the United States, while those on the right are used in other English-speaking countries (e.g., England, Australia). Try to match each term on the left with its non-U.S. counterpart.

___ biscuit	a. tomato sauce
___ 7-Up (or other lemon-lime drink)	b. scone
___ bag (as of potato chips)	c. crisps
___ butty	d. mince
___ candy	e. green mealies
___ canned	f. sweets
___ cookie	g. cream cracker
___ corn meal	h. lemonade
___ ears of corn	i. jelly
___ eggplant	j. maize meal
___ flavoring (such as vanilla)	k. tinned
___ French fries	l. treacle
___ ground beef	m. icing sugar
___ Jello™	n. aubergine
___ ketchup	o. courgette
___ molasses	p. banger
___ potato chips	q. mange-tout
___ powdered sugar	r. prawn
___ sausage	s. sandwich on a roll
___ shrimp	t. packet
___ soda cracker	u. essence
___ sugar peas, snap peas	v. chips
___ zucchini	w. biscuit

Regional Phonological Variation

The following are representative examples of regional variation in North American English.

Linking [r]. This feature, associated with eastern New England and New York City, refers to a pattern whereby a vowel-vowel sequence between words is "linked" with an [r]. In the phrase *That idea is crazy,* for example, *idea* ends in a vowel and the following word *is* begins with a vowel. A speaker whose dialect contains the "linking [r]" feature would pronounce this phrase as if *idea* ended in an [r] (*idear*). Speakers of this dialect presumably have the following rule in their phonological systems.

Ø → [r] / V _____ # V (recall that # indicates a word boundary)

In contrast, this rule would not insert the "linking [r]" in the phrase *That idea sounds crazy,* since there are no vowel-vowel sequences between words (*idea* ends in a vowel, but *sounds* begins with a consonant).

This type of process, whereby a consonant is inserted to break up a series of two vowels, is called **consonant epenthesis.** The mirror-image process, whereby a vowel (typically [ə]) is inserted to break up a series of two consonants, is called **vowel epenthesis** (e.g., *athlete* [ǽθəlit]). Both processes reflect that fact that languages gravitate toward CV syllable structure.

Vowel Neutralization before Nasals. For many speakers of Southern dialects, the phonemes /ɪ/ and /ɛ/ are both represented phonetically as [ɪ] before a nasal consonant. This process, whereby two segments lose their contrast in a particular phonetic environment, is known as **neutralization** or **merger.** So, for example, the words *pen* and *pin* would both be represented phonetically as [p^hɪ̃n] for speakers of this dialect. (For this reason, Southerners sometimes refer to pen as an *ink pen* to distinguish it from *pin.*) Such speakers apparently have a rule in their phonological systems which changes /ɛ/ to /ɪ/ before a nasal consonant, as follows.

/ɛ/ → [ɪ] / _____ C
[+nasal]

Before leaving this rule of Vowel Neutralization, we can give you a concrete example showing the practical effects of such dialect differences. One of the authors, Frank Parker, was visiting the National Zoo in Washington, D.C., which attracts tourists from all over the country. Because this zoo was displaying the famous pandas Hsing-Hsing and Ling-Ling (now deceased), it predictably sold a lot of "panda paraphernalia"—shirts, postcards, and so on. A man approached the clerk in a souvenir shop and asked for a "panda [p^hɪ̃n]." The clerk brought him a panda pin (i.e., a button designed to be worn on a shirt). The man promptly said, "No, I want a [p^hɪ̃n], like a ball point pen," and the clerk responded, "Oh, you want a [p^hɛ̃n]." Finally, the man got what he wanted: a pen decorated with panda pictures. However, neither the customer nor the clerk appeared to understand the source of the confusion. We, on the other hand, can explain this interchange by assuming a rule of Vowel Neutralization. The man (presumably from the South) pronounced *pen* as [p^hɪ̃n], which the clerk (presumably not from the South) interpreted as *pin.*

Vocalization. This rule, common among speakers in the deep South, substitutes [ə] for a post-vocalic liquid (i.e., an /l/ or /r/ following a vowel). In other words, the rule "vocalizes" the liquid (i.e., turns it into a vowel). For example, *there* /ðɛr/ may be pronounced [ðɛə].

Voicing Assimilation. This rule changes the voicing feature of an obstruent (i.e., a stop, fricative, or affricate) to match that of an adjacent segment. This rule, for example, accounts for the difference between *greasy* with an [s] in the North and a [z] in the South. In the Southern dialect, the [s] assimilates the voicing of the adjacent vowels to yield [z].

Monophthongization of /aɪ/. In general American speech, words like *tire* and *fire* are pronounced with the diphthong [aɪ]: [taɪr], [faɪr]. However, Southern dialect speakers typically **monophthongize,** or **unglide,** this dipthong so that the second element is lost. As a result, pronunciations of *fire* and *tire* may sound like General American pronunciations of *far* and *tar*—i.e., [far] and [tar]. Similarly, words like *five* and *guide* may be pronounced as [fav] and [gad]. This process tends to occur more when the following segment is voiced, as in these examples.

Canadian Raising. Traditionally, this term has been applied to variations on two diphthongs /aɪ/ and /aʊ/, although some research indicates that variations on these diphthongs are not equally associated with Canadian speech, with "Canadian Raising" occurring more prominently on /aʊ/ and variations on /aɪ/ occurring in the northern United States as well as in Canada (Chambers, 1989). This phenomenon raises the first member of the vowel diphthong from /a/ to /ʌ/, so that *fight* /faɪt/ is pronounced as [fʌɪt], and *out* /aʊt/ is pronounced as [ʌʊt]. Canadian Raising is more likely to occur when the diphthong is followed by a voiceless consonant. Speakers attempting to imitate this feature of the Canadian dialect often exaggerate the back diphthong by dropping the first element and tensing the second element, so that *out and about* is pronounced [utənəbut], and *about the house* is pronounced [əbutðəhus].

Stress. Several patterns also distinguish British and American English pronunciations. First of all, stress patterns may differ, resulting in a different pattern of full and reduced (/ə/) vowels. This pattern is evident in the following pairs.

	AMERICAN ENGLISH	BRITISH ENGLISH
laboratory	/lǽb(ə)rətɔri/	/ləbɔ́rətri/
garage	/gəráž/	/gǽraž/
massage	/məsáž/	/mǽsaž/
cervical	/sʌ́rvɪkəl/	/sərváɪkəl/

Second, the vowel used within a stressed syllable may differ. This pattern is illustrated in the following pairs.

	AMERICAN ENGLISH	BRITISH ENGLISH
process	/prásɛs/	/prósɛs/
patent	/pǽtənt/	/pétənt/
migraine	/máɪgren/	/mígren/
path	/pæθ/	/paθ/

We should point out that these examples illustrate differences between American English and only one variety of British English, the dialect often referred to as RP (for Received Pronunciation). This variety is actually more of a social dialect, since it is associated with educated, upper-class speakers rather than with one region of England. In reality, numerous regional dialects exist within British English as well.

Several additional points should be made before leaving this section on regional variation. First, regional dialects, at least in North America, differ primarily in vocabulary and pronunciation (i.e., lexically and phonologically). As we will see in the next section, social dialects may differ in pronunciation, word formation, and sentence structure (i.e., phonologically, morphologically, and syntactically). Second, many of the regional dialect differences detected by fieldworkers in the 1930s and 1940s are not as clear-cut as they once were. As a result, you may have noticed that some of the dialect features ascribed to your particular area of the country do not match the way you speak. For example, you may say *faucet* (Northern) rather than *spigot* (Southern), even though you're from Alabama! This should come as no great surprise; the mobility of the American population in the last half-century has blurred, if not obliterated, what were earlier distinct limits on many dialect features. Keep in mind that a dialect boundary exists solely by virtue of the fact that a number of different dialect features coincide there. For example, the fact that the boundaries of *bucket, sack, spigot, seed,* and so on coincide (or at least formerly did) justifies hypothesizing a Southern dialect area. A dialect area does not (and, in fact, cannot) exist apart from these individual dialect features.

Exercise D

1. The phonetic representations of words such as *absorb* and *Mrs.* contrast for some Northern and Southern speakers in the United States as follows.

NORTHERN	SOUTHERN
[əbsɔrb]	[əbzɔrb]
[mɪsɪz]	[mɪzɪz]

What systematic contrast occurs between the Northern and Southern dialects? How does the phonological environment account for the Southern forms?

†2. Certain regional dialects of English (e.g., eastern New England and the deep South) contain the following rule:

$/r/ \rightarrow \emptyset \ / \ V \ \_\_\_$

Which of the following words would not be affected by this rule?

a. forty **c.** pretty **e.** both (a) and (b)
b. four **d.** free **f.** both (c) and (d)

3. Many Southern varieties of English contain the following rule:

$$\underset{\begin{bmatrix}-\text{high}\\ -\text{low}\\ -\text{back}\\ -\text{tense}\end{bmatrix}}{V} \rightarrow [+\text{high}] \ / \ \_\_\_ \ \underset{[+\text{nas}]}{C}$$

Based on this rule, indicate the vowel that would occur in the phonetic form corresponding to each of the following phonemic forms.

a.	hem	/hɛm/	**e.**	strength	/strɛŋkθ/
b.	pin	/pɪn/	**f.**	teen	/tin/
c.	pant	/pænt/	**g.**	net	/nɛt/
d.	pen	/pɛn/	**h.**	neat	/nit/

Exercise D Continued

†4. Many dialects of the northeastern seaboard contain the following rule:

Ø → [r] / V ____ # V

Indicate how each of the following phrases would be affected by this rule (if at all):

a. Anna asked Neal **c.** Anna told Neal

b. Neal asked Anna **d.** Neal told Anna

5. How must the rule in Exercise (4) be restricted in order to correctly predict the following data?

Cuba is	[kyubrərɪz]	Linda ate	[lɪndəret]
Tahiti is	*[təhitirɪz]	Roscoe ate	*[raskoret]
Martha ate	[marθəret]		

Social Variation

Over the past 40 years or so, much research in language variation has shifted to **sociolinguistics.** This field is concerned with the interrelationship between the language of a group and its social characteristics (especially socioeconomic status and ethnicity). For example, working-class New Yorkers "drop their r's" (i.e., delete post-vocalic [r] in words like *forty-four*) more often than middle-class New Yorkers do. It would be misleading, however, to say that regional dialectology and sociolinguistics are mutually exclusive fields of study. On the contrary, researchers in regional dialectology often include sociological information about their informants such as age and education. Likewise, sociolinguists must often take into account regional influences on the social dialects they are studying. Nevertheless, we can draw a few generalizations about why research in language variation has gravitated toward sociolinguistics.

Several trends developed in the United States during the late 1950s and early 1960s that shifted attention to social variation. First, since regional dialectologists had been collecting information about social variables such as age and education, it was a natural step for linguists to become interested in social variables for their own sake. The one person who did the most to bring sociolinguistics to prominence was William Labov. His doctoral dissertation, completed in the mid-1960s, dealt with the social stratification of English in New York City. Labov correlated several different phonological variables (e.g., the deletion of post-vocalic [r]) with different social classes (upper-middle, lower-middle, upper-working, and lower-working). Among his innovations was the use of a preexisting sociological classification system for his informants. That is, he used a model of social stratification developed within sociology, whereas most regional dialectologists had classified their informants using relatively subjective criteria. Moreover, he collected data from four different styles of speech: casual, careful, reading, and formal. Finally, he tried to use the results of his studies to develop both linguistic and sociological theory, whereas many regional dialectologists were working without any particular attention to fundamental issues in linguistic theory.

Second, linguists found it impossible to deal with language variation without acknowledging the fact that listeners often make social judgments based on characteristics of a speaker's dialect. For example, someone who says *I ain't sorry* may be judged as coming from a lower socioeconomic status than another person who says *I'm not sorry.* Thus arose an interest in **standard** and **nonstandard** dialects. It is no simple matter to define the difference between a standard and a nonstandard variety of a language. However, for our purposes, we can define a standard dialect as one that draws no negative attention to itself; that is, educated people do not judge a person speaking such a dialect as coming from a lower socioeconomic status, lacking education, and so forth. On the other hand, a nonstandard dialect does draw negative attention to itself; educated people might judge the speaker of such a dialect as coming from a lower socioeconomic status, lacking education, and so on. Nonstandard forms such as *ain't,* which cause the listener to form a negative social judgment of the speaker, are referred to as **socially marked** forms.

Third, the interest in nonstandard dialects in the 1960s and 1970s led quite naturally to an interest in what is now called African American Vernacular English (AAVE), a variety spoken primarily by low-income blacks in urban areas. There were several reasons for this interest. For one thing, the civil rights movement and integration of the public schools brought the language differences between lower-class blacks and middle-class whites into noticeable contrast. This led to concerns about how best to administer public education. Research on nonstandard dialects in general and on AAVE in particular has been especially relevant to practical problems in public education. For example, a teacher is less likely to be concerned when a student says *tap* instead of *faucet* (a purely regional distinction) than when a student says *Can't nobody tell him what to do* instead of *Nobody can tell him what to do.* Likewise, nonstandard variations may result in a child's being diagnosed for language therapy or failing a standardized test. For example, a student who pronounces *these* with initial [d] instead of [ð] may be judged as having an "articulation problem." Because social variations in language are, rightly or wrongly, so strongly linked to how students are tested and evaluated, many sociolinguists have focused on communicating with teachers, test developers, and speech-language pathologists about the nature of nonstandard dialects.

Also, it seemed reasonable for linguists to begin their description of nonstandard dialects with AAVE, since it is thought to be the most distinct from standard English. Their interest was further fueled by the controversy surrounding the origins of AAVE. Some scholars maintained the traditional position that AAVE developed from the dialect spoken by poor Southern whites. Others, however, proposed that AAVE developed from a **creole.** A creole is a language that develops from a **pidgin,** a linguistic system used when speakers of different languages come into contact through trade or colonization—as, for example, when slaves on plantations came into contact with slaves from different language groups and with speakers of English. When the pidgin evolves into a more complex system and becomes the native language of a later generation, it has become a creole. Evidence for the **creole hypothesis** about the origin of AAVE came from researchers who were studying Caribbean creoles and who pointed out creole forms in modern-day AAVE.

A final reason for the increased interest in social dialects is that, while regional dialects are characterized largely by lexical variation, social dialects are more likely to reflect grammatical variation—variation in phonology, morphology, and syntax. Many linguists find these patterns more interesting than lexical variation because grammatical variation tends to be more systematic and predictable. For example, given the fact that *submarine* refers to a sandwich made on an oblong loaf of bread, no amount of theorizing would enable us to predict that other speakers might call the same object a *hero, hoagie, grinder,* or *poboy*! On the other hand, grammatical forms are more likely to reflect predictable variations, as we will see in the next three sections.

Before looking at specific examples of socially marked forms, we want to emphasize that identifying a dialect as standard or nonstandard is a sociological judgment, not a linguistic one. If we say that Dialect X is nonstandard, we are saying that the educated members of the society in which X is spoken judge the speakers of X as inferior in some way and associate this negative judgment with certain linguistic characteristics of X. We are not, however, saying that X is inferior linguistically in the sense of being cruder, less well developed, and so forth than the standard. All dialects of all natural languages are rule governed and systematic. None is more or less developed than another; all are equally complex.

Let's look at a concrete example of the difference between a linguistic judgment and a sociological one. Consider the reflexive pronouns in the following sentences.

(8) Lou hurt *himself.*

(9) Lou hurt *hisself.*

(10) *Lou hurt *heself.*

Both (8) and (9) are used by speakers of English, but (10) isn't. In other words, (8) and (9) are part of English, but (10) isn't. This is a linguistic fact that we can capture by using some terms that came up in our discussion of syntax: we can say that (8) and (9) are **grammatical,** meaning simply that each occurs regularly in some system of English, while (10) is **ungrammatical,** meaning that it is not part of any system. (Recall that the asterisk * designates an ungrammatical structure.) Second, (8) and (9) are used by different groups of speakers; they belong to different social dialects. In particular, (8) is not socially marked and would go unnoticed by educated speakers of the language. On the other hand, (9) is socially marked; educated speakers may make a negative sociological judgment about the speaker of (9). We can capture the difference between (8) and (9) by saying that, while both forms are grammatical, (8) is standard (not socially marked), while (9) is nonstandard (socially marked).

Exercise E

1. What criterion would a linguist use to determine that a language should be classified as a creole rather than as a pidgin?
2. Macauley (1994:174–75) cites the following forms from Tok Pisin, a pidgin language spoken in Papua, New Guinea.

TOK PISIN	ENGLISH
gras	grass
gras bilong fes	beard
gras bilong hed	hair
gras bilong pisin	feather
gras antap long ai	eyebrow
gras nogut	weed

   a. What strategies does Tok Pisin use to build vocabulary and to indicate possession?
   b. How does the meaning of *gras* in Tok Pisin differ from the meaning of *grass* in English?

Nonstandard Phonological Variation

As we have seen, not all phonological variation carries social weight. For example, a speaker who pronounces *caught* as [kʰɔt] would probably not form any negative social judgment about a speaker who pronounces the same word as [kʰat], at least not on the basis of this single form. Similarly, a speaker from New England whose dialect contains the Linking [r] rule would probably not form a social judgment about a speaker whose dialect lacks this feature. However, some phonological variation is socially marked. Let's look at some examples.

Substitution of [d] for [ð]. Consider the pronunciation of *this, that, these, those,* and so on with initial [d] instead of [ð]. A listener may associate such forms with speakers from, say, working-class sections of New York City. A listener who holds this group in low social esteem may label such forms as "bad" or "incorrect" English. As pointed out earlier, though, it is essential to try to separate social judgments from linguistic ones. Let's concentrate on examining such forms from a linguistic standpoint; that is, on discovering, from a phonological perspective, *why* these particular forms are used by some speakers.

First, in what sense is the pronunciation of *these* as [diz] a predicable and systematic phonological variation? To answer this question, we can begin by comparing the features for /ð/ and /d/. The phoneme /ð/ is a voiced interdental fricative; /d/ is a voiced alveolar stop. Intuitively, it seems more plausible for a substitution to occur between similar segments than between dissimilar segments. At first glance, /ð/ and /d/ seem to have little in common, since they differ in place and manner or articulation. On the other hand, both segments are voiced consonants. Moreover, /ð/ and /d/ are very close in their places of articulation. (To confirm this, consult the consonant chart in Chapter 6.) Therefore, the place of articulation contrast between these two segments is not so great as it may initially seem.

But what about the contrast in the manner of articulation? In order to understand why a dialect might replace /ð/, a fricative, with [d], a stop, some additional background is required. Several pieces of evidence suggest that stops are more "natural" than fricatives, especially interdental fricatives such as /ð/. For one thing, children acquire stops before they acquire fricatives, indicating that stops are somehow more "basic" than fricatives. A second piece of evidence comes from language change, the study of how languages evolve historically. As a rule, the likelihood of finding a language that had alveolar stops in its consonant inventory and then later added interdental fricatives is much greater than finding a language that had interdental fricatives and then later added alveolar stops. Again, this pattern indicates that alveolar stops are more basic than interdental fricatives. A third, related piece of evidence is that languages without interdental fricatives are relatively easy to find—French, German, and some dialects of Spanish are a few examples—whereas languages without at least one alveolar stop are extremely rare. All of these facts, then, suggest that a dialect which substitutes a stop such as [d] for a fricative such as /ð/ is following a "natural" linguistic trend. This process, whereby a stop is substituted for a corresponding fricative, is termed **stopping.**

Exercise F

1. Based on the preceding discussion of stopping, determine what substitution might occur for /θ/ in some nonstandard dialects (e.g., as the first segment of *think* and *throw*).
2. In some varieties of AAVE and in some nonstandard British English dialects, /θ/ and /ð/ are replaced by /f/ and /v/, respectively, so that *Ruth* is pronounced as [ruf], and *brother* is pronounced as [brʌvər]. In what way does this pattern resemble the stopping pattern just discussed? In what way is it different?

Consonant Cluster Reduction. Consonant Cluster Reduction deletes a consonant from a series of two or more word-final consonants. More specifically, the second member of a consonant cluster (typically a stop) is deleted if the following word starts with a consonant. For example, *iced tea* /aɪst ti/, which contains the cluster /st/ followed by another consonant /t/, would become [aɪs ti] by the rule of Consonant Cluster Reduction. (Note that *iced tea* is, not surprisingly, often spelled *ice tea.*) Such reduction occurs in the running speech even of speakers of standard dialects. This can be confirmed through introspection—try saying *iced tea* at a normal rate of speech—or by listening to another person say it at a normal rate of speech. It is very difficult to enunciate the final [t] of *iced* without pausing between words, thereby creating an artificial speaking style.

Nonstandard dialects, however, often create socially marked forms by extending the environment of a rule that applies in the standard dialect, so that the rule applies in additional contexts. As an illustration, consider how Consonant Cluster Reduction operates in standard English:

$$C \rightarrow \emptyset \,/\, C \,\underline{\quad\quad}\, \# C$$

Now consider a phrase like *He pushed the car* /hi pʊšt ðə kar/. Note that *pushed* ends in a consonant cluster /št/, and the next word starts with a consonant /ð/. Therefore, our standard English rule of Consonant Cluster Reduction would delete the /t/ in *pushed the car.* However, it would not delete the /t/ in *pushed a car,* since the /št/ cluster is followed by a word-initial vowel /ə/.

There are, however, nonstandard dialects of English in which *both* of the forms just mentioned would undergo Consonant Cluster Reduction. These dialects have generalized the Consonant Cluster Reduction rule so that it deletes the second member of a word-final consonant cluster, regardless of what segment begins the next word. The rule can be formalized as follows:

$$C \rightarrow \emptyset \,/\, C \,\underline{\quad\quad}\, \#$$

This nonstandard version of the rule still applies in the same contexts as the standard dialect rule. However, it also applies in contexts that the standard dialect rule does not, namely where the consonant cluster is followed by a word beginning with a vowel (e.g., *He pushed a car* → *He push a car*) or by nothing at all (e.g., *He got pushed* → *He got push*).

Other Nonstandard Phonological Features. There are many examples of socially marked phonological variation too numerous to mention here; the following, however, constitute a representative sample. One is the substitution of [t] for [k], and vice-versa: [kémark] for *K-Mart,* [krɛ́dɪk] for *credit,* [rɪsk] for *wrist,* [ot] for *oak,* [dɛst] for *desk,* and so on. The segments [t] and [k] are very similar acoustically, especially when they occur before another consonant, as in *K-Mart Plaza.* A speaker who is only semiliterate (i.e., unfamiliar with the spelling of a word) might understandably perceive a word like *K-Mart* as ending in the phoneme /k/.

Another example is **metathesis,** the reversal of two segments, one of which is typically a liquid (/l/ or /r/). This process results in forms like [číldərn] for *children,* [kǽlvəri] for *cavalry,* [nukyulər] for *nuclear,* and so on. Liquids may also be deleted following a vowel: [hɛp] for *help,* [hod] for *hold,* and so on. This process, known as **post-vocalic liquid deletion,** applies optionally in some nonstandard dialects. This process is responsible for the variant pronunciations of words like *Carol* /kǽrəl/: as /kǽrə/ (/l/ deleted), /kǽəl/ (/r/ deleted), and /kǽə/ (both liquids deleted).

A final example of socially marked phonological variation is the devoicing of a word-final obstruents (stop, fricative, or affricate): [kɪlt] for *killed,* [əhólt] for *ahold,* [hɛt] for *head,* and so on. This process, called **final devoicing,** is quite common among the world's languages. It applies in both German and Russian, and has applied selectively in English earlier in its history, as can be seen in the pairs *spilled/spilt, dreamed/dreamt, learned/learnt, burned/burnt,* and so on.

Exercise G

1. Mark the following statements true or false.
   - †**a.** T F [tʰɪs] is a possible pronunciation for *this* in nonstandard English.
   - **b.** T F [dɪŋk] is a possible form of *think* in some nonstandard dialects.
   - **c.** T F Consonant Cluster Reduction is found only in nonstandard spoken dialects.
   - **d.** T F [pʰæf] is a possible pronunciation of *path* in nonstandard English.
2. In all varieties of English, certain consonants are deleted phonetically in certain environments. Consider the following data.

	PHONEMIC	PHONETIC
most people	/most pipəl/	[mos pipəl]
most of us	/most əv əs/	[most əv əs]
iced tea	/aɪst ti/	[aɪs ti]
iced a cake	/aɪst ə kek/	[aɪst ə kek]
eight people	/et pipəl/	[et pipəl]
six people	/sɪks pipəl/	[sɪks pipəl]

   - **a.** Which forms show a systematic change between the phomemic and phonetic levels?
   - **b.** What do these forms have in common?
   - **c.** State in words the rule that describes this change.
   - **d.** Write the rule in formal notation.

Exercise G Continued

3. Assume that the rule of Consonant Cluster Reduction in English deletes the second member of a consonant cluster. What restrictions must be placed on this general rule so that it predicts the following data? In other words, how must the rule be restricted if we want to prevent it from applying to /læmp/, /bɛnt/, /hɛlp/, and /bʌlk/?

hand /hænd/ → [hæn]	help /hɛlp/ → *[hɛl]
lamp /læmp/ → *[læm]	hold /hold/ → [hol]
last /læst/ → [læs]	bulk /bʌlk/ → *[bʌl]
bent /bɛnt/ → *[bɛn]	

4. Which of the following phonological variations is not typically found in nonstandard English?
   - **a.** [kemark] for K-Mart /kemart/
   - **b.** [dɛst] for *desk* /dɛsk/
   - **c.** [saʊf] for *south* /saʊθ/
   - **d.** [hæθ] for *half* /hæf/
5. What phonological process accounts for the following forms, found in some nonstandard dialects of English?

	STANDARD	NONSTANDARD
business	[bíznɪs]	[bídnɪs]
wasn't he	[wʌ́zni]	[wʌ́dni]
Disney	[dízni]	[dídni]

6. Identify the phonological process reflected by each of the following.
   - **a.** Pulled /pʊld/ becomes the nonstandard form /pʊlt/.
   - **b.** Cassidy (1981) states that in some dialects *bronical* /bránɪkəl/ is substituted for *bronchial* /bráŋkiəl/.
   - **c.** *Tests* becomes the nonstandard form *tesses* /tɛsəz/. (Hint: Two processes are involved.)

Nonstandard Morphological Variation

Nonstandard patterns in word formation tend to involve the inflection of nouns and verbs. Whereas many phonological processes are common to all spoken dialects of English, variations in morphology tend to be restricted to particular social dialects. In general, morphological variation is more socially marked in speech than is phonological variation. However, morphological variation, like phonological variation, is also predictable and systematic. In fact, nonstandard morphological forms often reflect more regular treatments of the noun and verb systems of English than their standard counterparts do, as we will see in the following examples.

Reflexive Pronouns. One example of nonstandard morphological variation was given in the exercises for Chapter 5. In Supplementary Exercise 4, we observed that some nonstandard dialects of English use the following system of reflexive pronouns.

	SINGULAR	PLURAL
1st person	myself	ourselves
2nd person	yourself	yourselves
3rd person	herself/hisself	theirselves

This system is identical to the standard English system, with two exceptions: the third person singular form *hisself* is used, instead of the standard English form *himself;* and the third person plural form *theirselves* is used, instead of the standard English form *themselves.*

Again, if we set aside any social judgments that we may have about the nonstandard forms, we can see that these forms are highly systematic from a linguistic perspective (and, in fact, are more predictable than the standard English forms *himself* and *themselves*). Note that the first and second person reflexive pronouns have as their base a possessive pronoun: *my, our,* or *your.* (The third person singular feminine form, *herself,* can be interpreted as either possessive + *self* or objective + *self.*) In other words, given the first and second person forms, the principle for forming a reflexive pronoun in English appears to be the following: add *-self* or *-selves* to the possessive form. Following this rule would give us *hisself* and *theirselves* for the third person forms. Therefore, from a linguistic perspective, the nonstandard forms *hisself* and *theirselves* are actually more systematic than the standard forms *himself* and *themselves.* The reflexive pronoun system illustrates quite pointedly the systematic nature of nonstandard morphological variation.

Omission of Final *-s* on Verbs. Consider the sentence *He walk home every day.* We can begin by comparing this sentence to its standard English counterpart, *He walks home every day.* One way to account for the nonstandard form *walk* is to hypothesize that a morpheme has been deleted, namely the {PRES} inflection that occurs in standard English as *-s* on the third person singular form of present tense verbs. In order to understand why this morpheme is omitted in some nonstandard dialects, we need to look at the standard English system for the inflection of present tense verbs.

	SINGULAR	**PLURAL**
1st person	I walk	We walk
2nd person	You walk	You walk
3rd person	S/he walks	They walk

We can see immediately that most present tense verbs in standard English have no overt inflection for {PRES}. If we substitute the nonstandard forms *(S/he walk)* for the corresponding standard forms, we come out with a perfectly regular system (i.e., no present tense forms have an overt inflection). This regularization of the third person present tense verb forms generalizes to all main verbs and auxiliaries in some nonstandard dialects of English, yielding forms like *He do* for *He does, He don't* for *He doesn't,* and *He have* for *He has.*

It is interesting to note that the *-s* ending can represent three different morphemes in English, but that these morphemes are omitted with different frequencies in nonstandard dialects such as AAVE. Specifically, {PRES} (as in *She walks home every day*) is omitted more frequently than {POSS} (the possessive morpheme, as in *the girl's book*). In turn, {POSS} is omitted more frequently than {PLU} (the plural morpheme, as in *two friends*). This pattern indicates that the omission of *-s* is morphological rather than phonological—that is, speakers are omitting an inflection, not simply a segment. If the omission were phonological, all three morphemes would be omitted with equal frequency, since they are phonologically identical.

Other Nonstandard Verb Patterns. Divergences from standard English occur in several other verb inflections. One socially marked feature is the use of nonstandard past tense and past participial verb forms, especially on irregular verbs. For example, the verb *to see* in standard English has the past tense *saw* and the past participle *seen: I saw him yesterday; I've seen him three times this week.* Nonstandard dialects may regularize these forms by using one of several strategies. One is to form the past tense by using the regular inflection, spelled *-ed,* yielding a sentence like *I seed him yesterday.* Another is to use one form for both the past and past participle forms, yielding sentences like *I seen him yesterday* or *I've saw him three times this week.*

The irregular verb *to be* is highly variable in standard English, with seven different inflected forms depending on the number and person of the subject and the tense and aspect of the verb phrase: *am, are, is, was, were, been, being.* Perhaps not surprisingly, speakers of some nonstandard dialects regularize all present tense forms of *be* to one single form: for example, *I is, You is, We is,* and *They is.* Note that when this happens, *be* is no longer an irregular verb. This strategy and those discussed in the preceding paragraph have the effect of regularizing forms that are irregular, and therefore unpredictable, in the standard dialect.

Exercise H

1. *Ain't* fills a gap in the standard English system by providing an alternative contracted form for the phrase *I am not.* However, the use of *ain't* is not restricted to the first person subject in nonstandard dialects. Given the following data, in what way is the nonstandard system more regular than the standard one?

Standard System		Nonstandard System	
(no form)	we aren't	I ain't	we ain't
you aren't	you aren't	you ain't	you ain't
he/she/it isn't	they aren't	he/she/it ain't	they ain't

2. Some dialects of Appalachian English use the prefix {a} on certain forms. Based on the following data (adapted from Wolfram [1982]), state five constraints on the use of this prefix. (Some are phonological; others are morphological.)
   - **A.** She kept a-callin' my name.
   - **B.** She woke up a-screamin'.
   - **C.** The bear come a-runnin' out of the woods.
   - **D.** She kept a-waterin' the lawn.
   - **E.** *She kept a-forgettin' my name.
   - **F.** *She kept a-askin' my name.
   - **G.** *She woke up a-screaming.
   - **H.** *They like a-sailin'.
   - **I.** *They shot the a-runnin' bear.

†3. The following is taken from a church bulletin: *The deacon wives will be meeting on Thursday, April 11, in the uptown location.* Explain how the socially marked form in this passage arises. (Hint: The wives are not deacons.)

(continued)

***Exercise H** Continued*

†**4.** The morphemes {PRES}, {PLU}, and {POSS} are omitted with different frequencies in AAVE. Given the different frequencies of omission, the standard English sentence *Sam hates his sister's boyfriends* is most likely to show up in AAVE as _______.

a. Sam hate his sister's boyfriends.
b. Sam hate his sister boyfriends.
c. Sam hates his sister boyfriends.
d. Sam hates his sister's boyfriend.
e. either (a) or (b)

Nonstandard Syntactic Variation

Like morphological variations, syntactic variations tend to be more socially marked than phonological variations, some of which are regional as well as social. Let's take a look at some specific nonstandard syntactic constructions.

Inversion in *wh*-Interrogatives. In some nonstandard dialects of English, an interrogative such as *What is it?* may be phrased as *What it is?* In order to demonstrate the relation between these two syntactic forms, we will need to make use of several concepts discussed in Chapter 4 (Syntax), namely underlying structure, surface structure, and transformation. With these concepts at hand, we can begin by analyzing the **derivation** of the standard English form *What is it?;* that is, by looking at the transformations that relate its underlying and surface structures.

Let us assume that, in the underlying structure of this interrogative, we have a sequence of elements like the following:

it - is - what

This underlying structure differs from the surface form in two ways. First, the verb *(is)* follows the subject *(it)* in the underlying structure, but precedes it on the surface. Second, the *wh*-word *(what)* is in final position in the underlying structure, but in initial position on the surface. Each of these differences involves a transformation. Inflection Movement (I-Movement) moves the verb-form inflected for tense to the left of the subject. *Wh*-Movement moves the *wh*-word to clause-initial position. Applying these transformations yields the standard English form *What is it?*

How can we account for the nonstandard English structure *What it is?* Let's assume that this form has the same underlying structure as its standard counterpart: it - is -what. What transformational rules are needed to relate this underlying structure to the surface form *What it is?* Only one: *wh*-Movement. Applying this transformation to the underlying structure would yield the surface form *What it is?*

Let's compare the standard and nonstandard derivations side by side. As we have seen, the difference between them can be explained by assuming that I-Movement applies in the standard derivation, but not in the nonstandard derivation. This situation is summarized here.

	STANDARD ENGLISH	NONSTANDARD ENGLISH
Underlying structure:	it - is - what	it - is - what
I-Movement:	is - it - what	(does not apply)
wh-Movement:	what - is - it	what - it - is
	What is it?	*What it is?*

At this point, it should be clear that the nonstandard derivation omits a step (I-Movement) that appears in the standard derivation. This should not be interpreted to mean that the nonstandard derivation is "deficient" or "incomplete" in some way. Rather, a dialect containing this nonstandard feature is perfectly rule governed and differs from standard English in a systematic and predictable way.

Double Negatives. Let's now take a look at the infamous double negative construction, exemplified by sentences such as *I don't have no money* (cf. standard English *I don't have any money*). This construction is significant not so much because it is socially marked (which of course it is in Modern English), but because of the faulty reasoning usually associated with its prohibition.

Every school child is familiar with the following rule: Double negatives are incorrect because two negatives make a positive. This claim can largely be traced to a highly influential book written by Robert Lowth in 1762, *A Short Introduction to English Grammar.* Lowth's work appeared during the 18th-century **prescriptive grammar** movement, which produced many collections of "dos and don'ts" about the English language. Unfortunately, many of these proclamations were based on personal prejudices against certain structures (for example, Jonathan Swift objected to verb forms such as /dɪstʌ́rbd/ instead of /dɪstʌ́rbəd/ for *disturbed*) and on the notion that new forms (including words such as *banter, bully,* and *mob*) would corrupt the language. Moreover, many leaders of this movement believed that English should emulate Greek, Latin, and other systems that were perceived as more authoritative and rational than English.

Lowth's prohibition against double negatives illustrates this latter tendency, in that it attempted to make English conform to mathematical logic. According to Lowth, "Two Negatives in English destroy one another, or are equivalent to an Affirmative." Here Lowth was apparently generalizing the principle that the product of two negative numbers is a positive number: for example $(-2) \times (-2) = 4$. (Interestingly enough, Lowth could likewise have *defended* the double negative by analogy to mathematics, arguing that the sum of two negative numbers is itself a negative number: that is, two negatives reinforce, rather than cancel, each other.) The point is that Lowth proclaimed the double negative in English to be "illogical" not because it violates our linguistic system, but because it violates a principle from another system—mathematics.

If Lowth's reasoning were correct, we would expect certain things to follow from it. First, we would expect a sentence such as *I don't have no money* to mean 'I have some money.' Contrary to Lowth's prediction, however, this sentence means 'I don't have any money,' as any native speaker of English can point out. Second, we would expect human languages in general to shun double negative constructions. This, however, is not the case. If we turn to the present-day forms of languages other than English, we find that double negatives appear as a matter of course. For example, the standard English sentence *I don't want anything,* which contains one negative (the contracted form of *not*), has as its Spanish equivalent *No quiero nada,* where both *no* and *nada* indicate negation. Thus, there is nothing inherently deviant about the double negative construction. Moreover, if we look back at earlier stages of the English language, we find double negatives in the language of quite a few highly esteemed writers. The double negatives in (11–13) have been italicized.

(11) Old English (King Alfred, the *Orosius,* ca. 880–890): "*ne* bið ðær *nænig* ealo gebrowen mid Estum" (literally 'not is there not-any ale brewed among Estonians'; Modern English 'no ale is brewed among the Estonians').

(12) Middle English (Chaucer, the *Canterbury Tales,* ca. 1390): "he that is irous and wrooth, he *ne* may *nat* wel deme" (literally 'he that is angry and wrathful, he not may not well judge'; Modern English 'he cannot judge well').

(13) Early Modern English (Shakespeare, *2 Henry IV,* ca. 1600): "There's *never none* of these demure boys come to any proof" (Modern English 'Not one of these young boys amounts to anything').

From a historical perspective, then, it is difficult to say that the double negative construction was either socially or linguistically marked in earlier forms of English.

If Lowth's analysis of double negatives is inaccurate, what actually led to the socially marked status of double negatives in Modern English? Briefly, here's what seems to have happened. In Old English, double negatives were obligatory, as they are in Modern Spanish. That is, the Old English equivalent of *I don't have no money* would have been grammatical, and the equivalent of *I don't have any money* would have been ungrammatical. By Shakespeare's time, double negatives had become optional. That is, the Early Modern English equivalents of *I don't have no money* and *I don't have any money* existed side by side, both fully grammatical. Apparently, however, the single negative construction somehow became associated with educated speakers, while double negatives became associated with uneducated speakers. This, of course, eventually led to double negatives being socially marked in Modern English. The point to keep in mind, however, is that sociolinguistic phenomena are a function of the interaction of linguistic and sociological forces; mathematical and logical systems have no bearing on them whatsoever.

Nonstandard Treatments of *to be.* AAVE differs from standard English in several patterns that affect forms of *to be.* One of these patterns is *be*-deletion, the absence of what would occur in standard English as an inflected form of auxiliary or main verb *be:* for example, *He's looking for work* → *He looking for work,* or *Her hair is messed up* → *Her hair messed up.* Labov has determined that AAVE can omit an inflected form of *be* only in environments where standard English can contract it. For example, in the sentences below, standard English allows contraction of the first occurrence of *be,* but not the second occurrence. Similarly, AAVE allows deletion of the first occurrence of *be,* but not the second occurrence.

STANDARD ENGLISH: CONTRACTION	AAVE: *BE*-DELETION
Allowed: *It is his.* → *It's his.*	Allowed: *It is his.* → *It his.*
Not allowed: *What is it?* → **What's it?*	Not allowed: *What is it?* → **What it?*

Another nonstandard syntactic feature involves the treatment of main verb *be* in interrogatives such as *Do they be sick?* Standard English has a general rule for forming an interrogative: I-Movement applies to auxiliaries but not to main verbs. If there is no overt auxiliary verb, a form of *do* is used to form an interrogative. This distinction is shown below.

STANDARD ENGLISH: I-MOVEMENT ALLOWED ON AUXILIARIES BUT NOT ON MAIN VERB

They have gone to work. → Have they gone to work?

They went to work. → *Went they to work? (cf: Did they go to work?)

The exception to this rule in standard English is that main verb *be* behaves like an auxiliary verb for purposes of forming an interrogative. That is, it undergoes I-Movement, as shown below.

They are at work. → Are they at work?

Now consider what form we would get if main verb *be* in standard English behaved like all other verbs, that is, if it did not undergo I-Movement but instead required a form of *do* to form an interrogative. We would get exactly the structure that occurs in AAVE, as shown below.

They are at work. → Do they be at work?

In this case, the nonstandard dialect has regularized an exception in standard English, so that main verb *be* is treated exactly like all other main verbs.

Another pattern found in AAVE and some varieties of Southern rural white speech is **habitual *be*** (sometimes called **distributive *be***) as in *He be looking for work* 'He is always looking for work' (as opposed to 'He is looking for work right now'). This structure is reserved for utterances that refer to activities or states that occur over time (including the present) or are generally true. Taken together, *be*-deletion and habitual *be* form a system that allows for the same meaning distinctions found in Standard English. The following table shows instances of auxiliary *be* and main verb *be* in standard English and their counterparts in AAVE.

INTENDED REFERENT	STANDARD ENGLISH	AAVE	MEANING IN BOTH DIALECTS
Specific instance or point in time	He is looking for work.	He (is) looking for work.	'He is looking for work at this point in time.'
	Her hair is messed up.	Her hair (is) messed up.	'Her hair is messed up at this point in time.'
Ongoing or habitual occurrence	He is always looking for work.	He be looking for work.	'He is engaged in an ongoing search for work; every time I talk to him, he's looking for work.'
	Her hair is always messed up.	Her hair be messed up.	'Her hair is messed up all the time; every time I see her, her hair is messed up.'

To summarize this section, socially marked grammatical variations are highly systematic from a linguistic perspective. They reflect predictable variations of standard English forms and are by no means "illogical" from the standpoint of how language actually works. Any negative judgments that we may have about nonstandard forms are based more on our social biases about the speakers who use them than on their linguistic structure.

Does this mean that linguists take an "anything goes" attitude toward language? That is, do linguists advocate the use of double negatives and other socially marked forms? We cannot speak for all linguists, of course, but our own point of view is that social judgments are just as real as linguistic judgments. That is, a form like *What it is?* is likely to elicit a negative social judgment from many listeners, even though they understand the meaning of the sentence. It would be foolhardy to pretend that such social judgments are nonexistent or unimportant. On the other hand, it would be just as misguided to claim that a structure like *What it is?* constitutes an illogical or inferior linguistic form. We believe that anyone who is in the business of teaching language and evaluating the language of others should understand the distinction between social and linguistic judgments, as well as the underlying regularity of many socially marked forms.

Exercise I

1. One prescriptive rule states that the nominative case of a pronoun should be used after a form of main verb *be:* hence, *It is I, That is he,* and so on. However, most speakers, at least in an informal register, tend to use the objective case of a pronoun in these structures: *It's me, That's him.* Given the following data (where an asterisk marks an ungrammatical structure), what general principle do speakers appear to be following when they use the objective case pronoun following *be* instead of the nominative case?

A.1. The girl hit him.

A.2. *The girl hit he.

B.1. Please call me.

B.2. *Please call I.

C.1 I don't know her.

C.2. *I don't know she.

2. Consider the following sentence: *That is not where they are now.* Which occurrences of inflected *be* could be omitted in AAVE?

†3. A freshman composition teacher corrects a student's sentence from *I asked her what did she want* to *I asked her what she wanted.* What syntactic rule of English accounts for the difference between the original version of the sentence and the revised version?

4. Which of the following was a goal of prescriptive grammar?

a. To objectively describe the actual language of speakers.

b. To make English conform to classical languages such as Latin.

c. To indicate the geographical distribution of certain dialects.

d. To show how creole languages evolve from pidgin languages.

5. Consider the following data:

A. Are they sick? (standard)

B. Do they be sick? (nonstandard)

Exercise I *Continued*

C. Are they going? (standard)
D. Do they be going? (nonstandard)
E. Do they have a car? (both dialects)
F. Do they need money? (both dialects)

Label the following generalizations about *yes-no* questions as true or false.

a. T F SE treats main verb *be* like other main verbs.
b. T F NSE treats main verb *be* like other main verbs.
c. T F NSE treats auxiliary *be* like a main verb.
d. T F SE treats main verb *have* like an auxiliary verb.

6. Consider the following interchange between a judge and the foreman of a jury.

JUDGE: Have you reached a verdict?

FOREMAN: We have, Your Honor.

JUDGE: What say you?

The judge's grammar differs from that of Modern English in the formulation of one syntactic rule. What is that rule, and how is it different from Modern English?

7. Macauley (1994:76) writes:

In French it is the reduction of negative marking to a single form that is stigmatized. In "correct" (that is, socially approved) French the simple negative consists of two parts, *ne* and *pas,* as in *Je ne sais pas* ("I don't know"). Many French people now simply use *pas* alone for the negative in everyday conversation, much to the disgust of purists.

How does this fact present a problem for Lowth's proclamation about double negatives?

Language and Gender

So far we have dealt with linguistic variation that correlates with socioeconomic status and ethnicity. In addition to these social variables, linguists have also investigated the relation between language and **gender:** the social and psychological roles, attitudes, and traits associated with biological sex. The field of language and gender has focused on two questions. First, what correspondences can be drawn between a speaker's language and gender? (Can we generalize, for example, about the degree to which males and females use indirectness?) Second, is language sexist? That is, do certain linguistic forms (such as the use of *mankind* to refer to all people) reflect or promote an antifemale bias? In this section we focus on findings about the first question, referring the reader to supplementary readings for discussions of the second question.

Gender as a Social Variable

We have already seen that socioeconomic status and ethnicity are related to the use of standard and nonstandard linguistic forms. For instance, suppose we were to study two groups of 30-year-old white males: one upper-middle class and one lower-working class. A typical finding would be that lower-working-class speakers are more likely than upper-middle-class speakers to omit the *-s* on the third person singular form of the verb (e.g., *He don't* for *He doesn't*). This is the expected result: other things being equal (in this example, age and ethnicity), the use of nonstandard forms increases among speakers of lower socioeconomic status.

What happens, though, when gender is introduced as an additional variable? A number of studies have found that, within a given socioeconomic class, female speakers are more likely to use standard forms than male speakers. For example, lower-working class women are more likely than lower-working class men to retain third person singular *-s* (e.g., *He doesn't* rather than *He don't*). In some cases, in fact, the language of women patterns more like that of the men in the next-highest class.

This general tendency for women to use standard forms more often than men (or, stated conversely, for men to use nonstandard forms more often than women) has emerged in studies of a number of linguistic variables. For example, Labov (1966) found that New York City men were more likely than women to employ stopping (i.e., substitution of [t] and [d] for [θ] and [ð], respectively). Other forms that have been studied, with similar findings, include post-vocalic [r] deletion, the use of medial and word-final [ʔ] for /t/ (e.g., [baʔəl for *bottle*), Consonant Cluster Reduction, omission of the {POSS} and {PLU} morphemes, and multiple negatives.

Researchers such as Peter Trudgill have offered several explanations for gender differences in the frequency of standard and nonstandard forms. The greater use of standard forms may reflect women's traditional role as caregivers to children and a concern with transmitting more highly valued forms to the next generation. The use of standard forms may also offer women a way of achieving or signalling a higher social status when other paths (such as greater earning power) have been closed off to them. Along other lines, Trudgill has proposed that middle- and working-class men attach **covert prestige** to their use of nonstandard forms, associating these forms with masculinity and strength. This theory is supported by the fact that men tend to overreport their use of nonstandard forms; that is, they claim to use even more nonstandard forms than they actually do.

Gender Patterns within Standard English

In addition to differences in the use of standard and nonstandard forms, other differences between men and women's language have also been investigated, many of them as the result of Robin Lakoff's influential work *Language and Women's Place* (1975). Lakoff proposed that there is a set of traits which distinguish women's language from men's language, among them a greater use of tag questions, hedges (e.g., *sort of, you know, I guess*), question intonation on declarative structures, indirect speech acts, euphemisms (e.g., *powder room* for *toilet*), "empty" adjectives and intensifiers (e.g., *that is SUCH an ADORABLE puppy!*), and specialized vocabularies in domains such as color terms (e.g., *magenta* and *periwinkle* for shades of purple and blue).

Lakoff based her claims on her own impressions and personal observations rather than on empirical study. Consequently, much subsequent research has attempted to test the accuracy of her perceptions. One finding has been that Lakoff's claims do reflect common stereotypes about women's language. For example, people presented with a cartoon caption (minus the cartoon) like *That is SUCH an ADORABLE puppy!* and asked to guess the speaker's gender will usually identify the speaker as a woman. Other research has been more concerned with confirming whether or not women's language actually displays the traits proposed by Lakoff. This research has borne out some of her claims to varying degrees. In some studies, for example, women have been found to use comparatively more hedges, fewer taboo terms for sexual and bodily functions, and more indirect speech acts. On the other hand, studies of question intonation and tag questions have yielded mixed results, with some studies finding gender differences but others not.

In addition to the linguistic traits proposed by Lakoff, other patterns have also been studied, such as those involving conversation and other interaction. For example, a number of studies of classroom behavior have found that boys talk more than girls and that teachers are likely to give more attention (both positive and negative) to boys. Such differences persist to adulthood, when men tend to dominate situations such as question-and-answer periods after lectures. Studies of conversations between men and women have also revealed that men tend to take longer "turns" throughout the conversation and have a greater tendency to interrupt women than vice versa. Women, on the other hand, tend to ask more questions and provide frequent "support indicators" for the other speaker—expressions like *yeah, um-hm,* and *right.*

Gender patterns, where found, have naturally given rise to attempts at their explanation. Following Lakoff, some analysts have associated the (purported) traits of women's language with powerlessness, uncertainty, and deference. Under this view, for example, hedging is seen as a sign of the speaker's tentativeness. In fact, one extension of this view is that "women's" language is actually the language used by powerless speakers of either gender; "women's" language reflects the fact that women have tended to occupy less powerful positions. This hypothesis is supported by studies that have discovered "women's" language used by men in subordinate roles and "men's" language used by women in powerful roles.

Other analysts have taken a different approach, arguing that women's language reflects a social interaction style that is different from, but not inferior to, that of men. Under this view, women's language reflects a concern with building cooperation, showing empathy, and facilitating communication. This approach, for example, treats the more frequent use of questions among women not as a sign of deference and uncertainty, but instead as a strategy for showing interest in and engaging the other speaker. Similarly, studies of children playing have revealed that boys tend to give each other direct orders *(Put that piece here!),* while girls tend to use more indirect, "inclusive" language *(Why don't we see if this piece fits here?).* From a social interaction perspective, these linguistic differences may reflect differences between a more individualistic, competitive mode more typical of males and a more communal, cooperative mode more typical of females.

Some interest has developed in applying findings about language and gender to solving problems in cross-gender communication at the personal, institutional, and professional levels. For example, as discussed in Deborah Tannen's work *You Just Don't Understand,* many misunderstandings between couples can be traced to differences in male and female conversational styles. Similarly, language and gender studies have been applied in the teaching profession to promote more egalitarian treatment of male and female students. Differences in male and female communication styles have also been used to analyze communication problems encountered by females entering traditionally male fields such as management.

Exercise J

1. A catalogue uses the following terms to describe color selections for riding breeches: "beige, caramel, fawn, sage, moss, slate, and pearl." Is this catalogue designed to appeal primarily to men or women? Explain.
2. Man or woman? "That X is so cute!" Explain.
†3. Are men or women more likely to phrase an order in a restaurant as "Give me a cup of coffee" (as opposed to "I'd like a cup of coffee")? Explain.
4. Consider Figure 7.6, showing the percentage of times that *ain't* was substituted for other verb forms during casual conversation. The results are broken down by both socioeconomic status and gender.
   a. Based on this graph, what generalization can be made about the relative use of nonstandard forms among males and females?
   b. Among speakers of different socioeconomic status?
5. Tannen (1990:153–54) cites a study in which children (ages 6–14 years) produced the following utterances while they were engaged in making objects by hand. Speculate on whether each utterance was produced by a boy or a girl, and explain your choice.
   a. Gimme the pliers!
   b. Man, don't come *in* here where I *am.*
   c. Maybe we can slice them like that.
   d. We gotta find some more bottles.
   e. Get off my steps.
   f. Let's ask her, "Do you have any bottles?"
   g. Give me that, man. After that, after you chop 'em, give 'em to me.
   h. Let's move *these* out *first.*

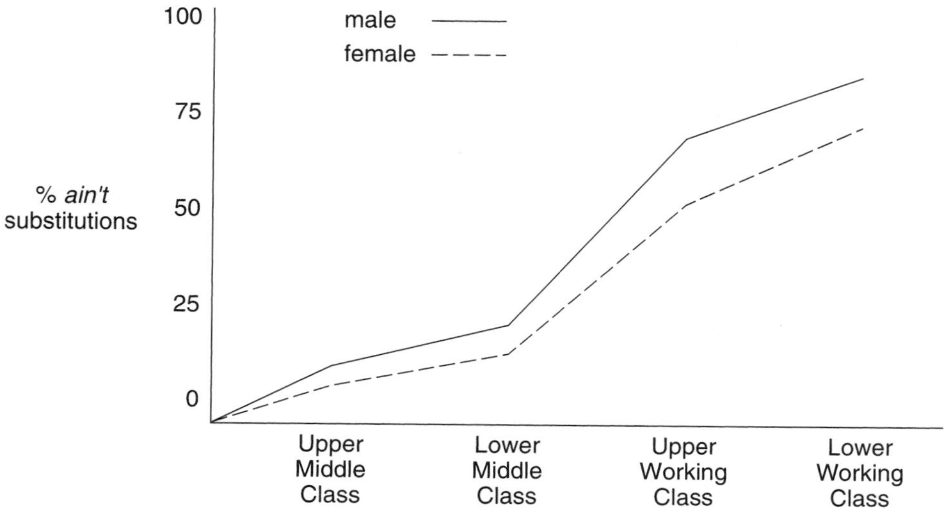

FIGURE 7.6 Substitutions of *ain't* for other verb forms during casual conversation

Exercise J Continued

6. Tannen (1990:242) cites the following passages that were used to describe vice-presidential candidate Geraldine Ferraro during the 1984 campaign:

   An article in *Newsweek* . . . quoted a Reagan aide who called Ferraro "a nasty woman" who would "claw Ronald Reagan's eyes out." . . . She was credited with "a striking gift for tart political rhetoric, needling Ronald Reagan on the fairness issue and twitting the Reagan-Bush campaign for its reluctance to let Bush debate her." . . . One headline [in another source] called her "spunky," another "feisty."

   Why did Tannen choose these passages to support her claim that "gender distinctions are built into the language. The words available to us to describe women and men are not the same words" (243)? (Hint: What particular words would seem odd or inappropriate if used to describe a male politician, and why?)

Stylistic Variation

Earlier in this chapter, we looked at linguistic features that vary from one group to the next. In this section, we will look at stylistic variation—that is, systematic variations within the language of any one speaker, depending upon the occasion and the participants in the interchange. Different styles or **registers** range from extremely formal to quite informal.

An analogy can be drawn between stylistic variation in language and variation in dress. For example, if Professor Smith goes on a job interview for a teaching position—a fairly formal encounter with an unfamiliar audience—he is likely to wear a blazer, a tie, and dress shoes. If he gets the job, however, it is unlikely that he will continue to dress in this same manner while teaching from day to day. Rather, he is likely to dress more informally, perhaps in a sweater, trousers, and loafers. And, if he goes to a backyard barbecue at the house of one of his colleagues, he is likely to wear shorts, a tee-shirt, and tennis shoes.

Smith's manner of dress changes according to the situation and the participants. These changes have in common the fact that they reflect what is appropriate for his role in each situation, the activities he expects to participate in, and the impression he wants to make on the other participants. In this regard, his navy blue blazer is not "better" than his shorts in any absolute sense. Rather, the blazer is more appropriate for the job interview, while the shorts are more appropriate for the backyard barbecue. (Anyone who has ever looked into a closetful of clothes and declared, "I don't have a thing to wear" was actually saying, "I don't have anything to wear that is appropriate for this particular occasion.") Moreover, variations in dress are largely automatic; that is, they do not require a lot of conscious thought. For example, while Smith might decide to wear sandals instead of tennis shoes to the barbecue, it would never occur to him to wear his sandals on his hands. Likewise, while he may have to make a conscious decision about which tie to wear to the job interview, the decision to wear some tie is relatively unconscious. In other words, we move from one style to another without giving it a lot of conscious thought, so long as we are familiar with the conventions of each style.

Similar observations can be made about stylistic variation in language. First of all, linguistic style is a matter of what is **appropriate.** Like variation in dress, stylistic variations in language cannot be judged as appropriate or not without reference to the participants (i.e., speaker and listener or reader and writer). For example, you would not speak to a 5-year-old child, an intimate friend, and a professor using the same style of speech. Using the term *eleemosynary* 'charitable' would probably be inappropriate for the child and the friend, while using *number one* 'urinate' would probably be inappropriate for the friend and the professor. Moreover, stylistic variations in language are largely automatic, in that we do not normally have to stop and think about which style to shift into next. For example, even though many Americans pepper their conversations with "four-letter words" occasionally, very few speakers have to consciously suppress such forms when they are talking to their mother, the president of their company, or a store clerk. In short, shifting styles is essentially automatic and unconscious, and is governed by the concept of appropriateness.

Differences in formality tend to form a continuum rather than a discrete set of categories. Therefore, even though it is fairly easy for an observer to determine when two styles are different, it is sometimes difficult to draw a clear boundary between two styles. The best we can do is identify the relative formality of a particular form (i.e., state the circumstances in which it would be appropriate) and determine the type of variation it represents: lexical, phonological, morphological, or syntactic. With these points in mind, let's look at some different types of stylistic variation.

Stylistic Lexical Variation

One rather obvious stylistic dimension that speakers vary from one situation to another is vocabulary. When speaking or writing in a more formal register, our word choice may lean toward multisyllabic words rather than their shorter equivalents. For example, someone writing a letter of application for a job may close with a phrase like *Thank you for your consideration.* In more informal correspondence, the same person may use *Thanks for your time* to express the same idea. In the same way, a person may use connectives such as *however, therefore,* and *thus* in a more formal register, and use *but* and *so* in a less formal one. Similarly, idiomatic expressions such as *let the cat out of the bag, kick the bucket, make the grade,* and *give me a break* are characteristic of more informal registers. Likewise, words borrowed from Latin and Greek tend to be more formal than native Germanic lexical items: for example, *canine* (from Latin) rather than *dog; thermal* (from Greek) rather than *heat; dental* (from Latin) rather than *tooth;* and *lexical* (from Greek) rather than *word.*

Stylistic Phonological Variation

The application (or nonapplication) of various phonological rules also correlates with changes in register. In particular, neutralization rules (i.e., those that obliterate the distinction between segments) and deletion rules tend to be suppressed in more formal types of speaking. For example, Flapping, which neutralizes /t/ and /d/ to [ɾ], may be suppressed, so that *latter* is pronounced with a [t] and *ladder* with a [d] (rather than both being pronounced [lǽɾər]. Likewise, English has a rule of Vowel Neutralization that reduces all unstressed vowels to [ə], so that *affect* /æfɛ́kt] and *effect* /ifɛ́kt/ are both ordinarily pronounced [əfɛkt]; speakers often suppress this rule in very formal registers. Likewise, Consonant Cluster Reduction may be suppressed, so that the /t/ in *soft drink* is pronounced. Finally, the **deletion of unstressed syllables** (e.g., [mɛ́mbər] for *remember*) may be suppressed, resulting in "hypercorrect" pronunciations such as [ɛləmɛ́ntəri] for *elementary* or [mæθəmǽɾɪks] for *mathematics.*

The suppression of such rules in informal settings, however, can have unintended effects. One of the authors, Frank Parker, had a colleague whom he first encountered in an informal conversation in the hallway. After listening to him speak for a few minutes, Parker inferred that he was not a native speaker of English. Later, after learning that this fellow was a native of Chicago, Parker realized what had given him his initial impression: the colleague systematically (and quite unnaturally) suppressed rules like Flapping, Consonant Cluster Reduction, and Vowel Neutralization in *all* styles of speech.

These examples illustrate two points worth emphasizing. First, pronunciations characterized by phonological neutralization and deletion do not reflect "careless" speech; on the contrary, they reflect a style of speech appropriate for informal registers. Second, it is easy to make the mistake of thinking that informal styles are appropriate only for informal occasions, but that formal styles are appropriate for all occasions. The latter half of this proposition is false, as we have seen from the example of the colleague from Chicago. Using a formal register in casual situations is just as inappropriate as using a casual style on formal occasions.

Stylistic Morphological Variation

The formation of words can also exhibit stylistic variation. One of the features most commonly associated with more informal registers is contraction: for example, *I'm* for *I am* and *you're* for *you are.* Note, however, that contraction of a lexical NP (e.g., *John'll* for *John will*) seems to be more informal than contraction of a pronoun (e.g., *he'll* for *he will*). Moreover, contraction in speech is characteristic of all but the most formal styles. For example, even when being interviewed for a job, you might be more likely to say *I'll do it immediately* rather than *I will do it immediately.* In fact, most people would have to concentrate very carefully in order to block contraction in speech.

Another morphological characteristic of informal registers is the use of clipped forms: for example, *psych* for *psychology, econ* for *economics,* and *comp lit* for *comparative literature.* Note that in an academic treatise on compulsive behavior you might find the term *sports fanatic,* but in the sports section of the newspaper you would see *sports fan.* Once again, contracted and shortened forms are no more "careless" than their lengthier counterparts; rather, they are perfectly appropriate in more informal speech and writing.

Stylistic Syntactic Variation

Changes in syntax may also occur as a function of changes in register. For example, a speaker in a job interview might ask *In which department will I be working?* Having gotten the job, however, the same speaker might ask a colleague *Which department do you work in?* Notice that in shifting from a relatively formal to a more informal register, the speaker has placed the preposition *in* at the end of the clause, rather than at its beginning. The more formal structure, with *in* in initial position, may reflect the speaker's awareness of a prescriptive rule: don't end a sentence with a preposition. This prohibition originated with the 18th-century prescriptive grammarians; it was based on an attempt to model English after Latin, a language in which prepositions cannot appear in sentence-final position. In fact, the word *preposition* comes from a combination of Latin morphemes meaning 'put before

(NPs).' Likewise, the use of *whom* for *who* in object position is characteristic of more formal styles. These two variables (moving a preposition to initial position and substituting *whom* for *who*) interact to form a continuum from formal to casual: for example, *For whom do you work?* → *Whom do you work for?* → *Who do you work for?*

Another informal syntactic pattern is omission in interrogatives. Such omission forms another continuum from relatively formal to more informal: for example, *Do you want another drink?* → *You want another drink?* → *Want another drink?* The rule here seems to be (a) omit the auxiliary (in this case *do*) and (b) omit *you*. It is clear, however, that these omissions are absolutely rule governed, since the subject *you* cannot be omitted unless the auxiliary has been omitted (cf. **Do want another drink?*). Once again, the more informal syntactic constructions discussed in this section do not constitute "careless," "sloppy," or "incorrect" English. The key to their use is appropriateness. Suppose, for example, that you knock on a friend's door and a voice from inside asks *Who's there?* You respond with *It is I* (rather than *It's me*). The use of this extremely formal construction (with a nominative case pronoun following an uncontracted form of *be*) is clearly inappropriate in this case.

Before leaving these examples of stylistic variation, we want to make one final point concerning the central concept of appropriateness. All of the examples we have covered in this section on stylistic variation involve standard English. The only difference between, say, *Who did you speak to?* and *To whom did you speak?* is a matter of register. There are times, however, when the use of even nonstandard forms is appropriate. For example, an African American adolescent from the inner city would in all likelihood be ostracized by his friends on the street if he were to address them in standard English, no matter how informal the style. He would be better off speaking AAVE under the circumstances, because anything else would be inappropriate. Roger Shuy, a well-known sociolinguist, has told a similar story about his experiences. While in college, he got a summer job working on a loading dock in his home town. At first, he was shunned by his co-workers, lower-working-class men who worked on the dock year round. The fact that he was excluded from their circle bothered him and pretty soon he figured out the problem: He was speaking standard English, which was inappropriate in this situation. Once he started using some nonstandard forms (e.g., *ain't, he don't, me and him went,* etc.), he was accepted into the group.

Exercise K

1. When a speaker attempts to emulate a stylistic register that he or she is not completely familiar with, a phenomenon known as **structural hypercorrection** may result. This term describes the use of a structure associated with a more formal register in a linguistic environment where it is not typically used. Now consider the following data.

    A. To whom should I speak?
    B. Whom did you see?
    C. Whom is taking you to dinner?

    a. Which sentence illustrates structural hypercorrection?
    b. What principle has the speaker of these sentences apparently learned?
    c. What principle has the speaker failed to learn?

Exercise K *Continued*

†**2.** In one of her comedy routines, Lily Tomlin introduced the character of Ernestine, a rather obnoxious telephone operator. A typical utterance from Ernestine might be *Is this the party to whom I was just speaking to?*

a. How would you render this utterance in a more informal style?

b. Which forms and constructions does Tomlin use to help characterize Ernestine's personality?

3. What changes might occur in the following sentence if it were spoken in a more informal style: *From whom is he taking a psychology course?*

Summary

The theory of language variation makes use of such concepts as regional, social, and stylistic variation; dialect; social markedness; standard and nonstandard forms; gender; and register. We have seen that one variety of language can differ from another in terms of its lexicon, phonology, morphology, and syntax. Perhaps most importantly, we have seen that language variation is highly systematic, with nonstandard forms often reflecting a more predictable system than their standard counterparts.

SUPPLEMENTARY READINGS

Cassidy, F., & Hall, J. H. (1985, 1992, 1996, 2002). *Dictionary of American regional English,* 4 vols. Cambridge, MA: Harvard University Press.

Eckert, P., & McConnell-Ginet, S. (2003). *Language and gender.* Cambridge, England: Cambridge University Press.

Fasold, R. (1984). *The sociolinguistics of society.* New York: Blackwell.

Fasold, R. (1990). *The sociolinguistics of language.* Cambridge, MA: Blackwell.

Green, L. J. (2002). *African American English: A linguistic introduction.* Cambridge, England: Cambridge University Press.

Tannen, D. (1990). *You just don't understand: Women and men in conversation.* New York: William Morrow.

Wolfram, W., Adger, C. T., & Christian, D. (1999). *Dialects in schools and communities.* Mahwah, NJ: Erlbaum.

Wolfram, W., & Schilling-Estes, N. (1998). *American English: Dialects and variation.* Malden, MA: Blackwell.

You are now prepared to read all of these works. Wolfram and Schilling-Estes is a recent introductory text offering treatments of regional, social, and gender variation in American English. The volumes of *DARE* (Cassidy and Hall) are the result of over 30 years of research on regional expressions found in the United States; these four volumes cover terms beginning with the letters A–Sk. The books by Fasold are in-depth texts covering the sociology of language (where linguistic factors are brought to bear on the study of society) and sociolinguistics (where social factors are brought to bear on the study of linguistics). The books by Eckert and McConnell-Ginet and by Green provide comprehensive introductions to language and gender and to African American English, respectively. Tannen's work also discusses language and gender issues. Wolfram, Adger, and Christian is an excellent discussion of dialect issues that concern professionals in the language arts and speech-language pathology.

Supplementary Exercises

1. Mark the following statements true or false.
   - **a.** T F Linking [r] is a phonological feature of Southern English.
   - **b.** T F Male speakers are more likely to use nonstandard forms (e.g., [dɪs] for *this*) than are female speakers.
   - **c.** T F Girls tend to use more direct directives (e.g., *Put that piece here*) than boys do.
   - **d.** T F Dialects of different languages are mutually unintelligible.
2. Consider the following dialects of English.

	Dialect A	Dialect B
police	/pəlís/	/pólis/
hotel	/hotέl/	/hótɛl/
July	/ǰəláɪ/	/ǰúlaɪ/
insurance	/ɪnšʊ́rəns/	/ɪ́nšərəns/
Detroit	/dətrɔ́ɪt/	/dítrɔɪt/

   - **a.** What is the principle for assigning stress in Dialect A? (Assume stress is assigned from the right.)
   - **b.** What is the principle for assigning stress in Dialect B? (Assume stress is assigned from the left.)
   - **c.** Which principle is simpler?
   - **d.** Which dialect is more socially marked?
3. Some nonstandard forms actually fill gaps or regularize exceptions in the standard English system, as was the case with *hisself* and *theirselves*. Now consider another case: all but one of the following phrases can be contracted in two different ways; the exceptional case has only one contracted form.
   - **A.** I am not
   - **B.** We are not
   - **C.** You are not
   - **D.** He/She is not
   - **E.** They are not
   - **a.** Which phrase has only one contracted form in standard English?
   - **b.** By analogy with the other four phrases, how would the "missing" contracted form for this phrase be constructed? Give a phonological representation for this form.
   - **c.** Assume, first, that two consecutive nasals cannot occur in the same syllable in English (e.g., *mnemonic* is represented phonemically as /nimánɪk/) and, second, that in some dialects of English the vowel before a nasal is raised (e.g., *can't* is pronounced as [kʰɛ̃nt] rather than as [kʰæ̃nt]). Apply these principles to the form you constructed for (b). What nonstandard form seems to fill the role of the "missing" contracted form?
4. Weasel Podowski handed in the following paragraph to his English teacher, Miss Movable Feast.

   Muffy pulled out her overnight case. She plan to go to her frien's house the nex day. She had been there before. She walked a mile to get there. She wish she did not have to walk all the way.

Miss Feast, who is a friend of yours, claims that Weasel has no sense of time, because he makes so many "tense errors." You realize Miss Feast's mistake.

a. What part of Weasel's grammatical system is responsible for these errors?

b. Write a rule (in formal notation) that accounts for these errors.

5. Consider the following vowel contrasts between General American English and certain South Midland dialects (southern Indiana down to northern Alabama, Maryland over to Arkansas).

	General American	South Midland
fish	[fɪš]	[fiš]
fifth	[fɪfθ]	[fɪfθ]
measure	[mɛžer]	[mežər]
left	[lɛft]	[lɛft]
push	[pʊš]	[puš]
itch	[ɪč]	[ič]
fresh	[frɛš]	[freš]
butcher	[bʊčər]	[bučər]
puss	[pʊs]	[pʊs]

a. What generalization can you state about the difference between the vowels in these two dialects?

b. Construct a formal rule that would change the relevant vowels in the General American dialect to those in the South Midland dialect.

6. Cassidy (1981) notes that in the South and Southwest *nother* is a separate word meaning 'other' as in *That's a whole nother thing.* Explain the origin of the form *nother.*

7. Dave says [vihɪgə] for *vehicle.* What two phonological processes is Dave applying that do not apply in the Standard English pronunciation of this word?

8. Wolfram and Fasold (1974:208–211) point out that some tests used to diagnose articulation problems in children contain items that may be biased against speakers of certain regional or social dialects. For example, if a child is asked to name a picture of a pie and says [pa] rather than [paɪ], this response may be scored as an error. Explain how each of the following forms might lead to similar problems if used on an articulation test, due to regional or social variations from the standard pronunciation. Include a phonemic transcription of how each word might be pronounced due to dialect influence, and identify the phonological process responsible for the variation.

a. death
b. felt
c. they
d. Ken
e. test

9. A bar in Baton Rouge has a sign over the jukebox that reads *Don't use nickels in judebox.* Explain how *jukebox* becomes *judebox* phonologically.

10. Assume a speaker has been told to say *running* instead of *runnin'*. The speaker then extends this treatment to forms like *mountain* and *button.*

a. What forms will result?

b. What principle has the speaker misinterpreted?

c. What general phenomenon do the forms in (a) illustrate?

11. In a study reported by Fasold (1984:258–59), college freshmen were tested to see whether they would use *is* or *are* in the frame *There* ________ *about five minutes left.* Following this performance test, they were asked to self-report on which verb they had used and also to judge one of the verbs as more "correct." Figure 7.7 shows the results (P = performance test, R = self-report, and C = judgment as correct).

    Based on the graph, mark the following statements true or false.

    a. T F The form judged "correct" by most speakers is the same one actually used by most speakers.

    b. T F Most speakers think that they actually use an "incorrect" form.

    c. T F The form judged "correct" is more formal than the form actually used by most speakers.

    d. T F It appears that most speakers are able to give a reliable report of the forms that they themselves use.

12. What forms might result from structural hypercorrection of the following forms?

    a. two children

    b. Bob Johnson's car

    c. I want a cookie.

13. The phrase *What can I do you for?* is sometimes used facetiously for *What can I do for you?* Explain how the underlying structure of the facetious phrase differs from that of its Standard English counterpart.

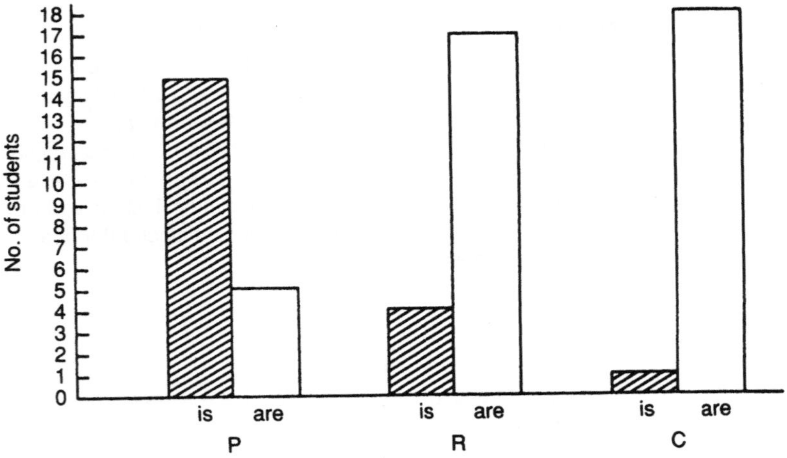

Number of subjects who used *is*/*are* in performance tests (P), who reported *is*/*are* as the form they used (R), and who considered *is*/*are* correct (C).

FIGURE 7.7 Results of performance test, self-reported usage, and judgments as correct

Source: From Ralph Fasold (1984), *The Sociolinguistics of Society.* New York: Blackwell. Reprinted with permission.

Exploratory Exercises

1. In addition to the forms noted in Exercise C.2, British English contains many informal words and phrases not used in the United States, such as those listed below. What is the U.S. equivalent of each item? Try to construct a sentence for each item that uses the word or expression idiomatically. You may want to consult a source like the British-American online dictionary at http://www.bbcamerica.com/britain/dictionary.jsp.

   Bob's your uncle
   cheeky
   chuffed
   doddle
   fancy
   flash
   give it some wellie
   Give over!
   gobsmacked
   knackered
   knickers in a twist
   over the moon
   posh
   toff
   twee
   whinging
   wind up

2. The following movies and TV series portray characters with regional, social, and ethnic dialects. Select one of these movies (or several episodes of a series) and prepare an inventory of some of the dialect features that you find. Focus on phonological and lexical features, although you may also be able to find morphological and syntactic features if social variation is involved.

   As a more advanced project, determine how accurately the dialect is portrayed if the actor is not a native speaker of it. For example, are any features exaggerated? You may also want to consider any personality or character traits that are associated with speakers of the dialect.

   The Andy Griffith Show
   Blown Away
   Clueless
   The Color Purple
   Eight Mile
   Fargo
   Ghosts of Mississippi
   Goodbye Columbus
   JFK
   Malibu's Most Wanted
   Mr. Saturday Night
   My Cousin Vinny
   My Fair Lady
   The Office (British version)
   Quiz Show
   Sling Blade
   The Sopranos
   Steel Magnolias
   Thirteen Days

3. Examine a catalog or website that sells clothing primarily for women (e.g., Talbots) and one that sells clothing primarily for men (e.g., Cabela's). What differences, if any, do you notice in their use of color terms?

4. An article analyzing the campaign strategies of 2004 Democratic presidential candidate Wesley Clark included the following statement: "Clark's embrace of flag, faith and family plays very well in Red State America, where the Democrats are hurting. Last week, as he traveled through eight Southern states on a two-day 'True Grits Tour,' wavin' the flag and droppin' his g's, he seemed exuberant" (Thomas & Klaidman 2004:23). Discuss this characterization of

Clark's language from a sociolinguistic perspective, looking in particular at how dialect features might be used as part of a campaign strategy. You may want to include data about other dialect features that you have heard used by this or other political candidates.

5. Review some of the findings from the dialect survey at http://hcs.harvard.edu/~golder/dialect/. Can you draw any inferences about the survey's methodology (i.e., the way that respondents were selected or solicited, the way that questions were constructed, and the medium through which the survey was conducted)? How might methodological considerations affect your interpretation of the survey results? What might you need to know about the methodology in order to judge how interpret the results? Explain.

6. Cockney Rhyming Slang is a system said to have its origins in the language of thieves in 19th-century London. It now survives as a dialect feature used to evoke "colorful" working-class characters in British media and as the basis for tourist items such as dictionaries of rhyming slang (similar to the books on "how to talk Southern" that one can find in parts of the United States). Consider the following classic examples of rhyming slang.

Cockney Rhyming Slang	Meaning
apples and pears	stairs
butcher's hook	look
grasshopper	copper
hit or miss	kiss
Lady Godiva	fiver (i.e., £5 note, a unit of currency)
trouble and strife	wife

The rhyming slang phrase may be used either in full or in an abbreviated form. Hence a speaker might say, "I caught him coming down the apples and pears with his trouble" or "Come and have a butcher's at this."

a. Based on these examples, write a rule for forming Cockney Rhyming Slang.

b. How are the supposed origins of Cockney Rhyming Slang related to its use?

c. What might a speaker mean who says "Use your loaf!"?

d. What does it mean to "grass on" someone? How might this term have evolved?

e. According to the Oxford dictionaries, a new genre called Popney Rhyming Slang is alive and well and being added to constantly. Examples of this genre include *Britney Spears* for *beers* and *Billy Ocean* for *suntan lotion.* Refer to an online dictionary of Cockney Rhyming Slang such as the one at http://www.cockneyrhymingslang.co.uk/ and find additional examples of the Popney variety. (Warning: Since slang terms often replace taboo words, the translations of some entries may contain offensive language!)

7. **Eye dialect** is a written strategy used by authors to suggest that a speaker is illiterate or otherwise not a speaker of standard English. However, the form used in eye dialect differs from the standard form only in spelling, not in pronunciation. For example, an author might record a character's utterance as "Sez who?" instead of "Says who?" Note that *sez* and *says* would both be pronounced [sɛz]. Hence the use of *sez* is an instance of eye dialect.

With this concept in mind, examine the following newspaper ad for a pizza shop in Duluth, Minnesota, a heavily Scandinavian area. (Sven & Ole's is a restaurant in northern Minnesota; the pizza shop referred to in the ad is a new branch of it.)

Sven & Ole
Vood Like Tew
Congradeulate
Jim & Renee
On Da Opening of Dere New
Store, Sven & Ole's Pizza
Express! Da Store iss Located
At 5 S. 13 Ave. E. inn Duluth's
Plaza Shopping Center and
Serves Da Finest Peetzahs and
Sandviches from Lake
Superior's North Shore

a. What forms in this ad qualify as eye dialect? What forms represent pronunciations that actually differ from standard English pronunciations?

b. Based on this sample, what would you infer to be some of the phonological properties of Scandinavian languages? That is, what are some ways in which the phonological system represented in this ad appears to differ from that of standard English?

c. What is the sociolinguistic purpose of using nonstandard spellings in this ad? That is, what effect do you think the advertiser is trying to achieve by deliberately using misspellings?

CHAPTER EIGHT

First-Language Acquisition

Language acquisition is the study of how human beings acquire a grammar: a set of semantic, syntactic, morphological, and phonological categories and rules that underlie their ability to speak and understand the language to which they are exposed. For example, a normal child born to English-speaking parents in the United States obviously is not born knowing English. By the age of 5, however, the child can speak and understand English with relative facility. Language acquisition is the study of how this transformation takes place—from a mental state in which the child does not possess a grammar of a particular language to a mental state in which the child does. As defined here, language acquisition does not include the process by which a person learns a language other than his or her native tongue. This process is called second-language acquisition and is discussed in Chapter 9. Keeping this distinction in mind, let's consider some observations we can make about the acquisition of a first language.

(1) A child acquiring English might form the plural of *foot* first as *foots,* then as *feets,* then as *feetses,* and finally as *feet.*

(2) A child acquiring English might form an interrogative as *Why I can't go?* instead of as *Why can't I go?*

(3) All normal children acquire a language, but not all children learn to read and write.

(4) Many children gain a fairly sophisticated facility with language before they master tasks such as tying their shoes, telling time, or adding numbers.

Observation (1) illustrates that language is acquired in stages. Observation (2) illustrates that language is not acquired through simple imitation: Adults don't say *Why I can't go?,* so the child cannot simply be mimicking the adult. Instead, the child infers a system of rules (i.e., a grammar) for forming sentences, based upon the language to which he or she is exposed. Observation (3) supports the hypothesis that human beings are genetically predisposed to acquire a language. That is, children do not *learn* a language in the way they learn to read and write, through conscious effort and instruction; rather they *acquire* a language in the same way they acquire their ability to walk, effortlessly and without instruction. Observation (4) suggests that language acquisition is subserved by a mental faculty designed specifically and solely for that purpose. In other words, language acquisition is not thought to be a function of intelligence or general intellectual abilities.

All of these phenomena have to do with language acquisition, the way we acquire the grammar of our first language. As usual, we will assume that the phenomena in observations (1–4) are systematic; that is, they are governed by a system of principles. What we will now try to do is construct a set of concepts that will account for these phenomena. Keep in mind that what follows is a theory designed to account for observations (1–4).

Prelinguistic Stages

In the first year of life, infants go through three stages of vocal production. The **crying** stage lasts from birth to around 2 months and includes other **reflexive,** or involuntary, sounds such as burping, coughing, sighing, and sneezing. Several types of cries may be distinguishable by caregivers—for example, cries signaling hunger, pain, anger, and loneliness. The **cooing** stage, characterized primarily by vowel-like sounds, lasts from about 2 to 5 months. Hulit and Howard note that cooing may be integrated into a simple turntaking routine with a caregiver: "In a typical exchange, the caregiver smiles and says something like 'Aren't you a sweetheart.' The infant responds with 'O-o-o-o-u-u-u-u,' and the caregiver imitates the coo. This cooing-imitation-cooing exchange can sometimes continue for fifteen minutes or longer, and most adults find it as delightful a communicative experience as the infant" (2002:115). Laughter also begins during this stage, at around 4 months.

The **babbling** stage, characterized by syllable-like consonant-vowel sounds, begins to develop at about the age of 5 months and is established by 6 months. Babbling lasts till about 12 months and continues into the early linguistic stages that begin around 12 months. There are several types of babbling. **Reduplicative** or **syllabic babbling** consists of repetitions of a syllable, such as [ba-ba-ba]. **Variegated babbling,** which occurs somewhat later in the babbling stage, is characterized by strings that vary a consonant or vowel, such as [pa-ga-ba-ga] or [pu-pi-pa-pi]. **Jargon babbling,** which also begins later, is characterized by prosodic or intonational patterns reminiscent of adult speech. These vocalizations may give an adult listener the impression that the child is "asking a question" or "making an announcement" because of the overall intonational pattern of the child's production. The babbling of babies acquiring English tends to contain stops, nasals, and glides found in the English consonant inventory, but not most fricatives, affricates, or liquids. Vocalizations during the babbling period are described as language-*like* rather than as language. This is because the vocalizations do not reflect a set of sounds used consistently to refer to a particular referent. However, toward the end of the babbling stage, babies start to use forms sometimes referred to as **protowords.** A protoword is a form that does not correspond to an adult form but that is used consistently by a particular child for a particular referent or situation. For example, a child might consistently say "uh-uh-uh" while trying to get food or drink (Hulit & Howard 2002:20).

Interestingly, recent studies indicate that deaf babies babble on the same timetable that hearing babies do—except in a different modality. Researcher Laura-Ann Petitto and colleagues have studied "manual" or "silent" babbling, a behavior exhibited both by deaf babies and by hearing babies of profoundly deaf parents. For both groups of babies, the primary exposure to language is the sign language used by their caregivers. Both groups of babies use hand activity that is distinctly different from other rhythmic hand activity and that has the same traits as vocal babbling: the manual babbling uses syllabic structure based on units from the larger inventory of signs; like vocal babbling, the manual babbling is used without meaning or reference. Petitto and colleagues (2001) hypothesize that the innate predisposition to acquire language may be attuned to structural and rhythmic features that characterize all natural human language, regardless of whether the infant encounters it in a spoken or a signed modality.

In addition to these productive capabilities, the infant's perceptual capabilities also develop during the first year of life. It is worth noting that infants are able to perceive differences between pairs of stimuli such as [ba] and [pa] or [ba] and [ga]. Several ingenious methods have been devised for testing the perception of infants as young as 1 month old. One method, known as **high-amplitude sucking** or **nonnutritive sucking,** involves having the child suck on a pacifier which is connected to a monitoring device. The child hears a repeated stimulus for several minutes (e.g., [ba-ba-ba-ba-ba]) and gradually attains a steady sucking rate (e.g., 25 sucks per minute). This "steady state" sucking is taken as a sign that the infant is used to the stimulus and no longer perceives it as a novelty. Then a new stimulus is presented (e.g., [pa-pa-pa-pa-pa]). The infant's sucking rate typically increases significantly at the onset of the new stimulus (e.g., to 50 sucks per minute) before subsiding to the previous "steady state." From this change, researchers can infer that the infant perceived the change from [ba] to [pa] and thus is capable of discriminating between [b] and [p].

The apparently innate ability of infants to perceive at least some auditory contrasts that correspond to differences in voicing, place, and manner of articulation may contribute to the relatively rapid pace at which language acquisition proceeds (a point discussed further toward the end of this chapter). At the same time, it would be misguided to conclude that infants can comprehend language; instead, it would be more accurate to say that they can discriminate between acoustic stimuli that also happen to be linguistically significant. For example, researchers have found that chinchillas are capable of perceiving these same contrasts, but we would not want to conclude from this that chinchillas can understand human language. Perhaps the best way to regard the ability to perceive auditory contrasts is that it forms a necessary, but not a sufficient, prerequisite to acquiring spoken language.

Exercise A

1. The word *infant* is generally used to describe a human under the age of 12 months. Look up the etymology (historical source) of the word *infant* in a dictionary. In what sense does the word's origin accurately reflect the state of, say, a child who is 1 month old? In what sense is it inaccurate?
2. Boysson-Bardies describes the following experiment: "we presented adults with sample pairs of babbling by eight-month-old French babies (recorded in Paris), Arab babies (recorded in Algiers), and Cantonese babies (recorded in Hong Kong). . . . The adults were asked to indicate—by guessing, if necessary—which one of two successively heard samples they thought was the babbling of the French baby. Their answers were correct more than 70 percent of the time" (1999:48).

   What do you conclude from these results? What additional information might you need about the experiment in order to refine your conclusions?

Linguistic Stages

In this section, we will look at the stages of language acquisition from the perspective of the four components of grammar: phonology, morphology, syntax, and semantics, in that order. However, before getting into details, we want to clarify several potential points of confusion.

First, in acquiring language, children go through more or less the same stages at more or less the same time. These stages, however, represent general trends, and every child does not follow them in lock-step fashion. For example, a child will typically acquire stops (/p, b, t, d, g, k/ in English) before liquids (/l, r/ in English). This does not mean, however, that every normal child will acquire all of the stops, completely and correctly, before any of the liquids. Likewise, a child will typically acquire grammatical morphemes (e.g., inflectional affixes, prepositions, articles, and so on in English) by the age of 5. Again, this does not mean that no normal child will acquire them earlier or later; rather, it is simply a general pattern.

Second, in this chapter we deal primarily with the acquisition of English. However, the principles discussed here typically apply, where they are relevant, to the acquisition of other first languages as well. For example, children tend to correctly interpret complex sentences in which the order of the clauses reflects the order of events before they correctly interpret sentences in which this ordering relation does not hold. As a result, a child acquiring English will typically be able to correctly interpret *John ate before he came home* at an earlier stage than *Before John came home, he ate.* This general principle, however, seems to apply to children acquiring any first language.

Third, it is much more difficult to draw inferences about first-language acquisition than about almost any other area of linguistics. This is because language acquisition researchers must deal with immature informants (i.e., infants and children). One problem for researchers is interpreting the structure underlying a child's utterance. For example, a child whose mother is trying to dress him may utter *No hat.* Is such an utterance a structured sentence, or just an unstructured string of words? Does it signal the absence of a hat (i.e., 'I don't have a hat') or the rejection of a hat (i.e., 'I don't want to wear that hat')? It is often impossible to answer such questions conclusively and without some reliance on nonlinguistic evidence such as context, the child's facial expression, and so forth. Another problem is that researchers cannot question a child as they can an adult speaker. For example, a linguist can ask an adult informant such questions as "Is the sentence *Mario put the car* acceptable in English?" and "Are the sentences *John ate the cake* and *The cake was eaten by John* paraphrases of each other?" In the example just mentioned, however, it would be quite difficult (to say the least) to elicit from the child whether *No hat* means 'I don't have a hat' or 'I don't want to wear that hat.' In short, keep in mind the inherent problems involved in using infants and children as research subjects.

Exercise B

1. Boysson-Bardies (1999:121) describes the following procedure for testing 2-year-old children's recognition of words, based on the duration of the child's gaze: "The children were seated on their mothers' knee and, from a speaker situated between two television screens, a woman's voice was heard asking 'Where is the truck?' Images then simultaneously

(continued)

Exercise B *Continued*

appeared on the two screens—on the left screen, a truck; on the right screen, a shoe. The woman's voice then said, 'Find the truck.' "

What problems might arise in this experimental procedure that could lead to "false positives"? If you were using this procedure, what might you do to eliminate the problem? You may want to draw a sketch of the experimental situation to help you visualize the procedure.

2. In "The Acquisition of Language," Breyne Moskowitz cites an interchange between researcher Ronald Scollon and a 19-month-old girl named Brenda.

BRENDA: [k^ha] (4 times)

SCOLLON: What?

BRENDA: Go. Go.

SCOLLON: (undecipherable)

BRENDA: [baɪš] (9 times)

SCOLLON: What? Oh, bicycle? Is that what you said?

BRENDA: [na]

SCOLLON: No?

BRENDA: Not.

SCOLLON: No. I got it wrong.

Now consider how Moskowitz interprets this exchange: "Brenda was not yet able to combine two words syntactically to express 'Hearing that car reminds me that we went on the bus yesterday. No, not on a bicycle.' She could express that concept, however, by combining words sequentially" (1979:91). Comment on how much of Moskowitz's interpretation is justified by Brenda's utterances.

Acquisition of Phonology

Let's look at some representative examples of the stages a child goes through in acquiring the phonology of his or her language. Note that when we say that a child *acquires* such-and-such a segment, we don't mean simply that he or she produces a sound that an adult observer perceives as that segment. Rather, we mean that the child has actually incorporated that segment into his or her phonological system. Such a judgment, of course, requires interpretation by the analyst—which, as we just saw, is a tricky business.

Vowels. Children exposed to English typically acquire /a, i, u/ at an early stage. This tendency reflects two principles. First, extreme values in the vowel system tend to be acquired before intermediate values. In this instance, the child is filling in the extreme points of the vowel triangle as shown in Figure 8.1. (For reference, see the vowel chart in Chapter 6.) Note that /a, i, u/ are maximally distinct from each other: /i/ and /u/ are maximally distinct from each other along the horizontal dimension [±back]; and both /i/ and /u/, in turn, are maximally distinct from /a/ along the vertical dimensions [±high] and [±low]. Second, children typically acquire segments common among the world's languages before they acquire those that are relatively rare. For example, /a/ is universal (it occurs in all languages), and /i, u/ are nearly

	[−back]	[+back]
[+high]	i	u
[+low]		a

FIGURE 8.1 The child's first vowels

universal (they occur in the vast majority of languages). Thus, the interaction of both principles predicts that /a, i, u/ will be acquired early, and the other intermediate vowels will come later.

Consonants. Children exposed to English typically acquire /p, b, m, w/ at a relatively early stage. This tendency reflects several principles. First, **place of articulation** tends to be acquired from the front of the mouth to the back. In particular, labials are generally acquired before alveolars, palatals, and velars. (For reference, consult the consonant chart in Chapter 6.) For example, the labial stop /p/ would be expected to appear before the velar /k/. Second, **manner of articulation** tends to be acquired from most to least consonant-like. In particular, stops and nasals, both of which require complete closure of the oral cavity, are generally acquired before liquids and fricatives. For example, among the alveolar consonants in English, we would expect /t/ before /l/.

Phonological processes affecting consonants are quite common in normal phonological development. Some of these processes involve substitution of one type of consonant for another. For example, the fact that liquids are acquired relatively late is evidenced by the phonological process of **gliding,** in which a glide, typically [w], substitutes for a liquid. A child using gliding may pronounce *room* as [wum] and *love* as [wʌv]. The interdental fricatives /θ, ð/ are also acquired relatively late, in addition to being rare segments among the world's languages. Thus, it is not surprising to find that children use **stopping**—the substitution of a stop consonant for a fricative—in forms such as [dæt] for *that.* Other fricatives may undergo stopping as well; for example, a child may produce *zoo* as [du]. Another process, **fronting,** replaces a palatal or velar consonant with one that has a more forward place of articulation. For example, a child may say [do] instead of [go]. Since velar consonants are especially susceptible to this process, it is sometimes called **velar fronting.**

Other processes reflect assimilation, which as you may recall from Chapter 6 involves modifying a segment to make it more similar to another segment in the environment. **Consonant harmony** is a common type of assimilation in child language. This is a process in which a consonant in one syllable assimilates to a consonant in another syllable. For example, the word *doggie* may be produced as [gɔgi].

Voicing changes may occur as well. In **prevocalic voicing,** a voiceless consonant in front of a vowel or other voiced segment is replaced by a voiced consonant. For example, *cow* may be pronounced as [gaʊ]. Note that prevocalic voicing can be analyzed as an instance of assimilation: all vowels are [+voice], so the substitution of the [+voice] consonant [g] for the [–voice] consonant [k] reflects assimilation to the [+voice] property of the vowel. Conversely, in **final devoicing,** a voiced consonant at the end of a word is replaced by a voiceless consonant. For example, a child may pronounce *bed* as [bɛt].

Let's now consider some of the forms predicted by the interaction of the principles governing the acquisition of vowels and consonants. Variations on *ma* /ma/ and *pa* /pa/ are extremely widespread as early forms for female and male parents, respectively. This is no accident: as we have just seen, /m, p, a/ are all acquired very early. Another predictable form is Dennis the Menace's *telebision* (with a /b/) for *television* (with a /v/). Even though Dennis is a fiction of Hank Ketchum's imagination, this example of stopping is based on fact. Our principles governing child phonology predict that the stop /b/, which is acquired early, will substitute for the fricative /v/, which is acquired somewhat later. Note, incidentally, that our theory predicts that /b/ alone (not just any stop) will substitute for /v/. The phoneme /b/ is the only stop in English that agrees with /v/ in both place of articulation and voicing, since both /b/ and /v/ are [+labial] and [+voice].

Likewise, these principles are often reflected in children's productions which become "lexicalized" into proper names. One child, for example, referred to his mother with a form perceived as /bámbi/, presumably for *mommy* /mámi/. This child had apparently acquired /b/ and was in the process of acquiring /m/, thus substituting the voiced labial stop for the voiced labial nasal in /mámi/, which became /bámbi/. In fact, the child's family began to refer to the mother as *Bombi.* Another example is the name *Teeter* /titɛr/ from *sister* /sɪstər/. In this case, the child had an aunt whom the mother called *Sister,* a nickname common in the South. The child, who apparently had acquired the stop /t/ but not the fricative /s/, substituted /t/ for /s/, since both are [+alveolar] and [–voice]. This resulted in a production that the adults perceived as /titɛr/, and the aunt from then on was known in the family as *Teeter.*

Syllable Structure. The simplest type of syllable found among the world's languages is CV, where C = consonant and V = vowel. All languages contain words made up of CV syllables. In fact, Japanese words, with a few predictable exceptions, are all of this form: for example, *Fujiyama* and *Hasegawa.* English, however, has a quite complex syllable structure; for example, we have words like *spy* (CCV), *ask* (VCC), *spry* (CCCV), *asked* (VCCC), and even *splints* (CCCVCCC). Thus, it comes as no surprise that a child will go through several stages in acquiring the full range of syllable types in English. This acquisition generally proceeds in the following order (McLeod et al., 2001):

(C) V	(initial C is optional)
CV	(initial C)
CVC	(final C)
CVCC	(final cluster)
CCVCC	(initial cluster)

For example, a child trying to pronounce *stoves* might proceed through the following stages: [o] or [t^ho], [t^ho], [t^hov], [t^hovz], and then [stovz]. As reflected by these forms, **simplification** or **reduction** of consonant clusters is quite common in child language. For example, we might hear [skǽmbəl] for *scramble* [skrǽmbəl], [dĩŋk] for [drĩŋk], and so on. Another example of a child's production becoming lexicalized as a new word is *tummy* /tʌ́mi/ for *stomach* /stʌ́mɪk/. Note, first, that *stomach* begins with an /st/ cluster. A child who has not yet acquired clusters will simplify /st/ to /t/. (Recall that stops are generally acquired before fricatives.) Note also that the second syllable of *stomach* ends in a final consonant /k/. If the child has not yet acquired syllable-final consonants, the /k/ will be omitted, resulting in /tʌ́mɪ/. Finally, English has a rule that tenses a lax vowel in word-final position. For example, *said* contains the lax vowel /ɛ/ followed by a consonant, but *say* contains the tense vowel /e/, since it is in word-final position. This vowel-tensing rule changes /ɪ/ to /i/, yielding /tʌ́mi/. Again, the point is that the child's acquisition of phonology is rule-governed and predictable.

As this example also illustrates, the stage at which a cluster is acquired depends to some extent not only on the number of consonants it contains but also on which consonants comprise it. Beginning around 2 years of age, children acquiring English begin to produce clusters like [fw], [pw], and [bw], even though adult forms containing these clusters are not present in the ambient language (McLeod et al. 2001:100). Hence we may hear a young child may say something like [pwi] for *pretty.* Stop + liquid clusters such as /pl/ are typically mastered earlier than fricative + liquid clusters such as /sl/. Before mastering such clusters, the child might either simplify the cluster by deleting the liquid, producing [pet] for *plate,* or use **epenthesis** (vowel insertion) to break up the cluster, producing [pəlet] for *plate.* At the later end of the spectrum, some word-initial clusters such as the /θr/ in *three,* the /spl/ in *splash,* and the /spr, str, skr/ sequences in *spring, string,* and *scrape* may not be mastered until the child is 7 or 8 years old, with 100 percent mastery coming as late as 9 years old (McLeod 2001:104). The tendency toward CV syllable structure also reflects the fact that a particular consonant phoneme is not typically acquired in all word positions at the same time. For example, a child may acquire /t/ in initial position by age 3½ years, but not acquire /t/ in final position until age 4½ years. Generally speaking, segments are first acquired in word-initial position.

Another common syllable process, especially among the child's first 50 words, is **reduplication** (syllable repetition). This process can be seen in forms like *mama, papa, peepee,* and so on. Partial reduplication (the repetition of part of a syllable) may also occur; very often an /i/ is substituted for the final vowel segment, as in *mommy* and *daddy.* Note that both types of reduplication result in CVCV word structure, which uses the universal CV syllable structure. Other phonological processes may also act to create basic CV syllable structure. **Final consonant reduction,** for example, deletes a post-vocalic, word-final obstruent, turning CVC into CV (e.g., *good* /gʊd/ pronounced [gʊ]). Likewise, **blending** combines features of two adjacent segments into a single segment, turning CCV into CV (e.g., *snow* /sno/ pronounced [n̥o]; an open circle under a segment indicates voicelessness).

Exercise C

1. For each set of structures (a–d), which construction would children exposed to English be most likely to acquire first?

   a. /ɪ/ /a/ /æ/

   b. /k/ /č/ /p/

   †c. /t/ /s/ /r/

   d. VC CV CVC

(continued)

Exercise C *Continued*

2. Assume a child is acquiring English. Which of the following representations of *stick* would be most likely to appear first: [tʰɪk] or [stɪ]? Why?
3. In terms of syllable structure alone, which word from each set would a child exposed to English be expected to acquire earliest? (Hint: Syllable structure is best determined from a phonemic transcription rather than from spelling.)
   - **a.** *dog, dough, stow, March*
   - **b.** *train, play, kick, past*
4. A child acquiring English produces the following forms.

	Adult Form	Child's Form
stop	/stap/	[tap]
slide	/slaɪd/	[laɪd]
Sue	/su/	[su]
Casey	/kési/	[kési]
house	/haʊs/	[haʊs]

   Formulate a phonological rule to describe the way that the child's forms differ from the adult's.

5. How would the child described in question (4) be expected to pronounce *smoke?*
   a. [mok] **b.** [smok] **c.** [smo] **d.** [mo]
6. Consider the forms /titi/, /pupu/, and /kaka/. These forms illustrate ________.
   - **a.** reduplication
   - **b.** the three earliest vowels acquired by children
   - **c.** blending
   - **d.** all of the above
   - **e.** (a) and (b) only
7. Identify the phonological process(es) illustrated by each of the following forms. If more than one process is involved, explain whether they would have to apply in any particular order.
   - **†a.** [sɪ́wi] for *silly*
   - **b.** [tíbí] for *TV*
   - **c.** [bǽŋki] for *blanket*
   - **d.** [bɛ́wi] for *very*
   - **e.** [l̥o] for *slow*
   - **†f.** [dɔ] for *dog*
   - **g.** [kwézi] for *crazy*
   - **h.** [gɪp] for *skip*
   - **i.** [pəlíz] for *please*
   - **j.** [sip] for *sheep*
   - **k.** [ti] for *key*
   - **l.** [gʌk] for *truck*
   - **m.** [bap] for *stop*
   - **n.** [dɪm] for *Jim*
   - **o.** [bɪk] for *big*

Acquisition of Morphology

We will now examine a few representative examples of the stages a child goes through in acquiring the morphology of his or her language. Around the age of 2 years, the child begins to form two-word utterances; around the age of 3 years, these gradually increase to more than two words. Grammatical morphemes gradually begin to appear during this multiword stage, although their acquisition is not usually complete until around age 5 years. The class of grammatical morphemes includes inflectional and derivational affixes, among other things. (See Chapter 5 for a review of these concepts.)

Roger Brown's classic study (1973) found the following order of acquisition for 14 common grammatical morphemes in English.

Order of acquisition for 14 grammatical morphemes (based on Brown, 1973:274–277)

	MORPHEME	EXAMPLE
1.	present progressive	Mommy cry*ing.*
2–3.	prepositions *in* and *on*	Juice *in* cup; Doggie *on* chair.
4.	plural regular	Book*s* fall.
5.	past irregular	Cup *fell.*
6.	possessive	That Eve'*s* book.
7.	uncontractible copula (main verb) *be*	There he *is.*
8.	articles *a* and *the*	Doggie on *the* chair.
9.	past regular	Doggie *walked.*
10.	3rd person singular regular	He *wants* juice.
11.	3rd person singular irregular (*has, does*)	Mommy *has* juice.
12.	uncontractible auxiliary *be.*	Who is crying? Mommy *is.*
13.	contractible auxiliary *be*	Mommy'*s* crying.
14.	contractible copula (main verb) *be*	That'*s* Adam's truck.

We will look in detail at several trends related to the acquisition of these morphemes.

Inflectional Affixes. In general, the {PRES PART} affix, spelled *-ing,* is acquired fairly early, presumably because this affix shows little phonological variation; that is, it always appears as /ɪŋ/ or /ɪn/. The morphemes {PAST}, {PLU}, {POSS}, and {PRES}, on the other hand, are all acquired somewhat later, presumably because they exhibit more phonological variation. For example, {PAST} shows up variously as /t/ (as in *walked*), /d/ (as in *hugged*), and /əd/ (as in *added*). The rule governing this alternation involves three simple principles.

- If a verb ends in a voiceless segment other than /t/, add the voiceless segment /t/; *walk* ends in the voiceless segment /k/, so {PAST} shows up as /t/.
- If the verb ends in a voiced segment other than /d/, add the voiced segment /d/; *hug* ends in the voiced segment /g/, so {PAST} shows up as /d/.
- If the verb already ends in /t/ or /d/, add /əd/; *hate* ends in /t/, so {PAST} shows up as /əd/.

Note that the third principle is purely functional. If we were to simply add /t/ to *hate,* we would get /hett/, which is indistinguishable from the uninflected form /het/. The insertion of /ə/, however, breaks up the two /t/'s and we get /hétəd/.

Because of this phonological variation, it makes sense that a child acquiring English will take some time to infer the rules governing the various forms of {PAST}, which can be summarized as follows.

FINAL SEGMENT OF ROOT	**PHONOLOGICAL FORM OF {PAST}**	**EXAMPLE**
[–voice] (other than /t/)	/t/	walk-walked
[+voice] (other than /d/)	/d/	hug-hugged
/t, d/	/əd/	hate-hated

However, the fact that the child is inferring rules is unarguable. This can be seen by examining the acquisition of irregular {PAST} forms in English, which despite being irregular are quite common. A child might first use adult irregular forms (e.g., *went* or *broke*). These, however, are apparently just memorized forms, since the child quickly moves to a second stage in which the past tense is formed following the rule just outlined. At this stage, the child often overgeneralizes the regular {PAST} morpheme to irregular verbs, resulting in forms like *goed, breaked,* and even *wented.* The point to note is that these are phonologically well-formed. For example, *go* ends in the voiced segment /o/; thus the past tense should be formed by the addition of /d/, yielding /god/. Finally, the child learns that verbs like *go* and *break* are exceptional in that they have irregular past tense forms, and his or her usage begins to conform to the adult's.

The acquisition of {PLU}, generally spelled *-(e)s,* follows the same progression as that of {PAST}. The morpheme {PLU} shows up variously as /s/ (as in *ducks*), /z/ (as in *dogs*), and /əz/ (as in *horses*). The rule governing this alternation involves three principles.

- If the noun ends in a voiceless segment other than /s, š, č/, add the voiceless segment /s/; *duck* ends in /k/, so {PLU} shows up as /s/.
- If the noun ends in a voiced segment other than /z, ž, ǰ/, add the voiced segment /z/; *dog* ends in /g/, so {PLU} shows up as /z/.
- If the noun ends in /s, z, š, ž, č, ǰ/, add /əz/; *horse* ends in /s/, so {PLU} shows up as /əz/.

As was the case with {PAST}, the third principle is purely functional. If we were to simply add /s/ to *horse,* we would get /hɔrss/, which is indistinguishable from the uninflected form /hɔrs/. The insertion of /ə/, however, breaks up this sequence and we get /hɔ́rsəz/.

Once again, it makes sense that a child exposed to English would take some time to infer the rules governing the various phonological forms of {PLU}, which are summarized here.

FINAL SEGMENT OF ROOT	**PHONOLOGICAL FORM OF {PLU}**	**EXAMPLE**
[–voice] (other than /s, š, č/)	/s/	duck-ducks
[+voice] (other than /z, ž, ǰ/)	/z/	dog-dogs
/s, z, š, ž, č, ǰ/	/əz/	horse-horses

As with {PAST}, the fact that the child is acquiring rules is clear from examining the acquisition of irregular plural forms. For example, a child acquiring the plural of *foot* might first use the adult form *feet.* Once again, this seems to be simply a memorized form, since the child moves rapidly to a second stage in which he or she forms the plural following the rule just outlined, namely as *foots* or *feets.* Note that *foot* ends in a voiceless segment; thus the plural should be formed by adding /s/, resulting in /fʊts/. A third stage often follows in which the child treats *foots* or *feets* as an uninflected form, thus constructing the plural following the rule, namely as *footses* (or *feetses*). Note that *foots* (and *feets*) ends in /s/; thus the plural should be formed by adding /əz/, yielding *footses* /fʊtsəz/ (or *feetses*). Finally, the child learns that *foot* is exceptional in English in that it has an irregular plural form, and his or her usage begins to conform to the adult's.

The morphemes {POSS} and {PRES}, usually spelled *-'s* and *-(e)s,* respectively, show the same phonological variation as {PLU}. This is illustrated in the following chart.

	{PLU}	**{POSS]**	**{PRES}**
/s/	cats	Bart's	waits
/z/	cads	Bud's	wades
/əz/	cases	Bess's	winces

What is interesting, however, is that these three morphemes are not acquired at the same time. Instead, a child exposed to English typically acquires them in the following order: {PLU}, {POSS}, and then {PRES}. This indicates that the child acquires them as a function of their morphological, rather than their phonological, structure. The late Roman Jakobson (1971), a Harvard linguist, suggested an explanation for this order of acquisition: the smaller the domain to which an affix applies, the earlier the affix is acquired. Thus, {PLU} is acquired first because it affixes to nouns (e.g., *kids*). {POSS} is acquired next because it affixes to NPs (e.g., *the kid next door's dog*). (See Chapter 5 for a detailed discussion of this distinction.) {PRES} is acquired last because, even though it is affixed to verbs, it is a function of the entire sentence. That is, the affixation of {PRES} to a verb depends on its subject, and a subject plus a verb is essentially a sentence. Only a third-person singular subject takes an overt affix on a present tense verb (e.g., *The kid plays there* versus *The kids play there*). The distinctions among {PLU}, {POSS}, and {PRES} are summarized in the following chart.

ORDER OF ACQUISITION	**MORPHEME**	**DOMAIN**
1	{PLU}	N
2	{POSS}	NP
3	{PRES}	S

Derivational Affixes. The acquisition of derivational affixes is not as well understood as the acquisition of inflectional affixes. This is because English has only eight inflectional affixes, but many more derivational affixes. Moreover, many derivational affixes in English have been borrowed from Latin and Greek, whereas all inflectional affixes are native to

English. Thus, derivational affixes are associated with more advanced vocabulary, which is acquired relatively late; for example, the word *inconsolable* (from Latin) will typically come later than *unhappy* (native English). Nonetheless, we can make one generalization concerning the acquisition of derivational affixes: the more productive they are, the earlier they are acquired. A more productive affix is one that can be attached to a relatively large number of roots. For example, the *-ly* suffix, which forms an adverb from the corresponding adjective, is very productive, yielding forms such as *quick-quickly, careful-carefully,* and *intelligent-intelligently.* Likewise, the agentive suffix *-er,* which forms a noun from the corresponding verb, is quite productive: *love-lover, farm-farmer, drive-driver,* and so on. A less productive affix is one that can be attached to relatively few roots. For example, the suffix *-hood,* which typically forms an abstract noun from a concrete noun, is relatively unproductive: we have *father-fatherhood* and *mother-motherhood,* but not *uncle-*unclehood, aunt-*aunthood,* or *cousin-*cousinhood.*

We can close this section by stating simply that a child's acquisition of morphology is for the most part systematic and rule governed, even though some domains, such as the acquisition of derivational morphology, are not well understood.

Exercise D

1. A child exposed to English might go through the following stages in acquiring the rule for forming the past tense of verbs. At which stage has the child actually acquired a rule similar to that in the adult grammar?

   STAGE I: eat

   STAGE II: ate

   STAGE III: eated

   STAGE IV: ate

†2. A child acquiring English who says *feetses* for *feet* has apparently misanalyzed the root form to which the {PLU} suffix is attached. What is the root of *feetses* for this child?

3. Consider the following exchange reported by Aitchison (1985:96):

   CHILD: My teacher holded the baby rabbits and we patted them.

   ADULT: Did you say your teacher held the baby rabbits?

   CHILD: Yes.

   ADULT: What did you say she did?

   CHILD: She holded the baby rabbits and we patted them.

   ADULT: Did you say she held them tightly?

   CHILD: No, she holded them loosely.

   What does this exchange illustrate about the relative processes of acquiring regular and irregular verbs?

4. A 3-year-old imitated a Folgers coffee commercial as follows: *The best part of waking up is* SOLDIERS *in your cup.* What word-formation process is the child utilizing? (Hint: See Chapter 5.)

Acquisition of Syntax

Children's progress toward adult-like syntax has traditionally been measured in a unit called **mean length of utterance (MLU).** MLU is a measurement of the average number of morphemes in a child's utterance. Brown (1973) defined five stages in the development of syntax, with each stage bringing the child closer to adult-like utterances. Here we will look closely at length of utterance and word order in three types of structures that develop as children proceed through these stages—declarative-like structures, questions, and negatives—and then close with a look at the "big picture" of how children progress through stages I–V.

Children generally proceed through these stages, with their characteristic linguistic structures, in the same sequence. It is important to note, however, that there is significant individual variability in the age at which children begin each stage, as well as in the length of time that each stage lasts. Thus, while we will provide some general guidelines for the onset of each stage, keep in mind that normal children may fall outside of these typical ages.

Exercise E

1. Brown argues that MLU is "an excellent simple index of grammatical development because almost every new kind of knowledge increases length: the number of semantic roles expressed in a sentence, the addition of obligatory morphemes, coding modulations of meaning, the addition of negative forms and auxiliaries used in interrogative and negative modalities, and, of course, embedding and coordinating" (1973:53–54).

   To calculate MLU, a researcher would have to set clear criteria for what "counts" as a morpheme. Consider the following utterances. The number in parentheses reflects Brown's criteria for counting morphemes in order to calculate MLU.

   Doggie went bye-bye. (3)

   Doggie go nite-nite. (3)

   Quack-quack on wawa. (3)

   B-b-babies wanna go bye-bye. (5)

   Doggie wented nite-nite. (4)

   Train goes choo-choo. (4)

   Allgone milk. (2)

   No see-saw. (2)

   Not gonna, um, Mommy not gonna go bye-bye. (5)

   Based on these examples, derive a set of general principles that could be used to determine the number of morphemes in new utterances. In particular, note any cases where the morpheme count for child utterances might differ from the morpheme count for adult utterances. How would you justify these differences?

Declarative-like Structures. Around the age of 12 months, when they utter their first words, children enter Stage I, which begins with **one-word** or **holophrastic** utterances. Words in early Stage I typically refer to some concrete object or entity in the child's environment (e.g., *shoe, milk, eye, ball, car, juice, Mommy, Daddy*), with the word's phonology modified along the lines discussed in that section. During late Stage I, around 18–24 months, children begin using the two-word utterances that mark the beginnings of syntax. During late Stage I, declarative-like utterances typically are interpretable as expressing the following relationships (Brown 1973:173):

RELATIONSHIP	**EXAMPLE**
agent + action	*Kendall go*
action + object	*drink juice*
agent + object	*Kendall juice*
action + locative	*sit chair*
entity + locative	*doggie chair*
possessor + possessed	*Mommy shoe*
attributive + entity	*big doggie*
demonstrative + entity	*that doggie*

At this stage, word order is not always consistent; thus *Kendall go* might be expressed as *go Kendall,* or *drink juice* as *juice drink.* These early two-word utterances tend to lack bound and free grammatical morphemes, which do not typically begin emerging until Stage II. For example, *Kendall go,* which we might interpret from context as meaning 'Kendall is going,' omits the auxiliary verb *is* and the present participle affix *-ing.* The child's strategy during Stage I appears to be one of focusing on content words (i.e., lexical morphemes). As a result, the absence of grammatical morphemes may result in some surface ambiguity. For example, *Mary chair* could, at various times, indicate possession ('Mary's chair'), location ('Mary is in the chair'), or a request ('Put Mary in the chair'). However, contextual clues would typically enable a listener to interpret the intended meaning.

Children begin using three-word utterances late in Stage I, around 26 months, moving into Stage II around 27 months. The most notable change in syntax in Stage II is the gradual addition of grammatical morphemes such as the present progressive *-ing* suffix, the prepositions *in* and *on,* and plurals. The child may also use some auxiliary-like forms such as *gonna, gotta, hafta,* and *wanna.* Stage II is associated with a MLU of 2.0–2.5 morphemes.

During Stage III, which begins around 31 months, the child continues adding grammatical morphemes, including wider use of personal pronouns and auxiliary verbs. Another feature that emerges during Stage III is the elaboration of NPs to include modifiers such as adjectives. Hence we might hear *That big doggie* or *That my doggie.* The MLU associated with Stage III is 2.5–3.0 morphemes.

Syntax continues to develop in Stage IV, which begins around 35 months, as the child introduces **embeddings** to produce **complex sentences** (i.e., sentences with more than one clause). For example, the child might produce sentences with embedded noun clauses, like the following: *I hope [you have a cookie]* or *Tell me [how do I make this].* During Stage IV, the child also begins using modals such as *could, might,* and *would.* The MLU associated with Stage IV is 3.0–3.75 morphemes.

Stage V, which begins around 41 months and ends around 46 months, is marked by the beginnings of **relative** (or **adjectival**) **clauses**—clauses that modify a noun. During this stage, a child might say *That's the book that I like.* Children also begin to **conjoin** clauses during this stage, typically by *and:* for example, *I had a cookie and I went to bed.* By the end of Stage V, it is typical for children to have mastered the first 9 of the 14 grammatical morphemes that were discussed in the section on acquisition of morphology.

Exercise F

1. Boysson-Bardies observes the following patterns in the early vocabulary of French, American, Swedish, and Japanese children, at the stage at which they have a vocabulary of 30–50 words (1999: 185).

	NOUNS	VERBS AND OTHERS
French	68.5%	31.5%
American	74.6	25.7
Swedish	67.9	32.1
Japanese	50.9	49.1

   a. What general trend occurs in all four groups?
   b. Which group shows the greatest discrepancy from the other three?
   c. Boysson-Bardies observes that Japanese "is often structured . . . around verbs that it puts at the end of sentences" (p. 187). In other words, Japanese is an SOV language, one in which the subject-object-verb elements occur in that order, as in *John his arm broke* instead of *John broke his arm.* What conclusions might you draw about the most salient sentence position for children, based on this fact?

Questions. Stages in the acquisition of questions by children acquiring English have been studied quite extensively by language acquisition researchers. As we look at these stages, keep in mind that English has two basic interrogative structures: *yes-no* interrogatives (e.g., *Is Big Bird hugging Ernie?*) and *wh*-interrogatives (e.g., *Who is Big Bird hugging?*). The formation of *yes-no* interrogatives involves I-Movement, a transformation which moves the tensed auxiliary verb to the left of the subject: for example, *Big Bird is hugging Ernie* → *Is Big Bird hugging Ernie?* The formation of *wh*-interrogatives involves both I-Movement and *wh*-Movement, which moves a *wh*-word to clause-initial position: for example, *Big Bird is hugging who* → *Is Big Bird hugging who?* → *Who is Big Bird hugging?*

A child exposed to English first signals questions simply by **intonation.** A declarative in English typically has falling intonation (—↘), whereas a *yes-no* interrogative has rising intonation (—↗). Thus, a child will first form *yes-no* interrogatives simply by adding a rising intonation contour to a declarative structure (e.g., *Daddy going* = 'Daddy is going' and *Daddy going?* = 'Is Daddy going?'). In the second stage, *wh*-interrogatives appear with the *wh*-word in clause-initial position (e.g., *Where Daddy going?*). At this stage, *yes-no* interrogatives are still marked only by intonation (e.g., *Daddy going?*). In the third stage, *yes-no* interrogatives are formed by I-Movement (e.g., *Is Daddy going?*). In this stage, however, *wh*-interrogatives are formed without I-Movement, even though an auxiliary may be present (e.g., *Where Daddy's going?*). In the fourth stage, the child finally forms *wh*-interrogatives with both *wh*-Movement and I-Movement (e.g., *Where's Daddy going?*). These stages may be summarized as follows.

STAGE	QUESTION TYPE	RULES	EXAMPLE
1	*yes-no*	Intonation	Daddy going?
	wh	—	—
2	*yes-no*	Intonation	Daddy going?
	wh	WHM	Where Daddy going?
3	*yes-no*	IM	Is Daddy going?
	wh	WHM	Where Daddy's going?
4	*yes-no*	IM	Is Daddy going?
	wh	WHM + IM	Where's Daddy going?

Progression through these stages makes perfect sense. First, the earliest linguistic structure acquired by a child seems to be the intonation contours of the language to which he or she is exposed, regardless of what that language may be. In fact, intonation seems to be acquired by about the age of 12 months. Second, *wh*-Movement is a structurally simpler rule than I-Movement. *Wh*-Movement moves any *wh*-item to clause-initial position, regardless of category (NP, PP, ADVP, and so on). I-Movement, on the other hand, is less general; it moves one specific category (tensed auxiliary) to the left of another specific category (subject NP). Thus, it makes some sense that *wh*-Movement would be acquired before I-Movement. Third, *yes-no* interrogatives are formed by applying one rule (I-Movement), whereas *wh*-interrogatives are formed by applying two rules (I-Movement and *wh*-Movement). Thus, it is predictable that the adult form of *yes-no* interrogatives would appear in a child's speech before the adult form of *wh*-interrogatives.

Negatives. As was the case with questions, stages in the acquisition of negative structures have been studied extensively. As we look at these stages, keep in mind that negative declarative sentences in the adult grammar place *not* immediately to the right of the first auxiliary: for example, *Big Bird will not hug Ernie, Big Bird could not play the game,* and so forth.

The use of negation begins fairly early. During the one- and two-word stages, at around age 2, the child may express negation with *no* or *not* as well as with semantically related terms like *all gone.* Negation at this stage involves juxtaposing the negative element and the term being negated (e.g., *no milk, all gone milk, no eat pudding, wear hat no*). At this stage it is typical for the subject to be omitted from the negative utterance. As the child's utterances become longer, the negative element gradually becomes incorporated into the sentence. Around age 2½ to 3 years, the contracted forms *can't* and *don't* (but not their uncontracted counterparts) may be added to the repertoire of negative elements. The exact semantic distinctions among *no, not, can't,* and *don't* may not be evident from the child's usage. At this stage, the negative element typically appears between the subject and the predicate (e.g., *It not hot* or *I don't like that*).

During the final stage in the acquisition of negatives, the negative element is consistently incorporated into the sentence. (The onset of this stage varies a great deal; some children may attain it as early as age 2, while others may be closer to 3½.) This stage corresponds to a further increase in the length of the child's utterances; other auxiliary verbs, such as *can't, won't,* and *didn't,* are also added. It is important to note that the child at this stage may not have acquired other auxiliary elements that are necessary for truly adult-like negatives. In particular, forms such as *wasn't, couldn't, wouldn't,* and *shouldn't* may be acquired relatively late. At this point, we may also hear forms like *I didn't told him,* indicating that the child has not yet internalized the principle for {PAST} inflection (note that both *didn't* and *told* are inflected for {PAST}, whereas in the adult grammar only the first verb form is inflected for {PAST}). The main point, though, is that the child has mastered the basic principle for negation in the adult grammar, which places *not* in sentence-internal position.

Again, this progression makes sense. If the child's early positive utterances form some sort of nucleus, then we would expect their negative counterparts to be formed by simply appending a negative item before or after this nucleus. Once a child begins to analyze utterances into subject and predicate, we would expect the negative item to appear between them, since this is its basic position within the adult grammar. Finally, since acquisition of the auxiliary system is relatively late (compared to major sentence constituents such as subject, object, and verb), we would expect relatively late acquisition of the adult rule for negatives, namely put *not* after the first auxiliary.

Once again, the point of this section is that a child's acquisition of syntactic categories and rules proceeds through orderly, systematic, and predictable stages. Table 8.1, based on Brown (1973) and Hulit and Howard (2002), summarizes milestones in the acquisition of syntax, morphology, and vocabulary.

Exercise G

1. For each set of structures (a–c), which construction would children exposed to English be most likely to acquire first?

a.	{POSS}	{PRES}	{PLU}
†b.	I-Movement	*wh*-Movement	Intonation
c.	*not*	*don't*	*do not*

2. Consider the following interchange between 4-year-old Muffin and her mother.

   MUFFIN: Why you don't eat?

   MOTHER: What?

   MUFFIN: Why don't you eat?

   These data illustrate that Muffin is in the process of acquiring a particular syntactic rule of English. Which one?

3. Which of the following forms would a child acquiring English be expected to produce first? Second? Third?

   A. Why he's crying?

   B. Why he crying?

   C. Why's he crying?

TABLE 8.1 Milestones in acquisition of syntax, morphology, and vocabulary

STAGE	I	II	III	IV	V
Age in months	*12–26*	*27–30*	*31–34*	*35–40*	*41–46*
MLU in morphemes	*1.0–2.0*	*2.0–2.5*	*2.5–3.0*	*3.0–3.75*	*3.75–4.5*
General syntactic characteristics	1st words around 12 mos. Late Stage I (18–24 mos): 2-word stage; MLU 1.5–2.0; beginnings of syntax. May begin 3-word utterances late in Stage I.	Mastery of present progressive, *in/on,* and plural; beginnings of other grammatical morphemes. Use of some auxiliary verbs and related forms like *gonna, gotta, hafta, wanna.*	Continues adding grammatical morphemes, including wider use of personal pronouns and auxiliary verbs, particularly the uncontractible copula. Elaboration of NPs to include modifiers such as adjectives.	Beginnings of embedding to produce complex sentences: e.g., *I hope you have a cookie; Tell me how do I make this.* Inclusion of modals such as *could, might, would.*	Beginnings of relative clauses: e.g., *Where's the book that I like?* Conjoining of clauses, especially by *and.* Mastery of 9 of the 14 grammatical morphemes by end of Stage V.
Negation	Negation signaled by *no/not* + word = *No chair; Not go.*	Late Stage II: Negatives formed by *no/not* in front of verb (e.g., *Mommy no go*).	Negative word integrated into adult-like structure with auxiliary verb: e.g., *Mommy is not crying.*	Addition of negative contractions: *aren't, didn't, doesn't, isn't.*	Negative past tense forms: *wasn't, couldn't, wouldn't, shouldn't*

Acquisition of Semantics

As we saw in Chapter 3, semantics is probably the most poorly understood component of grammar. Likewise, the way that children acquire semantics is also not well understood. Nonetheless, we can still draw some generalizations concerning this process. In doing so, it is convenient to distinguish between **lexical semantics** (meanings of individual words) and **sentence semantics** (the interpretation of entire sentences). Let's look at a few representative examples within each area.

Lexical Semantics. Two fairly clear processes that children go through in acquiring the meaning of individual words are **overgeneralization** and subsequent **narrowing.** These

TABLE 8.1 *Continued*

STAGE	I	II	III	IV	V
Age in months	*12–26*	*27–30*	*31–34*	*35–40*	*41–46*
MLU in morphemes	*1.0–2.0*	*2.0–2.5*	*2.5–3.0*	*3.0–3.75*	*3.75–4.5*
Questions	*Yes-no* questions signaled by rising intonation: e.g., *Daddy go?* Use of simple *wh-* questions: e.g., *Where Daddy? What that?*	Late Stage II: Still forming *yes-no* questions via intonation. *Wh*-questions formed without inversion: e.g., *Where doggie sit? Why Mommy sad?*	Inversion in *yes-no* questions: e.g., *Can I have juice?* Continued use of *wh-* questions, but not always with adult-like auxiliary verbs: e.g., *Where juice?*	Addition of *how* and *when* questions.	Addition of *why* questions.
Vocabulary	First words tend to be 1-syllable or reduplicated syllable (e.g., *dada*); mainly nouns; overextension common. First 50 words in productive vocabulary acquired by about 18 mos. Mainly lexical morphemes (nouns, verbs, adjectives), but also some pronouns, demonstratives. Productive vocabulary of about 200–300 words by end of 24 mos.	Productive vocabulary of about 400 words.	Productive vocabulary of about 1000 words.	Productive vocabulary of about 1500 words.	Productive vocabulary of about 2200 words.

processes can best be seen in the acquisition of concrete nouns. At first, the child will overgeneralize a word by using it to refer to more things than it does in the adult's lexicon. For example, *cookie* might be used to refer to anything round: a cookie, a cracker, a coin, a wheel, the moon, and so on. Over time, however, the meaning of *cookie* is narrowed so that it refers to only those items that an adult would call a *cookie.* Moreover, this narrowing often occurs in stages. For example, *dog* might be used at first to refer to any animal, then only to four-legged animals, then only to four-legged animals with fur, then only to relatively small four-legged animals with fur, and so on. (Note, incidentally, how well this process lends itself to analysis in terms of semantic features, which we discussed in Chapter 3.)

In addition, overgeneralization may affect the child's productions without affecting comprehension. For example, a child may use the term *daddy* to refer to any adult male, such as Uncle Fred or the mailman. However, if asked *Where's Daddy?* with other males present, the child may correctly point to his or her father. This is not as paradoxical as it sounds. It is a general characteristic of language acquisition that comprehension outdistances production; that is, a child can perceive distinctions that he or she cannot yet produce.

Consider another systematic stage that children seem to go through. In acquiring the meaning of individual words, children tend to acquire so-called **basic-level terms** like *house* before terms such as *building* or *cabin. House* is intermediate between a very general term such as *building* and a relatively specific term such as *cabin.* Along the same lines, children would be expected to acquire *bird* (basic-level) before *animal* (too general) or *robin* (too specific). Although the notion of "basic-level term" appeals to our intuitions, it is difficult to define exactly what distinguishes a basic-level term from one that is not "basic."

A third principle is that children typically acquire the **positive member** of a pair of opposites before the **negative member.** For example, when 3-year-olds are presented with two sticks of different lengths, they give more correct responses to questions like *Which stick is longer?* than to *Which stick is shorter?* The positive term of a pair of opposites is the unmarked member of the pair; that is, the one which carries the fewest presuppositions. For example, if a friend says that he just saw a new movie, you might ask *How long was it?* You would ask *How short was it?* only if you had some reason in advance for believing it was short. In this example, *long* is the positive term and *short* is the negative term. Likewise, we would expect a child exposed to English to acquire *tall* before *short, big* before *little, wide* before *narrow,* and *deep* before *shallow.*

Sentence Semantics. The way a child acquires the ability to interpret sentences is not purely a semantic phenomenon; it is inextricably bound up with syntax. Even our example concerning the acquisition of positive terms depends upon the child's ability to interpret an entire sentence: *Which stick is longer?* Thus, throughout this section, keep in mind that it is difficult to keep the acquisition of sentence semantics completely separate from syntax.

One interesting process is the way that children acquire the ability to interpret **passive** sentences. At one time, linguists thought that children acquired their entire linguistic system (except for vocabulary) perfectly and completely by about the age of 5 years. More recent research, however, indicates that some structures such as passives may not be acquired fully by some children until as late as 6 to 10 years of age. Some children as old as 4 and 5 years interpret passive sentences as if they were active. For instance, sentences such as *Elmo kissed Gina* (active) and *Elmo was kissed by Gina* (passive) are both interpreted as 'Elmo kissed Gina.' In such cases, it appears that the child is responding to the order of the major sentence constituents *(Elmo, kissed,* and *Gina)* and ignoring the grammatical morphemes *(was* and *by).* In other words, the child seems to be interpreting the first NP *(Elmo)* as the **agent,** the volitional actor, and the second NP *(Gina)* as the **patient,** the entity acted upon.

An imaginative method has been developed for testing a child's ability to interpret such sentences. In this method a child is given a set of toys and instructed to "act out" a sentence using the toys. For example, the child might be given two dolls, one "Elmo" and one

"Gina." Then the child is presented with a sentence like *Elmo was kissed by Gina* and ask to use the dolls to show what was said. If the child acts out the sentence by having "Elmo" kiss "Gina," then the researcher concludes that the child interprets the sentence as meaning 'Elmo kissed Gina.'

A child exposed to English must also acquire the ability to interpret **bare infinitives.** Like the interpretation of passives, this ability may be acquired relatively late. A bare infinitive is a subordinate clause containing an infinitive verb and no overt subject (thus, the infinitive is said to be "bare"). For example, the sentence *I told you where to sit* contains a subordinate clause *where to sit,* which has no overt subject NP; thus, *where to sit* is a bare infinitive clause. The strategy for interpreting the subject of such bare infinitives is called the **Minimum Distance Principle** (MDP), which can be stated as follows: interpret the subject of a bare infinitive as the closest NP to the left. Note that our sample sentence, *I told you where to sit,* has two NPs to the left of the bare infinitive: *I* and *you.* The closest NP to the left of the bare infinitive is *you.* Thus, the MDP predicts that the subject of the bare infinitive *where to sit* will be the closest NP to the left, *you.* This is exactly how speakers of English interpret this sentence: 'I told you where *you* should sit,' not 'I told you where *I* should sit.' In general, the MDP seems to work fairly well in the interpretation of English.

There are, however, exceptions. Consider, for example, the analogous sentence *I asked you where to sit.* The MDP predicts that the subject of the bare infinitive *where to sit* should be the closest NP to the left, *you.* This, however, is not the way speakers of English generally interpret this sentence. For most speakers, it is interpreted as 'I asked you where *I* should sit' rather than 'I asked you where *you* should sit.' Not surprisingly, Carol Chomsky, in her research on children's interpretation of such structures, found that children acquiring English can correctly interpret sentences that conform to the MDP earlier than sentences that don't. Consequently, a child will typically go through a stage in which *I told you where to sit* will be correctly interpreted as 'I told you where *you* should sit,' but *I asked you where to sit* will be incorrectly interpreted as 'I asked you where *you* should sit.'

A final ability that children acquire in systematic stages involves the interpretation of sentences containing the temporal connectives *before* and *after.* Consider, for example, the following synonymous sentences: *He came home before he ate lunch; Before he ate lunch, he came home; He ate lunch after he came home;* and *After he came home, he ate lunch.* Researcher Eve Clark found that children typically go through four different stages in learning to interpret such sentences. In the first stage, they interpret all the sentences according to the **order of mention** principle: the event reported in the first clause is interpreted as happening before the event reported in the second clause. Thus, *He came home before he ate lunch* will be interpreted correctly ('First he came home, then he ate lunch'), but *Before he ate lunch, he came home* will be interpreted incorrectly ('First he ate lunch, then he came home'). In the second stage, children interpret all sentences containing *before* correctly; however, they continue to interpret sentences containing *after* according to the order-of-mention strategy. Thus, *After he came home, he ate lunch* will be interpreted correctly ('First he came home, then he ate lunch'), but *He ate lunch after he came home* will be interpreted incorrectly ('First he ate lunch, then he came home'). In the third stage, they interpret both *before* and *after* as 'before.' Thus, *Before he ate lunch, he came home* will be interpreted correctly ('First he came home, then he ate lunch'), but *After he came home, he ate lunch* will be interpreted incorrectly ('First he ate lunch, then he came home'). In the fourth and final stage, the children interpret all four sentence types correctly; that is, *before* as 'before' and *after* as 'after.' This progression is summarized in the following chart.

STAGES

1	All sentences interpreted via order of mention (i.e., event in first clause happened first; event in second clause happened second).
2	*Before* interpreted correctly; *after* interpreted via order of mention.
3	*Before* and *after* interpreted as 'before.'
4	All sentences interpreted correctly.

EXAMPLES	*Stages (+ = correct; 0 = incorrect)*			
	I	II	III	IV
He came home *before* he ate lunch.	+	+	+	+
Before he ate lunch, he came home.	0	+	+	+
He ate lunch *after* he came home.	0	0	0	+
After he came home, he ate lunch.	+	+	0	+

One further point to note in this example is that children interpret more sentences correctly at Stage II than at Stage III. This illustrates the fact that a child acquiring a native language may appear to be regressing at certain points in his or her development. However, once language acquisition is seen as a series of rule-governed and systematic stages, it is clear that the child is not regressing at all, but simply revising his or her set of rules. Note the parallel between this example and the acquisition of the plural of *foot,* discussed earlier: *feet* → *foots/feet* → *footses/feetses* → *feet.* The child appears to be regressing, but actually is simply acquiring a rule.

After this discussion of the acquisition of phonology, morphology, syntax, and semantics, one point should be clear. The acquisition of a first language involves more than simply imitating and memorizing samples of the language to which a child is exposed. Rather, it involves constructing a grammar of the language. This grammar, in turn, is a system composed of categories and rules that essentially constitute a definition of that language. Moreover, this grammar is acquired in stages, each of which more and more closely resembles the adult system.

Exercise H

1. Consider the following sentences.

- **A.** I promised Mary to go.
- **B.** I persuaded Mary to go.
- **a.** Which of these sentences would be correctly interpreted first by a child acquiring English?
- **b.** What principle accounts for this?

†2. A child learns the meaning of *chair* before that of *recliner, rocker,* or *furniture.* What principle from the acquisition of semantics accounts for this?

Exercise H *Continued*

3. Clark (1975:83–84) describes the following overgeneralizations by children. For each one, determine the semantic property that is the basis for the overgeneralization.
   †a. A child used the word [bɔ] to refer to a ball, an apple, an egg, and a bell clapper.
   b. A child used the word *fly* to refer to a fly, a speck of dust, crumbs of bread, and her own toes.
   c. A child used the word [kotibaɪz] to refer to the bars of his cot, a large toy abacus, a toast rack, and a picture of a building with a columned facade.
4. A child uses *car* to refer to cars, trucks, and buses, but not to bicycles or airplanes. What semantic property does the child appear to associate with *car* at this stage?
5. For each pair of sentences, determine the one that a child acquiring English would typically interpret correctly at an earlier stage, and explain the principle that accounts for your answer.

   A.1. Tommy kicked Mary.
   A.2. Mary was kicked by Tommy.

   B.1. Which tree is taller?
   B.2. Which tree is shorter?

   C.1. We'll go to the movie as soon as we go to the store.
   C.2. As soon as we go to the store, we'll go to the movie.
6. Boysson-Bardies describes a child, Guy, who at 17 months "used the word *dog* for all mammals—and also for dinosaurs. He used the word *hen* for all birds and the word *fish* for all sea creatures" (1999:134).

   What strategy is Guy using? What appear to be the criteria that he uses to decide which name will be used for a particular animal? In particular, what criteria does Guy appear to use when he calls something a *dog*? What different criteria would an adult use? How can you account for the fact that Guy does not (yet) use the adult criteria?

Issues in Language Acquisition

In the first half of this chapter, we looked at some representative stages a child goes through in acquiring a first language, or, more specifically, a grammar of that language. In other words, we have considered how a child passes from an initial mental state through intermediate states until he or she reaches a final mental state (possessing a grammar more or less equivalent to an adult's). One thing we have not dealt with so far is the **initial state.** The second half of this chapter briefly discusses some positions that various researchers have held concerning this initial state.

Nativism and Empiricism

In general terms, there are basically two schools of thought on the nature of the initial mental state. On one side, we have what might be called **nativism.** Extreme nativism would hold that human beings are born with all of the knowledge that they will eventually have as adults.

With respect to language, this position would hold that a child is born knowing a language and this knowledge manifests itself during the first few years of life. On the other hand, we have what might be called **empiricism.** Extreme empiricism would hold that human beings are born with none of the knowledge that they will have as adults. With respect to language, this position would hold that a child is born with no linguistic knowledge whatsoever and that all language ability is somehow learned throughout life by making associations among events in the environment. These two positions are mutually exclusive.

It is fairly easy to see that the extreme nativist position cannot be correct. If human beings were born knowing, say, English, it would be impossible to explain the fact that most people in the world do not acquire English as a first language. Of course, the same could be said of Russian, Chinese, or any other language. On the other hand, it is not quite as easy to see that the extreme empiricist position is wrong, as indeed it is. The problem with this view is that it cannot explain how human beings ever acquire a language at all (or for that matter, any knowledge whatsoever). If human beings are born with absolutely nothing in their minds, how can they make even the simplest "associations" among events in their environment? Consequently, it should not come as a surprise that no serious researcher today could hold either of these extreme positions. Instead, most students of language and language acquisition hold a position of either modified nativism or modified empiricism. From now on we will refer to these modified positions as nativism and empiricism, respectively.

The nativist position (sometimes referred to as **mentalism**) focuses on the fact that much of human behavior is **biologically determined.** That is, much of our behavior is a function of the fact that we are human beings and our genes are structured in characteristic ways. Our ability to walk is an example of biologically determined behavior: we do not learn to walk, no one teaches us to walk; as normal human beings, we simply **acquire** the ability to walk because such ability is dictated by our genes. To use one of Chomsky's favorite examples, we do not "learn" to have arms any more than birds "learn" to have wings; rather, different species develop different attributes as a function of their different genetic structures.

The person most often associated with the nativist view of language acquisition is Chomsky. Quite simply, Chomsky holds the view that human beings are born already "knowing" something about the structure of human language. That is, human beings, by virtue of their characteristic genetic structure, are born in an initial mental state in which general properties of human language are already specified. (Note that this is different from saying that humans are born with properties of one particular human language already specified.) Candidates for this innate (inborn) knowledge would be those characteristics common to all human languages: for example, the fact that the phonology of every human language appears to operate in terms of segments, distinctive features, levels of representation, and phonological rules. In other words, according to this view, human beings are born with part of their grammar already in place. For example, they "know" that whatever language they are exposed to, they will have to organize the phonological component for that language in terms of segments, distinctive features, levels of representation, and phonological rules. It would probably be safe to say that nativism is the dominant (although certainly not exclusive) view of language acquisition among American linguists today. We will discuss the motivation for this position in more detail later on.

On the other hand, the empiricist position (sometimes referred to as **behaviorism**) focuses on the fact that much of human behavior is **culturally determined.** That is, much of our behavior is a function of specific environmental factors. The ability to write (among literate societies) is an example of culturally determined behavior. We **learn** to write by going through specific training; we do not simply acquire this ability spontaneously and naturally the same way we learn to walk. Witness the fact that all normal human beings learn to walk, just as they all acquire a first language; there are entire cultures, however, which do not use any writing system at all. A more transparent example of culturally determined knowledge would be learning the rules of, say, football. This game is played by two teams of 11 players each, on a field 100 yards long, and so on and so forth. (Note, incidentally, that in Canada the game is played with 12 players on each team on a field 110 yards long.) Knowledge of the game of football is obviously culturally determined. Human beings are clearly not born with any sort of knowledge of football. Instead, its rules must be learned in the same way we learn to tie our shoes or to drive on the proper side of the road: by conscious attention, specific training, and trial and error.

The person traditionally associated with the empiricist view of language acquisition is the late B. F. Skinner. In 1957, Skinner published *Verbal Behavior,* in which he set out his views in detail. In greatly oversimplified terms, Skinner proposed that language is learned essentially through vaguely defined powers of "association" and that human linguistic communication is a stimulus-response chain. That is, a stimulus in a person's environment causes him or her to speak (a response). In turn, this utterance (now a stimulus) causes another person to speak (a response), and so on. Under this view, the initial state has some innate structure (perhaps general powers of association and abstraction), but not much. Moreover, this view holds that language is not necessarily a human-specific capacity. That is, adherents to this position would not automatically assume that human languages are qualitatively different from animal communication systems (e.g., those found among bees, dolphins, and chimpanzees). However, since empiricism has been largely discredited within linguistics (see, for example, Chomsky's [1959] review of *Verbal Behavior*), at least in its present form and for the present time, there is little point in pursuing it here.

The main points of these two views are summarized in Figure 8.2. Keep in mind, however, that this represents a greatly oversimplified view. In reality, there are probably as many different views, representing points between what we have been calling nativism and empiricism, as there are people who have thought about the subject. Moreover, the controversy

FIGURE 8.2 Nativism versus empiricism

NATIVISM	EMPIRICISM
■ Mentalism	■ Behaviorism
■ Chomsky	■ Skinner
■ Mind has more innate structure	■ Mind has less innate structure
■ Language acquisition is primarily biologically determined	■ Language acquisition is primarily culturally determined
■ Language is acquired	■ Language is learned

surrounding these views is still very much alive; Chomsky's position is by no means universally held.

Language-Specific and General Cognitive Capacities

Even though both nativists and empiricists disagree on how much structure the human mind comes equipped with, they agree that there must be at least some innate structure in the initial state. This in turn raises another question: Is any of this innate structure specifically designed to facilitate language acquisition? In other words, does the initial state contain **language-specific capacities,** or does it contain only **general cognitive capacities?** Chomsky makes it quite clear that he believes the initial state to contain language-specific information. For example, the Subjacency Constraint, which essentially limits movement to adjacent clauses, has no known analog in any other domain of human knowledge. In contrast, others who have addressed this question, most notably the late French psychologist Jean Piaget, have held that the initial state does not contain language-specific information. Rather, language acquisition results from the interaction of various general cognitive capacities, such as memory, intelligence, motivation, and so on. If these "general cognitive capacities" sound vague, it is because they are. The state of the human mind as it enters the world is very poorly understood. This question of what kind of innate structure (i.e., language-specific versus general) is even harder to debate than that of how much structure (i.e., nativism versus empiricism). Here we will present one of the most clearly articulated positions on the subject, namely Chomsky's.

Chomsky's Position

As we have seen, Chomsky is essentially a nativist. He is convinced that human beings are born with a very rich fabric of mental structure already in place. Moreover, he is convinced that part of this mental structure is language-specific in nature. Chomsky has arrived at this position through what we might call a "what else" argument. That is, he starts with a number of observations about language and language acquisition and argues that the simplest way to explain them is to assume that human beings are born with a certain amount of language-specific knowledge already in place. In other words, according to Chomsky, if linguistic ability is not due to innate, language-specific knowledge, "what else" could explain it? Let's now consider some of the observations that have led Chomsky to this conclusion.

The Complexity of Acquired Structures. As we have seen throughout this chapter (indeed, throughout this entire book), the acquisition of a language is essentially the acquisition of a grammar: that is, a set of categories and rules for characterizing all and only the sentences of that language. By hypothesis, the semantic component consists of knowledge organized in terms of sense relations (antonymy, hyponymy, etc.), reference relations (anaphora, coreference, etc.), and logical relations (entailment and presupposition). The syntactic component consists of knowledge organized in terms of categories (NP, VP, etc.), constituent structure (i.e., bracketing of categories into higher units), and transformations (*wh*-Movement, NP-Movement, etc.). The morphological component consists of knowledge organized in terms of different types of morphemes (lexical or grammatical, free or bound, and inflectional or derivational). The phonological component consists of knowledge organized in terms of segments, distinctive features, levels of representation, and phonological rules. If this is a reasonably accurate representation of a grammar, then the final state achieved by a human being (i.e., an adult grammar) is exceedingly complex. From Chomsky's point of view, it is difficult to explain how human beings acquire such a complex system, unless we assume that they are genetically predisposed to do so.

Fixed Onset and Development. As we have seen in the first half of this chapter, the acquisition of language begins at about the same time for all normal children (i.e., it has a "fixed onset") and progresses through predictable stages, regardless of each child's particular environment or the specific language to which he or she is exposed. For example, a child typically acquires the intonational patterns of a language around the end of his or her first year. Efforts to speed up language acquisition are generally in vain. Specific studies have found that it is generally impossible to "teach" a child a detail of language until the child is ready to acquire it spontaneously. A case often cited in the literature concerns a little boy who told his mother *Nobody don't like me.* She tried to correct this double negative by responding with *Nobody likes me.* They repeated this interchange eight times, until the boy finally said *Oh! Nobody don't likes me.* Presumably, the boy eventually acquired the adult rule for forming negatives as well as the {PRES} morpheme, but only when he reached the appropriate stage of development.

In order to appreciate the systematic and uniform progression of language acquisition, it is useful to consider the errors children do *not* make in acquiring their native language. For example, part of the experience of a child exposed to English might be utterances such as *She is cooking dinner* and *Is she cooking dinner?* From these and many other such examples, a child might be expected to form a rule for forming interrogatives as follows: move the first occurrence of *is* to the beginning of the sentence. However, this rule would predict that at some stage in the child's acquisition of English syntax, he or she would make an error of the following sort. Given a sentence with two occurrences of *is* (e.g., *The spoon she is using is broken*), the child would form the interrogative by moving the first occurrence of *is* to the beginning of the sentence. This would yield **Is the spoon she using is broken?* rather than the correct form *Is the spoon she is using broken?*

The significant point is that children acquiring English (or any other language with such a rule) seem never to make such mistakes. It appears that children are constrained from forming a syntactic rule which is independent of structure; that is, a rule of the form: move the first, second, or *n*th word to, say, the beginning of the utterance. Rather, all syntactic rules for all languages seem to be structure-dependent; that is, they must be framed in structural terms, with reference to units such as NP, auxiliary, subject, main clause, and so forth. In our example, the rule would be something like the following: move the first occurrence of *is* following the subject NP of the main clause to initial position in that clause. Thus, in our sample structure, the rule would identify and move the occurrence of *is* in the main clause, while completely ignoring the occurrence of *is* in the subordinate clause. Details of this analysis aside, Chomsky argues that it is difficult to account for the uniform onset and quite narrowly constrained development of language unless we assume that children are genetically predisposed to acquire a grammar that meets certain criteria.

Rapidity of Acquisition. A child acquires his or her first language in remarkably rapid fashion. Even though some structures are acquired later than researchers had originally thought, the fact remains that a normal child acquires the majority of his or her grammar by about 5 years of age. This is amazing when you consider the nonlinguistic tasks that many children do not master until later (e.g., tying their shoes, telling time, learning the basic conventions of etiquette, throwing a ball, snapping their fingers, riding a bicycle, and so on). Moreover, the rapidity of first-language acquisition is brought into relief by considering the painstaking labor involved in learning a second language as an adult. Approximately half of the Americans who attend college are required at some point to take a foreign language. Very few, however, gain real facility in it.

Such facts suggest a genetic predisposition among humans that begins to dissipate around the age of puberty and falls off dramatically at the onset of adulthood. This view is supported by the fact that children who are exposed to two languages seem to acquire both of them with equal ease and rapidity, unlike adults learning a second language. Another piece of evidence comes from Genie, an abused girl discovered in Los Angeles in 1971 at the age of 13. Because her father isolated her from the rest of the family, Genie had reached puberty without being exposed to language. Subsequent attempts to teach English to Genie indicated that, although she was intelligent, she was unable to acquire English in the same way or as completely as a normal child. (See Susan Curtiss's [1977] book, *Genie.*) Once again, in Chomsky's view, it is difficult to explain both the rapidity of language acquisition and the rapid decline in this ability unless we assume that language acquisition is part of a human being's genetically programmed biological development.

Features Common to All Languages. On the face of things, it appears that human languages are wildly divergent. English and Japanese, for example, seem so different that it would be hard to find anything that they have in common. In fact, as recently as the late 1950s, many linguists believed that languages could differ without limit and in unpredictable ways. If, however, we look below the surface, we find that human languages are remarkably similar. As we discussed earlier, the grammars of all languages can be characterized in terms of four components—semantics, syntax, morphology, and phonology—each of which is organized in terms of the same types of categories and rules. Of course, it could be that grammars of all languages share these components and subcomponents because linguists analyze languages in terms of them; that is, linguists find what they are looking for. However, if we accept as inevitable the fact that theorists in any field must necessarily look at their subject through a theory of their own construction, languages still exhibit certain common properties that are by no means logically necessary. You may recall from the beginning of Chapter 7 that such common properties are called **language universals.**

During the past 40 years an enormous number of language universals have been proposed. Consider just a few examples. From the standpoint of phonology, all languages have at least one voiceless stop, such as /p, t, k/ in English, but not all languages have a voiced stop such as /b, d, g/. Similarly, all languages have syllables of the form CV, but not all languages have syllables of the form VC. From the standpoint of morphology, if a language inflects nouns for gender (i.e., masculine and feminine), it always inflects them for number (i.e., singular and plural). For example, Spanish inflects nouns for gender, as in *hermano* 'brother' versus *hermana* 'sister' (*-o* = masculine, *-a* = feminine). Thus, nouns in Spanish are necessarily inflected for number, as in *hermano* 'brother' versus *hermanos,* 'brothers.' On the other hand, a language that inflects for number does not necessarily inflect for gender. For example, English inflects nouns for number, as in *brother* versus *brothers,* but not for gender. From the standpoint of syntax, if a language moves *wh*-items (e.g., *who, what,* etc. in English), it moves them leftward to clause-initial position, never rightward to clause-final position. Similarly, in simple declarative sentences, the vast majority of languages (approximately 99 percent) order the subject before the object. And the list goes on and on.

Even though some of these universals are absolute (i.e., all languages have property X) and others are implicational (e.g., if a language has property X, then it will also have property Y), the fact is that none of these universals is logically necessary. For example, there is no logical reason that inflectional suffixes should follow derivational suffixes. It is perfectly possible to imagine a human language in which the opposite situation holds. Likewise, there is no logical reason that languages move *wh*-items to the left; they could just as easily move them to the right. Chomsky's view is once again straightforward: it is difficult to explain the vast number of common (but not logically necessary) features among languages unless we assume that such properties are specified by the genetically determined initial state.

Independence of Instruction. A normal child acquires the bulk of his or her first language (other than vocabulary) before ever starting school; thus, it is clear that teachers do not "teach" a child language. Indeed, children who never attend school in their lives acquire language. Likewise, parents do not "teach" their children language. In fact, most parents have no conscious knowledge of the rules of their language. What parent (other than one who has studied syntax) would be able to state, say, the rule of I-Movement? Even for those few adults who have conscious knowledge of (some of) the rules of their own language, it is hard to imagine how they could convey such information to a child. Consider an extremely simple example, often cited by Chomsky. Every native speaker of English knows that in the sentence *Bob proved that he is incompetent,* the pronoun *he* can refer either to Bob or to someone else. Likewise, every such speaker knows that in the sentence *Bob proved him to be incompetent,* the pronoun *him* must refer to someone other than Bob. This knowledge is clear-cut and acquired without training; yet imagine trying to explain the principle involved here to a 5- or even a 10-year-old child!

Moreover, much of our grammatical knowledge is acquired without appropriate experience; that is, we know things about our language for which we apparently have no relevant experience. A favorite example of Chomsky's involves what he calls **parasitic gaps.** In such constructions, a pronoun can be omitted without affecting the interpretation of the sentence—for example, *Who did you insult by ignoring him?* versus *Who did you insult by ignoring?* (Most speakers prefer one or the other of these sentences, but the point is that both of them can be interpreted as identical in meaning.) These parasitic gap constructions, however, are extremely rare in English. Compare, for example, the sentences *Who insulted Bob by ignoring him?* and **Who insulted Bob by ignoring?* In this pair, which is the typical case in English, the pronoun *him* cannot be optionally omitted. Chomsky's point is that constructions containing parasitic gaps are so uncommon that it is unlikely that a child would ever be exposed to one while acquiring the syntax of English. Nevertheless, all native speakers of English know exactly when a pronoun may and may not be omitted, and they apparently know this without training and without relevant experience.

From Chomsky's point of view, it is difficult to explain how such subtle grammatical distinctions are acquired independently of instruction and experience, unless we assume that the basic grammatical principles that underlie these distinctions are biologically determined and present in the initial state.

Independence of Intelligence and Motivation. Acquiring a first language does not seem to be a direct function of intelligence. The individual with an IQ of 70 acquires the grammar of the language to which he or she is exposed just as the individual with an IQ of 130 does. Even children with Down syndrome acquire a grammar. Likewise, language acquisition does not seem to be a function of motivation. Normal children do not "try" to acquire language; they do not have to work at it; they simply acquire it—effortlessly and spontaneously. In fact, it is impossible to interrupt or retard language acquisition short of isolating the child from language completely (as in the case of Genie mentioned earlier). Again, from Chomsky's perspective it is virtually impossible to explain the fact that language acquisition is independent of intelligence and motivation, unless we assume that it is a biologically determined process.

Since there has been so much controversy and misunderstanding over this line of reasoning, let us reiterate this argument in point form. Chomsky first makes the following observations.

- The final state achieved (i.e., an adult grammar) is extremely complex.
- Language acquisition is characterized by a fixed onset and uniform stages of development.
- Language acquisition is comparatively rapid (i.e., it is accomplished almost totally by age 5 or 6).
- All languages have numerous features in common—features which are not the product of logical necessity.
- Human language is not taught.
- Language acquisition is independent of intelligence and motivation.

Chomsky then concludes that these observations are difficult (if not impossible) to explain unless we make the following assumptions. First, human beings acquire a language because they are genetically programmed to do so. Second, this genetic endowment contains (among other things) language-specific capacities, present at birth. The only requirement for language acquisition external to the individual is exposure to a human language. In other words, language acquisition is both biologically and culturally determined. The biologically determined linguistic capacities present in the initial state interact with the culturally determined experience of the child (i.e., the particular language spoken around the child) to set off the acquisition of a human language.

This position, of course, may turn out to be either totally or partially incorrect. And, in fact, there is widespread controversy over its details. It is, however, the most clearly articulated and (for us, at least) the most convincing theory presently available to explain commonplace observations about language acquisition.

Exercise I

1. The empiricist approach to language acquisition would claim that children must base their grammar only on the language they hear spoken around them. Chomsky would say that this view is not entirely correct. What additional information would he claim that the child brings to the task of language acquisition?

Exercise I *Continued*

†2. Forms such as *comed* (for {come} + {PAST}), *wented* (for {go} + {PAST}), and *foots* (for {foot} + {PLU}) are common in child language. How do such forms bear on the views of language acquisition held by Skinner and Chomsky?

3. Brown (1973:358), in a longitudinal study of three children, tracked their acquisition of 14 grammatical morphemes, as well as the relative frequency with which their parents used the same morphemes. One of his findings was that the articles *a* and *the* were among the morphemes most frequently used by the parents, yet they were acquired eighth out of fourteen by the children. How does this finding constitute a problem for the behaviorist view of first-language acquisition?

4. Consider the following exchange between a father and his 3-year-old daughter about nursery school.

   FATHER: What is the name of the dog at your school?

   CHILD: Way.

   FATHER: Way?

   CHILD: No, Way.

   FATHER: Did you say Way?

   CHILD: No. (Angrily) I said WAY!

   FATHER: (Suddenly catching on) Oh, you mean Ray?

   CHILD: Yes, that's what I said—Way!

   This exchange illustrates the developmental relationship between comprehension and production. What is that relationship?

5. On an episode of the TV show *Family Feud,* host Ray Coombs asked the contestants, "Besides walking and talking, name something else parents teach their children to do."
   - **a.** Would Chomsky agree or disagree with the premises of this question?
   - **b.** Why would Chomsky agree or disagree?

†6. Moscowitz (1979) makes a number of claims concerning language acquisition. Which of the following claims is consistent with the nativist view of language acquisition?
   - **a.** "The child is confronted with the task of learning a language about which she knows nothing."
   - **b.** First language acquisition involves "intense effort."
   - **c.** "Any language specialization that exists in the child is only one aspect of more general cognitive capacities."
   - **d.** "People who learn at least two languages in early childhood appear to retain a greater flexibility of the vocal musculature."
   - **e.** none of the above

Summary

The theory of language acquisition makes use of such concepts as prelinguistic and linguistic stages, the latter of which constitutes grammars (i.e., systems of categories and rules) that more and more closely correspond to the adult's. The acquisition of language can be analyzed from the perspective of phonology, morphology, syntax, and semantics. We have also looked at some of the fundamental philosophical issues surrounding language acquisition. These issues reflect two positions regarding the initial mental state of the human organism: nativism (more innate structure) and empiricism (less innate structure). Controversy continues to exist over whether the initial state contains language-specific capacities or only general cognitive capacities.

SUPPLEMENTARY READINGS

Primary

Bloom, P. (Ed.). (1994). *Language acquisition: Core readings.* Cambridge, MA: MIT Press.
Chomsky, N. (1959). A review of B. F. Skinner's *Verbal behavior. Language, 35,* 26–58.
Chomsky, N. (1988). *Language and problems of knowledge: The Managua lectures.* Cambridge, MA: MIT Press.
Chomsky, N. (2002). *On nature and language.* New York: Cambridge University Press.
Curtiss, S. (1977). *Genie: A psycholinguistic study of a modern-day "wild child."* New York: Academic Press.
Flanagan, O. J. (1984). *The science of the mind.* Cambridge, MA: MIT Press.
Skinner, B. F. (1957). *Verbal behavior.* New York: Appleton-Century-Crofts.

Secondary

Boysson-Bardies, B. de. (1999). *How language comes to children: From birth to two years.* Trans. M. B. DeBevoise. Cambridge, MA: MIT Press.
Gleason, J. B. (1997). *The development of language* (4th ed.). Boston: Allyn and Bacon.
Hulit, L. M., & Howard, M. R. (2002). *Born to talk: An introduction to speech and language development* (3rd ed.). Boston: Allyn and Bacon.
Lenneberg, E. (1964). The capacity for language acquisition. In J. Katz and J. Fodor (Eds.), *The structure of language* (pp. 579–603). Englewood Cliffs, NJ: Prentice-Hall.
Moskowitz, B. A. (1979). The acquisition of language. *Scientific American* (November), 82–96.
Ninio, A., & Snow, C. E. (1996). *Pragmatic development.* Boulder: Westview Press.
Reed, V. A. (1994). *An introduction to children with language disorders* (2nd ed.). New York: Macmillan.

You are now prepared to read all of the secondary works. The works by Hulit and Howard and by Moskowitz provide good discussions of the stages that a child goes through in acquiring English. Boysson-Bardies is an accessible introduction that includes data from children acquiring other languages. Gleason provides a comprehensive review and synthesis of research on the acquisition of phonology, morphology, syntax, and semantics. Reed covers language disorders associated with mental retardation, learning disabilities, autism, hearing impairment, and aphasia. Ninio and Snow discuss the development of pragmatic ability in children. Lenneberg distinguishes between biologically determined and culturally determined behavior, and discusses the characteristics of each.

An introductory course in linguistics is probably necessary to fully appreciate the primary works. Bloom is a collection of 18 articles, most from scholarly journals, on the acquisition of morphology, syntax, and semantics. Chomsky (1988) and (2002) provide an excellent discussion of Chomsky's views. Curtiss is a classic study in the effects of depriving a child of linguistic stimuli. Flanagan provides a rich discussion of the intellectual traditions from which Skinner, Piaget, and Chomsky operate. Skinner and Chomsky (1959), however, are difficult going and are now primarily of historical interest. The former is the classic statement of the empiricist view of language, and the latter is Chomsky's detailed rejection of it.

Supplementary Exercises

1. Mark the following statements true or false.

a. T F Intelligence seems to play a major role in a child's ability to acquire a language.

b. T F It will generally take a child longer to acquire Japanese than to acquire English.

c. T F It is generally impossible for a parent to speed up the process of language acquisition.

d. T F To support the empiricist point of view, a researcher would be more likely to cite second-language acquisition by an adult rather than first-language acquisition by a child.

e. T F The babbling stage seems to be a necessary prerequisite for normal language acquisition.

f. T F Before a child exposed to English has acquired the ability to interpret passives, he or she would be likely to interpret *Tommy petted Bozo* and *Bozo was petted by Tommy* as having different meanings.

g. T F A child exposed to English would be likely to acquire the meaning of *old* before *young.*

2. Smith and Wilson (1985) report the case of a 3-year-old who produced the following forms. What property of the first syllable of these words might explain why it is the one replaced by [rə]?

[rətǽk]	'attack'	[rəǰɔ́ɪ]	'enjoy'
[rəstʌ́rb]	'disturb'	[rətár]	'guitar'
[rəlǽstɪk]	'elastic'	[rədʌ́ktər]	'conductor'

3. Explain how regular phonological processes account for the "humor" in the following riddles.

Q: How do you catch a unique rabbit?

A: "Unique" up on him.

Q: How do you catch a tame rabbit?

A: The "tame" way.

4. Name the phonological process(es) illustrated by each of the following child-language forms.

a. [tɛ́wəbižən] for *television*

b. [m̥ɛə] for *smell*

c. [trɪ́šə] for *Patricia*

d. [tʌ́mɪ] for *stomach*

e. [skɛ́ti] for *spaghetti* (be sure to explain where the /k/ comes from)

5. According to Clark and Clark (1977:399), the following rules are common in child language:

A. fricative + stop ⟶ stop (e.g., *stop* ⟶ [t^hap])

B. nasal + stop ⟶ stop (e.g., *lamp* ⟶ [læp])

C. fricative + liquid ⟶ fricative (e.g., *free* ⟶ [fi])

a. How does the order in which segments are acquired appear to relate to the order in which segments are omitted?

b. Explain in particular why the fricative is deleted in rule (A) but retained in rule (C).

6. The article "Say Rabbit, Not Wabbit" (1971) describes the following hypothesis put forth by Robert Ringel of Purdue University: "Persons with functional speech disorders [e.g., who say *wabbit* for *rabbit*] have faulty sensory perception in their mouths . . . they lack the oral sense of touch."
   a. Name one piece of evidence that this hypothesis is false. (Hint: If the hypothesis were true, what "mistakes" would you expect such people to make?)
   b. What feature do /r/ and /w/ have in common? (Hint: vowel feature.)
   c. How do /r/ and /w/ differ? (Hint: tongue.)
7. A child acquiring English systematically produces [tap] for stop rather than [t^hap]. What can you conclude about the child's phonemic representation of *stop?* Explain your reasoning.
8. Consider the following forms produced by children acquiring French as a first language (Boysson-Bardies 1999:143–45). What phonological processes are illustrated by these forms?

Target (with English translation)		Child's production
chaud	'hot'	[to]
lapin	'rabbit'	[papa]
sale	'dirty'	[tal]
éléphant	'elephant'	[tetefan]
canard	'duck'	[kaka]
clef	'key'	[ke]
chapeau	'hat'	[po]
chapeau	'hat'	[papo]
sapin	'pine tree'	[papẽ]
gateau	'cake'	[tato]
Jacques	'Jacques'	[kako]

9. In an early study by Berko and Fraser (cited in Ingram [1988:441–43]), 2- to 3-year-olds were asked to imitate sentences like the following:

   A. I showed you the book.
   B. I will read the book.
   C. Do I like to read books?
   D. Where does it go?

   Some of the different children's responses to each sentence are given below.

   A.1. I show book.
   A.2. I show you the book.
   B.1. Read book.
   B.2. I will read book.
   B.3. I read the book.
   C.1. To read book?
   C.2. I read books?
   C.3. I read book?
   D.1. Go?
   D.2. Does it go?
   D.3. Where do it go?

What generalizations can you draw about the types of morphemes that tend to be omitted in the children's repetitions? Retained? (If necessary, review the terms for different types of morphemes in Chapter 5.)

10. According to Clark and Clark (1977:355–56), children acquiring relative clauses find them easier to interpret if the relative pronoun cannot be deleted and if the relative clause does not interrupt the main clause. Based on these principles, which of the following sentences should be easiest for a child to interpret? Most difficult? (The relative clause in each sentence is italicized.)

a. The girl *that ran after the boy* caught the dog.
b. The girl *that the boy ran after* caught the dog.
c. The girl caught the dog *that ran after the boy.*
d. The girl caught the dog *that the boy ran after.*

11. According to Limber (1973:181), children first learning to produce sentences with relative clauses produce sentences like (A) before those like (B):

A. I want the doll Mary's got.
B. The doll Mary's got is pretty.

What structural difference between the placement of the relative clause in (A) and (B) might explain why (A) is acquired earlier?

12. Judy Reilly of UCLA (cited in Moskowitz [1979:94]) recorded the following interchange between 6-year-old Jamie and his mother. These data illustrate that Jamie has mastered a syntactic principle of English. Considering only these data, name the principle. (Hint: Consult Exercise F-2 in Chapter 4.)

JAMIE: Why are you doing that?
MOTHER: What?
JAMIE: Why are you writing what I say down?
MOTHER: What?
JAMIE: Why are you writing down what I say?

13. A child was observed saying *the upmost importance* for *the utmost importance.* What word-formation process is the child using here? (Hint: See Chapter 5.)

14. Why would children exposed to English be expected to learn the meaning of the prepositions *in* and *on* before *behind* and *in front of?* (Hint: Consider the speaker's perspective.)

15. Carol Chomsky (1969:24–32) conducted research on the ability of 5- to 10-year-olds to interpret certain syntactic structures. She showed the subjects a blindfolded doll and then asked, *Is this doll hard to see or easy to see?* Nearly all of the 5-year-olds (and some of the 6-, 7-, and 8-year-olds) responded *hard to see,* as in the following exchange:

CHOMSKY: Is this doll easy to see or hard to see?
LISA: Hard to see.
CHOMSKY: Will you make her easy to see?
LISA: If I can get this untied.
CHOMSKY: Will you explain why she was hard to see?
LISA (TO DOLL): Because you had a blindfold over your eyes.
CHOMSKY: And what did you do?
LISA: I took it off.

Explain how the children's interpretation of these structures differs from an adult's.

16. In research conducted by Bates (1976:295–326), pairs of sentences like the following were presented to 3-year-olds and 6-year-olds and they were asked to choose the more polite form:

A. Give me a candy.

B. Would you give me a candy?

The 3-year-olds judged (B) as more polite only about 50 percent of the time, while the 6-year-olds judged (B) as more polite about 80 percent of the time. What concept from pragmatics do the 6-year-olds appear to be more sensitive to?

17. Clark and Clark (1977:364–65) describe a study in which 7-year-olds were tested on their ability to produce speech acts for asking, ordering, and promising another child to do something. Over 90 percent of the children produced appropriate utterances for asking and ordering, but only 55 percent produced appropriate utterances for promising. Try to explain these results, using a principle from either pragmatics or semantics.

18. At an amusement park, a child and his parents are arguing about the child riding on the roller coaster. The child says, *I promise I won't throw up if you let me go on the ride.* The parents protest that the child cannot make such a promise. The child continues to scream, *I promise . . . I promise.* What felicity condition on promises has the child not yet learned?

19. Aitchison (1985:93–94) compares the case of Genie (see Curtiss 1977) to that of Isabelle, the child of a deaf mute, who was isolated from language until age 6½ years. Isabelle exhibited normal language behavior by age 8½, two years after her discovery. In contrast, Genie, who was nearly 14 years old when discovered, has never exhibited normal language behavior. What hypothesis about language acquisition might explain the different outcomes of these two cases?

20. Brian Albiser, deputy director of Clark County juvenile services, said of "C," a neglected 6-year-old who was found wandering the streets of Las Vegas and unable to speak: "Muscle development of the child's tongue is also critical to speaking" (Macy 1982:18-A). Which of the following quotations expresses the same general (mis)understanding of language that Albiser's comment does?

a. Dialect differences exist because "Many southerners suffer . . . from 'oral-facial muscular imbalance.' "

b. "Persons with functional speech disorders have faulty sensory perception in their mouths."

c. "People who learn at least two languages in early childhood appear to retain a greater flexibility of the vocal musculature."

d. all of the above

e. none of the above

21. In the article "How Genes Shape Personality" (1987), Stanford psychiatrist Herbert Leiderman is quoted as saying, "The pendulum is definitely swinging toward the side of the biologists and away from the environmentalists." The article explains that "scientists are turning up evidence that heredity has a greater influence on one's personality and behavior than either one's upbringing or the most crushing social pressure."

a. In terms of this passage, would Chomsky be more of a "biologist" or an "environmentalist"? How about Skinner?

b. According to the article, the science of sociobiology claims that the mind is not a *tabula rasa* (blank slate) "to be filled in from birth by family and society," but rather "is 'hard wired' before birth with a predisposed personality. This predisposition can be enhanced or suppressed, but not eliminated." Which of the following persons and concepts would be in basic agreement with the tenets of sociobiology?

i. mentalism
ii. nativism
iii. Chomsky
iv. Skinner
v. "environmentalists"
vi. "biologists"

c. The article quotes Harvard zoologist Edward O. Wilson as saying, "Genes hold the culture on a leash." Which of the following terms best describes Wilson?

i. behaviorist
ii. empiricist
iii. nativist
iv. Skinnerian
v. "environmentalist"

d. Assume that it turns out that the "biologists" are correct and that the "environmentalists" are wrong. The article says that some people fear that this might have an adverse effect on education. What would drive this fear?

Exploratory Exercises

1. Assume that a researcher wants to test a claim such as "Children acquire the phoneme /t/ by age 5." What issues arise in establishing criteria for whether a particular child has "acquired a phoneme"? That is, consider ways in which the way the term "acquired" might be defined differently by different researchers, and comment on how this might affect their findings. Consider whether a distinction needs to be made between "production" and "mastery" and, if so, what criteria should be used to determine "mastery." Keep in mind also that a particular phoneme such as /t/ will typically have different allophones in different positions (e.g., initial, medial, final, after /s/, and so on).
2. Assume that a researcher is studying the age at which children typically produce the sounds corresponding to particular phonemes. The researcher encounters a 3-year-old who consistently substitutes /s/ for /š/—so, for example, *fish* is produced as [fɪs] rather than as [fɪš]. As Hulit and Howard (2002:312) point out, the researcher then has to make certain decisions about how to classify data like this. Is it correct to state that the child has no knowledge of the target phoneme? Explain one argument against this statement, using concepts from phonology. What problems does this data suggest for a theory of language acquisition that assumes that children acquire their phonology one phoneme at a time?
3. Many nicknames start in childhood and persist to adulthood. Their structure can often be attributed to phonological processes used in child language. Compare each of the following nicknames to the full form on which it is based, and determine any phonological process(es) that have applied. Remember that you may first need to convert each full form and corresponding nickname to phonemic transcription in order to figure out what process(es) are involved. You may add to this list to include other nicknames that illustrate particular processes.

FULL NAME	NICKNAME	FULL NAME	NICKNAME
Katherine	Kathy	Elizabeth	Betty
Patricia	Trisha	Katherine	Kate
Patricia	Patty	Richard	Rick
William	Bill	Christopher	Kit
Margaret	Peggy	Martha	Marty
Elizabeth	Liz	Anthony	Tony

CHAPTER NINE

Second-Language Acquisition

Second-language acquisition is the study of how native speakers of one language acquire another language. (Hereafter, the native or source language will be referred to as the L1, and the second or target language as the L2.) In particular, second-language acquisition is concerned with explaining phenomena like the following:

(1) Norwegian forms negatives by placing the negative after the main verb (analogous to *He wrote not the book*). However, a speaker of Norwegian learning English may produce forms like *He not wrote the book,* even though such a construction never occurs in Norwegian or English.

(2) A speaker of Spanish learning English may pronounce *Spain* with an initial vowel [ɛspén], much as it would be pronounced in Spanish.

(3) A speaker of English learning German will have relatively little difficulty pronouncing *Tag* [tak] 'day' with a final [k], as native German speakers do. However, a speaker of German learning English will have relatively more difficulty pronouncing *bag* with a final [g], as native English speakers do.

(4) A speaker of Spanish learning English may produce *wh*-questions such as *Where she went?* just as children acquiring English as an L1 do.

Observation (1) suggests that speakers acquiring an L2 go through stages during which they construct a grammar different from that of either L1 or L2. Observation (2) suggests that some properties of this intermediate grammar reflect the influence of rules in the L1. Observation (3) suggests that apparent mirror-image differences between two languages are not equally easy to acquire. Observation (4) suggests that speakers acquiring an L2 go through stages similar to those that native speakers go through when acquiring that language as an L1.

The remainder of this chapter discusses research of two types. First, it reviews some basic issues in second-language acquisition, focusing on the intermediate grammar of the language learner and how it is formed. Second, it describes some specific patterns in phonology, morphology, syntax, and semantics that have been observed in speakers acquiring a second language. This chapter does not discuss classroom methods for facilitating second-language acquisition; however, the reader should be aware that a large body of research exists on teaching both foreign languages and English as a second language.

A note about terminology is in order. In Chapter 8, we were careful to note that children *acquire* their first language; they do not *learn* it. However, while some researchers refer to second-language *acquisition,* others use the term second-language *learning.* The variation in terminology arises from the fact that speakers are exposed to a second language at a much wider range of ages than speakers are exposed to their native language. For example, the task facing a 3-year-old native speaker of Japanese whose family moves to Italy might be more accurately described as that of *acquiring* Italian, while the task facing her adult parents would be more accurately described as that of *learning* Italian. In this chapter, we will use the term second-language *acquisition,* both for simplicity's sake and because it is somewhat more common in the research literature.

Issues in Second-Language Acquisition

Learning a second language involves more than just unlearning by trial and error the habits of one's native language. Between L1 and L2 the learner constructs a rule-governed **interlanguage,** arising from several different influences besides **language transfer,** that is, forms from the native language imposed on the second language. These include **language universals, markedness** relationships between L1 and L2, and **developmental processes** typical of first- (i.e., child) language acquisition. This section discusses each of these basic concepts needed to understand current issues in second-language acquisition.

Interlanguage Theory

The term *interlanguage,* first used by Larry Selinker (1972), refers to an intermediate grammar (i.e., linguistic system) that evolves as a learner acquires an L2. The interlanguage is characteristically distinct from both the L1 and the L2. A procedure known as **error analysis** attempts to identify regularities in interlanguage forms. These forms are viewed as reflecting the learner's hypotheses about the L2 and are believed to be rule-governed, just as the L1 and L2 are. For example, the learner may go through a stage of producing English negatives like *He not wrote the book.* Even though this is not a pattern found in the L1 or L2, the learner is forming negatives in a systematic way, by putting *not* before the main verb. At the same time, more recent studies of interlanguage have acknowledged that it has variation, just as variation exists in any natural language. For example, a learner may exhibit more native-like pronunciation of an L2 when reading a word list than when engaged in casual conversation. An English speaker learning Russian, for instance, might pronounce *czar* [tsar] as [dzar] in a word list, but as [zar] in conversation.

Language Transfer

The degree to which the L1 influences interlanguage is subject to debate. During the 1950s and 1960s, an approach known as **contrastive analysis** attempted to account for learner errors by examining similarities and differences (i.e., contrasts) between the L1 and L2. These contrasts were used to construct **hierarchies of difficulty,** predictions about the ease with which a particular L2 structure could be acquired, given facts about the L1. The most difficult type of contrast was predicted to be one in which the learner has to acquire a form that is nonexistent in the L1. For example, a speaker of English must learn Spanish [β] (a voiced bilabial fricative) as an allophone of /b/ after a vowel, as in *cabeza* [kaβesa] 'head.' At the other end of the hierarchy, contrastive analysis predicted that the least difficulty would result when a form or structure could be transferred with no change from L1 to L2. For example, both Spanish and English require that an /sw/ cluster be followed by a vowel.

Despite the commonsense appeal of contrastive analysis, its predictions of difficulty were not always borne out. For example, neither /ŋ/ nor /ž/ occurs word-initially in native English words. Yet speakers of English have much greater difficulty acquiring initial /ŋ/ (as in the Vietnamese name *Ngo*) than initial /ž/ (as in the French name *Jacques*). More generally, the contrastive analysis approach viewed language as a set of "habits," some of which must be "unlearned" during second-language acquisition. This essentially empiricist view was incompatible with subsequent nativist approaches that also took into account other forces, such as the learner's active contribution and the role of developmental processes in language acquisition and, by extension, second-language acquisition. (See Chapter 8 for a brief discussion of issues in first-language acquisition.)

At the same time, the influence of L1 on L2 acquisition cannot be ignored. The language learner may exhibit either **negative transfer** (also known as **interference**), in which some property of the L1 impedes acquisition of the L2, or **positive transfer** (also known as **facilitation**), in which some property of the L1 promotes the acquisition of the L2. An example of negative transfer would be a native speaker of English who, while acquiring French as an L2, transfers English subject-verb-pronominal object word order to French, as in *Il veut les* (he-wants-them) for *Il les veut* (he-them-wants). An example of positive transfer would be a native speaker of French who, while acquiring English as an L2, transfers French subject-verb-nominal object word order to English, as in *He wants the books.* The degree of L1 influence may also vary according to linguistic domain. For example, it is much easier to identify a nonnative speaker from pronunciation errors than from syntactic errors. That is, negative transfer from the L1 may be more apparent in phonology than in syntax: when we think of a "foreign accent," it is phonological interference that we are typically responding to.

Other Linguistic Factors

Other factors that cannot be attributed to language transfer from the L1 also affect second-language acquisition and the form of the interlanguage.

Language Universals. Language universals are those properties (i.e., categories and rules) that (nearly) all human languages have in common. (See Chapter 8.) The theory of language universals is intended primarily to explain first-language acquisition: universal properties of language are attributed to the child's initial state, thus relieving the child from having to learn these properties as idiosyncratic facts about the particular language to which he or she is exposed. Not surprisingly, researchers in second-language acquisition have also become interested in language universals. For one thing, L2 learners apparently face a **projection problem** similar to that faced by L1 learners: namely, they must acquire grammatical knowledge that cannot be inferred solely from the data they are exposed to. Language universals provide an explanation for this ability. In addition, controversy exists over the critical period hypothesis (i.e., the notion that language-acquisition abilities atrophy with age). This leaves open the possibility that adults may have access to language universals when acquiring an L2.

Universals can be classified as implicational or nonimplicational. An **implicational** universal is a property whose presence implies some other property. A commonly cited example concerns the distribution of voiced and voiceless stops among the world's languages. Some languages have only voiceless stops (e.g., Paiute and many other Native American languages); other languages have both voiced and voiceless stops (e.g., English and most western European languages); but no languages have only voiced stops. Based on this distribution, we can state that the presence of voiced stops in a language implies the presence of voiceless stops, but not vice versa. On the other hand, some universals are **nonimplicational.** For example, all languages have stop consonants, but this property alone does not imply the presence or absence of any other property.

Likewise, language universals can be classified as absolute or statistical. Universals are **absolute** if they are without exception. For example, all languages have syllables of the form CV, all languages have pronominal categories that include three persons and two numbers, and *wh*-movement always moves the *wh*-item leftward to clause-initial position. On the other hand, **statistical** universals, or tendencies, are properties that occur frequently but that do have exceptions. For example, verb-initial languages *generally* have prepositions (e.g., *in there*), while verb-final languages generally have postpositions (e.g., *therein*).

Finally, language universals can also be **parametric,** meaning that languages can vary according to the value they assign to a parameter. For example, languages vary in their setting for the so-called Pro-Drop Parameter, that is, in whether or not they allow the omission of subject pronouns in tensed clauses. For example, Spanish allows Pro-Drop, whereas English does not. The Spanish sentence *Está enfermo* translates literally as 'Is sick'; the referent of the subject is identified from the linguistic and nonlinguistic context. The English counterpart of this sentence, however, must have an overt subject, as in *He/She/It is sick.*

Markedness. The concept of **markedness** follows naturally from the concept of universals. Structures that are consistent with universals are considered **unmarked,** and those that are inconsistent with universals are considered **marked.** Marked structures are thought to be more difficult to acquire than are unmarked structures. Markedness can be viewed in an implicational sense: since voiced stops imply the presence of voiceless stops, but not vice versa, voiced stops are considered marked and voiceless stops are considered unmarked. Markedness may also be viewed in a statistical sense: property X is more marked than property Y if X is rarer than Y. Under this definition, the interdental fricative /θ/ is more marked than the alveolar fricative /s/, since /θ/ occurs in fewer of the world's languages. Markedness can also be viewed in a parametric sense: for example, heads of phrases (N is the head of NP, V the head of VP, etc.) tend to come at either the beginning or the end of each phrase in a given language. Thus, a language containing a VP made up of V-NP and a PP made up of P-NP is unmarked since both phrases are head-initial. In contrast, a language containing a VP made up of NP-V and a PP made up of P-NP is marked since one phrase is head-final and the other is head-initial.

The theory of markedness has been used to refine the contrastive analysis hypothesis and the notion of language transfer in general. As mentioned earlier, contrastive analysis in its initial form did not always make accurate predictions about second-language acquisition. For example, English and German differ in that English allows both voiced and voiceless obstruents (i.e., stops, fricatives, and affricates) word-finally (e.g., *tack/tag*), but German allows only voiceless obstruents word- finally (e.g., *Tag* 'day' is pronounced [tak]). Contrastive analysis would predict that English speakers learning German would have as much difficulty suppressing the voicing contrast as German speakers learning English would have mastering it. In fact, however, it is the L1 speakers of German who have the greater problem.

In order to predict more accurately when language differences will cause difficulty in second-language acquisition, Eckman (1987) proposed a **Markedness Differential Hypothesis** consisting of the following principles:

- Those properties of the L2 which differ from the L1 and are more marked than the L1 will be difficult.
- Among properties of the L2 that are more marked than the L1, the relative degree of difficulty will correspond to the relative degree of markedness.
- Those properties of the L2 which differ from the L1, but are not more marked than the L1, will not be difficult.

Evidence from language universals suggests that a word-final voicing contrast among obstruents, such as that found in English, is more marked than no such contrast. Therefore, the Markedness Differential Hypothesis correctly predicts the direction of difficulty between English and German for this particular property: L1 speakers of German will have relatively more difficulty learning the *marked* word-final voicing contrast in English; L1 speakers of English will have relatively less difficulty learning the *unmarked* word-final devoicing of obstruents in German.

Developmental Processes. It appears that an L2 learner may go through stages similar to those that speakers go through when acquiring their native language. For example, as discussed in Chapter 8, children acquiring English as an L1 break up or simplify consonant clusters (e.g., *tay* for *stay*); they acquire lexical morphemes before grammatical ones (e.g., *dog* before *the*) and inflectional affixes before derivational ones (e.g., tall*er* before sing*er*); in forming questions, they acquire *wh*-Movement before I-Movement (e.g., *Why I can't go?*); and they employ overgeneralization in the acquisition of lexical items (e.g., *Daddy* for all men). Speakers acquiring English as an L2 appear to go through these same stages and employ these same processes.

Exercise A

†1. Languages with front round vowels, like French, also have front unround vowels; but languages with front unround vowels, like English, don't necessarily have front round vowels. According to markedness theory, would the vowel system of French or English be harder for a speaker of the *other* language to learn? Explain.

2. Consider the following putative universal: I-Movement occurs in *yes-no* questions only if it occurs in *wh*-questions. This universal is ________.

a. implicational
b. statistical
c. parametric
d. both (a) and (b)
e. none of the above

Exercise A *Continued*

†**3.** There is a tendency for speakers acquiring English as an L2 to produce forms such as [pe] or [pəle] for *play* /ple/, even when attempting clusters that appear in their L1. Is this phenomenon an example of ________.

a. positive transfer
b. negative transfer
c. developmental process
d. a statistical universal
e. none of the above

4. Assume that languages with affricates also have stops and fricatives, but that not all languages with stops and fricatives have affricates. Which type(s) of consonants should be easiest to learn, according to markedness theory?

5. Assume that languages with nasalized vowels also have nonnasalized ones, but that not all languages with nonnasalized vowels have nasalized ones. Which type of vowel should be easier to learn, according to markedness theory?

6. Speakers of English as an L2 tend to go through the same stages as native English speakers do in acquiring negatives. Put the following forms in the order in which nonnative speakers are most likely to acquire them.

A. I no eat meat.
B. I don't eat meat.
C. No eat meat.

7. Speakers of English as an L2 tend to go through the same stages as native English speakers do in acquiring questions.

a. Put the following forms in the order in which nonnative speakers are most likely to acquire them.
b. What rule has applied in (C) that has not applied in (B)?
c. What rule has applied in (A) that has not applied in (C)?

A. Where do you come from?
B. You come from where?
C. Where you come from?

8. Spanish forms negatives as follows: *Pienso* 'I think' → *No pienso* 'I don't think.' Dulay and Burt (1983) report the following negative forms by Spanish speakers learning English:

A. He no wanna go.
B. It no cause too much trouble.
C. He look like a glass, but no is a glass.

These errors are due to ________.

a. positive transfer
b. negative transfer
c. a universal
d. a developmental process
e. either (b) or (d)

9. Consider the following putative universal: the subject occurs before the object in the vast majority of the world's languages. This universal is ________.

a. implicational
b. statistical
c. parametric
d. both (a) and (b)
e. none of the above

Patterns in Second-Language Acquisition

This section looks at four areas of linguistic theory—phonology, morphology, syntax, and semantics—and examines some specific L2 acquisition patterns within each area. It is important to emphasize that each of these areas has a different pattern of influence on interlanguage forms. In particular, interlanguage phonology shows perhaps the strongest L1 transfer influence. On the other hand, interlanguage morphology shows strong developmental influence, with clear resistance to transfer. Interlanguage syntax demonstrates a complex interaction of transfer (affected by universals and markedness) and developmental influences. Interlanguage semantics is strongly developmental, with some negative transfer; semantics is also influenced by developing cultural knowledge in ways that no other domain of interlanguage is.

Phonology

Speakers may transfer the segmental structure of L1 to L2. One situation in particular in which L1 interference is noticeable is when the L2 makes a phonemic distinction that does not exist in the L1. For example, Japanese has one phoneme /r/ with allophones [l] and [r]; thus, there is no phonemic distinction between [l] and [r]. In contrast, English maintains a phonemic distinction between /l/ and /r/. Therefore, the native speaker of Japanese learning English as an L2 would be expected to experience greater difficulty than an English speaker learning Japanese. The Japanese speaker has to learn to make a phonemic distinction not found in his or her native language. On the other hand, the English speaker's distinction between [l] and [r] will go unnoticed by Japanese listeners.

Speakers may also transfer phonological rules from L1 to L2. One example that we have already looked at is the rule of Final Devoicing in German, which states that word-final obstruents must be voiceless. Obstruents may display a voicing contrast in medial position (e.g., [p] in [lumpən] 'rascals' but [b] in [šterbən] 'to die'), but this contrast is neutralized in word-final position (e.g., [p] in [lump] 'rascal' and [p] in [štarp] 'died'). Consequently, it is common for native speakers of German to devoice final obstruents when they are learning English, pronouncing both *back* and *bag,* for example, as [bæk].

Speakers may also transfer **phonotactic constraints** (i.e., conditions on permissible sequences of segments) from their L1 to the L2. For example, English permits syllable-initial clusters of up to three consonants, as long as the first consonant is /s/, the second is a voiceless stop, and the third is a liquid (e.g., *street* /strit/, *splash* /splæš/). A speaker whose native language does not permit such initial clusters may insert a vowel that breaks up the cluster, making it conform to a syllable structure acceptable in the speaker's L1. For example, Broselow (1987) reports that native speakers of Egyptian Arabic and Iraqi Arabic produced the following forms:

ENGLISH TARGET		EGYPTIAN ARABIC	IRAQI ARABIC
floor	[flor]	[filor]	[iflor]
three	[θri]	[θiri]	[iθri]
Fred	[frɛd]	[firɛd]	[ifrɛd]
children	[čɪldrɛn]	[čildirɛn]	[čilidrɛn]

Note that native speakers of the two Arabic dialects employ different strategies for breaking up the unacceptable clusters. Egyptian Arabic speakers insert [i] between members of a consonant-liquid cluster, while Iraqi Arabic speakers insert [i] before a consonant-liquid cluster, allowing resyllabification (e.g., [flor] → [iflor]). Both of these strategies, however, achieve a similar end: they allow the consonant and liquid to be analyzed as members of *different* syllables. The resultant forms thus reflect an acceptable syllable structure in the L1.

Interference from the L1 and developmental processes may also interact during second-language acquisition. Research by Major (1987) suggests that L1 interference takes precedence during the earlier stages of phonological acquisition, and then developmental processes may predominate for a time. Finally, these processes are suppressed, yielding a form approximating that of the native speaker. For example, a Brazilian Portuguese speaker learning English as an L2 went through the following stages in producing the word *dog:*

[dɔgi]
[dɔgə]
[dɔk]
[dɔg]

The first form, [dɔgi], reflects the transfer of a phonotactic constraint from the L1. Portuguese does not permit any word-final obstruents except /s/; thus, the addition of [i] removes [g] from word-final position. The second form, [dɔgə], reflects a developmental process: reduction of unstressed vowels to [ə]. This cannot be a transfer from the L1, since Portuguese does not allow word-final [ə]. The third form, [dɔk], also reflects a developmental process: devoicing of word-final obstruents. The fourth form, [dɔg], approximates the pronunciation of a native English speaker.

Exercise B

†1. The cluster [ts] is not permitted in word-initial position in English. Thus, the form [tsitsi] *tsetse* may be modified to [titsi] or [sitsi]. What developmental process(es) is involved?

2. A native speaker of English learning German as an L2 may produce [kənɔf] for German /knɔpf/. What developmental process(es) is involved?

†3. Consider the following error produced by a native speaker of Arabic acquiring English as an L2: *Did you sail your boat?* for *Did you sell your boat?* What can be inferred about the phonology of Arabic from this error?

4. Consider the following error produced by a native speaker of Vietnamese acquiring English as an L2: *Did you forget your code?* for *Did you forget your coat?* What can be inferred about the phonology of Vietnamese from this error?

5. In the movie *Murder on the Orient Express,* the protagonist is a Belgian detective, Hercule Poirot. Poirot, a native speaker of French, speaks excellent English but regularly pronounces the word *pipe* as /pip/. Explain Poirot's pronunciation of this word.

6. Korean has the following phonological rule:

$$\underset{[+\text{alveolar}]}{\text{C}} \rightarrow [+\text{palatal}] \,/\, \underline{\qquad\quad}\, \underset{\begin{bmatrix}+\text{hi}\\ -\text{back}\end{bmatrix}}{\text{V}}$$

(continued)

Exercise B *Continued*

Assume a native speaker of Korean is learning English. How might this speaker pronounce the word *seat?*

7. Consider the following pronunciations by native speakers of Japanese acquiring English as an L2.

bus	[basu]	baby	[bebi]
bath	[basu]	gum	[gamu]

a. What can be inferred about the basic syllable structure of Japanese?

b. What English consonant phoneme(s) does Japanese lack?

c. What English vowel phoneme(s) does Japanese lack?

Morphology

Developmental processes play a major role in the acquisition of L2 morphology. For example, several studies have found similarities among both child and adult learners of English as an L2, in the order in which certain grammatical morphemes are acquired. For example, the {PLU} morpheme is acquired by both groups relatively early, whereas the {PRES} and the {POSS} morphemes are acquired later. The point to note is that these morphemes seem to be acquired in much the same way that they are acquired by native speakers. First, they are acquired in the same order—{PLU} first, then {POSS} and {PRES}. Second, they are acquired according to their morphological function rather than their phonological form. If they were acquired according to form, they would all be acquired at the same time.

Other research also indicates that L2 learners may exhibit developmental processes in expressing temporality, in the absence of verb morphology. Among these devices are temporal markers such as *yesterday* and *last night,* locatives such as *in Vietnam* and *at work,* calendar expressions such as *January* and *Tuesday,* and clause sequencing as in *I go to school Vietnam. [Then] I come U.S.* Once again, children acquiring English as an L1 go through similar stages.

Likewise, Dulay and Burt (1983) found that native speakers of Spanish employed strategies that are not found in Spanish but that do occur when children are acquiring English as their native language. Examples include the following:

(5) *He took her teeths off.* Here the irregular plural form *teeth* is misanalyzed as a root form and inflected again with the regular plural suffix.

(6) *I didn't weared any hat.* Here both verb forms are inflected for tense, rather than just the first verb form.

(7) *Me need crayons now.* Here the objective case pronoun is generalized to nominative position.

(8) *He didn't come yesterday* (*He* = a little girl). Here the masculine pronoun is generalized to a female referent.

(9) *He say he bring it to school.* Here the tense inflection is omitted from the first verb form in both the main clause and the subordinate clause.

Less research has been done on the acquisition of derivational morphology by L2 learners. However, Laufer (1990) reports that derivational complexity may be both a help and a hindrance to the nonnative speaker. For example, a learner's knowledge that {pre} means 'before' (as in *preview* and *premature*) may help the learner to understand the meaning of a newly encountered word such as *prenuptial.* On the other hand, the L2 learner also has to deal with **deceptive transparency**—morphemes that lead to a misinterpretation of a word. For example, Laufer describes nonnative speakers of English who interpreted *outline* as meaning 'out of line' and *discourse* as meaning 'without direction.'

Exercise C

1. Morphological information is missing from each of the following sentences. In each case, state how the speaker signals temporal information in the absence of relevant verb morphology.
   - **a.** I eat McDonald last night.
   - **b.** I say prayer, I go bed.
   - **c.** Already I fly San Francisco.

†2. Consider the following forms used by a speaker acquiring English as an L2. What can be inferred about the morphological structure of *gimme* in this person's lexicon?
   - **A.** Gimme that pencil to me.
   - **B.** Gimme that pencil to her.

3. Which of the following words exhibits "deceptive transparency"? For those that do, how would a nonnative speaker of English be likely to misinterpret them?
   - **†a.** upbraid
   - **b.** reanalyze
   - **c.** discover
   - **d.** underhanded
   - **e.** uncooperative
   - **f.** disability
   - **g.** uproar

Syntax

Along with phonology, syntax is one of the domains that has been studied the most by researchers in second-language acquisition, largely because of the concurrent interest in syntax that Chomsky generated within linguistics in general. Researchers have found transfer, markedness, and developmental processes to play a role in interlanguage syntax.

One area in which transfer commonly occurs is subcategorization—that is, restrictions on the syntactic categories that can co-occur with a particular lexical item. Consider the example of English speakers learning French as an L2. In English, the verb *listen* is subcategorized for a preposition *(listen to NP);* however, the equivalent French verb is not *(écouter NP).* Conversely, the English verb *obey* is not subcategorized for a preposition *(obey NP);*

however, the equivalent French verb is *(obéir à NP).* Adjémian (1983) reports that English speakers commonly transfer English subcategorization restrictions to French, producing interlanguage forms like the following:

INTERLANGUAGE FORM	ENGLISH GLOSS	CORRECT FRENCH FORM
écouter à	'listen to'	écouter
obéir	'obey'	obéir à

Negative transfer errors may also result when the L1 and L2 share a rule, but apply the rule under different circumstances. For example, Dulay and Burt (1983) report the following productions by Norwegian speakers learning English as an L2:

(10) *Like you* me not, Reidun?
(11) *Like you* ice cream?
(12) *Drive you* car yesterday?

They account for these data by observing that English inverts the subject and first *auxiliary verb* in questions, whereas Norwegian inverts the subject and the first *verb,* whether auxiliary or main verb.

It is important to remember that transfer between an L1 and L2 is not a simple bidirectional phenomena, indicating that factors other than simply "difference" come into play. For example, consider the case of English speakers learning French or Spanish as an L2. (The following data and analysis are adapted from Anderson [1983].) French and Spanish adhere to a subject-object-verb (SOV) order when the object is a pronoun:

(13a)	French:	Je *les* vois	(I-*them*-see)	'I see them'
(14a)	Spanish:	Yo no *la* vi	(I-not-*her*-see)	'I didn't see her'

However, English speakers learning Spanish or French often place the pronoun after the verb, reflecting English word order (SVO):

INTERLANGUAGE FORM	CORRECT TARGET	
(13b) Je vois *les*	Je *les* vois	'I see them'
(14b) Yo no vi *la*	Yo no *la* vi	'I didn't see her'

Conversely, one might predict that native speakers of French and Spanish learning English would reverse the process, producing forms like *I them see* and *I not her see.* However, forms like these do not appear in the interlanguage of Spanish or French speakers. That is, in sentences with pronominal objects, English speakers transfer SVO order, but French and Spanish speakers do not transfer SOV order.

One principle that accounts for this asymmetrical transfer is markedness. Consider the permissible word orders in English and in French and Spanish:

	ENGLISH	FRENCH/SPANISH
Nominal object	SVO	SVO
Pronominal object	SVO	SOV

With no alternative order, SVO is clearly unmarked in English. Thus, English speakers can be expected to transfer SVO to the L2. On the other hand, SOV is marked in French and Spanish. (Pronominal objects are the only elements of VP in French and Spanish that precede the verb, thus representing the exceptional or "marked" case.) Consequently, French and Spanish speakers would not be expected to transfer SOV to the L2.

Sometimes transfer and developmental processes appear to interact. For example, Anderson (1983) reports a study of two children learning English: one a native speaker of Spanish, the other a native speaker of Japanese. The native speaker of Spanish acquired English articles quite quickly, which can be attributed to positive transfer from Spanish, which also has articles. In contrast, the Japanese child went through a stage where articles were omitted, a stage which is also found among children acquiring English as their native language. However, this stage was prolonged for the Japanese child, since Japanese does not have articles. Thus negative transfer from the L1 may prolong an interlanguage feature associated with a developmental process.

The role of language universals in the acquisition of L2 syntax is still a controversial one. Some research indicates that L2 learners are able to acquire knowledge about the L2 which is derivable from neither L1 nor L2 input. For example, research reported by White (1989) investigated the ability of native Japanese speakers to recognize the Right Roof Constraint in English. This constraint on rightward movement prevents an element from being extraposed out of its original clause. For example, the Right Roof Constraint permits (15b), but not (15c), as a paraphrase of (15a).

(15a) That [[a book *by Chomsky*]$_{NP}$ has just come out]$_S$ is not surprising.
(15b) That [[a book]$_{NP}$ has just come out *by Chomsky*]$_S$ is not surprising.
(15c) *That [[a book]$_{NP}$ has just come out]$_S$ is not surprising *by Chomsky*.

Japanese speakers of English as an L2 were, in most cases, able to recognize sentences like (15c) as ungrammatical. This ability is significant because the Right Roof Constraint does not operate in Japanese, which is verb-final and does not allow rightward movement. What is even more significant, however, is that this constraint cannot be directly inferred from merely listening to English, since no violations of it ever occur. (Just because something *does not* occur in a corpus of data doesn't mean it *cannot* occur.) Thus, it may be that the Japanese speakers are able to infer the Right Roof Constraint from the putatively universal Subjacency constraint on movement, which essentially states that all movement must be within one clause or between adjacent clauses (i.e., a moved item cannot cross more than one S or NP). (For an exact statement of Subjacency, see Chapter 4.)

Exercise D

1. An English speaker learning French as an L2 produces the form *Le chien a mangé les* (the dog - ate - them) for *Le chien les a mangé* (the dog - them - ate). This error is caused by
   a. the positive transfer of an L1 feature to L2
   b. the negative transfer of an L1 feature to L2

(continued)

Exercise D Continued

- **c.** subcategorization restriction in L1
- **d.** a developmental process
- **e.** a universal

†2. A French speaker acquiring English as an L2 uses the form *Look that plane* for *Look at that plane.* The French verb that corresponds to *look at* is *regarder.* Explain the error.

3. All languages allow relativization of the subject (e.g., *the teacher <u>who</u> taught me*). However, not all languages allow relativization of the object of a preposition (e.g., *the teacher <u>to whom</u> I talked*); even fewer allow relativization of the possessive (e.g., *the teacher <u>whose course</u> I took*). Which of these constructions is most marked? Explain.

4. In an example cited by Adjémian (1983), French speakers acquiring English as an L2 produced forms like the following. What can be inferred about French from such errors?

- **A.** He stopped *to defend* himself. (Target [apparent from context]: *defending*)
- **B.** We just enjoyed *to move* and *to play.* (Target: *moving* and *playing*)

†5. An English speaker acquiring French as an L2 uses the form *entrer* 'enter' for *entrer dans* 'enter into.' Explain the error.

6. Consider the following forms, produced by a native speaker of German acquiring English as an L2. Based on these examples, what can you infer about the process of forming questions in German? How does it differ from the same process in English?

- **A.** Can you go with me?
- **B.** Has he drunk the beer?
- **C.** Came you home early?

7. Justin Wilson, a Cajun comedian from Louisiana, is famous for the greeting *How y'all are?* (instead of *How are y'all?*). Wilson's greeting suggests that English has a syntactic rule not found in Cajun French. What is the rule?

Semantics

Semantics has received somewhat less attention in research on second-language acquisition than have phonology and syntax. Nonetheless, it is possible to draw some generalizations about processes that occur when speakers attempt to acquire the vocabulary of an L2. The following phenomena are based on studies by Laufer (1990) and Zughoul (1991); all deal with speakers learning English as a second language.

One developmental strategy such speakers employ is the overgeneralization of superordinates, much as children overgeneralize in acquiring the lexicon of their native language. Because of their limited vocabulary, speakers may rely on superordinate terms (e.g., *animal* where native speakers would use the hyponym *dog*). The learner's strategy here seems to be to use words that are generalizable to more contexts. In addition, some speakers may rely heavily on the modifiers *good, bad, big, small, very,* and *many,* generalizing their use to inappropriate contexts (e.g., *I have small money* for *I have little money*).

Another common developmental strategy is the inappropriate use of synonyms. Two or more words may have similar meanings, but differ in their selectional restrictions (i.e., in the semantic features of the words with which they co-occur), in their subcategorization restrictions (i.e., in the categories of words with which they co-occur), in their connotations (i.e., in the emotional associations of the word), and in their register restrictions (i.e., in their level of formality). The nonnative speaker may use a word whose literal meaning is appropriate but which violates one of the restrictions just described. Sometimes this use may reflect the fact that two synonyms are equivalent to one word in the speaker's L1. For example, *tall* and *long* are subsumed by one Arabic word, *tawīl*. Consequently, an Arabic speaker learning English may produce a sentence like *My father is a long thin man,* not realizing that *long* is not used with [+human] nouns. Or the learner may rely on a bilingual dictionary that simply lists synonyms (e.g., *career, job, occupation, work*) without explaining their restrictions. This strategy may lead the L2 learner to produce sentences like *There are not many occupations in the village* or *There are many works in the city.* Similarly, the nonnative speaker who says *I want to grow my knowledge* may have found *grow* as a synonym for *develop* in a dictionary or thesaurus.

Another semantic relation that may cause difficulty has to do with converses: a pair of words that express a reciprocal relation. For example, *teach* and *learn* are converses: if X teaches Y, Y learns from X. It is not unusual for a nonnative speaker to confuse the members of a pair of converses, producing sentences like *It learns them independence.* This phenomenon appears to be developmental and is similar to the stages a child goes through in acquiring the positive member of a pair of opposites (e.g., *long*) before the negative member (e.g., *short*).

Yet another developmental strategy is the use of **circumlocutions,** which involve substituting a descriptive phrase for a word that the learner has not yet acquired or cannot retrieve: for example, a student who did not know the word *pregnant* wrote *Smoking cigarettes has a bad effect, especially on a lady who is carrying an infant.*

Another common problem in the semantic domain is difficulty with **idioms,** expressions whose meaning cannot be derived from their component words—for example, *kick the bucket* for 'die,' *pull one's leg* for 'joke,' and *blow one's top* for 'get angry.' Not surprisingly, idioms are often incomprehensible for the nonnative speaker, who may also prefer to use nonidiomatic equivalents in expressive tasks. The difficulty seems to be compounded by the degree of mismatch between the literal and figurative meanings of the idiom. For example, an idiomatic expression like *flying high* 'exuberant' would probably present fewer difficulties than *chewing the fat* 'talking.' Related problems may arise with the numerous phrasal verbs in English. For example, we have *run up* 'incur,' *run down* 'find,' and *run out* 'expire.' Here again, the nonnative speaker may prefer the one-word equivalent to the phrasal verb.

Finally, confusion of words with similar sounds or spelling may also occur. For example, in the following sentences the target words are in brackets: *People are unable to work and earn efficient [sufficient] money; They are reasonable [responsible] for the loss of our land.* A related problem may arise with **polysemes** (one form with related meanings, e.g., *mouth* 'orifice for eating' and *mouth* 'opening of a river into another body of water') and **homonyms** (one form with unrelated meanings, e.g., *swallow* 'ingest' and *swallow* 'small, long-winged bird'). For example, a learner may mistakenly interpret *state* in a sentence like *He is in a critical state* in its geopolitical sense, rather than as 'situation.'

Exercise E

1. Some researchers have noticed that L2 learners of English prefer *decide* to *make up your mind, postpone* to *put off,* and *reprimand* to *tell off.* What principle from semantics appears to explain this preference?

(continued)

***Exercise E** Continued*

†**2.** Assume that an ESL student writes *I returned the books I lent from the library.* What principle from semantics explains this error?

3. Speculate on the intended word in each of the following sentences. The word used and the one intended are covered by one form in the writer's native language:

   a. *Most works require the applicant to speak English.*

   b. *I am for coeducation because of two reasons. The first is that friendship grows up among the two races. Coeducation also teaches students to improve their ability to deal with the other kind.*

Non-Linguistic Influences on Second-Language Acquisition

While this chapter has focused on the role of linguistic variables in second-language acquisition, other forces are believed to play a role as well. A few of these are treated briefly here.

Age. The traditional view of the role of age in second-language acquisition has been that acquiring an L2 is more difficult for an older (i.e., post-pubescent) learner than for a younger one. This view derives largely from the Critical Period Hypothesis, developed by the neurobiologist Eric Lenneberg. According to Lenneberg (1964), the critical period for language acquisition is between years 2 and 12, after which plasticity of the brain's left hemisphere declines. However, the Critical Period Hypothesis in general and its implications for second-language acquisition in particular are not universally agreed upon by researchers. For example, Hatch (1983) reviews findings which suggest that adult L2 learners actually achieve higher levels of proficiency than younger learners, at least initially, and learn more efficiently than younger learners (i.e., with relatively less exposure). It is generally agreed, however, that phonology is the one domain where adult learners lag behind younger learners, in that a native-like accent is difficult to acquire if L2 acquisition begins beyond the age of puberty.

The role of age is a complex issue because age interacts with other nonlinguistic variables that may also affect second-language acquisition. For example, length of exposure has been shown to correlate positively with proficiency. Thus, if two learners started studying an L2 at different ages, the learner who started at an earlier age may display superior proficiency simply because of having studied the L2 for a longer period of time, not necessarily because of having begun at an earlier age. Also, younger learners may be less self-conscious about learning an L2, which can promote acquisition. On the other hand, older learners bring to the acquisition process more mature cognitive skills in analysis and problem-solving—skills which, though not strictly linguistic, may be profitably applied to the task of language acquisition.

Cognitive Style. Cognitive style reflects the learner's approach to problem-solving and to conceptualizing and organizing information. There are two types of cognitive style. **Field independence** is a relatively analytical style in which the learner imposes structure on individual parts, distinguishing the irrelevant from the essential. **Field dependence** is a relatively global or holistic style in which the learner does not differentiate individual parts. Field independence has been found to correlate somewhat with success in second-language acquisition (although this may reflect the fact that most teaching techniques emphasize analysis).

Personality Traits. Traits found to correlate with success in second-language acquisition include extroversion and a willingness to take risks. Extroversion has been found to be more of an advantage in naturalistic settings than in formal learning settings. Risk-taking may be both social (e.g., a willingness to engage in conversations) and linguistic (e.g., a willingness to try new vocabulary).

Social-Psychological Forces. Factors such as the learner's motivation and attitude toward the L2 have also been hypothesized to play a role in second-language acquisition. Two types of motivation have been identified. **Integrative motivation** reflects the language learner's desire to become part of the community or culture represented by the L2. **Instrumental motivation** reflects the language learner's desire to learn the language for practical purposes, such as getting a job. Integrative motivation is seen as the more important component in second language acquisition.

Exercise F

Bilingual speakers sometimes engage in **code-switching,** that is, changing from one language to the other in the course of a conversation. The following excerpt, adapted from Preston (1989:216–18), illustrates code-switching between English and Spanish. Answer questions (1–4) based on this excerpt.

BOSS: Carmen . . . I have a letter to dictate to you.

SECY: Fine. Let me get my pen and pad.

BOSS: Ah, this man William Bolger got his organization to contribute a lot of money to the Puerto Rican parade. . . .¿Tú fuiste a la parada? [Did you go to the parade?]

SECY: Sí, yo fuí. . . . [Yes, I went.]

BOSS: ¿Y cómo te estuvo? [And how did you like it?]

SECY: Y, lo más bonita. [Oh, very pretty.]

BOSS: Fuí con mi señora y con mis nenes. . . . y tuve día bien agradable. Ahora lo que me molesta a mi es que las personas cuando viene una cosa así, la parada Puertorriqueña . . . corren de la casa a participar porque es una actividad festiva, . . . y sin embargo, cuando tienen que ir a la iglesia, o la misa para pedirle [secretary laughs] a Diós entonces no van.

[I went with my wife and my children. . . . And I had a pleasant day. Now what bothers me is that people when something like this comes along, the Puerto Rican parade, . . . they run from the house to participate because it is a festive activity, . . . and then, when they have to go to church or mass to ask God then they don't go.]

SECY: Sí, entonces no van. [Yes, then they don't go.]

BOSS: Pero, así es la vida, caramba. [But that's life, you know.] Do you think you could get this letter out today?

SECY: Oh yes, I'll have it this afternoon for you.

1. Form a generalization about where code-switching takes place.
2. Which nonlinguistic factor seems to be the most important in this case of code-switching?
   - **a.** age
   - **b.** cognitive style
   - **c.** personality traits
   - **d.** social-psychological factors
   - **e.** both (b) and (d)
   - **f.** none of the above

(continued)

Exercise F Continued

3. Which of the following factors seems to be most important in switching from English to Spanish?
   - **a.** age
   - **b.** field independence
   - **c.** field dependence
   - **d.** extroversion
   - **e.** integrative motivation
   - **f.** instrumental motivation
4. Assume both speakers are L1 speakers of Spanish and L2 speakers of English. Which of the factors in question (3) are likely to be most important in their learning English?

Summary

The theory of second-language acquisition makes use of such concepts as interlanguage, language transfer (both positive and negative), language universals, markedness, and developmental processes. Second-language acquisition can be viewed from the perspective of phonology, morphology, syntax, and semantics. We have also looked briefly at some of the nonlinguistic influences on second-language acquisition, including age, cognitive style, personality, and other social-psychological forces such as motivation and attitude.

SUPPLEMENTARY READINGS

Bialystok, E., & Hakuta, K. (1994). *In other words: The science and psychology of second-language acquisition.* New York: Basic Books.

Cook, V. (1996). *Second language learning and language teaching* (2nd ed.). London: Edward Arnold.

Dicker, S. J. (1996). *Languages in America: A pluralist view.* Clevedon, England: Multilingual Matters.

Gass, S., & Schachter, J. (1989). *Linguistic perspectives on second language acquisition.* Cambridge, England: Cambridge University Press.

Gass, S. M., & Selinker, L. (2001). *Second language acquisition: An introductory course.* Mahwah, NJ: Erlbaum.

Hadley, A. O. (1993). *Research on language learning: Principles, processes, and prospects.* Lincolnwood, IL: National Textbook Co.

Hatch, E. (1983). *Psycholinguistics: A second language perspective.* Rowley, MA: Newbury House.

White, L. (1989). *Universal grammar and second language acquisition.* Amsterdam: John Benjamins.

You are now prepared to read the works by Bialystok and Hakuta, Cook, Dicker, and Gass and Selinker. These works review basic concepts in linguistics and demonstrate their applicability to second-language acquisition. Dicker addresses many of the cultural and political issues associated with language diversity.

The other works are more advanced and would therefore be more accessible to readers with additional coursework in syntax or phonology. Gass and Schachter is a collection of studies on second-language acquisition, most of them experimental, by researchers in syntax, semantics, and phonology. White investigates the role of universal grammar in second-language acquisition.

Supplementary Exercises

1. Consider the following forms produced by nonnative speakers acquiring English as an L2. Classify the errors by domain of linguistics (i.e., phonology, morphology, syntax, or semantics).
   - **a.** Why you gave him your paper?
   - **b.** She caught two fishes.
   - **c.** Hand me the pincers (i.e., pliers).
   - **d.** Do you play any [ɛspórts] (i.e., sports)?

2. In English, [p] and [pʰ] are allophones of one phoneme, /p/. In contrast, Hindi maintains a phonemic distinction between /p/ and /pʰ/: [p] is an allophone of /p/, while [pʰ] is an allophone of /pʰ/. Who will have more difficulty—a native English speaker learning Hindi, or a native Hindi speaker learning English? Explain.
3. Broselow (1987:14) reports that the following forms were produced by Arabic students learning English. Construct a phonological rule that describes where the students insert vowels.

floor	[iflor]	*study*	[istadi]
plane	[iblen]	*Fred*	[ifred]
snow	[isno]	*children*	[čilidren]
three	[iθri]		

4. Native speakers of Spanish learning English often produce forms like the following:

school	[ɛskúl]	spell	[ɛspɛ́l]
stop	[ɛstáp]	Spanish	[ɛspǽnɪš]
sell	[sɛl]	soup	[sup]

   a. These data illustrate that Spanish has a phonotactic constraint not found in English. State the constraint.
   b. What is the function of the epenthetic /ɛ/ in some of these forms?
5. Hungarian has the following rule of Regressive Voicing Assimilation:

$$[+\text{obstruent}] \rightarrow [-\text{voice}] \; / \; \underline{\qquad\quad} \; (\#) \begin{bmatrix} +\text{obstruent} \\ -\text{voice} \end{bmatrix}$$

   How might an L1 speaker of Hungarian pronounce the following English phrases?
   a. said that **b.** have tried
6. Consider the following riddle:
   Q: What do you call the jelly beans that get left in the bottom of your Easter basket because they're a flavor you didn't like?
   A: "Has beans."
   The "humor" here might escape someone acquiring English as an L2.
   a. What concept from semantics would help explain the nonnative speaker's failure to "get" it?
   b. What phonological distinction might add to the confusion?
7. Speakers acquiring English as an L2 often make *wanna*-contraction errors such as *Who do you wanna go?* Based on the following examples, determine the circumstances under which *wanna*-contraction is blocked. (Hint: Where does *who* originate in the underlying structure of each sentence?)
   A.1. Who do you *want to* go?
   A.2. *Who do you *wanna* go?
   B.1. Who do you *want to* go with?
   B.2. Who do you *wanna* go with?
8. Dulay and Burt (1983) report forms like *I finished to watch TV when it was four o'clock* instead of *I finished watching TV when it was four o'clock.* What can be inferred about Spanish from this error?
9. Assume the following hierarchy of markedness (> = "is more marked than"): final voicing contrast > medial voicing contrast > initial voicing contrast
   a. How does this hierarchy explain the relative ease with which L1 speakers of English are able to acquire the initial /ž/-/š/ contrast in French, as in *jais* [žɛ] 'jet' versus *chez* [še] 'at'?
   b. Arrange the following patterns from least marked to most marked.

i. a voicing contrast among obstruents in all syllable positions (i.e., initial, medial, final)
ii. a voicing contrast among obstruents in initial position only
iii. a voicing contrast among obstruents in initial and medial position only

10. Speakers acquiring English as an L2 often make subject-verb agreement errors such as *Where does the spiders go?* for *Where do the spiders go?* These same speakers, however, typically produce correct forms such as *The spiders go* and *The spider goes.* How might the incorrect forms be explained?

11. Some languages adhere to the Adjacency Principle, which requires noun phrases to be next to the item (e.g., verb or preposition) that assigns them case. Other languages do not adhere to this principle. Now consider the following data:

FRENCH:

A.1. Marie a mangé le dîner rapidement. [Marie-ate-the dinner-quickly]
A.2. Marie a mangé rapidement le dîner. [Marie-ate-quickly-the dinner]

ENGLISH:

B.1. Mary ate her dinner quickly.
B.2. *Mary ate quickly her dinner.

a. Which language, French or English, adheres to the Adjacency Principle?
b. If you assume negative transfer from L1, who is likely to make more errors: an English speaker acquiring French, or a French speaker acquiring English? Explain.

12. All languages with agentive passives like (B) have agentless passives like (A). However, some languages have structures like (A) but not like (B).

A. The door was closed.
B. The door was closed by the janitor.
a. Which structure is more marked?
b. Arabic has structures like (A), but not like (B). Japanese has structures like (A) and (B). Which language learner is likely to have greater difficulty: an L1 Arabic speaker learning Japanese as an L2, or an L1 Japanese speaker learning Arabic as an L2? Explain.

13. Consider the following table from Eckman (1987:63), which describes the use of pronominal reflexes in five different languages. A pronominal reflex is an item that marks the underlying position of a relativized NP. (If English had pronominal reflexes, it would have structures like *the boy that he came* for *the boy that came,* and *the boy that John hit him* for *the boy that John hit.*) Relativization without a pronominal reflex is more marked than relativization with a pronominal reflex.

	SUBJECT	DIRECT OBJECT	INDIRECT OBJECT	OBJECT OF A PREPOSITION
PERSIAN	(+)	+	+	+
ARABIC	(+)	(+)	+	+
CHINESE	–	–	+	+
JAPANESE	–	–	–	(+)
ENGLISH	–	–	–	–

[+ = relativization with obligatory reflex, (+) = relativization with optional reflex, – = relativization without reflex.]

a. Which of these languages is most marked with respect to relativization? Least marked? Explain.

b. Given this table, would Persian speakers or Chinese speakers be expected to make more errors in producing relative clauses in English?

c. How does the Markedness Differential Hypothesis account for your analysis in question (b)?

d. Across languages, which position (e.g., subject, direct object, etc.) is most likely to allow relativization without a pronominal reflex?

e. Native speakers of which of these languages would be expected to have difficulty with a relative clause like *He's the person that I was counting on?*

f. Native speakers of which of these languages would be expected to have difficulty with a relative clause like *She's the one that told me?*

g. Native speakers of which of these languages would be expected to have difficulty with a relative clause like *That's the one I saw?*

14. Speakers acquiring English as an L2 often make subject-verb contraction errors such as *Do you know where she's today?* Based on the following examples, determine the circumstances under which subject-verb contraction is blocked.

A.1. Do you know where she is today?

A.2. *Do you know where she's today?

B.1. You've eaten more than I have.

B.2. *You've eaten more than I've.

C.1. You've eaten more than I have eaten.

C.2. *You've eaten more than I've eaten.

15. There is a putative universal that heads of phrases tend to occur either first in the phrase or last in the phrase. Now consider four languages, each of which has a different combination of adjective-noun (AN) order within NP and verb-object (VO) order within VP.

JAPANESE:	AN + OV	ENGLISH:	AN + VO
MODERN IRISH:	NA + VO	PERSIAN:	NA + OV

a. Which combinations, if any, are marked?

b. Which combinations, if any, are unmarked?

c. In the unmarked languages, where would prepositions/postpositions be expected to occur with respect to their objects? (A postposition is essentially a preposition that follows its object.)

16. Forms like the following were produced by Spanish speakers learning English. What principle might explain the common error found in all of these examples?

A. In my country isn't army, navy, and air force.

B. The fountain of work in Venezula is petroleo; is our principle fountain of work.

C. In Venezuela is holiday both days.

Exploratory Exercises

1. Cook (1996:87) claims that codeswitching usually occurs when the speaker is doing one of the following:
   - Repeating what someone has said
   - Highlighting something

- Discussing particular topics
- Emphasizing a particular social role

Examine the following examples of codeswitching and decide which of these categories each fits into. Can you draw any more specific conclusions about the nature of the second, third, and fourth categories that Cook offers?

A. *"Suami daya dulu* slim and trim *tapi sekarang* plump like drum" ('Before my husband was slim and trim, but now he is plump like drum'). Bahasa Malaysia/English (Cook 1996:84)

B. *"Todos los Mexicanos* were riled up" ('All the Mexicans were riled up'). Spanish/English (Cook 1996:84)

C. *"Ik he been kop* of tea, tea or something" ('I had a cup of tea or something'). Dutch/English (Cook 1996:84)

D. *"Chustzovali, chto* le vin est tire et qu'il faut le boire" ('They felt that the wine is uncorked and it should be drunk'). Russian/French (Cook 1996:84)

E. *"Lapun man ia cam na tok* 'oh you poor pussiket' " ('The man came and said "You poor pussycat" '). Tok Pisin/English (Cook 1996:84)

F. *"La consulta èra* eight dollars" ('The visit cost eight dollars'). Spanish/English (Cook 1996, p. 85)

G. *"Ven acá! Ven acá! Come here, you!"* ('Come here! Come here!'). Spanish/English; parent to child (cited in Fasold 1984:205)

2. Researchers Ana Celia Zentella and Richard Otheguy have studied the use of pronouns by speakers of New York Spanish, a group that includes speakers from Puerto Rico, the Dominican Republic, Cuba, and Mexico. Consider the following excerpt from an article about their research (Scott 2002):

> [In Spanish,] "where an English speaker would say 'We sing,' a Spanish speaker could say either 'Nosotros cantamos' or simply 'Cantamos.' Linguists say Spanish speakers from the Caribbean tend to use a lot of pronouns; people from Central and South American countries use them less. . . .
>
> "It's interesting to compare Puerto Ricans, Dominicans and Cubans with the Mexicans, who use few pronouns," he [Otheguy] said. "And communities are different in their exposure to English. The Mexican community in New York is new; the Puerto Rican community is well settled."

Consider the following possible findings that this research might lead to, and discuss the conclusions that might you draw from each finding, especially with respect to group identity.

- A finding that speakers of New York Spanish are converging to a style that uses a lot of pronouns
- A finding that speakers of New York Spanish are maintaining the different styles described in the excerpt
- A finding that speakers of New York Spanish are converging to a style that uses relatively few pronouns

CHAPTER TEN

Written Language

This chapter focuses on the question of how language is represented in writing. We will start by looking at some of the different writing systems used by languages other than English, and then look in some detail at English spelling. Let's begin by considering some observations about written language.

(1) A t-shirt message reading *I ♥ New York* is interpreted as 'I love New York.'
(2) The phoneme /i/ may be represented in English spelling in several different ways: for example, *key, see, me, tea,* and *receive.*
(3) A 9-year-old girl writes an essay in which *drowned* is spelled *deround.*
(4) A college student in a basic writing course writes *Las yere I seen the basketbal teme play.*

Observation (1) illustrates the fact that language (even the English language) may be represented in ways other than the alphabetic spelling that we usually associate with English. Observation (2) illustrates the fact that English spelling is not entirely systematic, although it is more systematic than it is often given credit for. Observations (3–4) illustrate that language development and language variation may affect the way that writers encode language. All of these phenomena can be accounted for by some aspect of a theory of written language. What we will now do is attempt to articulate the linguistic principles that will account for these observations.

Writing Systems

It may be useful to start by discussing the various types of writing systems in use among the world's languages. Writing systems developed from drawing, in particular from pictographs, both of which are **iconic** (i.e., an actual depiction of an object in the real world). A **pictograph** is essentially a drawing of an object. For example, a drawing of the sun represents the sun (e.g., ☼ = sun). Over time, an individual pictograph may be used to represent not only an object but also other related concepts. For example, a drawing of the sun might represent not only the sun, but also heat, light, daytime, warmth, and so on. (A pictograph used in this manner is sometimes called an **ideograph,** since it can refer to abstract ideas as well as to concrete objects.) Drawing, unlike writing, is not peculiar to a specific language. Any human can interpret pictographs regardless of the language he or she speaks. For example, the ancient Sumerians who lived in what is now Iraq left records in the form of pictographs, which date from around 4000 B.C. Modern English speakers, however, can learn to interpret these pictographs without having to learn to speak Sumerian. For example, in the Sumerian pictography, a profile of a head stood for 'head,' and two parallel wavy lines stood for 'water.' When used together, they stood for 'drink,' as follows.

 = 'head' ≈ = 'water'  ≈ = 'drink'

(based on Malmkjaer 1991:498)

Pictography is widespread today. For example, a sign indicating 'no smoking' that shows a cigarette with a line through it, a road sign indicating a deer crossing that shows a silhouette of a jumping deer, and a cartoon indicating two people in love without dialogue or a caption are all pictographs, as follows.

In contrast, the symbols in a writing system are noniconic (i.e., they do not look like the objects they stand for). For example, the written English word *sun* bears no resemblance to the sun itself. Since writing is not iconic, each writing system is peculiar to a specific language. This means that in order to interpret a writing system, one must speak a language that the writing system represents. There are essentially three types of writing systems in use today, each based on a particular unit of linguistic structure: the morpheme, the syllable, and the phonological segment. In **morphographic** writing, each symbol represents a single morpheme—as, for example, when we use the ampersand symbol & to stand for the morpheme {and}. Morphographic writing is thought to have grown directly out of pictography, around 3000 B.C. Over time, pictographs became more stylized and less iconic (i.e., they looked less and less like the objects they represented). For example, the Chinese morphograph for {sun} is believed to have developed as follows:

Note that two simultaneous changes are occurring here: as the pictograph becomes less iconic and more stylized, it shifts from representing the object sun (a nonlinguistic entity) to representing the morpheme {sun} (a linguistic entity). These two changes working hand in hand are the essential steps in the development of writing.

Morphographic characters can be modified to shape meaning, as illustrated by the Chinese character for {tree}. (See Halpern 2001, for discussion.)

木 {tree} = 'tree'

林 two {tree} = 'woods'

森 three {tree} = 'forest'

本 {tree} with line across bottom = 'root' or 'origin'

日 {sun} + 木 {tree} = 東 'east'

人 {person} + 木 {tree} = 休 'rest'

The various Chinese languages (e.g., Cantonese and Mandarin) are the only widely used languages today that are still written with a morphographic writing system. However, we regularly use morphographic symbols when writing English. For example, in a road sign saying *Deer X-ing,* the symbol *X* stands for the morpheme {cross}. We use the symbol ♂ for {male}, ¢ for {cent}, + for {plus}, and V for {five}.

Exercise A

1. In the preceding illustration, explain how the Chinese morphographs for {sun} and {tree} combine semantically to produce 'east.' How do those for {person} and {tree} produce 'rest'?
2. Consider the following emoticons used in email: ☺ for 'joking/happy' and ☹ for 'unhappy.' Are these primarily drawing or writing? What is your reasoning? What difference does it make if the emoticons are turned on their sides, as they often are—i.e., as :) instead of ☺ and :(instead of ☹?
3. The symbol for KOA (Kampgrounds of America) is a drawing of a tent, similar to the one below. What type of representational or writing system is being used in a roadside sign that depicts a tent and stands for 'camping facilities'? Explain.

4. In Morse Code, the letter *A* is represented by a dot followed by a dash (i.e., a short burst of noise followed by a longer one). In American Sign Language, the letter *A* is represented by a raised, closed fist. Are these representations iconic or not? Explain.
5. Consider the following sign on a bottle of cleaning fluid. What type of representational or writing system is this an example of? Explain.

6. You go to a steak house for dinner and discover that the men's room has a drawing of a bull on the door, while the women's room has a drawing of a cow on the door. What type of representational or writing system is being used here? Explain.
7. You go to a farm and discover that the barn for bulls has a drawing of a bull on the door, while the barn for cows has a drawing of a cow on the door. What type of representational or writing system is being used here? Explain.
8. The following symbols are used to represent signs of the zodiac (i.e., horoscope signs). Try to match each symbol with the zodiac sign that it represents. Are some easier than

(continued)

Exercise A *Continued*

others? How does your ability to match a symbol to a sign relate to the symbol's degree of iconicity?

a. ♐	___ Aquarius (the water-bearer)
b. ♈	___ Aries (the ram)
c. ♉	___ Cancer (the crab)
d. ♊	___ Capricorn (the goat)
e. ♒	___ Gemini (the twins)
f. ♋	___ Leo (the lion)
g. ♏	___ Libra (the scales)
h. ♌	___ Pisces (the fish)
i. ♍	___ Sagittarius (the archer)
j. ♑	___ Scorpio (the scorpion)
k. ♓	___ Taurus (the bull)
l. ♎	___ Virgo (the virgin)

In the second type of writing system, **syllabic,** each symbol represents a single syllable—as, for example, when we use the symbols *4T* for the syllables /for/ + /ti/ in *forty.* Syllabic writing can develop from morphographic writing when a particular symbol shifts from standing for the *meaning* of a word to standing for the *sound* of a word. Once that shift occurs, then that symbol can be used for that sound anywhere it occurs in the language. Suppose, for example, that we have morphograph **6** which represents {bee}. If the symbol becomes associated with the sound of the word it represents (i.e., /bi/), then this symbol can be used to represent not only the word *bee* but also the word *be,* the first syllable in *beaker,* the second syllable in *baby,* and so on. In this way, we have the beginnings of a **syllabary:** a symbol being used to represent sound rather than meaning. (Note: we don't mean to imply that all syllabaries necessarily develop from morphographic writing. For example, syllabaries for the North American Indian languages Cherokee and Cree were invented in the 19th century.)

Probably the most well-known syllabic writing system in the world today is that used by the Japanese. The situation with Japanese, however, is complex. The Japanese, having no writing system of their own, borrowed Chinese characters in the 4th century A.D. However, the Chinese languages and Japanese are structurally quite different. Chinese words are mostly monosyllabic (note proper names such as *Chen, Wang,* and *Li*) and exhibit very little inflectional morphology—characteristics that lend themselves to morphographic writing (i.e., 1 word = 1 morpheme = 1 symbol). In contrast, Japanese words are multisyllabic with very simple and regular CV syllable structure (again, note proper names such as *Fujiyama, Nakajima,* and *Toyota*), and the verbs, in particular, have complex inflectional morphology (i.e., lots of endings). Because of these differences, as the Japanese began to adopt Chinese morphographic characters for writing their own language, they tended to associate some characters with a meaning (as in the Chinese morphographic system) and other characters with a sound, especially the sound of a whole syllable.

This transplantation of a Chinese morphographic system to Japanese led to a complex writing system made up of both morphographic and syllabic symbols. The morphographic symbols, known as *kanji,* are basically Chinese morphographs used to represent the core lexical morphemes of Japanese. The syllabic symbols, known as *kana,* are of two types: *hiragana,* used to write grammatical elements such as inflectional endings, and *katakana,* used to write Western loanwords. So, for example, in the word 見た pronounced /mita/, meaning 'saw' (past tense of *see*), 見 is a kanji character representing the root meaning of the verb 'see,' and た is a hiragana symbol representing the syllable /ta/, which here is a verb inflection indicating past tense. In contrast, consider the Western loanword プリンタ pronounced /purɪnta/, meaning 'printer' (Halpern 2001). Each of these is a katakana symbol representing the syllables /pu/, /rɪ/, /n/, and /ta/, respectively. Moreover, note that the final syllable in both /mita/ 'saw' and /purinta/ 'printer' is /ta/. However, the former, since it is a native verbal inflection, is written in hiragana (た), and the latter, since it is part of a Western loanword, is written in katakana (タ). We occasionally use syllabic symbols when writing English. For example, in a personalized license plate spelled *IMMT,* the sequence *MT* stands for the syllables /ɛm/ and /ti/, which constitute the word *empty.*

Exercise B

1. What type of representational or writing system is illustrated by the dollar sign in *Shirts $25.00*? Explain.
2. Consider a T-shirt that reads *I ♥ New York.* What type of representational or writing system does the heart symbol illustrate? Explain.

†3. A company in Duluth, Minnesota, specializes in mailing out discount coupons for local businesses to residents of the city. The company calls itself *Q-pon Express.* What type of representational or writing system does the *Q* represent? Explain.

4. Consider the *U* in the trademark *U-Haul.* What type of representational or writing system is this an example of? Is there more than one possible answer to this question? How do you decide?
5. You're driving along and see a car parked on the side of the road with a handwritten sign on it saying *4 Sale.* What type of representational or writing system is being used here with *4*? Is there more than one possible answer to this question? How do you decide?
6. What kind of representational or writing system are punctuation marks (e.g., periods, question marks, quotation marks, apostrophes)?

The third type of writing system, and the most common, is **alphabetic,** where each symbol of the writing system represents a single phonological segment. English, like most modern languages, is written with an alphabetic system. For example, the word *top* contains three symbols—*t, o,* and *p*—each representing a single segment—/t/, /a/, and /p/. Writing systems tend to evolve toward alphabets because they are less complicated than either morphographic or syllabic writing, at least for most languages. The Greek alphabet has 24 letters, and the Roman and Cyrillic (i.e., Russian) alphabets (both of which developed separately from the Greek) contain 26 and 31 letters, respectively. These few symbols are all it takes to represent the several hundred thousand words in each of these languages. In contrast, Chinese is estimated to have as many as 50,000 characters, 2,000 of which a child learns by the age of ten. (It is no accident that in 1958 the Chinese government developed a method for writing Chinese in the Roman alphabet, known as **pinyin.**) In short, morphographic writing, as the exclusive means of representing any given language, is extremely inefficient. Such a system requires a unique symbol for every morpheme in the language, and this can run into tens of thousands. Thus, it is not surprising that morphographic writing systems are rare.

Likewise, syllabic systems like those used by Japanese (and a few others like Cherokee and Cree) are rare for a similar reason, namely, the proliferation of syllable types in many languages. Even though Japanese has only around 100 syllables, all of which are essentially CV, most languages, like English, have many, many more. For example, English can have up to three consonants at both the beginning and the end of a syllable (e.g., *splints*). Consider this limiting case. American English has 14 vowels, 23 consonants that can begin a syllable, and 21 consonants that can end a syllable; that alone yields 6,762 syllables just of the form CVC. Imagine how many symbols you would need in a syllabary for a language that has (C)(C)(C)V(C)(C)(C) syllable structure! Thus, the scarcity of morphographic and syllabic writing systems along with the ubiquity of alphabetic systems is really a consequence of the structure of language: many morphemes and syllable types, relatively few segments.

Before leaving alphabetic systems, however, we should point out that some languages (e.g., Arabic, Hebrew, Sanskrit) use alphabetic systems that, for ordinary purposes, indicate consonants but not vowels. This is sometimes called **consonantal** writing. For example, the Hebrew alphabet consists solely of 22 consonants, and is written from right to left without vowels. Thus the Hebrew word *kelev* 'dog' would be written (in their Hebrew equivalents) as *vlk.* Vowels can be indicated with dots and dashes placed above and below the consonants, as follows.

ד = /d/
דִ = /di/
דֵ = /de/
דָ = /da/

However, vowels are indicated only in textbooks or prayer books; they do not typically appear in newspapers or magazines. This absence of vowels may seem like it would make reading difficult. However, in a language like Hebrew (or English) in which consonants predominate, the vowels are easy to infer from the consonants. For example, consider the following English phrase where only vowels are indicated:

E IO O E EI AUAE

This vocalic representation is virtually impossible to read. Now consider the same phrase where only consonants are indicated:

TH HSTRY F TH NGLSH LNGG

This consonantal representation, in contrast, is much easier to interpret, since the majority of the information needed to interpret the writing is conveyed by the consonants.

The various representational and writing systems we have discussed are summarized in the following chart.

DOMAIN	TYPE	SYMBOL	REFERENT	FAMILIAR EXAMPLE
Drawing	Pictographic	☼	sun	🚺 = woman
Drawing	Ideographic	☼	sun, heat, light	♥ = love
Writing	Morphographic	日 (Chinese)	{sun}	♂ = {male}
Writing	Syllabic	タ (Japanese)	/ta/	*4T* = /forti/
Writing	Alphabetic	*t* (English)	/t/	Standard spelling
Writing	Consonantal	ד (Hebrew)	/d/	bcs = 'because' (shorthand)

The English Spelling System

We have just stated that English uses an alphabetic writing system. However, a caveat is in order before we proceed. First, the alphabetic system we use to write English only *approximates* a segmental system. In a purely segmental system, each segment would be represented by a unique grapheme. However, English has about 38 phonemes, but the Roman alphabet we use has only 26 letters. This means there is not a unique match in English between phoneme and grapheme. For example, the word *box* consists of four phonemes (/baks/), but is written with three symbols. In this case, the symbol *x* represents the two phonemes /ks/. Moreover, in other words *x* represents only a single phoneme, but neither /k/ nor /s/. For example, the *x* in *xylophone* represents the phoneme /z/. Clearly, then, there is an imperfect relation between segment and grapheme in English.

Exercise C

1. Identify at least four words that illustrate the different ways that the phoneme /e/ can be represented in English spelling.
2. Identify at least three words that illustrate the different phonemes that the English grapheme *e* can represent. Limit yourself to words in which *e* appears in a stressed syllable.
3. Identify at least three words that illustrate the different ways that the phoneme /f/ can be represented in English spelling.

†4. Identify at least two words that illustrate the different phonemes that the English grapheme *c* can represent.

Reasons for Inconsistency in English Spelling

The imperfect relation between segment and symbol in English spelling has several causes. One is historical. When English writing was standardized in the fifteenth century, it was nearly perfectly segmental. For example, each letter in the word *knife* corresponded to the Middle English phonemic representation /knifə/. Over time, the phonemic representation of the word has changed from /knifə/ to /naɪf/, but the spelling has not. Similarly, the words *name* and *right* were pronounced /namə/ and /rixt/, respectively, in Old English (/x/ is a voiceless velar fricative). Over time, the phonemic representations of these words have changed to /nem/ and /raɪt/; however, their spellings reflect the older phonemic representations.

One historical change that causes some inconsistency in Modern English spelling is the Great Vowel Shift, which occurred during the transition from Middle English (c. 1400) to Early Modern English (c. 1600). The following chart compares the phonemic representation of some words in Middle English (before the Great Vowel Shift) and Modern English (after the Great Vowel Shift).

	MIDDLE ENGLISH	MODERN ENGLISH
mice	/mis/	/maɪs/
mouse	/mus/	/maʊs/
geese	/ges/	/gis/
broke	/brɔk/	/brok/
name	/nam/	/nem/

The so-called "silent *e*" at the end of words like *name* was pronounced (as [ə]) at least through the Middle English period.

Exercise D

1. The word *write* is derived from an Old English form. Based on its spelling, what can you conclude about the phonemic representation of this word in earlier forms of English?
2. Examine the vowels in the chart illustrating the effects of the Great Vowel Shift.
   a. What was the general direction in which vowels moved during the Great Vowel Shift? (Consult the vowel chart in Chapter 6 if you need to review vowel features.)
   b. What type of vowels were affected by the Great Vowel Shift—that is, what feature is shared by the vowels that underwent the shift?

In addition to language change throughout its history, English has borrowed much of its vocabulary from Latin and Greek. Consequently, we have had to make these borrowings fit our writing system. For example, English borrowed its word *phone* from Greek, which has a unique symbol ϕ, *phi,* to represent the initial consonant in *phone.* When brought into English, the initial consonant was spelled *ph* to indicate its Greek origin.

Exercise E

1. The letters ch can represent either /c/ or /k/ in Modern English.
   a. After examining the data below (based on Wolfram and Johnson 1982), complete the following statement: "The letters *ch* represent /k/ when ________."

chrome	*chore*	*chloride*	*chicken*	*Chuck*
choke	*chip*	*check*	*chlorophyll*	*choose*
chlorine	*chrysanthemum*	*chronic*	*cherish*	*Christian*

Exercise E *Continued*

b. Using a dictionary that gives you information about word origins, look up the words in which *ch* represents /k/. What do they have in common in terms of their history?

2. Identify some words in which *ps* represents /s/, then look up the words in a dictionary that gives you information about word origins. What do they have in common in terms of their history?

English Spelling and Morphophonemics

Earlier, we said that English spelling is alphabetic, which means that each grapheme represents a single phonological segment, at least in principle. There are, however, three separate levels of phonological representation upon which orthography could be based: morphophonemic, phonemic, and phonetic.

In **morphophonemic** spelling, each morpheme would have a unique graphemic representation. For example, the plural morpheme would have a unique graphemic representation (i.e., *s*), even though it appears as two different phonemes (i.e., /s/ and /z/) in words such as *caps* and *cabs.*

In **phonemic** spelling, each phoneme would have a unique symbolic representation. If English spelling were phonemic, *caps* and *cabs* would be written *caps* and *cabz.* The different spellings of the plural morpheme would reflect the fact that it appears as two different phonemes in these two words.

Finally, in **phonetic** spelling, each allophone would have a unique symbolic representation. If English spelling were phonetic, *caps* and *cabs* would be written *caps* and *caabz* to reflect the fact that the vowel in *cabs* is longer than the vowel in *caps* (due to the Vowel Lengthening rule discussed in Chapter 6).

It is obvious from these examples that English spelling is primarily morphophonemic, in that each morpheme is given a unique segmental representation. That is, the level of representation on which English spelling is based is (primarily) that of the morphophoneme. For example, consider the spelling of the three words *photo, photograph,* and *photography.* Each contains an instance of the morpheme {photo}, spelled *p-h-o-t-o* in each case. Note, however, that these three instances of {photo} are phonemically different: *photo* /fóto/, *photograph* /fótə/, and *photography* /fətá/. If English spelling were phonemic rather than morphophonemic, the morpheme {photo} in these three words would have different spellings, say, *photo, photugraph,* and *phutagraphy.*

On the other hand, it is equally clear that the English spelling system is not *purely* morphophonemic. It has some phonemic elements, as for example in the spelling of *wife* and *wives.* Here the morpheme {wife} is spelled phonemically, with an *f* in the singular and *v* in the plural to reflect the fact that the singular form has undergone Final Devoicing (i.e., the word-final /v/ is devoiced to /f/ in the singular). If these two words were spelled morphophonemically, they would be represented as, for example, *wive* and *wives.*

The morphophonemic basis of English spelling is one reason that it is sometimes characterized as confusing: the morphophonemic representation of a word like *photography* is not as close to its pronunciation as its phonemic representation is. It might seem less confusing, then, if spelling reflected pronunciation more closely. However, the morphophonemic system is not as chaotic as it might initially seem. The fact that *photo, photograph,* and *photography* all contain the same spelled sequence *p-h-o-t-o* allows us to recognize that they share a common element of meaning, the morpheme {photo}.

Exercise F

1. Consider the spelled sequence *g-r-a-p-h* in *photograph* and *photography,* in particular the spelling of the vowel. What level of representation does this spelling reflect: phonetic, phonemic, or morphophonemic? How would the vowel be spelled if a different level of representation were the basis for the spelling?
2. The following words all contain a "silent" consonant in their spellings. For each word, think of a word that is related in meaning and in which the "silent" letter is pronounced (e.g., *solemn - solemnity*). Consult a dictionary if necessary.

†**a.** *column*	**e.** *reign*
b. *hymn*	**f.** *damn*
c. *debt*	**g.** *thumb*
d. *sign*	

Analyzing Errors in Written English

Phonology and Spelling

Many spelling errors are a direct consequence of the phonology of English. In particular, phonological rules that affect the pronunciation of a word can cause confusion for writers who are basing their spelling on pronunciation. For example, one regular phonological process in English is that unstressed vowels tend to neutralize to [ə], as we saw with the first and third syllables of *photography*. If a speller is unfamiliar with the written form of the word, this neutralization can make it difficult to reconstruct the unneutralized form of the vowel. (Here we can see that the morphophonemic nature of English spelling might help the speller, who might be able to reconstruct the *o*'s from a form like *photo.*)

Another example of a phonological process that can affect spelling is **unstressed syllable deletion,** which deletes a completely unstressed vowel (typically [ə]) and optionally deletes the adjacent consonants in the same syllable. The deleted syllable may be in initial, medial, or final position within a word. For example, in the phrase *reading, writing, and 'rithmetic,* the unstressed initial syllable of *arithmetic* is deleted by this process. The same process can affect spelling as well as pronunciation. For example, a 6-year-old girl wrote *guvment* for *government.* Note that if the medial syllable in /gʌ́vərnmənt/ is removed, the result is [gʌ́vmənt].

Other phonological processes that can account for misspellings have been discussed in Chapter 7 (Language Variation). Among them are vowel epenthesis (e.g., *thero* for *throw*), metathesis (e.g., *Southren* for *Southern*), consonant cluster reduction (e.g., *attrac* for *attract*), post-vocalic liquid deletion (e.g., *ho* for *whole*), voicing assimilation (e.g., *haf to* for *have to*), and vowel neutralization before nasals (e.g., *whin* for *when*).

Aside from errors caused by applying phonological rules, spelling deviations may also be caused by attaching the orthography to the wrong level of phonological representation. Children, as well as adults just learning to spell, will often construct a phonemic rather than a morphophonemic orthography. For example, a 7-year-old wrote *u lot uv mune* for *a lot of money.* Note the consistent use of the symbol *u* for the phonemes /ə/ and /ʌ/. The point to keep in mind about such errors is that they are not the result of phonological processes but rather the result of attaching letters of the alphabet to the wrong level of phonological representation.

Note finally that some orthographic errors have nothing to do with phonology or any other domain of linguistics. **Capitalization,** for example, is not linguistically driven in English orthography; its use is strictly a convention that has nothing directly to do with phonology. For instance, in writing English, we capitalize the first letter of the first word in a sentence, the pronoun *I* (but, interestingly enough, not *you* or *me*), and proper nouns. That capitalization is arbitrary is evidenced by the fact that other languages written in the Roman alphabet capitalize quite differently. For example, in Spanish many proper nouns are *not* capitalized (e.g., *inglés* 'English'), whereas in German *all* nouns are capitalized, including common nouns (e.g., *Kirche* 'church').

Exercise G

†1. A 7-year-old boy wrote the following sentence about Flash (a comic book hero): *flsh is a god man becaz he savz pepl and he iz nis he diznot kil pepl.* What level of phonological representation is he basing his spelling on, in general?

2. The following data is from Shaughnessy (1977), which analyzes the writing of college students in basic writing classes at the City University of New York. For each of the following examples, state the phonological process that accounts for the misspelling.

a. motvation (target: *motivation*)
b. inaccute (target: *inaccurate*)
c. impluses (target: *impulses*)

3. The following spellings were found on bulletin board notices and commercial signs (some of which must have been quite expensive to construct!). For each one, determine the standard spelling and identify the phonological process(es) that account for the misspelling. Pictures of some of the signs are given below.

a. A roadside sign in east Tennessee announced *Jamboree Augest 16th.*
b. An advertisement for *Leg Quaters* was seen in a grocery store in Wallace, North Carolina.
c. The following was written on a placard worn by a woman soliciting donations in front of a Kroger's store in Knoxville, Tennessee: *HELP ABUSE CHILDREN.*
†d. The following sign was seen in a grocery store window: *Hunderds of Prizes.*
e. A bakery in New Orleans advertised *Fresh Pasteries.*
f. A bulletin board notice advertised the following: *Experience babysitter needed.*
†g. A sign at a mall announced *No Parking Pass This Point.*
h. A candy store advertised a sale on Cuccia brand *Choclates.*
i. A bulletin board notice told readers to *Call 555-1234 for more imformation.*
j. A gift shop advertised a *Clearence Sale.*
k. A sign in a supermarket advertised *cha-broiled steaks.*

(continued)

Exercise G *Continued*

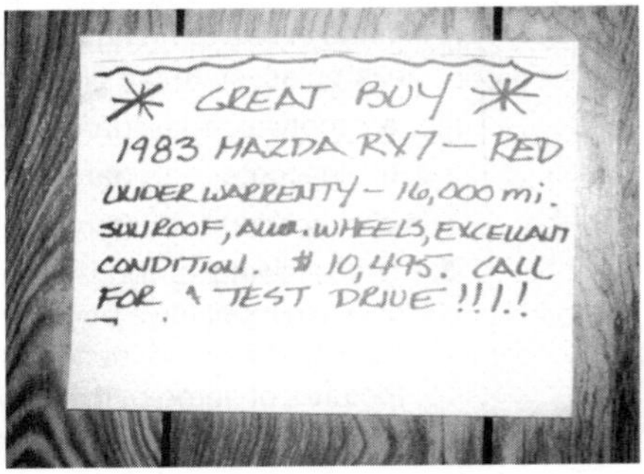

l. A sign in front of a palm-reader advertised *spiritualis reader.*

m. A sign in front of a clothing store read *bran new.*

n. A hand-lettered sign advertised *Carpentery* work and *Hot Tubes.*

o. A billboard advertised a *Truck Stop and Restraunt.*

p. A hand-painted sign on a building in Baton Rouge read exactly as follows: *No loit^{e}ring.*

q. A sign seen in a driveway in Tennessee warned There Is No Turn Aroun.

†r. A sign in a men's clothing store in Savannah read *Tuxsedo Rental.*

s. A bulletin board notice advertised a car *under warrenty* and in *excellant condition.*

Morphology and Writing

Some errors in how English words are represented in writing can be attributed to morphology rather than phonology. One source for such errors is the misanalysis of verb morphology; that is, in the analysis of a verb form or its associated affixes. For example, a child who writes *drownded* for *drowned* is misanalyzing the final /d/ of /draʊnd/ as part of the root of the verb rather than as a suffix representing {PAST}. Consequently, the child adds an additional past tense suffix to the root (i.e., {drownd} + {PAST} = **drownded*). Note, incidentally, that the additional past tense suffix is formed according to rule: since the new root ends in a /d/, the past tense suffix will be /əd/. Another common morphological deviation is the absence of the {PRES} inflection on third-person singular verb forms (e.g., *He do it without thinking*). As we saw in Chapter 7, this phenomenon is characteristic of some nonstandard dialects of English.

Many apparent verb-form errors can be analyzed as either morphological or syntactic in origin. In contrast to a morphological error, a syntactic error involves more than one word or is caused by an element outside of the word affected. Consider, for example, a student who writes *He come over here twice before. Come* is a morphological error if the target is *came:* someone who systematically substitutes *come* for *came* has internalized the incorrect past tense form. On the other hand, *come* is a syntactic error if the target is *has come.* That is, someone who systematically omits the auxiliary *have* may leave a past participial form in first position within the verb phrase, a position normally filled by a tensed verb.

In addition to verb morphology, errors in the analysis of noun morphology may result in writing errors. One type of morphological error in nouns is the treatment of a noncount noun as though it were a count noun. **Count nouns** are those that can take the {PLU} suffix (e.g., *job/jobs*); **noncount nouns** cannot. Now consider the college student who wrote *Machines can easily perform many manual labors. Manual labor* is noncount, but the student is treating it as if it were a count noun by modifying it with *many* and pluralizing *labor.* Moreover, singular count nouns require an article (e.g., *A man appeared/*Man appeared*), whereas noncount nouns cannot take the singular indefinite article (e.g., *furniture/*a furniture*). Other common morphological deviations are the absence of the {PLU} inflection on a plural count noun (e.g., *two book*) and of the {POSS} inflection (e.g., *John car*).

A final type of morphological error is the misformation of the comparative and superlative degrees of adjectives. Consider, for example, the form **foolishest* for *most foolish.* In general, the more syllables an adjective has, the more pressure there is to form the comparative and superlative with *more/most* rather than with *-er/-est.* Thus, we have *taller* rather than **more tall,* but *more abrupt* rather than **abrupter.* However, not all multisyllabic adjectives require *more/most* in the comparative and superlative. Consider, for example, the two-syllable adjectives ending in *-y: funny/funnier, silly/sillier,* and *happy/happier.* Another tendency seems to be that non-Germanic (i.e., nonnative) adjectives form their comparative and superlative degrees with *more/most.* For example, *more chic* seems preferable to *chicer.*

Exercise H

1. The following passage (adapted from Shaughnessy 1977:247) was written by a college student in a basic writing course. The numbers in parentheses indicate places where an English teacher might mark an error.

(continued)

Exercise H Continued

A child playing alone can become very involve (1) in a (2) animal or object. Walking through Kings (3) Park (4) I notice (5) a little boy sitting on a bench, (6) he had a bag with something in it resting between his leg. (7) A bird (8) sitting on the edge of the bench. It look (9) as though from the expression on the little boy (10) face that he was quit (11) surprise (12) at the bird. He start (13) feeding the bird something from the bag. Although the boy (14) alone, he (15) having a good time with the bird.

a. Identify four errors that have a principled, linguistic explanation.

b. Identify four errors that do not have a linguistic explanation.

Summary

A theory of written language includes different types of writing systems (morphographic, syllabic, and alphabetic) and spelling systems (morphophonemic, phonemic, and phonetic). We have also seen that other domains such as morphology are relevant to analyzing the way that English words are represented in writing.

SUPPLEMENTARY READINGS

Daniels, P. T., & Bright, W. (Eds.). (1996). *The world's writing systems.* New York: Oxford University Press.
Gelb, I. J. (1963). *A study of writing.* Chicago: University of Chicago Press.
Katzner, K. (1995). *The languages of the world* (rev. ed.). London: Routledge.
Sampson, G. (1985). *Writing systems.* London: Hutchinson.

You are now prepared to read all but the first of these works. Gelb is the first linguistically sophisticated treatment of writing. Katzner is very accessible for the beginner and offers a thumbnail sketch of each language and its writing system. Sampson, at a little over 200 pages, is a good introduction to the theory of writing systems. Daniels and Bright is a recent scholarly treatment and, at 900 pages, is exhaustive and primarily for specialists.

Supplementary Exercises

1. Consider a personalized license plate that reads *NGNR,* meaning "engineer." What type of writing system does this license plate rely on, primarily?
2. What type of representational or writing system is illustrated by the division sign in, for example, 20 ÷ 5 = 4?
3. What type of representational or writing system is used in the italicized part of the following interchange?

   JOE: *M R* ducks.

   BOB: *M R* not ducks.

   JOE: *O S A R.*

   BOB: *L I B, M R* ducks.

4. When Barry Goldwater was running for president in 1964, his campaign bumper stickers read *AuH_2O*. What type of representational or writing system is this an example of?
5. You visit a gas station/convenience store called the "EZ Stop." What type of representational or writing system does the *EZ* represent? (Thanks to John Spartz for this and the next two exercises.)
6. While reading the weather section of the daily newspaper, you come across a drawing of a cloud. What type of representational or writing system is being used in the paper?
7. At a gubernatorial debate, you see two signs, one with a depiction of a donkey, and one with a depiction of an elephant. What representational or writing system do the depictions illustrate?
8. What concept from this chapter accounts for the vowel differences in the stressed syllables of the following pairs? Explain.

divine/divinity	*serene/serenity*	*sane/sanity*
sublime/sublimity	*obscene/obscenity*	*profane/profanity*
line/linear	*hygiene/hygienic*	*humane/humanity*

9. The vowels in the morpheme {photo} are always represented by the grapheme *o,* regardless of what word the morpheme appears in. Can you think of a reason to justify this choice? That is, why not represent them with a letter that would reflect the pronunciation of *photography* or *photographic?*
10. Identify some words in which /š/ is represented by *ti* or *ss.* Then look up the words in a dictionary that gives you information about word origins. Can you draw any generalization about the language from which they were borrowed into English?
11. According to one researcher cited in Gleason (1997:424), many young children delete nasal consonants in spelling, especially when another consonant follows. Thus they write forms like *dot* (for *don't*), *mostr* (for *monster*), and *nooiglid* (for *New England*). What phonological rule can be used to account for these misspellings? (Hint: *banter* pronounced [bæ̃ɾər].)
12. A "linguistics" teacher once claimed that the misspelling *would of* for *would have* is caused by Final Devoicing. Explain how the teacher was fooled into making this faulty analysis. What is the correct analysis?
13. The following data is from Shaughnessy (1977). In each of the following examples, state the linguistic principle that accounts for the italicized error.
    a. My older brothers and sisters *founded* life not very much different.
    b. They don't see and hear things the same way as *they* children do.
    c. There *is* only 97,000 openings per year.
14. The following message was printed on a chopsticks wrapper:

    Welcome to Chinese Restaurant.

    Please try your Nice Chinese Food with Chopsticks, the traditional and typical of Chinese glorious history and cultual.

    PRODUCT OF CHINA

    a. *Chinese Restaurant* should be *our Chinese Restaurant* or *this Chinese Restaurant,* or something similar. What morphological principle accounts for this error?
    b. *Cultual* should be *cultural.* What phonological process accounts for this error?
15. The following passage from Wolfram and Schilling-Estes (1998:306), like the passage from Shaughnessy in Exercise H, contains some errors that can be explained by principles from

phonology or morphology and others that cannot. Identify the errors in the passage, then identify the phonological or morphological principles that account for some of the errors.

I tel you bout me and my fren basebal team. wen we together we do all kinds of things he play basketball and I play basebal. Las yere I seen the basketbal teme play and it look like I didnt have a chanc of making it. Im a prety good baseball player tho and the coch knowed it. James the best player we miss him when he couldnt play last weak.

Exploratory Exercises

1. Consider some shortcuts that you and your friends use when you take notes, send emails, or use instant messaging (e.g., the use of *bcs* instead of *because*). Look in particular at usages that depart from a full standard English spelling of words or phrases. What kinds of writing or representational system does each one represent? Explain.
2. Punctuation is an integral part of the writing system of English. Visit the Gallery of "Misused" Quotation Marks at http://www.juvalamu.com/qmarks and analyze some of the data there. Can you draw any generalizations about subgroups within the "misused" quotation marks? You may also want to visit the Abused Apostrophes site at http://www.suepalmer.co.uk/apostf.php and perform a similar analysis on some of the data there.
3. See Chapter 11, Exploratory Exercise 1, which also has to do with spelling.

CHAPTER ELEVEN

Language Processing

This chapter looks at language processing, focusing in particular on how humans **decode,** or understand, the language that they hear or read in "real-time," actual instances of language use. Analyses of language processing have come from several applied fields within linguistics. Among the topics studied by researchers in the field of **psycholinguistics** is the ease with which humans can decode different types of sentence structures. Among those studied by researchers in the field of **discourse analysis** is how readers process extended passages of written text. The phenomena that researchers in these fields might attempt to analyze include the following.

(1) A newspaper reader is confused by the headline *Democrats Urge President Not to Veto Ban.*

(2) The sentence *The old man was hit by the blue car* is easier for a group of subjects to understand than the sentence *The green car was hit by the blue car,* even though both are in passive voice.

(3) You are reading experimental reports in a scientific journal and notice that they all use the same headings: Introduction, Method, Results, and Discussion.

Observation (1) illustrates the fact that some sentence structures are easier to process than others, at least in isolation. Observation (2) suggests that syntactic structure alone does not account for all observations about sentence processing. Observation (3) indicates that readers rely on structural cues to help them process longer texts. What we will now do is articulate the principles that will account for these observations and some others related to language processing.

Sentence-Level Phenomena in Language Processing

Psycholinguistic studies use several different ways to evaluate how easily different structures are processed. One strategy is to compare the **reaction time** that research participants need to process different structures. For example, the researcher might present a research participant with active and passive sentences that describe a picture and ask the person to judge the sentences as true or false. Reaction time is a measurement of how quickly research participants are able to respond to a question or make judgments about a linguistic stimulus.

Another factor that researchers look at is the **accuracy** with which research participants process various structures. For example, a researcher might present a picture of a square on top of a circle and ask, "True or false: The square is not on top of the circle." A third variable studied in language processing is **memorability.** For example, a researcher might have participants read a narrative and then paraphrase it from memory, perhaps immediately after reading it and again a week later.

Resolving Syntactic Ambiguity

One phenomenon that psycholinguists have studied extensively is the way that people process ambiguous sentences. You may recall from earlier chapters that ambiguity can be one of two types. Semantic, or lexical, ambiguity occurs when a word has more than one meaning. For example, the word *bank* in *Meet me at the bank* can refer to either a financial institution or the edge of a river. Syntactic, or structural, ambiguity occurs when a word can be assigned to more than one category or constituent. In the phrase *abnormal psychology professor,* for example, the word *abnormal* can be interpreted as modifying either *psychology* (i.e., 'a professor of abnormal psychology') or *professor* (i.e., 'a psychology professor who is abnormal'). Much of the research in language processing has been concerned with how people resolve syntactic ambiguity.

One type of ambiguity is found in a structure known as a **garden path sentence:** one that causes readers to **parse** the sentence (i.e., assign it a syntactic structure) in a way that must then be rejected and replaced by a different syntactic structure. The classic garden path sentence is the following:

(1a) The horse raced past the barn fell.

You probably found this sentence confusing on first reading. This is because the first reading leads you "down the garden path"—that is, to an initial misinterpretation of the sentence's structure. You first interpret *raced* as the main verb, and then later find out that *fall* is the main verb.

Why is this sentence confusing? Let's start by looking at how this sentence's structure must be interpreted in order to make sense. Compare sentence (1b), which is not a "garden path" sentence and consequently is easier to process than (1a).

(1b) The horse that was raced past the barn fell.

Sentence (1b) has a **relative clause,** *that was raced past the barn,* modifying the subject *the horse.* A relative clause is one that modifies a preceding NP and is typically introduced by the relative pronouns *that, which,* or *who(m).* In this case, the relative clause contains a past participle *(raced)* that is part of a passive structure from which the agent has been deleted *(that was raced past the barn).* In other words, the relative clause is the agentless passive counterpart of *Someone raced the horse past the barn.*

In (1a), however, we have a **reduced relative clause**—one from which the relative pronoun *that* and the auxiliary verb *was* have been deleted. This is a common structure, also found in (1d), which is a reduced version of (1c):

(1c) The horse that was chosen for the Kentucky Derby fell. (full relative clause)
(1d) The horse chosen for the Kentucky Derby fell. (reduced relative clause)

The problem in our original sentence, (1a), is that the verb in the relative clause, *raced,* is ambiguous on first reading as to whether it is a past tense form or a past participle form. In the absence of the structural cues for a relative clause (i.e., *that was*), readers initially misinterpret the verb *raced* in (1a) as the main verb of the sentence. That is, they interpret it as a past tense verb for the subject *the horse.*

The problem arises when readers hit a second past tense verb, *fell,* that can also be interpreted as the verb for *the horse.* That verb slot has already been filled by *raced,* so readers have to reanalyze the sentence in order to find a role for *fell.*

The garden path nature of (1a) has been attributed to the fact that it violates a principle called the Canonical Sentoid Strategy (Fodor, Bever, & Garrett, 1974): Namely, when we encounter a sequence of noun-verb-(noun), we assume that those items fill certain semantic roles. We assign the first noun to the role of **agent:** the volitional performer of some **action,** which we assume is described by the verb. We tend to assign a noun following the verb to the role of **patient,** the entity or thing affected by the action. Thus, the reader (or listener) who encounters *The horse raced* will assign those items to agent-action roles—but in (1a), this default assumption turns out to be incorrect.

A more general way to account for the problematic nature of (1a) is to assume a parsing strategy of **minimal attachment.** This strategy predicts that we will parse the sentence in the simplest structure that is permitted by the grammar. In the case of *The horse raced . . . ,* it is simpler to assign these items to the structure NP-V (i.e., to interpret *The horse* as the subject of the verb *raced*). In the absence of any cues that a relative clause is starting—i.e., in the absence of the relative pronoun *that,* which we find in the easier-to-process sentence (1b)—it is more complex to assign *raced* to a separate clause from *The horse.* In other words, the subject-verb sequence reflects a simpler assumption about structure than does the subject-relative clause sequence.

Another principle involved in sentence parsing is **late closure,** which predicts that we will assign "incoming" material to the phrase currently being processed. For example, consider the following sentence:

(2a) The man talked to the father of the girl who was at the store.

This sentence is ambiguous as to whether the relative clause *who was at the store* modifies *the father of the girl* or simply *the girl.* Under one reading, the father was at the store; under the other reading, the girl was at the store. Late closure predicts that readers will prefer the latter reading, since *the girl* is the NP being processed when the reader encounters *who was at the store.*

In resolving ambiguity, however, readers make use not only of syntactic strategies but also semantic information. For example, consider the following sentence.

(3a) The computer purchased by the student crashed.

Structurally, this sentence is identical to (1a), *The horse raced past the barn fell.* It consists of a reduced relative clause, *purchased by the student,* that modifies the subject NP, *The computer.* However, it does not present nearly the garden-path difficulties that (1a) does. We can account for this by observing that the subject of (3a), *The computer,* is inanimate and therefore not a suitable subject for *purchased,* which requires an animate subject. In other words, the semantics of (3a) prevents the reader/listener from going "down the garden path."

Exercise A

1. Consider the aphorism *A penny saved is a penny earned.* What properties of this expression would lead you to predict that it would or wouldn't behave like a garden-path sentence?

Resolving Ambiguous Pronoun Reference

Another type of ambiguity that arises in language processing has to do with assigning an antecedent to a pronoun. You will recall from the introductory chapter that the antecedent of a pronoun is the linguistic expression to which the pronoun refers. In the sentence *Carla went to class, then she went to work,* the pronoun *she* has only one possible antecedent in the sentence: *Carla.* Other sentences, though, illustrate ambiguous pronoun reference:

(4a) Carla went to class with Gina, but she didn't come home with her.

This sentence is ambiguous in that each pronoun has two possible referents within the sentence, giving rise to two possible interpretations:

(4b) Carla_1 went to class with Gina_2, but she_1 didn't come home with her_2 (i.e., Carla didn't come home with Gina).

(4c) Carla_1 went to class with Gina_2, but she_2 didn't come home with her_1 (i.e., Gina didn't come home with Carla).

Before reading the next paragraph, you might introspect on which interpretation seems more natural to you.

It turns out that speakers favor interpretation (4b) over (4c). We can account for this by assuming that readers try to resolve ambiguity by assigning **parallel function** to the pronouns (Sheldon, 1974). Notice that in (4b), the nouns and their associated pronouns occur in the same position within each clause, as represented in the following diagram.

(4b) **Carla_1** went to class with **Gina_2,** but

↓ ↓

she_1 didn't come home with **her_2.**

That is, both *Carla* and *she* occur in subject position, so they occupy a parallel function within their respective clauses. Likewise, both *Gina* and *her* occur as objects of a preposition *(with),* so they occupy a parallel function within their respective clauses.

In contrast, interpretation (4c) violates this parallel function principle, as shown in the following diagram.

(4c) **Carla**$_1$ went to class with **Gina**$_2$, but

she$_2$ didn't come home with **her**$_1$.

Thus the parallel function principle predicts that readers will favor (4b) over (4c).

Another principle that affects the reader's ability to match a pronoun with its antecedent is **proximity:** how close the pronoun and antecedent are, with closer antecedents being favored over more distant antecedents. Consider the following passage.

(5) Charlotte wanted Debbie to meet her at the restaurant at noon. Debbie got there at 12:15. Charlotte was upset because she had to be back at work by 1:00.

This passage contains two possible antecedent NPs, *Charlotte* and *Debbie.* At the point at which the pronoun *she* appears, the most recent candidate antecedent is *Charlotte.* Therefore, readers are more likely to interpret *she* as referring back to *Charlotte* rather than to *Debbie.*

Exercise B

1. Examine interpretations (4b) and (4c) in light of the two principles just discussed, parallel function and proximity. Do both principles make the same prediction about which interpretation readers will favor? Explain. Assuming that (4b) is favored over (4c), which of the two principles appears to take priority?

As in resolving structural ambiguity, readers and listeners make use of semantic and real-world knowledge in resolving ambiguous pronoun reference. For example, consider the following sentences (discussed in Singer 1990:127):

(6) Donna punished Alice because she confessed to shoplifting.
(7) Donna phoned Alice because she needed money.

Although the pronoun *she* is, technically, ambiguous in both of these sentences, readers will tend to interpret *Alice* as the antecedent of *she* in (6), but *Donna* as the antecedent of *she* in (7). These interpretations indicate that readers are using not simply structural strategies but also assumptions about cause-effect relationships that are likely to exist in each sentence. In (6), for example, we are likely to make a connection between a person's being punished and their committing a crime such as shoplifting. In (7), we are likely to assume that a borrower is more likely to contact a potential lender, rather than vice versa.

Understanding Negative Sentences

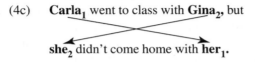

Negative sentences (for example, those containing *not* or a contraction of it) take longer to process than their positive counterparts. Some of the classic studies on negative sentences involve presenting research participants with a picture and then asking them to judge particular statements about the picture as true or false. For example, Clark and Clark (1977) describe a study in which participants were presented with pictures of either a square or a circle and asked to judge the truth or falsity of sentences such as *The circle is present.* If you are looking at a square and are asked to judge a sentence like *The circle is present,* two factors come into play. One is whether the sentence is affirmative or negative, and the other is whether it is true or false. For example, *The circle is present* is an affirmative sentence (it asserts a positive proposition), but it is false (if you are looking at a square).

When participants were looking at the square, their response times for judging the following sentences as true or false were as follows:

GENERAL PATTERN	± EXPLICIT NEGATIVE	RESPONSE TIME
True affirmative	*The square is present.*	Fastest
False affirmative	*The circle is present.*	↓
False negative	*The square isn't present.*	↓
True negative	*The circle isn't present.*	Slowest

Interestingly, similar results emerge for sentences containing **inherent negatives.** Instead of an overt negative word like *not,* an inherently negative sentence contains a word whose meaning includes negation. For example, the inherent negative *The maintenance people at the factory are* ***striking*** is equivalent in meaning to *The maintenance people at that factory are* ***not working.*** Inherent negatives do not take quite as long to process as explicit negatives, but both types take longer than their affirmative counterparts. In the study described above, the following results emerged when people were looking at the square and judging the sentences with inherent negatives as true or false (Clark and Clark 1977:454–455).

GENERAL PATTERN	± INHERENT NEGATIVE	RESPONSE TIME
True affirmative	*The square is present.*	*Fastest*
False affirmative	*The circle is present.*	↓
False negative	*The square is absent.*	↓
True negative	*The circle is absent.*	Slowest

Exercise C

1. Suppose you were setting up a study of response times to sentences containing inherent negatives. Identify an inherent negative for each of the following items: *arrive, find, remember, same, good, high, deep, many, big, fast, wide, long.*
2. Consider the following passages from news accounts about different pieces of legislation.
   - **A.** Voters will decide November 3 whether the state constitution should include the right to keep and bear arms. Advocates say the amendment could be used to lobby for abolition of the state's concealed-weapons ban.
   - **B.** Opponents of a bill to prohibit cameras in the courtroom received another setback today.

Exercise C *Continued*

C. [Headline]: Judge Revokes Welfare-Cut Block.

D. The state Assembly failed to get enough votes to override the governor's veto of the bill.

a. Does the group referred to in passage (A) support or oppose the right to carry concealed weapons? What specific words impede or enhance your conclusion?

b. Identify the inherent negatives in these passages.

c. Choose two of the passages and revise them to make them easier to comprehend.

3. Consider the following excerpt from a news account that appeared during Clinton's administration.

A. A group urged Congress to override President Clinton's veto of the partial-birth abortion ban.

a. Does the group referred to in passage (A) support or oppose this abortion process? How many times did you have to read the passage to arrive at your answer? What factors cause the processing difficulties?

b. Consider a revised version of the passage, given as (B) below. Would you predict that readers would have equal difficulty with it, compared to (A)? Why or why not?

B. A group of Catholic priests urged Congress to override President Clinton's veto of the partial-birth abortion bans.

Processing Passive Sentences

The difference between active and passive sentences was introduced in Chapter 4. By way of review, an active sentence (e.g., *Nicole wrote that essay*) and its passive counterpart (e.g., *That essay was written by Nicole*) differ in the following ways.

- In an active sentence, the **agent** (the entity or thing performing the action) is in subject position. In a passive sentence, the agent is the object of a *by*-phrase in the predicate (verb phrase).
- In an active sentence, the **patient** (the entity or thing affected by the action) is the direct object of the main verb. In a passive sentence, the patient is in subject position.
- An active sentence never contains a form of auxiliary *be* followed by a past participle main verb. A passive sentence always contains a form of *be* immediately followed by a past participle (e.g., *was used*).

In isolation, active sentences are easier to process than their passive counterparts. For example, (8a) is easier to process than (8b).

(8a) The car hit the truck. (active)
(8b) The truck was hit by the car. (passive)

We might hypothesize that active sentences are easier to process simply because they are shorter—the passive counterpart adds an auxiliary verb (a form of *be*) and a preposition *(by)*, thus making it a longer sentence. However, even when sentence length is taken into account, passive sentences still present processing difficulties that are related to structure rather than length. Humans appear to use a word-order processing strategy that interprets a sequence of noun-verb-noun as agent-action-patient. In other words, our "default" expectation is that the agent will occupy subject position. This is the pattern we find in an active sentence. In a passive sentence, however, the patient occupies subject position. Therefore, when we encounter the structural cues present in passive sentences (i.e., a form of *be* followed by a past participle), we have to revise our general processing strategy, thus slowing down comprehension time.

Interestingly, though, (9a) and (9b) are equivalent in their processing difficulty, even though (9a) is active and (9b) is passive.

(9a) The car hit the telephone pole.
(9b) The telephone pole was hit by the car.

This is because only *the car* can be interpreted as the agent in either (9a) or (9b). In this case, our knowledge of the real world (i.e., that cars can hit telephone poles, but not vice versa) allows us to interpret (9b) as quickly as (9a). Sentence (9b) is called a **nonreversible passive,** because the agent and patient cannot logically be reversed (it does not make sense, under ordinary circumstances, to say *The car was hit by the telephone pole*). In contrast, sentence (8b) is called a **reversible passive** because it is possible to reverse the agent and patient in (8b) *(The car was hit by the truck).*

Exercise D

1. Identify each sentence as active or passive. (Remember that a past tense verb does not necessarily indicate a passive voice sentence, or vice versa.) If a sentence is passive, further identify it as either reversible or nonreversible.
   †a. That book was written by a famous author.
   b. Lightning struck a tree by the river.
   c. The cat was chased by the dog.
   †d. A lion is being chased by a tiger.
   e. The patient could have been saved by the doctor.
   f. Carla is sending an e-mail to the members of the department.
   g. The homeowner was killed by an intruder.

Because passive sentences are longer and relatively harder to process than active sentences, writers are often advised to "Avoid the passive voice." However, keep in mind that the processing difficulties described above are based primarily on studies of sentences in isolation. As we will see later, the choice of active or passive voice within an extended passage often depends on the structure of the surrounding sentences; there are times when the passive voice will actually enhance a reader's comprehension.

Processing Complex Sentences

Clause order affects the processing of some types of **complex sentences.** A complex sentence contains a main clause and a subordinate clause; a subordinate clause is introduced by a **subordinating conjunction** such as *after, although, because, before, because, since,* or *when.* One principle is that sentences describing events ordered in time are easier to process if the events are mentioned in the order in which they occurred. (Note that this order-of-mention principle also applies in language acquisition, as discussed in Chapter 8.) This principle predicts that (10a) will be easier to process than (10b).

(10a) Save your document before running a spell-check.
(10b) Before you run a spell-check, save your document.

Another principle is that complex sentences are easier to process if the subordinate clause follows the main clause. This principle predicts that (11a) will be easier to process than (11b).

(11a) These students graduated in four years because they took 15 credits each semester.
(11b) Because these students took 15 credits each semester, they graduated in four years.

Exercise E

1. Assume you are writing a set of instructions for students applying for financial aid. They have to (1) fill out an application form and (2) take it to Matthews Hall.
   †a. Write a complex sentence that meets both principles described above: the events are described in the order in which they should occur, and the subordinate clause follows the main clause.
   b. Write another complex sentence that meets only the first principle described above: the events are described in the order in which they should occur, but the subordinate clause precedes the main clause.
   c. Write a third complex sentence that meets only the second principle described above: the events are not described in the order in which they should occur, but the subordinate clause follows the main clause.
   d. Which of sentences (b) and (c) do you prefer? In other words, which principle seems more important to follow, if one of them is violated?

Processing Heavy NPs

A **heavy NP** is a noun phrase that is long or internally complex, such as a **noun clause** (one serving an NP function such as subject or object) or a **relative clause** (one modifying an NP). Heavy NPs are easier to process if they appear in sentence-final position than if they appear earlier in the sentence. For example, (12b) is easier to process than (12a).

(12a) *That she got a perfect score on the exam* is impressive.
(12b) It's impressive *that she got a perfect score on the exam.*

The heavy NP in (12a) is the noun clause *that she got a perfect score on the exam,* which serves as the subject of (12a). In (12b), the noun clause has been moved to sentence-final position, and the subject slot filled by the "dummy" subject *it.*

Likewise, an NP containing a lengthy relative clause is easier to process in sentence-final position. For example, (13b) is easier to process than (13a).

(13a) I sent the article *that just appeared in Newsweek* to Mom.
(13b) I sent Mom the article *that just appeared in Newsweek.*

In (13a) the heavy NP is followed by a prepositional phrase, *to Mom.* In (13b) the heavy NP appears as the last element in the sentence. Note that the same effect can sometimes be achieved by moving just the relative clause to the end of the sentence without moving the NP it modifies, as in (13c).

(13c) I sent the article to Mom *that just appeared in Newsweek.*

Exercise F

1. Identify the heavy NP in each of the following sentences. Then revise the sentence so that the heavy NP is in final position.
   - **†a.** How she got a perfect score on such a difficult exam is what I'd like to know.
   - **b.** The candidate who spent the least amount of money on television advertising won.
   - **c.** The researchers gave the patients who volunteered for the study free medication.
   - **d.** The professor gave an incredibly complicated math problem with no apparent solution to the students.

Discourse-Level Phenomena in Language Processing

In the preceding section, we reviewed findings about language processing related to sentence-level phenomena. However, much research, especially in the field of discourse analysis, has also examined how humans process larger units of discourse. In this section, we will look at some of the main findings from this research, much of which focuses on how readers process written texts.

Readability

A number of **readability formulas** have been proposed to gauge the relative difficulty of processing a written text. For example, the Flesch Index (developed by Rudolph Flesch) is calculated as follows.

STEP I: Start with a 100-word sample.

STEP II: Count the average number of affixes (prefixes and suffixes) per 100 words.

STEP III: Subtract the number of personal references (proper names and pronouns) per 100 words.

STEP IV: Divide the number arrived at in step (3) by two.

STEP V: Add the average number of words per sentence.

The number arrived at in step (V) is measured against the following scale:

0–13	Very easy	36–43	Fairly difficult
13–20	Easy	43–52	Difficult
20–29	Fairly easy	52+	Unreadable
29–36	Standard		

Exercise G

1. Calculate the Flesch Index for the following 100-word passage (adapted from Gleason 1997:376). (Sentences have been numbered for easier reference.)

   [1]Many speech disorders in children have traditionally been termed **functional articulation disorders.** [2]There is growing evidence that **chronic otitis media** may predispose some children to delayed or disordered speech development, but this possible etiological factor has not been firmly established. [3]At one point, problems with **auditory discrimination** were suspected in this population: it was hypothesized that children did not articulate sounds properly because they could not discriminate between their defective productions and the correct model. [4]However, this theory has been criticized by a number of researchers, who find that the majority of articulation-disordered children appear to have normal perceptual abilities.

   Does the index reflect your subjective judgment of the passage's difficulty? How would you account for any difference? (In other words, what variables are **not** taken into account by the index?)

It is clear that sentence length alone does not always account for comprehension. For example, consider (14a) and (14b), cited in Anderson and Davison (1988:34).

(14a) An essential factor in contributory negligence is that it contributes as a proximate cause of the injury.

(14b) If the plaintiff was contributorily negligent, he actually helped cause his own injury, through his own negligence.

Each sentence consists of 17 words and would measure roughly the same according to some readability formulas. Yet subjects in an experiment found (14b) significantly easier to recall and paraphrase accurately. Some of the features that make it easier to comprehend include the use of the *if . . . then* structure in (14b) and the fact that it puts an abstract definition (i.e., *contributory negligence*) in human terms (i.e., *the plaintiff was contributorily negligent; he actually helped cause his own injury*).

Schemata and Scripts

A **schema** (plural: **schemata**) is a framework for organizing knowledge about the world. According to schema theory, readers are able to understand a text better when they can integrate information in the text with preexisting knowledge (represented in the schema). One type of schema is a **script,** a prototypical sequence of events in a familiar situation. For example, it has been hypothesized that a "restaurant script" would be organized according to the following **scene headers:** Entering, Ordering, Eating, and Exiting.

Schemata and scripts provide us with a structured framework for processing the information encountered in a text. As an illustration, consider passage (15), from Singer (1990:209).

(15) Don decided to have lunch at a restaurant. He took his seat, and ordered his favorite, the tuna sandwich. He straightened his collar while he waited. When the food arrived, Don ate hungrily. When the waiter brought the check, he accidentally spilled coffee on Don. Don was very upset and left without paying.

The information in (15) can be classified in the following ways:

- Presented, Central: Some information in the text makes an explicit reference to scene headers in the script, which are of central importance. For example, *He . . . ordered his favorite* explicitly mentions the scene header Ordering. Likewise, *Don ate hungrily* explicitly mentions the scene header Eating.
- Unpresented, Central: The information that corresponds to the scene header Entering is implied rather than presented. That is, *Don decided to have lunch at a restaurant. He took his seat, and ordered his favorite* implies that he entered the restaurant.
- Presented, Peripheral: Some information is explicitly stated in the text but does not relate to the script at all, namely *He straightened his collar.*

Experiments on the recall of passages such as (15) suggest that readers draw upon both the text itself and the script upon which it is based. The results of recall tests done after a short time (e.g., 30 minutes after reading) and after a longer time (e.g., several days after reading) are quite interesting. In short-term tests, participants recalled about an equal percentage of Presented Central and Presented Peripheral statements. They recalled more Unpresented Central statements than Unpresented Peripheral statements. In long-term tests, the recall of Unpresented Central statements *increased* over time. In contrast, the recall of both Presented and Unpresented Peripheral statements *decreased* over time. These results suggest that readers consult not just their memory of the text, but also their knowledge of the script. As recall of the text itself erodes, readers rely more and more on their knowledge of the script—they "remember" central statements that weren't actually in the text, and forget peripheral statements that were.

Exercise H

1. What elements in the story about Don should be classified as Presented, Peripheral? Would you predict that these elements would be recalled (or not recalled) at similar rates? Why or why not? If not, how would you suggest further subdividing the Presented, Peripheral category?
2. Construct scene headers for a script for each of the following activities.
   †a. going to the supermarket
   b. going to the movies

Exercise H *Continued*

3. Many types of writing (especially nonfiction genres) have scripts; that is, readers expect certain topics to be addressed in a certain order. Compose some scene headers that appear to be relevant to the script for each of the following genres.
   a. recipes
   b. instructions for assembling a partially assembled object (e.g., a piece of furniture or a lawnmower)
   c. scientific articles that report experimental results

Cohesion

Halliday and Hasan (1976) developed a theory of how listeners and readers establish relationships between different parts of a text. The reader's sense that the parts of a text "hang together" in a clear relationship is referred to as **cohesion.** According to Halliday and Hasan, writers can establish cohesion through several means. One is **reference,** which is achieved through the use of items such as personal and demonstrative pronouns (e.g., *him, this*). A related method is **substitution,** which is achieved through the use of pro-forms such as *one* and *ones* (which substitute for noun phrases) and forms of *do* (which substitute for verb phrases). Passage (16) illustrates both of these strategies.

(16) There was a fire in a downtown apartment building last night. The morning paper didn't carry a story about *it,* but the evening paper has *one.*

Here *it* is a pronoun that refers back to *a fire,* and *one* is a pro-form that refers back to *a story about it.*

A third way in which cohesion can be established is through **ellipsis,** which Halliday and Hasan define as "substitution by zero" (p. 143). In (17), the elliptical item *(coffee)* is indicated by a blank.

(17) I've drunk a lot of *coffee* in my time, but this is the worst _____ I've ever tasted.

Ellipsis can also apply to part of a VP, as in the following case:

(18) Evening classes were *canceled because of the snowstorm.* Daytime classes were not _____, however.

Here the elliptical item is *canceled because of the snowstorm.*

A fourth strategy for building cohesion is the use of **conjunctions.** Halliday and Hasan outline four categories of conjunctions, illustrated here with some examples.

- **Additive:** *and, furthermore, for instance, likewise*
- **Adversative:** *yet, in fact, however, on the other hand, instead*
- **Causal:** *so, therefore, as a result, because*
- **Temporal:** *then, first, second, third, finally, in conclusion*

Fifth, cohesion can be established through the use of **lexical cohesion:** either repeating a word or phrase from an earlier part of the discourse, using a synonym (e.g., *youngsters* for *children*), or using a superordinate term (e.g., *trees* for *elms*). Lexical cohesion may also be achieved through **collocation,** the use of lexical items that regularly appear in the same context. For example, *students, school, teacher,* and *test* are collocative items, as are *restaurant, food, waiter,* and *eat.*

Some of these strategies are illustrated in passage (19).

(19) [1]The essence of ritual is that it provides order and often marks periods of transition. [2]That's what makes public rites of birth, marriage, and death so important. [3]But acknowledging the smaller transitions of daily life may be just as vital—perhaps even more so. [4]Even activities that aren't blatantly ceremonial or religious may provide a comforting sense of structure if they're regularly done in similar fashion or at similar times of day. [5]For example, reading before bedtime makes it easier to relax and fall asleep. [6]Eating regular meals helps you track the hours of the day. (Adapted from Laliberte 1998:66)

An example of ellipsis occurs in sentence (4), where the phrase *regularly done* is omitted before *at similar times of day.* An example of an additive conjunction, *for example,* occurs in sentence (5). An example of collocation is illustrated by the words *ritual, public rites, ceremonial,* and *religious.*

Exercise I

1. Find examples of cohesion-building strategies in the following passage, adapted from Gleason (1997:376). (Sentences have been numbered for easier reference.)

   [1]A large proportion of speech disorders in children have traditionally been termed **functional articulation disorders** (i.e., their etiology is unknown). [2]There is growing evidence that **chronic otitis media** (middle ear infections) may predispose some children to delayed or disordered speech development, but this possible etiological factor has yet to be firmly established. [3]At one point, problems with **auditory discrimination** were suspected in this population; that is, it was hypothesized that children did not articulate sounds properly because they could not discriminate the difference between their defective productions and the correct model. [4]However, this theory has been criticized by a number of researchers, who find that the majority of articulation-disordered children appear to have normal perceptual abilities.

   You should be able to find at least the following:

   - two examples of reference
   - one example of ellipsis
   - two examples of repetition
   - one example of a synonym
   - one example of a superordinate term
   - one example of a collocative series

Thematic Roles

Each NP in a sentence plays a particular thematic role in relation to the verb in that sentence. For example, (20) illustrates four of these thematic roles.

(20) Sam$_1$ trimmed the shrubs$_2$ for his mother$_3$ with the new hedge clipper$_4$.

NP$_1$ functions as the **agent,** the volitional performer of the action described by the verb. NP$_2$ functions as the **patient,** the thing affected by the action of the verb. NP$_3$ functions as the **beneficiary,** the entity which benefits from the action. Finally, NP$_4$ functions as the **instrument,** the thing used to carry out the action.

A given thematic role (e.g., agent, patient, etc.) can occur in a number of syntactic positions (subject, object, etc.). In sentences (20a–c), for example, the semantic role of instrument occurs in three different syntactic positions.

(20a) Subject—*The new hedge clipper* was used to trim the shrubs.
(20b) Direct Object—Sam used *the new hedge clipper* to trim the shrubs.
(20c) Object of Preposition—Sam trimmed the shrubs with *the new hedge clipper.*

Conversely, a given syntactic position can be filled by a number of thematic roles. In sentences (20d–f), for example, the subject is filled by three different thematic roles.

(20d) Agent—*Sam* trimmed the shrubs with the new hedge clipper.
(20e) Patient—*The shrubs* were trimmed by Sam.
(20f) Instrument—*The hedge clipper* was used to trim the shrubs.

The flow of information in a discourse is facilitated when a particular thematic role always occupies the same syntactic position. Consider sentences (21a–b), from a proposal to develop software for a bookstore. In (21a–b) there is no consistent relationship between thematic role and syntactic position.

(21a) *The development team* will first determine the inventory functions needed in the software.
(21b) A survey of the bookstore staff's computer skills will also be conducted by *the team.*

In (21a) the agent is the subject; in (21b) it is the object of the passive *by*-phrase. Compare (22a–b), revised versions of the same sentences.

(22a) *The development team* will first determine the inventory functions needed in the software.
(22b) *The team* will also conduct a survey of the bookstore staff's computer skills.

In (22a–b) the subject position of each sentence is filled by the agent, thereby enhancing the flow of information.

Exercise J

1. State the thematic role played by each of the italicized NPs in the following examples.
   a. *The Gomosaygiama Agency* has launched *a new advertising campaign* for *the Katznelson Corporation.*
   b. *A new advertising campaign* has been launched by *the Gomosaygiama Agency.*
   c. *The Katznelson Corporation* is benefiting from *a new advertising campaign.*

The Given-New Contract

A sentence can be divided into two information units—**given information** (i.e., that which the writer assumes is known to the reader) and **new information** (i.e., that which the writer assumes is not known to the reader). Given information is normally expressed as the subject, and new information is normally expressed in the predicate (verb phrase). For example, consider sentence (23).

(23) Most patients with heart disease are overweight.

In (23), the subject *Most patients with heart disease* is the given information. By putting it in subject position, the writer is treating it as information that is already under discussion in the discourse. Even if it appeared as the first sentence of an article, the writer is still assuming that the reader understands heart disease to be the topic—perhaps because of the article's title. The predicate *are overweight* expresses the new information about the topic.

The arrangement of given and new information from sentence to sentence forms a larger organization called **thematic progression** or the **Given-New Contract.** Studies have shown that passages are easier to comprehend and remember if new information follows given information.

A **linear** progression of given and new information can be represented as AB:BC, where the new information (B) in one sentence becomes the given information (B) in the next, as in (24a) and (24b).

(24a) Most patients with heart disease are *overweight.* (AB)
(24b) *Extra weight* around the waist is an especially high risk factor. (BC)

The new information in (24a) includes *overweight,* which becomes the given information in (24b), *Extra weight.* In contrast, a **hierarchical** progression of given and new information can be represented as AB:AC, where the given information (A) in one sentence is retained as the given information (A) in the next, as in (25a) and (25b).

(25a) *An angiogram* may be used to diagnose a patient with severe heart attack symptoms. (AB)
(25b) During *this painless procedure,* dye is injected into the coronary arteries. (AC)

The given information in (25a), *An angiogram,* is repeated as the given information in (25b), *This painless procedure.*

Note that given information may be restated from one sentence to the next in several ways. The writer may repeat the information exactly, use a synonym (e.g., *overweight* and *extra pounds*), use a pronoun (e.g., *an angiogram* and *it*), or use a superordinate (e.g., *an angiogram* and *this painless procedure*).

Both the linear and hierarchical varieties of thematic progression adhere to the Given-New Contract. You can check this by noting that in both the linear (AB:BC) and hierarchical (AB:AC) patterns, earlier letters of the alphabet always precede later ones, within each pairing. Conversely, a progression violates the contract if an earlier letter follows a later one (e.g., AB:CA), as illustrated in (26a–b).

(26a) *An angiogram* may be used to diagnose a patient with severe heart attack symptoms. (AB)
(26b) Dye is injected into the coronary arteries during this *painless procedure.* (CA)

Exercise K

1. Identify the type of thematic progression illustrated in each of the following examples (AB:AC, AB:BC, or neither).
   †**a.** S&S Lighting was established in Omaha in 1968. S&S was incorporated in 1970.
   b. The annual Wellness Fair will be held this Saturday. We hope everyone will attend.
   c. We apologize for the delay in shipping your books. They will be sent within two weeks.
2. The two varieties of thematic progression may be combined in one passage, as in the following example. Label the given-new patterns found between each pair of sentences. (Sentences have been numbered for easy reference.)
   [1]An angiogram may be used to diagnose a patient with severe heart attack symptoms. [2]This painless procedure involves injecting dye into the coronary arteries. [3]The dye allows the doctor to examine the patient's circulation.
3. Analyze the given-new patterns used in the following passages. (Sentences have been numbered for easy reference.) Do the writers use primarily AB:BC, AB:AC, or a mixture? Also identify some of the different techniques used to restate given information (repetition, pronouns, synonyms, superordinates).
   a. [1]The U.S. Consumer Product Safety Commission compiles figures on horse-related injuries. [2]These numbers come from hospital emergency rooms, so they reflect only injuries that wind up there. [3]They show that the number of horse-related injuries has declined; however, they don't show a decrease in head injuries as a percentage of the total. [4]Nor do they indicate if injured riders were wearing helmets—and many riders, especially in Western disciplines, still don't. (Pascoe 1998:60)
   b. [1]For a few days after installation, all new carpets emit volatile organic compounds (VOCs), air pollutants associated with carpet manufacture. [2]Though emissions are generally at a very low level, not everyone agrees what level is "safe." [3]Ronald Gots, a medical doctor and toxicologist who heads a Rockville, MD, consulting firm on indoor air quality, says carpet emissions aren't known to cause irritation, but theoretically people with asthma or allergies "might be more sensitive than most." [4]The same people may also be affected by dirt, dust mites, and mildew that can build up in carpeting. ("The Retail Carpet Ride" 1998:37)

(continued)

Exercise K *Continued*

4. Examine the passage in question (3b) again. At what point is the passive voice used to sustain the Given-New Contract?
5. Revise the following passages so that they adhere to the given-new contract.
   †a. Some fruits contain more oil than others. The amount of oil in a fruit determines the fruit's caloric value. Birds' fruit preferences correlate with this caloric value. In other words, one way that birds choose the foods they eat is through caloric value.
   b. I have proposed that a standardized crew cycle be developed and used in the production of future mission time lines. The amount of time and labor currently required to produce a mission time line would be greatly reduced by the use of such a crew cycle.

Reading between the Lines

The preceding discussion of schema theory and cohesion should make clear that language processing goes far beyond simply "receiving information." Instead, language perception involves the unconscious, immediate interpretation of the text being heard or read. In particular, we frequently construct inferences that allow us to "read between the lines" and supply information that has not actually been stated. These inferences may be needed to maintain a coherent text and may also reflect assumptions based on our knowledge of the world. Harley (2001:318) discusses three types of inferences that readers may draw. **Logical inferences** are related to the ideas of **analytic truth** and **entailment** discussed in Chapter 3 (Semantics). For example, consider the text in (27).

(27) Mia recently moved to a new apartment. She wanted to hang some pictures on the walls, but the manager wouldn't let her.

Readers of this passage can readily associate *the walls* with *apartment,* since walls are a necessary part of an apartment (i.e., every apartment has walls).

By comparison, consider (28).

(28) Mia recently moved to a new apartment. The garbage disposal was broken, so the manager sent out a plumber to fix it.

A garbage disposal is a probable component of an apartment, but not a necessary one. In this instance, we have an example of a **bridging** inference. Note that the "bridge" metaphor, developed in an influential essay by Clark (1977), implies that we are building a connection between two distinct things. Passage (29) illustrates a case requiring an even longer bridge.

(29) Mia recently moved to a new apartment. She had some trouble getting past the security guard before she got a gate pass.

Security guards, while certainly a possible feature of an apartment, are by no means a necessary, common, or even probable feature. Hence we might expect readers to take longer to process (29) and to "build the bridge" between the new apartment and the mention of the security guard.

Finally, **elaborative inferences** are those that bring in real-world knowledge not mentioned in the text. For example, assume that participants in a study are asked to read (30).

(30) Mia recently changed jobs and moved to a new city. Her co-workers are great, and her new apartment is much nicer than her old one. She also traded in her old car and updated her wardrobe. She is now contributing $100 a week toward a retirement fund.

Readers questioned later may believe that they read the sentence "She got a raise when she took her new job"—even though this is mentioned nowhere in the text. Although this is an erroneous response about the text, the inference is plausible based on what we know about the real world.

Summary

The theory of language processing draws upon research in psycholinguistics and discourse analysis, both of which use concepts from linguistics to explain patterns in how humans process language. We have seen that research from these fields can explain several types of phenomena. First, concepts from language processing, such as minimal attachment and late closure, can explain why human have problems with structures like "garden path" sentences. Concepts like the principle of parallel function can explain how we resolve ambiguous pronoun reference. Research in language processing also reveals that readers and listeners may encounter processing difficulties with certain types of negative sentences, passive sentences, complex sentences, and heavy NPs. Second, we have looked at concepts related to how humans process longer texts. Among the concepts we have looked at are readability formulas, the role of schemata and scripts, cohesion, thematic roles, given and new information, and "reading between the lines."

SUPPLEMENTARY READINGS

Donnelly, C. (1994). *Linguistics for writers.* Albany: State University of New York Press.

Halliday, M. A. K., & Hasan, R. (1976). *Cohesion in English.* London: Longman.

Harley, T. (2001). *The psychology of language: From data to theory* (2nd ed.). New York: Taylor & Francis.

Riley, K. (1991). Passive voice and rhetorical role in scientific writing. *Journal of Technical Writing and Communication, 21,* 239–257.

Singer, M. (1990). *Psychology of language: An introduction to sentence and discourse processes.* Hillsdale, NJ: Erlbaum.

Vande Kopple, W. J. (1982). Functional sentence perspective, composition, and reading. *College Composition and Communication, 33,* 50–63.

You are now prepared to read all of these works. The textbooks by Harley and Singer provide comprehensive introductions to research in the psychology of language. Halliday and Hasan is the classic work on cohesion in English. The articles by Riley and Vande Kopple apply syntactic principles to the analysis of how writers and readers approach texts. Donnelly uses concepts from psycholinguistics, discourse analysis, and other linguistic fields to analyze effective and ineffective writing.

Supplementary Exercises

1. Principles of sentence comprehension may interact with, and sometimes contradict, each other. For example, consider the following sentences.
   - **A.** The incumbent from the fifth district, who has been campaigning extensively for the past two weeks, won the election.
   - **B.** The election was won by the incumbent from the fifth district, who has been campaigning extensively for the past two weeks.
   - **a.** What principle would predict that (A) will be easier to comprehend?
   - **b.** What principle would predict that (B) will be easier to comprehend?
   - **c.** Which principle do you think should take precedence in this case?
2. Consider the following passage cited by Duin (1989:97):

   The procedure is actually quite simple. First, you arrange things into different groups. Of course, one pile may be sufficient depending on how much there is to do. If you have to go somewhere else due to lack of facilities, that is the next step; otherwise you are pretty well set. It is important not to overdo things. That is, it is better to do too few things at once than too many. In the short run this may not seem important, but complications can arise. A mistake can be expensive as well. At first the whole procedure will seem complicated. Soon, however, it will become just another fact of life. . . .

   Subjects in an experiment were asked to read the passage quickly, put it aside, and recall as many facts from it as possible. One group of subjects was given the title of the passage before they started reading: "Washing Clothes." Another group of subjects was not given the title.
   - **a.** Based on schema theory, which group of subjects would you expect to be able to recall more information? Why?
   - **b.** Try an informal re-creation of the experiment described above. Ask one group of friends to read the passage (with its title), put it aside, and recall as many details as possible. Ask another group of friends to read the passage (without its title), put it aside, and recall as many details as possible. What results do you obtain?
   - **c.** Propose at least four scene headers for a "washing clothes" script.
3. The following pair of sentences conforms to the AB:AC pattern of thematic progression. Rewrite them so that the pair follows the AB:BC pattern.

   Budget reviews will now be conducted by a Budget Review Committee made up of department heads. In this way, our future budgets should better reflect the needs of each of the individual departments.
4. Consider the following paragraphs, adapted from Vande Kopple (1982:53–54). Paragraph (A) has been shown to be more readable and memorable than paragraph (B).
   - **A.** Epic poems usually include a long narrative or story. This story is almost always marked by certain conventions. These conventions are normally used to enhance the stature of a great hero. Such a hero personifies the ideals of particular societies.
   - **B.** A long narrative or story is usually included in epic poems. Certain conventions almost always mark this story. The stature of a great hero is enhanced through the use of these conventions. The ideals of particular societies are personified in such a hero.
   - **a.** State the thematic progression of paragraph (A).
   - **b.** State the thematic progression of paragraph (B).

c. Explain why (A) is more "readable and memorable" than (B).

d. How is passive voice used at several points in passage (A) to enhance the flow of given-new information? What is the problem with telling writers to always "avoid the passive voice"?

5. In experiments conducted by Warden (1976), subjects of different ages were asked to look at drawings and construct a story from them. Over half of the 3-year-olds began their stories with structures like (A).

A. The cat was chasing the bird. The bird flew away from the cat.

In contrast, over 80 percent of the 9-year-olds and 100 percent of the adults began their stories with structures like (B).

B. A cat was chasing a bird. The bird flew away from the cat.

Note the way that the 3-year-olds differ from the older subjects in their use of definite and indefinite articles. What pattern do the older subjects follow that the 3-year-olds have not acquired?

Exploratory Exercises

1. In 2004, the item below circulated widely on the Internet. While the assertion made in the message seems to work fairly well here, what other information is the reader using to decode this message? Consider, for example, the contribution that the surrounding discourse might be making to the reader's ability to decipher the misspelled words. If you wanted to test the assertion made in the message, what are some different strategies that you might use to rule out the effects of these variables?

The phaomnneel pweor of the hmuan mnid:

Aoccdrnig to a rscheraeer at Cmabrigde Uinervtisy, it deosn't mttaer in waht oredr the ltteers in a wrod are, the olny iprmoetnt tihng is taht the frist and lsat ltteer be at the rghit pclae. The rset can be a total mses and you can sitll raed it wouthit porbelm. Tihs is bcuseae the huamn mnid deos not raed ervey lteter by istlef, but the wrod as a wlohe.

Amzanig huh?

2. Visit at least a half-dozen websites for the same type of business or organization (e.g., airlines, car dealerships, universities, clothing catalogs), focusing on their homepages and navigational links. As you compare different websites for the same type of business or organization, do you find common elements among them that indicate the development of a genre for that type of business site? That is, do website designers seem to assume that visitors have developed a schema—a set of expectations about content and organization—for that type of site? If so, what are the elements of that schema?

3. While this chapter has focused on the receptive modalities of language (reading and listening), much research in language processing also studies the way that humans produce language. One interesting area is the study of **slips of the tongue** (also known as spoonerisms)—i.e., unintentional errors that people produce when they are speaking. Below are some reported by Fromkin (1971). In each case, the target, or intended utterance, is followed by the slip of the tongue—what the speaker said instead of the target.

A. *cup of coffee* → *cuff of coffee*

B. *gave the boy* → *gave the goy*

C. *the zipper is narrow* → *the nipper is zarrow*

D. *big and fat* → *pig and vat*

E. *pitch and stress* → *piss and stretch*

F. *Cedars of Lebanon* → *Cedars of Lemadon*

G. *one fell swoop* → *one swell foop*

H. *the flags hung out* → *the hags flung out*

Analyze these errors according to whether the error involves **anticipation** (a segment that occurs later in an utterance is repeated in an earlier position), **perseveration** (a segment that occurs earlier in an utterance is repeated in a later position), or **metathesis** (reversal of two segments). Also consider whether the error involves an entire segment (i.e., phoneme), or whether it is better analyzed as involving part of a phoneme (i.e., a feature) or something larger than a phoneme (such as a syllable).

4. See also Chapter 6, Exploratory Exercise 3, which deals with misperceptions of song lyrics.

CHAPTER TWELVE

The Neurology of Language

The **neurology of language,** also known as **neurolinguistics,** is the study of how the brain processes language. Let's consider some observations we can make about language and the brain.

(1) Damage to the brain can affect a person's ability to process language; damage to the heart, lungs, or kidneys (short of killing the person) does not.

(2) Damage to the left side of the brain is more likely to cause language processing difficulties (e.g., being able to hear speech but unable to comprehend it) than is damage to the right side of the brain.

(3) Damage to the front part of the brain is more likely to affect the production of language through speaking and writing. Damage to the rear part of the brain is more likely to affect the comprehension of language through listening and reading.

Observation (1) illustrates the fact that the physical organ underlying the ability to process language is the brain; in particular, brain damage can result in a language-specific dysfunction called **aphasia.** Observation (2) indicates that most human beings process language in the left cerebral hemisphere. This tendency reflects **hemispherical specialization:** the left hemisphere controls one set of abilities, among them language processing, while the right controls other abilities, such as orientation in space and visuospatial processing. Observation (3) indicates that different parts of each hemisphere control different cognitive functions. This is sometimes referred to as **localization of function.**

Before getting into the details of neurolinguistics, we should address three points concerning the nature of research in this field. First, neurolinguists commonly observe the language of patients who have suffered brain damage (i.e., a lesion) from a stroke, a tumor, or trauma. A stroke causes damage by disrupting the blood supply, and thus the oxygen supply, to part of the brain. A tumor causes damage by putting pressure on part of the brain from the inside, in effect "squeezing" the brain between the tumor and the skull. Trauma to the brain is caused by some sort of external force, such as a blow to the head. Of these three types of damage, stroke damage is typically of more interest to the neurolinguists than damage caused by tumor or trauma. This is because a stroke is capable of damaging a very specific, localized part of the brain, whereas damage caused by tumor or trauma tends to be more global, affecting a greater part of the brain.

Second, neurolinguistics is basically a correlational and statistical enterprise. It is correlational in that it tries to find correspondences between particular language functions and particular parts of the brain. The neurolinguist draws inferences of the following type: patients 1, 3, and 5 all have had strokes in area A of the brain and all exhibit language dysfunction Y; patients 2, 4, and 6 all have had strokes in area B of the brain and all exhibit language dysfunction Z; therefore, it appears that brain area A controls function Y and that brain area B controls function Z. Neurolinguistics is statistical in that the researcher cannot draw absolute correlations between a particular part of the brain and a particular language dysfunction for all human beings. For example, given 10 patients with damage to brain area A, only 8 may exhibit language dysfunction Y. On this basis, the neurolinguist could hypothesize that there is an 80 percent probability that damage to brain area A will lead to language dysfunction Y. In short, then, neurolinguists essentially make statistical correlations between localized brain damage and particular language processing deficits.

Third, as was the case with first-language acquisition, the research methods used in neurolinguistics present some inherent challenges. As we have just seen, one main avenue for studying neurolinguistics is through pathology; that is, through studying patients with brain damage. Obviously, however, the neurolinguist cannot inflict damage on a normal subject in order to see what happens, but instead must wait for a suitable subject to come along. Moreover, the patient must have relatively localized brain damage and must also exhibit fairly specific behavioral abnormalities. If the brain damage is global or if the behavioral abnormalities are too general, the analyst will have difficulty correlating a particular area of the brain with a particular behavioral deficit. In short, the neurolinguist is constrained to some extent by having to draw inferences on the basis of what nature provides.

In order to convey a better understanding of how research in neurolinguistics is carried out, this chapter is divided into three areas: the anatomy of the central nervous system, including the major areas related to the neurology of language; a discussion of the different functions performed by each of the cerebral hemispheres; and a survey of brain disorders affecting language.

Exercise A

1. Most patients cited in the neurolinguistics literature have incurred brain damage from strokes rather than from tumors or trauma. Why would stroke patients provide the most interesting evidence for the localization of linguistic function in the brain?

Anatomy of the Nervous System

The basic unit of the nervous system is the **neuron;** there are about 12 billion neurons in the nervous system. Each neuron is made up of three parts: a **cell body;** an **axon,** which transmits nervous impulses away from the cell body; and **dendrites,** which receive impulses coming in to the cell body. The point at which the nervous impulse passes from the axon of one neuron to the dendrites of another is called a **synapse.** Thus, neurons communicate with each other by transmitting information through this complex of axons, dendrites, and synapses.

The part of the nervous system that is of primary interest to neurolinguists is the **central nervous system (CNS),** composed of the brain and the spinal cord. The diagram of the CNS in Figure 12.1 illustrates the major landmarks which will be of interest to us in this chapter.

The **spinal cord** (1) transmits messages between the brain and the peripheral nervous system extending throughout the rest of the body. The spinal cord transmits the message from the brain that says, for example, to cross your right leg over your left. The spinal cord, however, plays no role in language processing. The **lower brain stem** (2) consists of the **medulla oblongata** and the **pons.** These structures serve essentially as a bridge between the spinal cord and the higher brain stem. (In fact, *pons* is Latin for 'bridge.') Damage to the lower brain stem can cause a speech disorder known as **dysarthria.** This is not a language deficit, but rather the inability to produce articulate speech.

The **higher brain stem** (3) consists of the **thalamus** and **midbrain.** These structures control involuntary regulatory functions such as breathing, heart rate, and body temperature. In addition, the thalamus receives all incoming sensory stimuli (except for the sense of smell) and transmits each stimulus to the part of the brain where it is processed. The **cerebellum** (4), which lies to the rear of the brain stem, controls equilibrium. The cerebellum plays no known role, however, in language processing.

The **cerebrum** (5) is the part of the brain on top of the brain stem and cerebellum. The cerebrum is divided into two hemispheres, the left and the right, and exhibits what is known as **contralateral control.** That is, each hemisphere controls the opposite side of the body. For example, if you raise your right arm, the message to do so originates in the left cerebral hemisphere. Likewise, if you step on a tack with your left foot, the sensation of pain is processed by your right cerebral hemisphere.

Each cerebral hemisphere consists of a mass of **white fiber tracts** covered by the **cortex,** which is approximately 0.25 inch thick and contains about 10 billion neurons.

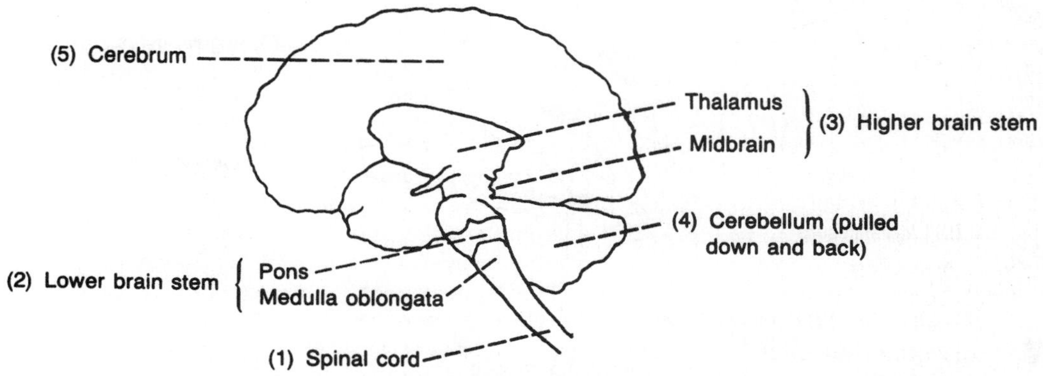

FIGURE 12.1 Cross-section of the central nervous system, facing left

(Recall that the entire nervous system contains only about 12 billion neurons; thus, the cortex is by far the most powerful processing center within the nervous system.) The white fiber tracts are divided into three types, according to their function. **Association fibers** connect different parts of the cortex within one hemisphere, enabling these parts to communicate with each other. **Projection fibers** connect the cortex to the brain stem and spinal cord, enabling the cortex to communicate with the peripheral nervous system. **Commissural fibers** connect the two cerebral hemispheres, enabling them to communicate with each other. The largest group of commissural fibers is known collectively as the **corpus callosum**.

Let's now turn our attention to the cortex itself, which is essentially the central storehouse of the brain and controls all voluntary activity, including the ability to process language. The diagram of the human cortex in Figure 12.2 illustrates the major landmarks which we will refer to throughout the rest of this chapter.

Lobes

The cerebrum (i.e., the cortex and the white fiber tracts serving it) is divided into four lobes: the **frontal lobe** (1) in the anterior (front) part; the **parietal lobe** (2) in the superior (top) part; the **occipital lobe** (3) in the posterior (back) part; and the **temporal lobe** (4) in the inferior (bottom) part. Each lobe, in turn, subserves somewhat different functions. For example, the frontal lobe processes olfactory stimuli; the parietal lobe processes tactile and visuospatial stimuli; the occipital lobe processes visual stimuli; and the temporal lobe

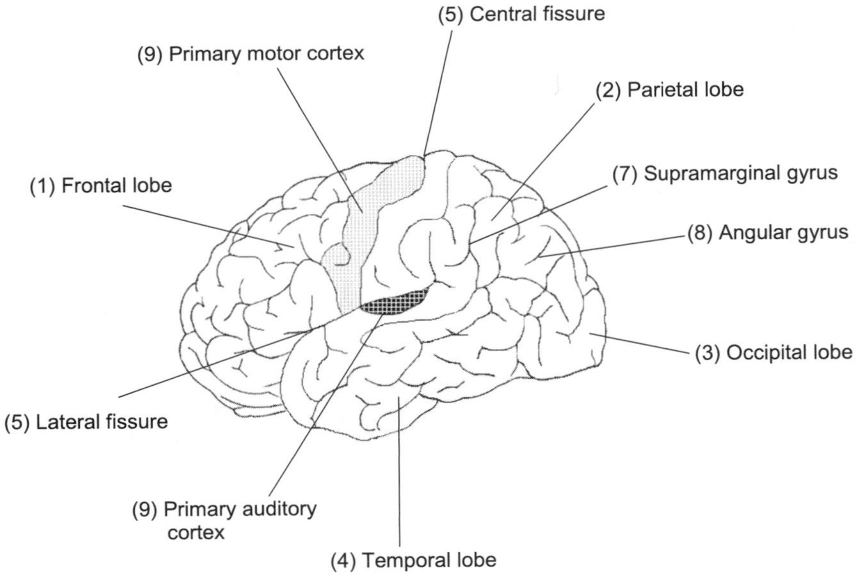

FIGURE 12.2 Human cortex, facing left

processes auditory stimuli. Each cerebral hemisphere has these four lobes, so we can speak of the left temporal lobe, the right occipital lobe, and so on. We will see later that the left frontal and temporal lobes house the major language processing centers for most humans.

Convolutions and Fissures

The cortex of the human brain has a wrinkled appearance. The indentations are called **fissures** or **sulci,** and the bulges are called **convolutions** or **gyri.** Certain fissures and convolutions serve as important anatomical landmarks. The **lateral fissure** (5), also known as the **fissure of Sylvius,** separates the frontal and temporal lobes. The **central fissure,** also called the **central sulcus** or **fissure of Rolando,** separates the frontal and parietal lobes. The **supramarginal gyrus** (7) and the **angular gyrus** (8) lie in the inferior part of the parietal lobe. And the **primary auditory cortex** (9), also known as **Heschl's gyrus** or the **transverse temporal gyrus,** receives all incoming auditory stimuli. One function of the primary auditory cortex is to separate different types of auditory stimuli (e.g., environmental noises such as buzzes, clicks, and whistles versus linguistic stimuli such as speech) and send them to the different parts of the cortex where they are interpreted.

The **primary motor cortex** is a strip of cortex about two centimeters wide, lying immediately anterior to the central fissure. Each point in the primary motor cortex controls a discrete set of muscles. For example, stimulating the superior (top) part of the primary motor cortex will cause the leg muscles on the opposite side of the body to contract. Movements of the lips, tongue, and jaw are controlled by the inferior (bottom) part of the primary motor cortex, near the lateral fissure. In general, the more fine-grained the movement, the larger the cortical area devoted to it. Thus, movement of the trunk has less cortex devoted to it than does movement of the fingers.

Exercise B

1. When you go to sleep, you become unconscious, which suggests a decrease in cortical activity. However, you continue to breathe and your heart continues to beat. Does this mean that these functions are not controlled by the central nervous system? Explain.
2. Nonlinguistic dysfunctions such as dysmetria ("overshoot" and "undershoot") and ataxia (lack of muscular coordination) may result from damage to the ________, which lies posterior to the brain stem.
3. Identify the part of the brain that does each of the following.
   - **a.** controls vision
   - **b.** connects the left and right hemispheres
   - **c.** separates linguistic and nonlinguistic auditory stimuli
   - **d.** controls the voluntary motor movements of the tongue and lips
4. Mark the following statements true or false.
   - **a.** T F The cerebrum is essentially made up of the two hemispheres of the brain.
   - **b.** T F The cerebrum controls equilibrium.
   - **c.** T F Neurons are composed of a cell body, an axon, and synapses.

Broca's Area

During the early 19th century, scientists hotly debated the question of whether different parts of the brain serve different mental functions. **Localizationists** believed that specific parts of the brain controlled different mental functions. **Holists,** on the other hand, believed that different mental functions were not localized in specific parts of the brain. The localization of cortical function was finally demonstrated to the satisfaction of most neuroscientists by the French physician Pierre Paul Broca (1824–1880).

Broca's evidence was based primarily on two patients. First was Leborgne, a 51-year-old man who had had brain seizures since his youth. At age 30, he lost most of his ability to produce language, but not to comprehend it. At age 40, Leborgne developed paralysis on the right side and became bedridden. Upon his death, an autopsy revealed extensive degeneration of the left hemisphere. Broca argued that the lesion had begun in the third convolution of the frontal lobe in the left hemisphere. In short, Broca correlated Leborgne's expressive aphasia—that is, his inability to produce linguistic output—with what began as localized damage in the third frontal convolution. In 1861 Broca reported his findings in a paper later translated into English as "Remarks on the Seat of the Faculty of Articulate Language, followed by an Observation of *Aphemia.*" (The term *aphasia* was later introduced by Trousseau.) Leborgne's case, however, was not completely conclusive since the patient's condition had degenerated slowly over the years, resulting in numerous, diffuse brain lesions at his death.

Broca offered additional evidence in 1861 based on a second patient, Lelong, an 84-year-old man who had had expressive aphasia for the previous nine and a half years. His motor power was intact; in other words, his inability to speak and write was not due to paralysis. After his death, an autopsy revealed localized damage to the third convolution of the left frontal lobe, the same general area that Broca had argued was the site of Leborgne's original lesion.

Shortly thereafter, other neurologists reported a total of 10 cases of aphasia with damage to the third frontal convolution in the left hemisphere, essentially replicating Broca's findings. At the same time, a patient was reported with damage to the third frontal convolution in the right hemisphere, but no language disturbance. Based on such cases, Broca contended that the left frontal lobe is specialized for language. Because of Broca's contributions, the area of the third frontal convolution in the left hemisphere is known as **Broca's area,** as shown in Figure 12.3.

Wernicke's Area

The German neurologist and psychiatrist Carl Wernicke (1848–1904) studied patients whose language disorders differed markedly from those described by Broca. Wernicke published his theories in 1874 as *Der aphasische Symptomenkomplex (The Aphasic Complex).* In general terms, Broca's patients could comprehend speech but could not produce it; moreover, they displayed varying degrees of right-sided paralysis. In contrast, the patients studied by Wernicke could not comprehend speech, but they could produce it (although it was characterized by errors); moreover, they exhibited a general absence of paralysis. Wernicke correlated this type of sensory disturbance with damage to the first convolution of the temporal lobe in the left hemisphere. This area, which is adjacent to the primary auditory cortex in the left hemisphere, is known as **Wernicke's area** and is shown in Figure 12.3.

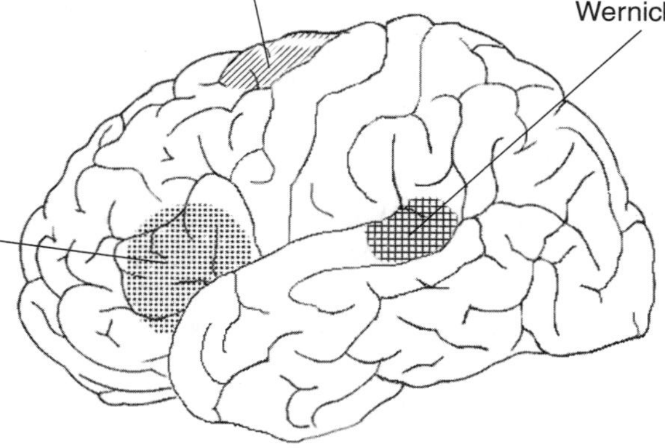

FIGURE 12.3 Three major language areas of the cortex

In sum, whereas Broca localized language in the left hemisphere, Wernicke subdivided that hemisphere as subserving two different language functions: the frontal lobe controls expression, and the temporal lobe controls comprehension. Wernicke's division makes perfect sense anatomically. The expressive aphasia described by Broca results from damage near the motor cortex, which controls outgoing motor movements, including the articulation of speech. The receptive aphasia described by Wernicke results from damage near the primary auditory cortex, which processes incoming auditory stimuli, including speech.

Exercise C

1. Broca's aphasia is more likely than Wernicke's aphasia to be accompanied by paralysis. Why? (Hint: Consider the areas surrounding the lesion site.)
†2. Patients with Broca's aphasia often exhibit an inability to perform voluntary facial movements. Why? (Hint: What is the common denominator in the two disorders?)
3. Broca'a patient Leborgne developed right-sided paralysis. Explain why this symptom is consistent with his language symptoms, considering the site of the lesion responsible for the problems.

Supplementary Motor Cortex

During the 20th century, research in the neurology of language was advanced by Wilder Penfield and LaMar Roberts, two neurologists working at the Montreal Neurological Institute in the 1940s and 1950s. Penfield and Roberts were treating patients for epilepsy, a disorder characterized by abnormal electrical discharges in the brain. One treatment method they used was to remove those areas of the brain that were the sources for these discharges. However, they did not want to remove a part of the brain that subserved some necessary cognitive function such as language. In other words, they didn't want the cure for epilepsy to be worse than the disease itself.

To determine the function of different parts of the brain, Penfield and Roberts stimulated specific parts of the exposed cortex with a weak electrical current transmitted through silver probes. Since the cortex itself cannot feel pain, it was possible for them to remove part of the patient's skull under a local anesthetic and have the patient remain conscious throughout the procedure. During stimulation they would have the patient perform such tasks as naming an object in a picture. When they stimulated an area of the cortex subserving language, the patient would experience some sort of linguistic difficulty such as total arrest of speech, halting and slurred speech, repetitions, confusions of numbers while counting, or inability to name. Penfield and Roberts describe some responses as follows.

> An example is . . . "Oh, I know what it is. That is what you put in your shoes." After withdrawal of the stimulating electrodes, the patient immediately said "foot." Still another example is the inability to name a comb. When asked its use, he said, "I comb my hair." When asked again to name it, he couldn't until the electrode was removed. (1959:123–124)

It is interesting to note in passing that this last patient was apparently able to access the verb *comb* (as in *I comb my hair*), but not the noun *comb*.

Using this technique on numerous patients, Penfield and Roberts "mapped" the entire cortex, publishing their results in 1959 as *Speech and Brain Mechanisms*. They were able to identify three discrete language centers in the brain. Their findings coincided, in general, with the earlier theories of Broca and Wernicke, except that they identified language centers in the cortex surrounding Wernicke's area and extending up to the supramarginal and angular gyri in the parietal lobe. In addition, they identified a third language area known as the **supplementary motor cortex,** which lies in the superior region of the frontal lobe anterior to the primary motor cortex. These areas are illustrated in Figure 12.3. Moreover, they ranked these areas according to the degree of language dysfunction that damage to each area could be expected to cause. In descending order of importance, they are Wernicke's area, Broca's area, and the supplementary motor cortex. Keep in mind, however, that neuroscientists continue to investigate the role that various areas of the brain play in language processing, as well as the way in which these areas interact with one another.

Hemispherical Specialization

One interesting finding from the study of language and brain is that the left and right hemispheres are specialized to carry out separate but complementary functions, a property apparently unique to humans. A central concept necessary to understanding the specific functions of each hemisphere is what is known as **dominance.**

Left-Hemisphere Dominance for Language

Penfield and Roberts estimated that 98 percent of the population have their language centers in the left hemisphere. Thus we might say that approximately 98 percent of the population is **left dominant,** and approximately 2 percent is **right dominant.** (This is an oversimplification since a very small number of people have **bilateral dominance,** where language function seems to be shared more or less equally by both hemispheres.) The term *dominance* as used here refers solely to the location of the primary language centers. The evidence for left-hemisphere dominance among humans comes from several sources.

Aphasia. Damage to the left hemisphere has been estimated to cause some form of aphasia in approximately 70 percent of adults with brain damage. Damage to the right hemisphere causes an aphasic disturbance in only about 1 percent of adults with brain damage.

Hemispherectomies. Adults undergoing a left hemispherectomy (surgical removal of the left hemisphere) generally suffer a permanent loss of their ability to process language. Right hemispherectomies among adults are less likely to cause complete or permanent loss of language function.

Planum Temporal. The planum temporal is a white fiber tract underneath the left and right temporal lobes. This structure is larger in the left hemisphere in approximately 65 percent of adults. Moreover, the planum temporal in fetuses is larger in the left hemisphere. Such findings may indicate that left-hemisphere dominance in humans in biologically determined; that is, the genetic program actually builds more neuronal structure into the left hemisphere to "enable" it to acquire language.

Subcortical System. The thalamus, part of the higher brain stem, is the lowest structure in the central nervous system to have a left and right hemisphere. Damage to the left side of the thalamus causes such linguistic dysfunctions as involuntary repetitions and naming difficulties; damage to the right side of the thalamus, however, generally does not.

Wada Test. In 1949 Juhn Wada reported on a new procedure for determining an individual's brain dominance. In this procedure, the patient lies in a comfortable position and is instructed to count and move the fingers of both hands rapidly. At this point, sodium amytal, a sedative, is injected into the left or right internal carotid artery in the neck. If the sodium amytal is injected into the left internal carotid, it will depress activity in the left hemisphere, and vice versa. It also temporarily paralyzes the opposite site of the body. If the affected hemisphere is nondominant, then the counting stops and starts again within 30 seconds. The patient is able to speak, name, and read correctly, and remembers the paralysis. However, if the affected hemisphere is dominant, the patient stops counting for one minute or longer, has difficulty in speaking, naming, and reading, and does not recall the paralysis. The results of this test indicate that the vast majority of humans are left dominant.

Dichotic Listening. In the 1960s, Doreen Kimura developed a technique called dichotic listening. In this procedure, a normal subject receives two auditory signals simultaneously through headphones. Even though each ear has neural connections to both hemispheres, the most direct pathway is to the contralateral hemisphere. Thus, for all practical purposes, a signal fed to the right ear goes to the left hemisphere for processing, and vice versa. When the two stimuli are linguistic (i.e., words), the listener reports hearing the word that was presented to the right ear. For example, a person presented with *boy* to the right ear and *girl* to the left ear would report hearing *boy* but not *girl.* Most people have this **right ear advantage** for linguistic stimuli, which supports the claim that most people are left dominant.

Subsequent dichotic listening experiments have shown that most people have a right ear (i.e., left hemisphere) advantage for all types of linguistic stimuli: speech, nonsense syllables (e.g., /kɛb/, /lʌb/), synthetic speech, speech played backward, CV syllables, and even Morse code. On the other hand, these same listeners have a **left ear advantage** (i.e., right hemisphere) for environmental sounds: clicks, tones, buzzes, laughter, coughing, and so on. In short, it seems that any auditory signal that is perceived as language or language-like is processed in the left hemisphere by most people; any other sort of auditory signal will be processed by the right hemisphere. Once again, this evidence suggests that the left hemisphere in most people is specialized for language processing.

Exercise D

1. A normal subject is presented with two auditory stimuli simultaneously, *see* in the left ear and *saw* in the right ear. The subject reports hearing *saw* but not *see.* Is this person left dominant, right dominant, bilaterally dominant, or nondominant?
2. Mark the following statements true or false.
   - †a. T F Approximately 89 percent of all humans are left dominant.
   - b. T F A right-ear advantage for nonlinguistic sounds during a dichotic listening test would indicate left hemisphere dominance for language.
   - c. T F A left-ear advantage for linguistic stimuli during a dichotic listening test would indicate right hemisphere dominance for language.

Split Brains. In the 1960s, another major breakthrough in the theory of left hemispherical dominance was made by Roger Sperry and his colleagues, most notably Michael Gazzaniga. Work on epilepsy had shown that seizures originating in one cerebral hemisphere would travel to the other via the corpus callosum (the white fiber tract connecting the two hemispheres). A surgical treatment was developed that severed the corpus callosum in patients with severe epilepsy. This treatment confined the abnormal electrical discharges to one hemisphere and, in fact, seizures dramatically decreased in both hemispheres. Thus, the normal brain can send information back and forth between hemispheres, but the "split brain" cannot.

The effects of severing the corpus callosum might seem devastating; remarkably, however, they are not. In fact, the overt behavior of a split-brain patient does not differ significantly from that of a normal person. This is because under ordinary circumstances, both hemispheres receive sensory information simultaneously. For example, when you look at an object, each eye sends information to both hemispheres simultaneously.

However, Sperry and his colleagues discovered a way to send visual information selectively to only one hemisphere. Unlike a normal brain, a split brain cannot transmit this information to the other hemisphere because the corpus callosum has been severed. In effect, the information is "trapped" in one hemisphere. By covering one of the patient's eyes completely and temporarily blocking the left or right visual field of the other eye, Sperry could control which hemisphere received the information. This method depends on the fact that each eye has both a left and a right visual field; information from each visual field is transmitted to the contralateral hemisphere. Thus, if the left visual field of the split-brain patient were blocked, information (e.g., a written word) could be presented to the right visual field and thereby sent only to the left hemisphere. If the right visual field were blocked, information could be presented to the left visual field and thereby sent only to the right hemisphere. This procedure is diagrammed in Figure 12.4.

Now that we have some idea of how split-brain patients allow us to examine the processing capacity of each hemisphere independently of the other, let's look at some of the studies that Sperry and his colleagues conducted. (In the following discussion, when we say that a stimulus was presented to either the left or right hemisphere, keep in mind that the stimulus was presented to one visual field, as just described.)

One procedure that Sperry used was to seat the patient at a desk, facing a screen. Hidden from view beneath the desk was a tray of small objects. Sperry flashed a word onto the screen to one of the hemispheres. The patient was then instructed to reach into the tray with the opposite hand (remember: contralateral control) and retrieve the appropriate object.

When Sperry presented a word such as *key* to the left hemisphere, the patient would retrieve a key from the hidden tray with his or her right hand. Then, when asked to name the object, the patient would say *key.* However, when Sperry presented a word to the right hemisphere, the patient would be able to retrieve the object with the left hand, but *would not be able to name the object.* In fact, the patient had no conscious knowledge of what the left hand was doing. This suggests that the dominant hemisphere (the left, in Sperry's patients) can process language both passively and actively; that is, it can both comprehend and produce linguistic stimuli. In contrast, the nondominant (i.e., right) hemisphere can process language

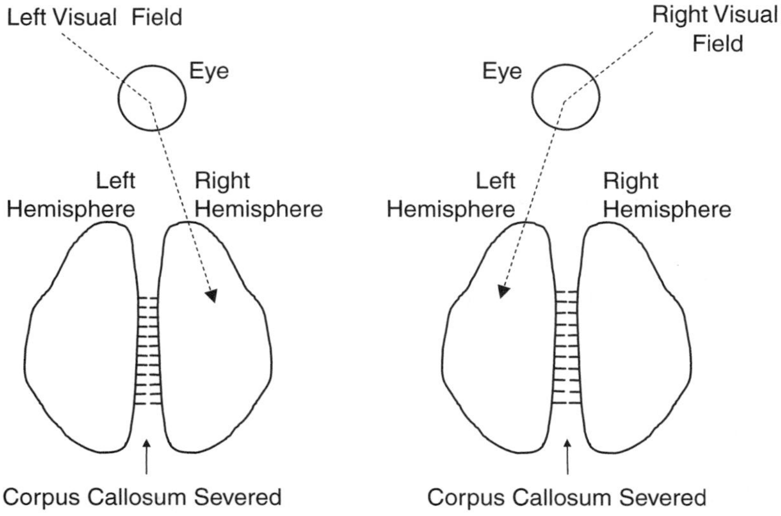

FIGURE 12.4 Presentation of visual stimulus selectively to right and left hemispheres

passively but not actively. It can "recognize" a word such as *key,* but cannot "produce" the word. This indicates that for a human to be conscious of a linguistic stimulus, the dominant hemisphere must have access to that stimulus.

In another study, Sperry presented verbs such as *nod* and *smile* to one hemisphere of split-brain patients and instructed the patient to carry out the command. (Note that this would require a nonlinguistic response, as did the object-finding task in the first experiment.) When the verb was presented to the left hemisphere, the patient carried out the command, as expected. However, when the verb was presented to the right hemisphere, the patient not only failed to carry out the command, but also behaved as if he or she had seen nothing. Earlier we saw that the nondominant hemisphere can process nouns at least passively (e.g., pick an object from a tray hidden from view). The results of this experiment, however, suggest that the nondominant hemisphere cannot process verbs at all, either actively or passively.

In another study, Sperry presented incomplete sentences (e.g., *Mother loves the* ___) to one hemisphere of the patients. The patient was instructed to complete the sentence by pointing with the opposite hand to one of four words (e.g., *nail, baby, broom, stone*). When the stimuli were fed to the left hemisphere, the patients correctly pointed to *baby* without hesitation. However, when the stimuli were fed to the right hemisphere, the patients only randomly pointed to *baby.* This experiment requires patients to choose a noun and then integrate the noun into a sentence in order to make an appropriate choice. This task requires processing syntactic information, namely that the correct noun can serve as the direct object of the structure *Mother loves the* ____. The results of this experiment suggest that the nondominant hemisphere cannot process syntactic information.

In sum, these and other studies provide rather dramatic evidence that the left hemisphere is specialized for language in most humans. In particular, this research suggests that only the dominant hemisphere can process language actively. The nondominant hemisphere appears to have some capacity for processing noun-like stimuli passively.

Exercise E

1. Assume that a normal subject has the input to the right visual field blocked. A written command (e.g., *Smile*) is presented to the left visual field. The subject smiles when presented with the stimulus. Explain how the subject is able to do this.

Left Brain versus Right Brain

So far we have looked at evidence that most human beings are left dominant; that is, the left hemisphere exercises primary control for the processing of language. In fact, each hemisphere is specialized for carrying out certain specific yet complementary types of tasks, summarized below.

Left Hemisphere. As we have seen, the left hemisphere is specialized for language. This includes not only speaking and listening, but also reading and writing. In addition, the left hemisphere is specialized for temporal order perception, the processing of any stimuli that arrive at different points in time. Suppose, for example, you are presented with a sequence of two tones, a buzz, and three more tones. If you are asked to determine where the buzz occurred in the series (i.e., third), your answer will require left-hemisphere processing. Similarly, the left hemisphere seems to be specialized for arithmetical calculations, such as determining that 1 + 2 + 3 = 6. Related to this is logical reasoning; for example, determining that if A is greater than B and B is greater than C, then A is greater than C.

Note that all of these functions involve step-by-step processing. In order to process the sentence *Denny eats ketchup on fried chicken,* you need to know that *Denny* precedes *eats* and *eats* precedes *ketchup.* In order to determine when a buzz occurs amid a series of tones, you need to keep track of the tones. In order to determine that 1 + 2 + 3 = 6, you need to know that 1 + 2 = 3 and that 3 + 3 = 6. In order to determine that A is greater than C, you need to know that A is greater than B and B is greater than C. All of these tasks require at least two sequential steps.

Right Hemisphere. In contrast to the left hemisphere, the right hemisphere is specialized for nonlinguistic auditory stimuli. This includes environmental sounds such as horns, whistles, laughter, the squeal of tires, waves breaking on the beach, musical instruments, melodies, and so on. In short, any sound that is perceived as nonlinguistic is apparently processed by the right hemisphere. Likewise, the right hemisphere is specialized for visuospatial processing. This includes depth perception; spatial orientation; the perception of pictures, paintings, photographs, and patterns; face recognition; and even the ability to dress oneself. Similarly, the right hemisphere seems to be specialized for tactile recognition tasks such as **stereognosis** (the ability to perceive an object's weight and form by handling or lifting it).

All of these right hemisphere functions involve holistic processing. To process the sound of a horn or a laugh, you do not need to divide it into meaningful parts. To recognize a familiar face, you presumably do not do it piece by piece but rather as an integrated unit. To tell that a box of feathers is lighter than a box of lead, you do not go through a series of mental calculations to determine their respective densities. Rather, all of these tasks require simultaneous integration of information.

By way of summary, we can make the following generalization: the left hemisphere is specialized for analysis, or breaking a whole into its parts, while the right hemisphere is specialized for synthesis, or combining the parts into a whole. Because the study of hemispherical specialization is an ongoing field of inquiry, much of what is now being hypothesized is subject to debate and further investigation. However, what we have covered here is summarized in the following table.

LEFT HEMISPHERE	RIGHT HEMISPHERE
Language	Nonlinguistic auditory processing
Temporal order perception	Visuospatial processing
Calculation	Stereognosis
Analysis	Synthesis

Although the left hemisphere is dominant for language in most humans, the right hemisphere does subserve some language processing functions. One of these is the ability to produce and comprehend intonational patterns—for example, modulations of tone that express emotion. Right-hemisphere damage may also lead to difficulties in interpreting discourse. For example, consider the sentences *Linda bought a puppy for her daughter Susan. It barks when you wind it up.* A correct inference is 'Susan has a new toy'; an incorrect inference is 'Susan has a new pet.' Patients with right-hemisphere damage can recognize a correct inference; however, they are also more likely to accept an incorrect inference. Right-hemisphere damage can also lead to deficits in understanding humor, metaphor, and indirect speech acts. For example, a patient may give a literal interpretation to an expression like *He lost his shirt* to describe an unlucky gambler. Some studies have also found that patients with right-hemisphere damage produce relatively rambling, noncohesive narratives (for example, when asked to describe a picture), which although detailed seem to miss the point of the depicted event.

Exercise F

1. Stereognosis refers to ________.
  a. visual recognition of patterns
  b. temporal order processing
  c. recognition of form and weight through touch
  d. the ability to hear sounds through both ears

2. Identify each of the following as typically a right or left hemisphere function.
  †a. ability to report when a buzz occurs in a sequence of tone-buzz-tone-tone
  b. recognition of environmental noises such as horns, whistles, and screeching tires
  c. ability to orient oneself in space
  d. ability to determine that 1 + 2 + 3 = 6

†3. Assume you are left-hemisphere dominant, you are not a musician, and you are listening to an orchestral composition by Beethoven. Which hemisphere is most likely to process this stimulus?

4. Ornstein (1973:92) notes that "increased alpha [rhythm] production is a sign of decreased information processing." Assume you are left dominant and you are listening to an orchestral composition by Beethoven. What happens to the alpha rhythm in your left hemisphere?

Handedness

Before leaving this section on hemispherical specialization, we want to say something about the relationship between dominance and handedness. This topic is important because, according to Penfield and Roberts (1959:89), Broca introduced a misconception about this relationship, which unfortunately persists even today. Broca inferred from one of his patients that left-handed people are right dominant, just as most right-handed people are left dominant.

About 95 percent of the population is right-handed, and about 5 percent is left-handed. In general, there is a high correlation between right-handedness and left dominance. However, most evidence indicates that left-handers are divided: about 40 percent (2 percent of the total population) are left dominant, and 60 percent (3 percent of the total population) are right dominant.

Two additional factors seem to affect the relationship between handedness and dominance. One is familial left-handedness: the more left-handed people in a family, the greater the likelihood of their right dominance. (Familial left-handedness also increases the likelihood of bilateral dominance in right-handers.) The second factor is strength of handedness (i.e., the number of tasks one does with the same hand). For example, someone who throws and bats with the left hand is more likely to be right dominant than someone who throws with the right hand but bats with the left. The correlation between these handedness factors and dominance is illustrated here.

LEFT DOMINANCE **BILATERAL DOMINANCE** **RIGHT DOMINANCE**

Strong right-handedness
Weak right-handedness
Weak right-handedness and familial left-handedness
Weak left-handedness
Weak left-handedness and familial left-handedness
Strong left-handedness
Strong left-handedness and familial left-handedness

The farther to the right that a particular individual falls on this list of factors, the more likely that person is to have bilateral or right-hemisphere dominance.

Exercise G

1. Assume you are left-handed and have a history of left-handedness in your family. A team of neurologists performs the Wada test on your left and right hemispheres. In neither case do you have much trouble in speaking, reading, or naming. What is your cerebral dominance likely to be?
2. Mark the following statements true or false.
   - **a.** T F Someone who is "strongly" left-handed is more likely to be left dominant than someone who is "weakly" left-handed.
   - **b.** T F Someone who is "weakly" left-handed is more likely to be bilaterally dominant than someone who is "strongly" right-handed.
   - **†c.** T F The more left-handed people in a family, the greater the likelihood of right dominance in those left-handers.
3. According to Heny (1985:179) "left-handed speakers are eight times more likely than right-handers to suffer from aphasia after damage to the right hemisphere only. For right-handers, the incidence of such aphasia is 3 percent, compared to 25 percent in their left-handed counterparts." Based on these observations, what generalizations might one make about cerebral dominance in left- and right-handers?

Aphasia

Aphasia is an acquired disorder of language due to cortical damage. It is important to note that aphasia is acquired; that is, only a person who has already developed a linguistic system can be stricken with aphasia. For example, a person with brain damage present at birth (or sustained immediately afterward) which prevents the acquisition of language would not properly be said to have aphasia. Moreover, aphasia is specifically a language disorder. Finally, aphasia is due to cortical damage, or to damage to the white fiber tracts immediately underlying language centers in the cortex. Thus, for example, a person sustaining damage to the brain stem that results in inarticulate speech would not properly be said to have aphasia.

Numerous types of aphasia have been proposed and discussed. Here, we look at three of the most common types (Broca's, Wernicke's, and conduction), as well as three other types found in the literature (anomia, semantic aphasia, and word deafness).

Broca's Aphasia. This disorder, also known as **motor** or **expressive aphasia** (because it affects linguistic output rather than comprehension) typically involves a lesion in the third frontal convolution of the dominant hemisphere. Note that this lesion is close to the motor cortex controlling the speech musculature. Symptoms usually include the following. First, motor function is normal; that is, the articulators such as the tongue and lips are fully functioning. However, there is typically some paralysis on the side opposite the dominant hemisphere. Second, the patient's speech output is hesitant, halting, labored, and lacks normal intonation. For this reason, Broca's aphasia is classified as a **nonfluent aphasia.** Third, the output is "telegraphic" in that it generally lacks grammatical morphemes, such as articles, prepositions, plural and possessive markers, tense markers on verbs, and so on. Thus, patients who speak a more highly inflected language (e.g., German) appear to have a more severe disturbance. Fourth, reading and writing usually exhibit the same deficiencies as speech. On the other hand, the patient's comprehension is typically fairly good. And the patient is usually self-monitoring, that is, aware of his or her mistakes and difficulties in speaking.

Let's now look at some examples of actual speech produced by patients with Broca's aphasia. Myrna Schwartz (1987:169) cites examples of such patients trying to describe a picture of a girl giving flowers to her teacher. Here is a sample of responses.

(4) *Girl is handing flowers to teacher.* Note the sporadic omission of grammatical morphemes. (Cf. *The girl is handing the flowers to her teacher.*)

(5) *The young . . . the girl . . . the little girl is . . . the flower.* Note the hesitant style. At each pause the patient seems to be giving up and starting over.

(6) *The girl is . . . is roses. The girl is rosing. The woman and the little girl was rosed.* Note here the use of *rose* as a verb.

Wernicke's Aphasia. This disorder is also known as **receptive aphasia** (because it affects linguistic comprehension rather than output) or **sensory aphasia** (because the damage site is near the sensory cortex). It typically involves a lesion in the first temporal convolution of the dominant hemisphere. Note that this lesion is near the primary auditory cortex (Heschl's gyrus). Symptoms usually include the following. First, hearing is normal. Second, the patient's speech output is typically fluent, rather than hesitant or halting, and has normal intonation. Hence Wernicke's aphasia is classified as a **fluent aphasia.** Third, the patient's language consists of anywhere from 30 to 80 percent **neologistic jargon.** This term refers to "new words"—utterances that conform to the phonological structure of the patient's language, but are meaningless—for example, *bliven, glover,* and *devable.* Consequently, Wernicke's aphasia is sometimes called **neologistic jargon aphasia** (or simply **jargon aphasia**). In addition, the output is riddled with **phonemic paraphasia,** which includes repetition and reversal of phonemes. For example, *bowling shirt* might come out *bowling birt* or *showling birt.* (Phonemic paraphasia is sometimes called **literal paraphasia,** due to confusion in the older neurological literature between phonemes and letters of the alphabet. Patients were said to confuse "letters"; thus, "literal" paraphasia.) Fourth, the patient's comprehension is generally quite poor. Fifth, the patient is not self-monitoring; that is, the patient seems unaware that much of his or her output is error-ridden and incomprehensible.

On the other hand, the patient's syntax is relatively normal: within a sentence, nouns appear where we would expect nouns, adjectives where we would expect adjectives, and so forth. For example, Brown cites a patient who responded to the question *What does "swell-headed" mean?* with *She is selfice on purpiten* (1972:65). Note that the syntactic structure of this sentence is perfectly normal: A subject (*she*) is followed by a verb (*is*) and a complement (*selfice on purpiten*). The problem is that in the complement, we get jargon where we would expect a lexical morpheme like *conceited* or a phrase like *in love with herself.*

Let's consider some more examples of the speech produced by patients with Wernicke's aphasia. In response to the question *What is your speech problem*? Brown's patient answered *Because no one gotta scotta gowan thwa, thirst, gell, gerst, derund, gystrol, that's all.* Note the phonemic repetition: *gotta, scotta; thwa, thirst; gell, gerst;* and *gystrol, that's all.* Hugh Buckingham (1981:54) gives examples of patients describing a picture of a boy taking a cookie out of a cookie jar; the boy's mother and sister are standing nearby. One patient's description is given in (7).

(7) You mean like this boy? I mean [noy], and this, uh, [mɛoy]. This is a [kénət kákən]. I don't say it. I'm not getting anything from it. . . . These were [ɛkspɛ́šəz], [əgrǽšənz], and with the type of mechanic is standing like this. . . . And this is [dɛ́li] this one is the one and this one and this one and . . . I don't know.

Note that the output is fluent; it is not labored and there are few hesitations. Likewise, the syntax is relatively normal (*You mean like this boy? . . . I'm not getting anything from it. . . . I don't know,* etc.). On the other hand, the output is so jargon-ridden that it is unintelligible.

Before leaving this section, let us try to clear up one point of potential confusion. We have drawn a distinction between Broca's aphasia, which is primarily a deficit in linguistic expression, and Wernicke's aphasia, which is primarily a deficit in linguistic comprehension. It is clear, however, that a major symptom of Wernicke's aphasia is the production of neologistic jargon, which appears to be a problem in expression. This is not a contradiction: The expression problem in Wernicke's aphasia is thought to be primarily a *result* of the fundamental deficit in comprehension.

Exercise H

1. Neurogenic deficits in reading and writing are known, respectively, as **alexia** and **agraphia.** What type of aphasia would you speculate is associated with each type of agraphia described below (Benson and Ardila 1996:218–219)? Why?
   - **A.** Written output is easily produced, with normal sentence length; the handwriting is well-formed; there is a lack of substantive words; frequent letter substitutions occur.
   - **B.** Written output is sparse, abbreviated, and effortful; the handwriting is clumsy; grammatical morphemes are often omitted; spelling is poor.

Conduction Aphasia. This disorder typically involves the **arcuate fasciculus,** the association fibers connecting Broca's area and Wernicke's area and the adjacent cortex. The primary symptom is the inability to repeat utterances, a problem exacerbated by long or unfamiliar targets. This problem makes sense anatomically, since linguistic input can be received (in Wernicke's area), but cannot be transmitted to the linguistic expression center (in Broca's area). Likewise, reading aloud is difficult for someone with conduction aphasia. On the other hand, output is generally fluent, in contrast to Broca's aphasia, but comprehension is typically normal or only mildly disturbed, in contrast to Wernicke's aphasia. Also, patients are generally self-monitoring. For example, one of Brown's patients interjected such comments as *Your baby could do better than I can* (1972:87).

Another of Brown's patients, when asked *Have you any headaches?* responded *Had one three to four week . . . days, Monday, Tuesday, Wednesday, Thursday, and Thursday it started to go away* (1972:87–88). Apparently, this patient was trying to access the word *Thursday* but could not do so directly. Thus, she started at the beginning of the week, went through the days of the week, and was able to continue when she got to *Thursday.* Note that this pathological behavior is an exaggeration of normal behavior. For example, if you were asked which letter of the alphabet precedes *L,* you might access *K* indirectly by reciting the alphabet up through *L.* Brown asked the same patient, *Can you give me the date (February 6)?* She replied, *It's the fu . . . 1-2-3-4-5, oh I don't know, there seems to me there must be something I could do but I don't know what it is* (1972:88).

The major symptoms of Broca's, Wernicke's, and conduction aphasia are summarized in the following table.

	BROCA'S	WERNICKE'S	CONDUCTION
Lesion Site	Third frontal convolution	First temporal convolution	Arcuate fasciculus
Language Output	Nonfluent	Fluent	Fluent
Comprehension	Unimpaired	Severely impaired	Unimpaired
Self-Monitoring	Yes	No	Yes
Paralysis	Yes (contralateral)	No	Contralateral weakness
Main Characteristic	Labored "telegraphic" output	Neologistic jargon	Severely impaired repetition

Anomia. This disorder has been associated with a lesion of the angular gyrus in the dominant hemisphere, along with diffuse lesions in the temporal lobe. The primary symptom involves the inability to name objects and general problems in accessing specific words. Consequently, the speech output appears empty, vague, and ridden with clichés. Patients tend to use an abundance of indefinite nouns, such as *gismo, thingamabob, whatchamacallit,* and *thing.* Their speech contains numerous circumlocutions, for example *what you drink out of* for *cup.* On the other hand, the output is fluent (unlike in Broca's aphasia), comprehension is normal (unlike in Wernicke's aphasia), and repetition is normal (unlike in conduction aphasia).

Semantic Aphasia. This disorder has been associated with lesions in the dominant temporal lobe. In fact, some specialists consider this disorder to be a mild form of Wernicke's aphasia. The primary symptom, **semantic paraphasia,** refers to the inappropriate use of words. For example, one of Brown's patients said *My son is just home from Ireland. He is a flying man* (1972:32). Note the use of *flying man* for what appears to be *pilot.* Brown also cites this written example: *There are certain incidence which unfolded from my last living time in England. Therefore I would rather not inform people of the last month of my last England life* (1972:45). Note *my last living time in England* and *my last England life* for something like *the last time I lived in England.*

Word Deafness. This disorder has been associated with the border of Heschl's gyrus and Wernicke's area in the temporal lobe of the dominant hemisphere. Patients with this disorder have normal hearing but cannot understand speech. Obviously, they have a severe comprehension problem, and their ability to repeat is profoundly disrupted. On the other hand, their self-generated speech output is fluent and correct. Patients' comments on their disorder are especially revealing. Brown cites one patient who said *I can hear quite well but I don't understand; I can hear a fly flying past me* (1972:127). Brown reports another patient as saying *Voice comes but no words. I can hear, sound comes, but words don't separate* (1972:129).

Exercise I

1. An adult, right-handed stroke patient exhibits the following symptoms: normal (or near-normal) comprehension, fluent output, and the inability to repeat words and sentences.
   - **a.** What type of aphasia is this most likely to be?
   - **b.** Where is the lesion most likely to be?
2. What type of aphasia is illustrated by each of the following utterances?
   - **†a.** A patient states: *Why my fytisset for, whattim tim saying got dok arne gimmen my suit, suit to Friday. . . . I ayre here what takes zwei the cuppen seffer effer sepped. . . .* (Brown 1972:64–65).
   - **b.** A stroke patient is asked to name the President of the United States. The patient responds, *I can't say his name. I know the man, but I just can't come out and say it.*
   - **†c.** An examiner shows a patient a clock and asks, *What do you call this*? The patient responds, *That's a timing machine.*
   - **d.** An examiner asks a patient to describe a picture of a boy taking a cookie. The patient responds, *Boy . . . cook . . . cookie . . . take . . . cookie.*
   - **e.** An examiner shows a patient a picture of a gun and asks, *What do you call this*? The patient responds, *That's a* [pínərəs pǽkrəs] . . . a [rǽkə]. *I'm sure it's* [nʌ́məri rébu].
   - **†f.** An examiner asks a patient to say the word *rifle.* The patient responds, [rífəl] . . . [rídəl] . . . *Oh, I mean gun.*
   - **g.** A patient states: *I should have then convolve to the particular asculation . . . which would give me particulars to tendon* (Davis 1983:14).
   - **h.** A patient, asked to explain how to drive a car, responded: *When you get into the car, close your door. Put your feet on those two things on the floor. . . . You just put your*

(continued)

Exercise I *Continued*

thing which I know of which I cannot say right now but I can make a picture of it . . . you put it in . . . on your . . . inside the thing that turns the car on. You put your foot on the thing that makes the, uh, stuff come on. It's called the, uh . . . (Davis 1983: 21).

i. A patient called a pencil *blacking* or *black lead* (Head 1926, Vol. 1: 232).

3. Which of the following is not typically associated with Broca's aphasia?

a. halting, telegraphic speech
b. damage to the left frontal lobe
c. neologistic jargon
d. absence of inflections
e. generally good comprehension

4. Which of the following is not typically associated with Wernicke's aphasia?

a. fluent speech
b. relatively good comprehension
c. damage to the left temporal lobe
d. neologistic jargon
e. retention of inflections

5. Which of the following illustrates phonemic paraphasia? Semantic paraphasia?

a. *bowling birt* for *bowling shirt*
b. *He is a flying man* for *He is a pilot*
c. *Girl is handing flowers to teacher* for *The girl is handing the flowers to the teacher*
d. *She is selfice on purpiten* for *She is swell-headed*
e. use of indefinite nouns like *gismo, thingamabob,* and *whachamacallit*

Summary

The theory of neurolinguistics is based in part on the anatomy of the central nervous system, in particular, the left and right hemispheres and the frontal, temporal, occipital, and parietal lobes. In addition, this theory uses such concepts as localization of function, hemispherical dominance, and hemispherical specialization. Cortical damage can cause aphasia, an acquired disorder of language. Within this general category, different damage sites typically coincide with different syndromes, most notably Broca's aphasia, Wernicke's aphasia, and conduction aphasia.

SUPPLEMENTARY READINGS

Brookshire, R. H. (2003). *Introduction to neurogenic communication disorders* (6th ed.). St. Louis: Mosby.
Brown, J. W. (1972). *Aphasia, apraxia, and agnosia.* Springfield, IL: Charles Thomas.
Luria, A. R. (1973). *The working brain.* New York: Basic Books.
Penfield, W., & Roberts, L. (1959). *Speech and brain mechanisms.* Princeton, NJ: Princeton University Press.
Pinker, S. (1997). *How the mind works.* New York: W. W. Norton.
Springer, S. P., & Deutsch, G. (1985). *Left brain, right brain* (rev. ed.). New York: W. H. Freeman & Company.
Young, R. (1970). *Mind, brain and adaptation in the nineteenth century.* Oxford: Clarendon Press.

You are now prepared to read the relevant sections of all these works. Luria provides a basic introduction to the brain sciences and it should be read first. Young is a rich source of information concerning advances in cerebral localization during the nineteenth century. Penfield and Roberts is a complete report of 10 years of research on cerebral dominance and aphasia, using electrical stimulation of the cortex. Brown provides a detailed source of clinical information on aphasia. Brookshire, a comprehensive introductory text for speech-language pathologists, covers basic research on aphasia and information about its diagnosis and treatment. Springer and Deutsch is an interesting and readable discussion of hemispherical asymmetry in normal and brain-damaged subjects, including chapters on split-brain research, handedness, and sex and age differences in brain asymmetry. Pinker is a fascinating, wide-ranging work that focuses not on language but on the neurological foundations of perception, reasoning, emotion, and social relations.

Supplementary Exercises

1. Mark the following statements true or false.
   - **a.** T F Ataxia is a type of aphasia characterized by the inability to name objects.
   - **b.** T F Broca's aphasia is characterized by the absence of lexical morphemes.
   - **c.** T F Dysarthria is the loss of motor power to speak distinctly; it typically involves damage to the lower brain stem.
   - **d.** T F Right-handed people with a family history of left-handedness are more likely to be bilaterally dominant than other right-handed people.
   - **e.** T F A patient with cortical blindness would be expected to have lesions in the parietal lobes.
   - **f.** T F Wernicke was the first researcher to correlate expressive aphasia with a specific area of the brain.
   - **g.** T F The left hemisphere of most "split-brain" patients can process nouns both actively and passively.
2. Consider a left dominant patient with a severe disturbance in spatial awareness, in musical ability, and in the recognition of other people, but with no paralysis or weakness. This patient's damage is most likely to be to which lobe of which hemisphere?
3. Heny (1985:171) reports research on the linguistic ability of a 10-year-old child whose left hemisphere had been removed shortly after birth. The child had difficulty distinguishing (A) and (B) below and in recognizing the ambiguity of (C):
   - **A.** The boy kissed the girl.
   - **B.** The boy was kissed by the girl.
   - **C.** He gave her dog biscuits.
   - **a.** What area of the grammar do these tasks reveal a deficit in?
   - **b.** What is the specific relation between (A) and (B)?
   - **c.** What type of ambiguity does (C) exhibit?
4. Ornstein (1973:92) states that scientists have concluded that in humans "the left hemisphere is organized in a focal manner and the right hemisphere is organized in a more diffuse manner." Which of the following facts can be used as evidence for this conclusion?
   - **a.** The human brain exhibits contralateral control.
   - **b.** Damage to the left hemisphere is more likely to cause an aphasic disturbance than damage to the right hemisphere.
   - **c.** Injuries in specific areas of the left hemisphere interfere with specific tasks, but no such specific disruptions are found following right-hemisphere lesions.
   - **d.** Split-brain patients are able to process more information at once than normal people can.

5. A stroke patient is asked to name several common objects. The patient gives the following responses:

PAD OF PAPER: the stuff you write on

FORK: it's the thing you use to eat with

SCREWDRIVER: that's one of those gismos . . . you know . . . I have one in my garage

a. What type of language disorder does this patient appear to have?

b. What area of the brain is associated with this disorder?

6. Identify the disorder illustrated by each of the following.

a. A patient is asked to name the following objects: a key, a button, a spoon, and a fork. The patient calls them *key, cutty, skoon,* and *sfork* (Eisenson 1984:95).

b. A patient refers to a kitten as a *little fur-child* (Head 1926, Vol. 1:52).

c. A patient refers to her eyeglasses as her *lights.*

7. A stroke patient utters the following: *I've* [tʌŋd] *it a little, but* [wítən dəvédən]. *I would say that* [mɪkdésəs nósɪs] *are* [spíktərz].

a. What disorder is this type of output characteristic of?

b. What area of the brain is associated with this disorder?

c. What is normal about the patient's output?

8. Heny (1985) notes that polyglots (i.e., speakers of more than one language) are five times more likely to exhibit aphasic symptoms from right-hemisphere damage than are monolinguals. What does this observation suggest about cerebral dominance in monolingual and polyglot speakers?

9. Research by Caramazza and colleagues (1976) compared the ability of normal subjects and subjects with right-hemisphere damage to solve problems of the following types:

TYPE 1: John is taller than Bill; who is taller?

TYPE 2: John is taller than Bill; who is shorter?

Normal and right-hemisphere-damaged subjects performed equally well on Type 1 problems. However, the right-hemisphere-damaged patients performed much more poorly on the Type 2 problems. Based on these results, what semantic relation appears to require an unimpaired right hemisphere?

10. What disorder is illustrated by the patient's responses in the following interchange (reported by Eisenson [1984:21])?

EXAMINER: On what do you sleep?

PATIENT: Alarm clock, wake up.

EXAMINER: What's ink for?

PATIENT: To do with a pen.

11. Gardner (1985:185) reports the following exchange with an aphasic patient. What disorder does Mr. Johnson's speech appear to reflect?

GARDNER: What kind of work have you done, Mr. Johnson?

MR. JOHNSON: We, the kids, all of us, and I, we were working for a long time in the . . . you know . . . it's the kind of space, I mean place rear to the spedwan . . .

GARDNER: Excuse me, but I wanted to know what work you have been doing.

MR. JOHNSON: If you had said that, we had said that, poomer, near the fortunate, forpunate, tamppoo, all around the fourth of martz. Oh, I get all confused.

12. Gardner (1985:186) reports the following exchange with an aphasic patient. What disorder is Mr. Cooper's response typical of?

GARDNER: [Asks patient what kind of work he's been doing]

MR. COOPER: Me . . . build—ing . . . chairs, no, no cab–in—nets. (This reply takes about 40 seconds.)

GARDNER: Can you tell me how you would go about building a cabinet?

MR. COOPER: One, saw . . . then, cutting wood . . . working . . . Jesus Christ, oh boy.

13. Head (1926, Vol. 2:141–42) describes a patient who was asked to read the following newspaper passage aloud:

SHIPBUILDING STOPPAGE. SUSPENSION OF LOCK-OUT NOTICES

Steps towards the settlement of two big labour disputes were taken yesterday. Lock-out notices to the forty-seven engineering units which have broken away, have been suspended pending negotiations, which will open on Monday afternoon. The notices which would have expired today affected 600,000 men.

The patient read as follows. What disorder does this patient's response typify?

Ship . . . buildin . . . stoppages . . . See . . . pep . . . I don't know the word . . . of lock-out notice . . . Steps . . . to-fore . . . to-ward . . . settle . . . of two big . . . Labour . . . despeds . . . are taken yesterday . . . Lock-out notice to the . . . forty-seven . . . inde . . . inder . . . unions which will have broke away . . . have been . . . sus-pes-ed . . . I don't know that . . . which will . . . open on Monday afternoon . . . The notice which will have . . . expied . . . to-day . . . affect . . . six unded thousand men.

14. Head (1926, Vol. 2:93) reports on a patient with a wound to the left parietal region around the left angular gyrus. The patient was asked to repeat the names of the months of the year as Head said each one aloud. This task produced the following results:

JANUARY:	Jan-jer-ley, Jan, Jan.
FEBRUARY:	Fenchurch, Jan-jey, Jan-jey.
MARCH:	Mart, Mar, Mar, Marts.
APRIL:	What was it? Aper, Aperl.
MAY:	Mage, Made, Mage.
JUNE:	Ju, June.
JULY:	June, June, June-eye.
AUGUST:	Orgeons, Or-just.
SEPTEMBER:	Eps-ten, Ex-pent, Ex-penst.
OCTOBER:	Ex, Ox, Ox, Ox-toe, Ox-tove.
NOVEMBER:	No-vendl, New-vender.
DECEMBER:	Ex. What was it? Ex-pend. Ex-cembr.

a. What disorder does this patient's response typify?

b. What type of behavior occurs in some of the responses (e.g., the naming of February and July)?

15. Head (1926, Vol. 2:8) describes a patient as follows: "He had recovered sufficient words to tell the time; but he was not only extremely slow in utterance, but confused 'past' and 'to' and stumbled over two of the numbers correcting himself each time." What disorder does this patient's behavior typify?

16. Winner and Gardner (1977) conducted research on patients with aphasia and on patients with right-hemisphere damage. The patients were shown different pictures for the same expression and asked to choose the most appropriate picture. For example, for the expression *he has a heavy heart,* the pictures included one of a crying person and another of a man carrying a huge heart-shaped object. Patients with aphasia (i.e., with left-hemisphere damage) were more likely to choose the first picture and to laugh at the second picture, rejecting it as inappropriate. In contrast, patients with right-hemisphere damage were equally likely to choose either picture and found nothing humorous about the second one. Given these responses, what capacity appears to be lost by patients with right-hemisphere damage?

17. Consider the following news account of an accident victim. What type of aphasia does the accident victim appear to have? List five symptoms mentioned in the passage that would support your answer.

Boston (AP)—A man whose brain was impaled by a 7-foot crowbar is home from the hospital, asking about neighborhood events and rousting slugabed teen-aged sons, his wife said Tuesday . . .

Thompson's head was pierced by the metal crowbar when the station wagon he was driving struck a tree and the crowbar hurled forward from the back seat.

When rescuers reached Thompson after the May 1 accident, the crowbar was extended three feet from his forehead and three feet from the back of his head.

The ends of the 40-pound tool had to be sawed off before he could be removed from the car, but the rest of the crowbar remained in his head until he got to the hospital. The injury was on the left side of the brain, which controls speech.

Doctors say Thompson's vision and hearing were not impaired in the accident and he can understand everything that is said to him. . . . "His speech is still halted and requires a good deal of effort, but we are very encouraged that he keeps doing better."

Thompson is able to work, though his right leg is weak. His right arm is paralyzed, but he is gradually learning to move it. (Source unknown)

18. Consider the following passage from Ohanian (1989:76), "The Lost Words of Joseph Chaikin":

When Chaikin woke up after the surgery, words like "piddle-poodle" popped out of his mouth. "His speech was all blather," says van Itallie, who was one of the first people to see him. Chaikin couldn't understand what was being said to him and didn't know that others didn't understand him. If he could have spoken, he would have told his doctors that he felt . . . "very pain my right."

The operation had left his heart stronger than ever. But it had also sent a blood clot shooting into . . . his brain. . . . He couldn't read music, do mathematical functions, use sign language, or speak.

Use evidence from the passage itself to answer the following questions.

a. What is the evidence that Chaikin was non-self-monitoring?

b. What is the evidence that Chaikin had a sensory type of aphasia?

c. What hemisphere was the blood clot in?

d. What is the evidence for your answer to (c)?

e. What type of aphasia did Chaikin most likely have?

Exploratory Exercises

1. At the Nobel e-Museum, you can read about the background to Sperry's split-brain experiments and work through a cartoon simulation of the split-brain experiments to test your understanding of the procedure. Visit http://www.nobel.se/medicine/educational/split-brain/index.html and report on your findings.
2. Brookshire (2003:208–209) cites the following factors (among others) that affect comprehension in adults with aphasia. For each of these categories, construct a pair of sentences or short passages that would illustrate a relatively easy item and a relatively difficult item.
   - Syntactically complex sentences are more difficult to comprehend.
   - Reversibility and plausibility: Semantically reversible sentences are more difficult to comprehend. Plausible sentences may be easier to comprehend.
   - Personally relevant sentences are easier to comprehend.
   - Directly stated (rather than implied) information is easier to comprehend.
   - Cohesive ties within discourse increase comprehension.
3. Brookshire (2003:294) cites a hierarchy of difficulty for spoken directions issued by clinicians to patients with aphasia. Assume that the patient is sitting in front of a table that contains four common objects: a knife, a fork, a toothbrush, and a pencil. The number in parentheses shows the average score for each activity on a 16-point scale, after the directions were administered to a number of patients with aphasia.
   - **a.** Point to one object by name. (14.30)
   - **b.** Point to one object by function. (14.02)
   - **c.** Point in sequence to two objects by function. (12.90)
   - **d.** Point in sequence to two objects by name. (12.67)
   - **e.** Point to one object spelled by the examiner. (12.51)
   - **f.** Point to one object described by the examiner with three descriptors. (12.23)
   - **g.** Follow instructions containing one verb. (12.05)
   - **h.** Point in sequence to three objects by name. (10.74)
   - **i.** Point in sequence to three objects by function. (10.72)
   - **j.** Follow instructions that involve putting one object in a new location relative to another. (10.20)
   - **k.** Follow two-verb instructions (i.e., do X and do Y). (9.77)
   - **l.** Follow two-verb instructions ordered in time (e.g., "Before you do X, do Y"). (8.60)
   - **m.** Follow three-verb instructions (i.e., do X, Y, and Z). (7.53)

   Prepare a statement that the examiner could use to cue each activity (example: for (a), the examiner could say, "Point to the toothbrush").

   What patterns do you see that might explain why some directions are more difficult to follow than other related directions? That is, what *types* of directions seem relatively difficult?

CHAPTER THIRTEEN

Conclusion

In Chapter 1, we discussed some examples of linguistic phenomena that specialists in allied fields might encounter and also outlined the general methodology that underlies theory construction in linguistics. In subsequent chapters, we continued this dual emphasis on data and theory. Each chapter began with some observations (data) that an adequate theory of linguistics should be able to explain and proceeded to construct a partial theory to account for these observations. In short, this book has continually emphasized the interdependence of data and theory that is at the heart of linguistics (as well as any other empirical field of inquiry). In this chapter, we would like to elaborate a little on two contributions that linguistic theory can make to related disciplines. The more obvious one is that linguistic theory provides a way of explaining a vast array of phenomena that professionals in allied fields encounter on a daily basis. Somewhat less obvious is the fact that linguistic theory provides a model for explanation that professionals in neighboring fields may be able to transfer to their own disciplines. In short, linguistic theory can benefit allied fields on two levels: a practical level, by providing explanations for particular observations, and a theoretical level, by providing a model for analyzing data. We will take these up one at a time.

First, let's consider the practical contribution: explanation of data. By way of illustration, let us return briefly to the phenomena mentioned at the beginning of Chapter 1 and consider how the discussion in Chapters 2 through 12 might enable us to explain these phenomena. We started with the hypothetical case of a researcher in business communication who is trying to characterize how different management styles are reflected in the way that managers give directions to their employees. The researcher notes that one group of managers tends to give instructions like *Type this memo,* while another group gives instructions like *Could you type this memo?* Principles from pragmatics, in particular the distinction between direct and indirect speech acts, can be used to characterize these two different styles of giving directions. In this case, the researcher might note that the first group of managers tends toward direct speech acts, those in which the syntactic form (an imperative) matches the illocutionary force (a directive). In contrast, the second group tends toward indirect speech acts, those in which the syntactic form (a *yes-no* interrogative) does not match the illocutionary force (a directive).

We also looked at phenomena that might be encountered in the fields of education and composition. We saw that a kindergarten teacher might observe that students tend to give more correct responses to questions like *Which of these girls is taller?* than to questions like *Which of these girls is shorter?* The teacher might draw upon semantic theory and principles of language acquisition in order to explain this phenomenon, noting that children tend to acquire the positive member of a pair of antonyms *(tall)* earlier than the negative member *(short).* Note that *tall* carries fewer presuppositions than *short.* The question *How tall was the girl?* presupposes nothing about the girl's height—she might be 7 feet tall or only 4 feet tall. On the other hand, the question *How short was the girl?* presupposes that the girl is relatively short.

Principles from linguistic theory would also enable a composition instructor to understand the source of a syntactic structure like *I wanted to know what could I do* when encountered in a student's writing. The difference between this form and the standard form *I wanted to know what I could do* has a straightforward syntactic explanation. In standard English, *wh*-interrogatives in subordinate clauses do not undergo the rule of I-Movement (i.e., move the tensed auxiliary to the left of the subject). Some speakers, however, do apply this rule in indirect *wh*-interrogatives, leading to forms such as *I wanted to know what could I do.* (Note that the tensed auxiliary verb, *could,* has been moved to the left of the subject NP, *I.*) Furthermore, the instructor would note that such forms, because they are somewhat socially marked, may reflect negatively on the writer.

The last two phenomena mentioned in Chapter 1 were drawn from ESL and speech-language pathology. We pointed out that an ESL teacher might encounter a student who writes *I will taking physics next semester.* In trying to offer the student an explicit principle for constructing sentences of this type, the teacher can draw upon morphological and syntactic principles governing the relation between auxiliary verbs and the affix on the following verb form. The relevant rules here are (i) within a single clause the verb form following a modal (e.g., *will*) is always uninflected (e.g., *take*) and (ii) the verb form preceding a present participle (e.g., *taking*) is always a form of *be.* The first principle alone would yield *I will take;* the second alone would yield *I am taking;* and the two together would yield *I will be taking.* Thus, any combination of principles that the student tries will result in an acceptable form.

Turning to speech-language pathology, we saw that a specialist in this field might encounter a child who says *tay* for *stay.* In order to evaluate and explain this form, the speech-language pathologist can draw upon principles from phonology and language acquisition. Here, for example, the omission of the /s/ in the /st/ cluster reflects the principle that single consonants are generally acquired before clusters. In fact, CV syllables are apparently universal, whereas CCV syllables are not. Moreover, the omission of the /s/ rather than the /t/ is explained by the tendency for stops (/t/) to be acquired before fricatives (/s/).

In short, language-related phenomena similar to those just described are encountered every day by researchers and teachers in the fields that neighbor linguistics. Linguistic theory, in turn, provides a system of categories and rules which can be used to analyze and explain such phenomena.

Now let's turn to the theoretical contribution that linguistic theory can make to specialists in allied fields: it may provide them with a model for analyzing the nonlinguistic (or quasilinguistic) phenomena within their fields. This, however, is not just speculation about a future state of affairs. During the last 40 years, a number of fields in the humanities and social sciences have looked to linguistic theory as a model for analyzing phenomena within their respective domains. Among these fields are those as diverse as folklore and anthropology, literary criticism, and rhetoric and composition.

Representative examples of this interest in linguistics among those outside the field are not hard to find. For instance, Robert Georges, a folklorist, states that "the theory and work of generative-transformational grammarians has direct implications for the study of traditional narrative [i.e., folktales]" (1970:14). Similarly, Roger Fowler, a literary critic, states that "description *per se* is not the only way in which linguistics has been . . . employed in literary studies. . . . linguistic concepts have often been used . . . metaphorically to provide *models* of textual structure rather than *accounts* of the specific structures of sentences and texts" (1981:19). Likewise, Ross Winterowd, a rhetorician, states that since the publication of Chomsky's *Syntactic Structures* in 1957, "composition teachers have been dazzled by the elegance of the notational system of the new grammar . . . , have been intrigued by the complexity and ingenuity of grammatical arguments; and . . . have allowed themselves to hope that from the new field would emerge *the* panacea for the ills of teaching composition" (1976:197). The attraction that linguistic theory has had for specialists in other disciplines is summed up by the folklorist Lauri Honko, who states that "the only success-story in the humanities in the recent past [is] modern linguistic theor[y]" (1979–1980:6). Even though some of these high expectations have met with disappointment (see Newmeyer, 1983, Chapter 5, for discussion), there has nonetheless been a sustained interest in linguistic theory from practitioners in neighboring fields. Let's now take a look at some of the properties which the theory presented in this book has (or at least should have) and which may be applicable to other fields in the humanities and social sciences.

First, the theory should be **testable;** and therefore, it must necessarily be **explicit.** This criterion is necessary in order to make empirical (testable) claims about the structure of the phenomenon of interest; vague, inexplicit claims are impossible to test. Consider, for example, the following hypothetical statements.

(1) We are living in the most corrupt era this country has ever seen.
(2) More elected officials were indicted for felonies during the 1980s than during the entire first half of the twentieth century.

The claim in statement (1) is simply too inexplicit to test. What indices is the writer using to define "corruption"? What length of time constitutes an "era"? The claim can be supported or denied only if these terms are made explicit. The claim in statement (2), on the other hand, is explicit enough to be tested. The subjects are well defined (elected officials), the criterion is well defined (felonies), and the time frames are well defined (1980 through 1989 and 1900 through 1949).

Consider how this principle applies to linguistic theory. You may recall from Chapter 1 that we tried to develop a theory of the distribution of antecedents for personal and reflexive pronouns: a personal pronoun cannot have an antecedent within its clause, and a reflexive pronoun must have an antecedent within its clause. Note that the statement of these two rules depends crucially on the concept of **clause.** Without a precise definition of this term, it is not possible to test our rules to see if they work (indeed, it would be impossible to hypothesize such rules in the first place). Even though we didn't define clause in Chapter 1, we could start with the following working definition: a clause is a syntactic structure consisting of one and only one main verb and its optional NP arguments (subject, object, indirect object, and so forth). Regardless of whether this definition is completely accurate, the point is that a precise definition of clause is absolutely essential for us to be able to test our theory.

The main point of this discussion is that demands of testability force linguists into stating their theories in precise, explicit terms. This, in turn, accounts for the widespread use of formal notation in linguistic theory. Even though nothing can be put into formal notation that cannot be put into words, the notation encourages the analyst to be precise and explicit.

Second, the theory should be **revealing:** that is, it should capture significant generalizations. This criterion is necessary because revelation is the primary reason for constructing a model in the first place; any analysis that is opaque or unrevealing is by definition useless. Failure to meet this criterion is similar to the freshman classification theme that sorts the seasons of the year into four and proceeds to point out that one follows the other in the order spring, summer, fall, and winter. Even though it is impossible to give a precise definition of what constitutes a revealing analysis, it is worth noting that we have relied on this concept, at least implicitly, throughout this book in choosing one analysis over another.

For example, in Chapter 4 we discussed the syntax of the following sentences.

(3) Tiny Abner has concealed the document.
(4) Has Tiny Abner concealed the document?
(5) What has Tiny Abner concealed?

Based on such sentences (among others), we constructed two theories concerning whether or not *conceal* takes an object. In our first theory, we proposed that if *conceal* appears in a declarative sentence (3) or a *yes-no* interrogative (4), it must have a direct object; however, if *conceal* appears in a *wh*-interrogative (5), it cannot have a direct object. This theory accounts for the data in (3–5), as well as all of the related data we discussed in Chapter 4. This theory, however, is not revealing. That is, it does not provide us with a clue as to why *conceal* sometimes is required to have an object and other times is prohibited from having one. Moreover, under this theory, it is completely unclear why one type of interrogative *(yes-no)* is required to have an object, while another type of interrogative *(wh)* may not have one.

On the other hand, our second theory proposed that in sentence (5), *what* originated in direct object position and was moved into clause-initial position by a transformation. This theory, in contrast to our first, is revealing. That is, it does explain why *conceal* appears to have an object in some cases but not in others. In particular, this theory provides the following explanation: *conceal* has a direct object in all cases. If the object is not a *wh*-item (e.g., *the document*), it remains in object position. If, however, the object is a *wh*-item (e.g., *what*), it moves to clause-initial position. Even though this theory does not explain why a language would have a rule of *wh*-Movement in the first place, it is nonetheless revealing in that it provides a straightforward and intuitively satisfying account of some rather perplexing data.

Third, the theory should be restricted to a characterization of **systematic** phenomena. This criterion is necessary because a theory is a model of a system that can't be observed directly, and only predictable, rule-governed phenomena can be modelled. Failure to meet this criterion results in a description in which the analyst "can't see the forest for the trees." In other words, the systematic properties of the phenomenon at hand are camouflaged by attention to unassociated detail. It would be like a theory of the game of baseball which, in addition to modelling systematic properties of the game such as the number of players, the number of innings, and the number of outs per inning, tried to account for idiosyncratic properties of the game such as depth of the outfield, the playing surface (grass versus astro-turf), or the color of the players' uniforms or eyes.

It is just as difficult to give a precise definition of systematic phenomena as it was to define a revealing analysis earlier. One reason is that what may be systematic within one field may not be systematic within another. For example, the color of baseball players' eyes may be perfectly systematic within a theory of genetics, but it isn't systematic within a theory of baseball. Another difficulty is that the notion of systematic phenomena is somewhat dependent on the point of view of the researcher. No researcher is going to study a phenomenon that he or she believes is not governed by principles which can be inferred through examination. The problem, of course, is that analysts sometimes disagree over what seems to be rule governed and principled versus what seems to be random and idiosyncratic.

Aside from such problems in defining the term, it is worth pointing out that we have relied on the concept of systematic phenomena throughout this book. For example, in our discussion of phonology in Chapter 6, we hypothesized that English has two systematic vowel lengths: relatively long and relatively short. This we characterized by means of the feature [±long]; and, through examining some relevant data, we postulated that a vowel is [+long] before a voiced consonant and [–long] before a voiceless consonant. At the same time, it is a well-documented fact that two speakers of English will pronounce the same vowel in the same phonological environment with different absolute lengths. Moreover, even the same speaker pronouncing the same word over and over will vary the vowel length. How then can we say that English has two degrees of vowel length? The answer is simple. We can do this by stipulating that the two degrees of vowel length are *systematic*. By using this term, we are essentially claiming that within the system of any speaker, there will be two types of vowels: relatively long and relatively short. Moreover, the relative length of the vowel is determined by the voicing characteristics of the following segment. The reason we don't try to model vowel lengths for individual speakers is that we assume that variation from speaker to speaker is idiosyncratic and for the most part unprincipled, at least within a theory of language. In short, by trying to account for all facets of some range of phenomena, the analyst risks confusing the systematic with the unsystematic and the relevant with the irrelevant.

At this point, it is appropriate to discuss how linguistic theory attempts to distill the abstract system from the raw data. The theory articulated by Chomsky is what is termed a **competence** model. That is, it is a theory of the psychological system of unconscious knowledge that underlies our ability to produce and interpret utterances in a language. (You will recall that this is how we defined language in the first chapter.) In contrast to a competence model is a **performance** model; that is, a theory of the actual physical and psychological processes that a speaker might go through in producing and interpreting an utterance. Some 40 years ago, Chomsky made this distinction in a landmark book entitled *Aspects of the Theory of Syntax:*

> We thus make a fundamental distinction between *competence* (the speaker-hearer's knowledge of his language) and *performance* (the actual use of language in concrete situations). . . . linguistic theory is mentalistic, since it is concerned with discovering a mental reality [i.e., competence] underlying actual behavior [i.e., performance]. (1965:4)

This is not to say that linguists have no interest in performance; certainly, performance data provides a way of studying competence. Instead, the point is that the central goal of linguistic theory, at least according to Chomsky, is to model the psychological system of unconscious knowledge that underlies behavior (competence) rather than the behavior itself (performance).

A good example of this distinction is provided by comparing two different interpretations of our rule of *wh*-Movement (move a *wh*-item to sentence-initial position). One interpretation of this rule would be to take it as a statement about performance. That is, when speakers of English produce an utterance such as *What did Tiny Abner conceal?* they actually go through the following steps. First, they formulate a mental structure in which *what* is the direct object of *conceal* (did-Tiny Abner-conceal-what). Then they move *what* to sentence-initial position, thus creating another mental structure (what-did-Tiny Abner-conceal). Finally, they utter the sentence.

This, however, is not the way that *wh*-Movement is understood within linguistic theory. Instead, this rule is interpreted as part of competence. In postulating such a rule, the linguist is actually making a statement of the following sort: In order to make the judgments that speakers of English do in fact make about *wh*-interrogatives, they need to know that certain verbs (e.g., *conceal*) require a direct object. Moreover, they need to know that if the direct object is a non-*wh*-item (e.g., *document*), it is uttered in direct object position; however, if it is a *wh*-item (e.g., *what*), it is uttered in clause-initial position. The linguist will try to explain this state of affairs by using the metaphor of movement; that is, the *wh*-item is "moved" from direct object position to clause-initial position. In a competence model, the linguist is not claiming that speakers of English actually move *wh*-items from one position to another when they utter *wh*-interrogatives. Instead, "movement" is a convenient metaphor for describing the psychological system of unconscious knowledge which speakers possess, at least with respect to the distribution of *wh*-items and non-*wh*-items in English.

At this point it is appropriate to bring up a final concept closely associated with the study of competence, namely **generative grammar.** Simply put, a generative grammar is a theory of competence: a model of the psychological system of unconscious knowledge that underlies a speaker's ability to produce and interpret utterances in a language. Chomsky defines a generative grammar as follows:

> a generative grammar is not a model for a speaker or a hearer. It attempts to characterize in the most neutral possible terms the knowledge of the language [i.e., competence] that provides the basis for actual use of language by a speaker-hearer. . . . When we say that a sentence has a certain derivation with respect to a particular generative grammar, we say nothing about how the speaker or hearer might proceed . . . to construct such a derivation. These questions belong to . . . the theory of performance. No doubt, a reasonable model of language use will incorporate, as a basic component, the generative grammar that expresses the speaker-hearer's knowledge of the language; but this generative grammar does not, in itself, prescribe the character or functioning of a perceptual model or a model of speech production. (1965:9)

A good way of trying to understand Chomsky's point is to think of a generative grammar as essentially a *definition* of competence: a set of criteria that linguistic structures must meet to be judged acceptable.

An analogy might make the point clearer. In *Transformational Grammar,* Andrew Radford compares a generative grammar to a municipal housing code, where the housing code is essentially a definition of house: that is, a set of criteria that housing structures must meet to be judged acceptable. Radford states:

> To interpret generative rules as well-formedness . . . conditions [i.e., as a definition of competence] . . . is to disclaim any implications about the processes and mechanisms by which sentence-structures might be formed. . . . Municipal regulations specify certain conditions that houses must meet: viz. they must be built out of certain materials, not others; they must contain so many windows of such-and-such a size, and so many doors; they must have a roof which conforms to certain standards . . . and so on and so forth. Such regulations are in effect well-formedness conditions on houses. What they do not do is tell you HOW to go about building a house; for that you need a completely different set of instructions, such as might be found e.g. in *Teach Yourself Housebuilding.* (1981:90–91)

The analogy between a generative grammar and a municipal housing code is summarized in Figure 13.1. In short, to produce an acceptable sentence, a speaker needs *both* the step-by-step instructions specifying how to proceed *and* a generative grammar identifying the criteria linguistic structures must meet. Likewise, to construct an acceptable house, a builder needs *both* the step-by-step instructions specifying how to proceed *and* a municipal housing code identifying the criteria that housing structures must meet.

Let's review what we have covered in this chapter. We discussed two levels on which linguistic theory might benefit specialists in related fields. First, it is of practical use in that it provides explanations for phenomena that crop up every day in language-related disciplines. Second, it is of theoretical use in that it provides a model that professionals in allied fields may find helpful in analyzing nonlinguistic or quasilinguistic phenomena. In particular, linguistic theory attempts to be testable, revealing, and restricted to systematic phenom-

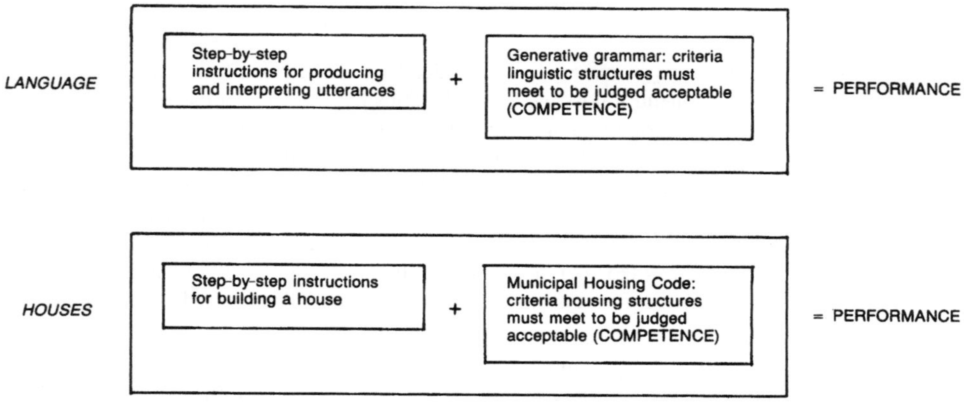

FIGURE 13.1 Relationship between competence and performance

ena. Specifically, it attempts to model linguistic competence (the psychological system of unconscious knowledge that underlies our ability to produce and interpret utterances in a language) by constructing a generative grammar (a set of criteria that linguistic structures must meet to be judged acceptable).

Supplementary Exercises

1. Consider the following claim: A personal pronoun cannot have an antecedent within its clause, and a reflexive pronoun must have an antecedent within its clause. This claim crucially depends on having a precise definition of the term *clause.* Having such a definition makes the claim ________.
   - **a.** systematic
   - **b.** revealing
   - **c.** testable
   - **d.** a production model
   - **e.** a performance model
   - **f.** none of the above
2. Vowels in English are considered to be [+long] and [–long] phonetically. Linguists propose this division even though no two speakers produce vocalic sounds of exactly the same length. The feature [±long] allows linguists to restrict their theory to ________ phenomena.
   - **a.** systematic
   - **b.** revealing
   - **c.** testable
   - **d.** production
   - **e.** performance
   - **f.** none of the above
3. Consider the following interpretation of the rule of *wh*-Movement: When English speakers produce an utterance such as *What hath God wrought?* they actually go through the following steps. First, they formulate a mental structure in which *what is* the direct object of *wrought.* Then they move *what* to clause-initial position. Then they utter the sentence. This interpretation assumes that *wh*-Movement is part of ________.
   - **a.** the unconscious knowledge that underlies behavior
   - **b.** a performance model
   - **c.** a competence model
   - **d.** a generative grammar
   - **e.** both (a) and (d)
   - **f.** none of the above
4. Which of the following is an instance of competence (rather than performance)?
   - **a.** a Beethoven symphony as put on by the Boston Pops
   - **b.** the 1993 Boston Marathon
   - **c.** the rules of the game show *Jeopardy*
   - **d.** a yodeling contest held in Austria
   - **e.** all of the above
   - **f.** (a) and (b) only

REFERENCES

Adams, V. (1973). *An introduction to modern English word formation.* London: Longman.

Adjémian, C. (1983). The transferability of lexical properties. In Gass & Selinker, pp. 250–268.

Aitchison, J. (1985). Predestinate grooves: Is there a preordained language "program"? In Clark et al., pp. 90–110.

Akmajian, A., & Heny, F. W. (1975). *An introduction to the principles of transformational syntax.* Cambridge, MA: MIT Press.

Allan, K. (2001). *Natural language semantics.* Oxford: Blackwell.

Allen, H. B. (1973). *The linguistic atlas of the Upper Midwest,* 3 vols. Minneapolis: University of Minnesota Press. Copyright 1982, Gale Research Inc., Detroit.

Allwood, J., Andersson, L.-G., & Dahl, Ö. (1977). *Logic in linguistics.* Cambridge, England: Cambridge University Press.

Anderson, R. (1983). Transfer to somewhere. In Gass & Selinker, pp. 177–201.

Anderson, R., & Davison, A. (1988). Conceptual and empirical bases of readability formulas. In Davison & Green, pp. 23–53.

Anderson, S. R. (1985). *Phonology in the twentieth century.* Chicago: University of Chicago Press.

Aronoff, M. (1976). *Word formation in generative grammar.* Cambridge, MA: MIT Press.

Austin, J. L. (1962). *How to do things with words.* Oxford: Clarendon Press.

Bates, E. (1976). *Language and context. The acquisition of pragmatics.* New York: Academic Press.

Bauer, L. (1983). *English word-formation.* Cambridge, England: Cambridge University Press.

Benson, D. F., & Ardila, A. (1996). *Aphasia: A clinical perspective.* New York: Oxford University Press.

Bialystok, E., & Hakuta, K. (1994). *In other words: The science and psychology of second-language acquisition.* New York: Basic Books.

Bloom, P. (Ed.). (1994). *Language acquisition: Core readings.* Cambridge, MA: MIT Press.

Boysson-Bardies, B. de. (1999). *How language comes to children: From birth to two years.* Trans. M. B. De Bevoise. Cambridge, MA: MIT Press.

Braganti, N. L., & Devine, E. (1984). *The travelers' guide to European customs and manners.* Deep Haven, MN: Meadowbrook.

Broca, P. P. (1861). Remarks on the seat of the faculty of articulate language, followed by an observation of aphemia. In G. von Bonin (Trans.), *Some papers on the cerebral cortex,* pp. 49–72. Springfield, IL: Charles Thomas.

Brookshire, R. H. (2003). *Introduction to neurogenic communication disorders* (6th ed.). St. Louis: Mosby.

Broselow, E. (1987). Non-obvious transfer: On predicting epenthesis errors. In Ioup & Weinberger, pp. 292–304.

Brown, J. W. (1972). *Aphasia, apraxia, and agnosia: Clinical and theoretical aspects.* Springfield, IL: Charles Thomas.

Brown, J. W. (Ed.). (1981). *Jargonaphasia.* New York: Academic Press.

Brown, P., and Levinson, S. C. (1987). *Politeness: Some universals in language use.* Cambridge, England: Cambridge University Press.

Brown, R. (1973). *A first language: The early stages.* Cambridge, MA: Harvard University Press.

Buckingham, H. W. (1981). Where do neologisms come from? In J. W. Brown, pp. 39–62.

Caramazza, A., Gordon, J., Zurif, E. B., & DeLuca, D. (1976). Right-hemispheric damage and verbal problem solving behavior. *Brain and Language, 3,* 41–46.

Carr, P. (1993). *Phonology.* New York: St. Martin's Press.

Carver, C. M. (1987). *American regional dialects: A word geography.* Ann Arbor: University of Michigan.

Cassidy, F. (1981). DARE. *National Forum* (Summer), 36–37.

Cassidy, F., & Hall, J. H. (1985, 1992, 1996, 2002). *Dictionary of American regional English,* 4 vols. Cambridge, MA: Harvard University Press.

Chambers, J. K. (1989). Canadian raising: Blocking, fronting, etc. *American Speech, 64,* 75–88.

Chierchia, G., & McConnell-Ginet, S. (1991). *Meaning and grammar: An introduction to semantics.* Cambridge, MA: MIT Press.

Chomsky, C. (1969). *The acquisition of syntax in children from 5 to 10.* Cambridge, MA: MIT Press.

Chomsky, N. (1959). A review of B. F. Skinner's *Verbal Behavior. Language, 35,* 26–58.

Chomsky, N. (1965). *Aspects of the theory of syntax.* Cambridge, MA: MIT Press.

Chomsky, N. (1988). *Language and problems of knowledge: The Managua lectures.* Cambridge, MA: MIT Press.

Chomsky, N. (2002). *On nature and language.* New York: Cambridge University Press.

Chomsky, N., & Halle, M. (1968). *The sound pattern of English.* New York: Harper & Row.

Clark, E. V. (1975). Knowledge, context, and strategy in the acquisition of meaning. In Dato, pp. 77–98.

Clark, H. H. (1977). Bridging. In Johnson-Laird & Wason, pp. 411–420.

Clark, H. H., and Clark, E. V. (1977). *Psychology and language: An introduction to psycholinguistics.* New York: Harcourt Brace Jovanovich.

Clark, V. P., Escholz, P. A., & Rosa, F. (Eds.). (1985). *Language: Introductory readings* (4th ed.). New York: St. Martin's Press.

Cole, P., & Morgan, J. L. (Eds.). (1975). *Syntax and semantics 3: Speech acts.* New York: Academic Press.

Coltheart, M., Sartori, G., & Job, R. (Eds.). (1987). *The cognitive neuropsychology of language.* London: Erlbaum.

Cook, V. (1996). *Second language learning and language teaching* (2nd ed.). London: Edward Arnold.

Coulthard, M. (1977). *Discourse analysis.* London: Longman.

Cruse, D. A. (1986). *Lexical semantics.* Cambridge, England: Cambridge University Press.

Cruse, D. A. (2000). *Meaning in language.* New York: Oxford University Press.

Culicover, P. (1997). *Principles and parameters: An introduction to syntactic theory.* New York: Oxford University Press.

Curtiss, S. (1977). *Genie: A psycholinguistic study of a modern-day "wild child."* New York: Academic Press.

Daniels, P. T., & Bright, W. (Eds.). (1996). *The world's writing systems.* New York: Oxford University Press.

Dato, D. P. (Ed.). (1975). *Georgetown University round table on languages and linguistics 1975.* Washington, DC: Georgetown University Press.

Davenport, M., & Hannahs, S. (1998). *Introducing phonetics and phonology.* London: Arnold.

Davis, G. A. (1983). *A survey of adult aphasia.* Englewood Cliffs, NJ: Prentice-Hall.

Davison, A., & Green, G. M. (Eds.). (1988). *Linguistic complexity and text comprehension: Readability issues reconsidered.* Hillsdale, NJ: Erlbaum.

Dicker, S. J. (1996). *Languages in America: A pluralist view.* Clevedon, England: Multilingual Matters.

Donnelly, C. (1994). *Linguistics for writers.* Albany: State University of New York Press.

Duin, A. (1989). Factors that influence how readers learn from text: Guidelines for structuring technical documents. *Technical Communication, 36,* 97–101.

Dulay, H., & Burt, M. (1983). Goofing: An indicator of children's second language learning and strategies. In Gass & Selinker, pp. 54–68.

Eckert, P., & McConnell-Ginet, S. (2003). *Language and gender.* Cambridge, England: Cambridge University Press.

Eckman, F. (1987). Markedness and the contrastive analysis hypothesis. In Ioup & Weinberger, pp. 55–69.

Einstein, A., & Infeld, L. (1938). *The evolution of physics.* New York: Simon & Schuster.

Eisenson, J. (1984). *Adult aphasia* (2nd ed.). Englewood Cliffs, NJ: Prentice-Hall.

Fasold, R. (1984). *The sociolinguistics of society.* New York: Blackwell.

Fasold, R. (1990). *The sociolinguistics of language.* Cambridge, MA: Blackwell.

Ferguson, C. A., & Heath, S. B. (1981). *Language in the USA.* Cambridge, England: Cambridge University Press.

Flanagan, O. J. (1984). *The science of the mind.* Cambridge, MA: MIT Press.

Fodor, J. A., Bever, T. G., & Garrett, M. F. (1974). *The psychology of language: An introduction to psycholinguistics and generative grammar.* New York: McGraw-Hill.

Fowler, R. (1981). *Literature as social discourse.* Bloomington: Indiana University Press.

Francis, W. N. (Ed.). (1958). *The structure of American English.* New York: Ronald Press.

Fromkin, V. A. (1971). The non-anomalous nature of anomalous utterances. *Language, 47,* 27–52.

Gardner, H. (1985). The loss of language. In Clark et al., pp. 184–194.

Gass, S., & Schachter, J. (1989). *Linguistic perspectives on second language acquisition.* Cambridge, England: Cambridge University Press.

Gass, S., & Selinker, L. (1983). *Language transfer in language learning.* Rowley, MA: Newbury House.

Gass, S. M., & Selinker, L. (2001). *Second language acquisition: An introductory course.* Mahwah, NJ: Erlbaum.

Gazzaniga, M. S., & Sperry, R. W. (1967). Language after section of the cerebral commissures. *Brain, 90,* 131–148.

Gelb, I. J. (1963). *A study of writing.* Chicago: University of Chicago Press.

Georges, R. (1970). Structure in folktales: A generative-transformational approach. *The Conch, II,* #2 (September), 4–17.

Gleason, J. B. (1997). *The development of language* (4th ed.). Boston: Allyn & Bacon.

Green, L. J. (2002). *African American English: A linguistic introduction.* Cambridge, England: Cambridge University Press.

Grice, H. P. (1975). Logic and conversation. In Cole & Morgan, pp. 41–58.

Grundy, P. (2000). *Doing pragmatics* (2nd ed.). New York: Oxford University Press.

Hadley, A. O. (1993). *Research on language learning: Principles, processes, and prospects.* Lincolnwood, IL: National Textbook Co.

Halle, M. (1985). The rules of language. In Clark et al., pp. 236–248.

Halliday, M. A. K., & Hasan, R. (1976). *Cohesion in English.* London: Longman.

Halpern, J. (2001). *Outline of Japanese writing system.* Retrived Dec. 18, 2003, from Kanji Dictionary Publishing Society website: http://www.kangi.org/kangi/japanese/writing/outline.htm

Harley, T. (2001). *The psychology of language: From data to theory* (2nd ed.). New York: Taylor & Francis.

Haspelmath, M. (2002). *Understanding morphology.* New York: Arnold and Oxford University Press.

Hatch, E. (1983). *Psycholinguistics: A second language perspective.* Rowley, MA: Newbury House.

Head, H. (1926). *Aphasia and kindred disorders of speech,* 2 vols. Cambridge, England: Cambridge University Press.

Heny, J. (1985). Brain and language. In Clark et al., pp. 159–182.

Hogg, R., & McCully, C. B. (1987). *Metrical phonology: A coursebook.* Cambridge, England: Cambridge University Press.
Honko, L. (1979–1980). Methods in folk-narrative research. *Ethnologica Europaea, 11,* 6–27.
How genes shape personality. (1987). *US News and World Report* (April 13), 58–62.
Hulit, L. M., & Howard, M. R. (2002). *Born to talk: An introduction to speech and language development* (3rd. ed.). Boston: Allyn & Bacon.
Hurford, J. R., & Heasley, B. (1983). *Semantics: A coursebook.* New York: Cambridge University Press.
Hyman, L. M. (1975). *Phonology: Theory and analysis.* New York: Holt, Rinehart & Winston.
Ingram, D. (1988). *First language acquisition: Method, description, and explanation.* Cambridge, England: Cambridge University Press.
Ioup, G., & Weinberger, S. (1987). *Interlanguage phonology: The acquisition of a second language sound system.* Cambridge, MA: MIT Press.
Jakobson, R. (1971). *Studies on child language and aphasia.* The Hague: Mouton.
Jakobson, R., Fant, G., & Halle, M. (1963). *Preliminaries to speech analysis.* Cambridge, MA: MIT Press.
Johnson-Laird, P. N., & Wason, P. C. (Eds). (1977). *Thinking: Readings in cognitive science.* London: Cambridge University Press.
Katamba, F. (1989). *An introduction to phonology.* Essex, England: Longman.
Katamba, F. (1993). *Morphology.* New York: St. Martin's Press.
Katz, J., & Fodor, J. (Eds.). (1964). *The structure of language.* Englewood Cliffs, NJ: Prentice-Hall.
Katzner, K. (1995). *The languages of the world* (rev. ed.). New York: Funk & Wagnalls.
Kempson, R. (1977). *Semantic theory.* Cambridge, England: Cambridge University Press.
Kreidler, C. (1998). *Introducing English semantics.* London: Routledge.
Labov, W. (1966). *The social stratification of English in New York City.* Washington, DC: Center for Applied Linguistics.
Labov, W., Ash., S., & Boberg, C. (Forthcoming). *Atlas of North American English.* Berlin and New York: Mouton de Gruyter.
Lakoff, R. (1975). *Language and women's place.* New York: Harper & Row.
Laliberte, R. (1998). Routine appreciation. *Cooking Light* (November), 66–68.
Laufer, B. (1990). Why are some words more difficult than others? Some intralexical factors that affect the learning of words. *IRAL, 28,* 293–307.
Lenneberg, E. (1964). The capacity for language acquisition. In Katz & Fodor, pp. 579–603.
Levinson, S. (1983). *Pragmatics.* Cambridge, England: Cambridge University Press.
Limber, J. (1973). The genesis of complex sentences. In Moore, pp. 169–185.
Luria, A. R. (1973). *The working brain.* New York: Basic Books.
Lyons, J. (1977a). *Noam Chomsky.* New York: Penguin.
Lyons, J. (1977b). *Semantics,* 2 vols. New York: Cambridge University Press.
Macauley, R. (1994). *The social art: Language and its uses.* New York: Oxford University Press.
Macy, R. (1982). Neglected 6-year-old may never fully recover. Baton Rouge *Morning Advocate* (April 24), 1-A, 18-A.
Major, R. (1987). A model for interlanguage phonology. In Ioup & Weinberger, pp. 101–124.
Malmkjær, K. (Ed.) (1991). *The linguistics encyclopedia.* London: Routledge.
Marchand, H. (1969). *The categories and types of present-day English word-formation* (2nd ed.). Munich: Beck.
McLeod, S., van Doorn, J., & Reed, V. A. (2001). Normal acquisition of consonant clusters. *American Journal of Speech-Language Pathology, 10,* 99–110.
Moore, T. E. (Ed.). (1973). *Cognitive development and the acquisition of language.* New York: Academic Press.

Moskowitz, B. A. (1979). The acquisition of language. *Scientific American* (November), 82–96.
Newmeyer, F. J. (1983). *Grammatical theory.* Chicago: University of Chicago Press.
Newmeyer, F. J. (1986). *Linguistic theory in America* (2nd ed.). Orlando: Academic Press.
Ninio, A., & Snow, C. E. (1996). *Pragmatic development.* Boulder, CO: Westview Press.
O'Barr, W. M. (1981). The language of the law. In Ferguson & Heath, pp. 386–406.
Ohanian, B. (1989). The lost words of Joseph Chaikin. *Hippocrates* (January/February), 74–80.
Ornstein, R. (1973). Right and left thinking. *Psychology Today* (May), 87–92.
Parker, F., & Riley, K. (2005). *A short introduction to generative grammar.* Superior, WI: Parlay Press.
Pascoe, E. (1998). Hats on! *Practical Horseman* (November), 56–61.
Penfield, W., & Roberts, L. (1959). *Speech and brain mechanisms.* Princeton, NJ: Princeton University Press.
Petitto, L. A., Holowka, S., Sergio, L. E., & Ostry, D. (2001). Language rhythms in baby hand movements. *Nature* (Sept. 6), 35–36.
Petitto, L. A., & Marentette, P. A. (1991). Babbling in the manual mode: Evidence for the ontogeny of language. *Science, 251,* 1493–1496.
Pinker, S. (1997). *How the mind works.* New York: W. W. Norton.
Preston, D. (1989). *Sociolinguistcs and second language acquisition.* Oxford: Blackwell.
Radford, A. (1981). *Transformational syntax.* Cambridge, England: Cambridge University Press.
Radford, A. (1997). *Syntax: A minimalist introduction.* Cambridge, England: Cambridge University Press.
Reed, V. A. (1994). *An introduction to children with language disorders* (2nd ed.). New York: Macmillan.
The retail carpet ride. (1998). *Consumer Reports* (August), 35–39.
Riley, K. (1991). Passive voice and rhetorical role in scientific writing. *Journal of Technical Writing and Communication, 21,* 239–257.
Riley, K., & Parker, F. (1988). Tone as a function of presupposition in technical and business writing. *Journal of Technical Writing and Communication, 18,* 325–343.
Riley, K., & Parker, F. (2005). *A short introduction to descriptive grammar.* Superior, WI: Parlay Press.
Salmon, W. C. (1973). *Logic* (2nd ed.). Englewood Cliffs, NJ: Prentice-Hall.
Sampson, G. (1985). *Writing systems.* London: Hutchinson.
Say rabbit, not wabbit. (1971). *Newsweek* (March 22), 98.
Schane, S. (1973). *Generative phonology.* Englewood Cliffs, NJ: Prentice-Hall.
Schane, S., & Bendixen, B. (1978). *Workbook in generative phonology.* Englewood Cliffs, NJ: Prentice-Hall.
Schwartz, M. F. (1987). Patterns of speech production deficit within and across aphasic syndromes: Application of a psycholinguistic model. In Coltheart, Sartori, & Job, pp. 163–199.
Scott, J. (2002). In simple pronouns, clues to shifting Latino identity. *New York Times* (Dec. 5), B-1.
Searle, J. R. (1969). *Speech acts.* Cambridge, England: Cambridge University Press.
Searle, J. R. (1975). Indirect speech acts. In Cole & Morgan, pp. 59–82.
Searle, J. R. (1976). The classification of illocutionary acts. *Language in Society, 5,* 1–24.
Selinker, L. (1972). Interlanguage. *IRAL, 10,* 210–231.
Shaughnessy, M. P. (1977). *Errors and expectations.* New York: Oxford University Press.
Sheldon, A. (1974). The role of parallel function in the acquisition of relative clauses in England. *Journal of Verbal Learning and Verbal Behavior, 13,* 272–281.
Singer, M. (1990). *Psychology of language: An introduction to sentence and discourse processes.* Hillsdale, NJ: Erlbaum.
Skinner, B. F. (1957). *Verbal behavior.* New York: Appleton-Century-Crofts.
Smith, N., & Wilson, D. (1985). What is a language? In Clark et al., pp. 325–339.
Sperber, D., & Wilson, D. (1986). *Relevance.* Cambridge, MA: Harvard University Press.

Springer, S. P., & Deutsch, G. (1985). *Left brain, right brain* (rev. ed.). New York: W. H. Freeman & Company.

Tannen, D. (1990). *You just don't understand: Women and men in conversation.* New York: William Morrow & Company.

Tate, G. (Ed.). (1976). *Teaching composition.* Fort Worth: Texas Christian University Press.

Thomas, E., & Klaidman, D. (2004). The general's new stripes. *Newsweek* (Jan. 12), 22–23.

Traugott, E. C., & Pratt, M. L. (1980). *Linguistics for students of literature.* San Diego: Harcourt Brace Jovanovich.

Trudgill, P. (1972). Sex, covert prestige, and linguistic change in the urban British English of Norwich. *Language in Society, 1,* 179–95.

Vande Kopple, W. J. (1982). Functional sentence perspective, composition, and reading. *College Composition and Communication, 33,* 50–63.

Walsh, T. (1998). *A short introduction to formal discourse analysis.* Superior, WI: Parlay Enterprises.

Walsh, T. (2000). *A short introduction to x-bar syntax and transformations* (2nd ed.). Superior, WI: Parlay Enterprises.

Warden, D. A. (1976). The influence of context on children's use of identifying expressions and references. *British Journal of Psychology, 67,* 101–112.

White, L. (1989). *Universal grammar and second language acquisition.* Amsterdam: John Benjamins.

Winner, E., & Gardner, H. (1977). The comprehension of metaphor in brain-damaged persons. *Brain, 100,* 719–727.

Winterowd, R. (1976). Linguistics and composition. In Tate, pp. 197–221.

Wolfram, W. (1982). Language knowledge and other dialects. *American Speech, 57,* 3–18.

Wolfram, W., Adger, C. T., & Christian, D. (1999). *Dialects in schools and communities.* Mahwah, NJ: Erlbaum.

Wolfram, W., & Fasold, R. (1974). *The study of social dialects in American English.* Englewood Cliffs, NJ: Prentice-Hall.

Wolfram, W., & Johnson, R. (1982). *Phonological analysis: Focus in American English.* Washington, DC: Center for Applied Linguistics.

Wolfram, W., & Schilling-Estes, N. (1998). *American English: Dialects and variation.* Malden, MA: Blackwell.

Young, R. (1970). *Mind, brain and adaptation in the nineteenth century.* Oxford: Clarendon Press.

Zughoul, M. (1991). Lexical choice: Towards writing problematic word lists. *IRAL, 29,* 45–60.

GLOSSARY

active sentence One that does *not* contain a form of *be* followed by a past participle (cf. **passive**).

additive conjunction A **conjunction** that introduces information that elaborates on the first element being conjoined (e.g., *and, for instance*).

adjunct In **X-bar syntax,** a modifier that occurs between any **specifier** and **complement** within a phrase (e.g., the adjective *tall* in the NP *the tall math student*). The term adjunct designates a position (like **subject, direct object,** etc.), not a class of words (like **determiner, adjective,** etc.).

adversative conjunction A **conjunction** that introduces information that runs counter to the first element being conjoined (e.g., *however, on the other hand*).

affix The category of **bound, grammatical morphemes,** including both prefixes and suffixes.

affricate A **segment** associated with complete closure in the vocal tract (i.e., a stop) followed by restricted airflow (i.e., a fricative) (e.g., /č/).

agent An NP representing an entity capable of acting under its own volition (e.g., *John* but not *lightning*).

allophone A **segment** that is a systematic variant of a **phoneme** (e.g., [t^h] is an allophone of /t/ in English because any time /t/ is syllable-initial before a stressed vowel, it is aspirated).

alphabetic Describing a writing system in which each symbol represents a phonological **segment** (e.g., *c-a-t*).

analytic sentence One that is necessarily true as a result of the words in it (e.g., *A triangle has three sides*).

anaphora Describing a linguistic expression (the anaphor) that must have another expression to refer to (the **antecedent**) (e.g., all **reflexive pronouns** are anaphors).

anomia A type of **aphasia** characterized by the inability to name objects and difficulty in accessing nouns.

antecedent A linguistic expression that another expression refers to (e.g., *They* is the antecedent of *each other* in *They ran into each other*).

anticipation Accessing an item that occurs *later* in a series (e.g., *tig and tall* for *big and tall*).

antonymy Two words whose senses differ only in the value of a single **semantic feature** (e.g., *man* and *boy* differ only in [±adult]).

aphasia An acquired language dysfunction caused by cortical damage.

assimilation Any phonological process by which one **segment** becomes more like a neighboring segment (e.g., Vowel Nasalization).

auxiliary verb Any verb preceding the right-most verb in a simple sentence; auxiliaries in English are the **modals** and forms of *be, have,* and *do.*

babbling A prelinguistic stage in language acquisition characterized by syllable-like sounds.

bare infinitive An infinitive verb form (e.g., *to go*) with no overt subject (e.g., *John told you where to go*).

basic-level terms Words of intermediate generality, typically acquired first (e.g., *car* is acquired before *vehicle* [general] or *four-by-four* [specific]).

beneficiary An NP representing an entity that benefits from an action (e.g., *Mary* in *John baked a cake for Mary*).

binary antonyms Antonyms that describe all possibilities along a single dimension (e.g., *sane* and *insane*).

blending A phonological process combining features of two adjacent **segments** into one (e.g., [m̥ok] for *smoke*).

bound morpheme One that cannot stand alone as a word (e.g., *un-*).

bridging inference One that results from probable or possible connections rather than from logically necessary ones (e.g., from *John entered the room. The chandelier burned brightly,* we can infer that the room contained a chandelier).

Broca's aphasia A type of **aphasia** characterized by labored, "telegraphic" output; caused by damage to **Broca's area.** Also known as **motor** or **expressive aphasia.**

Broca's area The area in the frontal lobe of the **dominant hemisphere,** near the primary motor cortex (which controls movement).

category A class of words that share a characteristic (e.g., nouns can be made plural, verbs can be inflected for tense, etc.).

category extension A word-formation process whereby a word in one category is extended to a new category, at which point it can also be inflected like other members of the new category (e.g., *table* (N) → *table* (V) enables *The committee* ***tabled*** *the discussion*).

causal conjunction A **conjunction** that signals a cause-effect relation between the items being conjoined (e.g., *therefore, because*).

circumlocution A descriptive phrase substituted for a single word the speaker either has not yet learned or is unable to retrieve (e.g., *thing you write with* for *pencil*).

clause A syntactic unit having both a subject and predicate (verb phrase). Clauses are of two types: independent (can stand alone as a sentence) and dependent (cannot stand alone as a sentence).

coda One or more consonants ending a syllable.

code-switching A bilingual speaker changing from one language to another during the course of a conversation; often triggered by a change in topic or attitude.

cohesion The impression that different parts of a text "hang together" into a related whole.

collocation The appearance within a discourse of words or phrases that regularly co-occur (e.g., *salt* and *pepper*); can be used to establish **cohesion.**

commissive An utterance used to commit the speaker to do something (e.g., a promise).

common noun Any noun not a **proper noun** (e.g., *actress, city*).

competence The psychological system of unconscious knowledge that underlies a speaker's ability to produce and interpret utterances in a language (cf. **performance**).

complement In **X-bar syntax,** a modifier that always occurs next to the head of the phrase, whether it precedes or follows the head (e.g., the noun *math* in *the tall math student*). The term **complement** designates a position (like **subject, direct object,** etc.), not a class of words (like **determiner, adjective,** etc.).

complementary distribution The relation between two items that never occur in the same environment (e.g., in English [t^h] always occurs before a stressed vowel, but [ɾ] never does).

complex sentence A sentence consisting of both a dependent and an independent clause (e.g., *When I opened the door, the cat ran out*).

conduction aphasia A type of **aphasia** characterized by the inability to repeat words; caused by damage to the arcuate fasciculus.

conjunction The part of speech that connects words, phrases, or clauses (e.g., *or*). *Conjunction* is from the Latin phrase for 'join with.'

connotation The associations attached to a word, apart from its core sense (e.g., *train* and *choo-choo* have different connotations) (cf. **denotation**).

consonant epenthesis Insertion of a consonant, typically to break up a series of two vowels (e.g., *Ramada Inn* [rəmadə ɪn] → [rəmadərɪn]).

constancy under negation A test for **presupposition:** Sentence A presupposes sentence B if both "A" and "not A" assume the truth of B (e.g., *Ralph regrets buying an SUV* and *Ralph doesn't regret buying an SUV* both assume the truth of *Ralph bought an SUV*).

constituent Two or more words dominated entirely and exclusively by a single **node** (i.e., the node dominates those words and no others).

constraint In **generative grammar** (especially government and binding theory), a limitation on where a **transformation** can move an item.

contradictory sentence One that is necessarily false as a result of the words in it (e.g., *A triangle has four sides*).

contralateral control The property of the brain (not peculiar to humans) such that each hemisphere controls activity on the opposite side of the body.

contrast Two **segments** contrast if substituting one for the other causes a change in meaning. The **phonemes** of a language are all and only those segments that contrast with each other.

contrastive analysis A point-by-point comparison of the grammars of two languages.

conversational maxims Four principles (Quality, Quantity, Relation, and Manner) in terms of which speakers interpret utterances.

converse antonyms Antonyms that describe the relationship between two entities from opposite perspectives (e.g., *employer* and *employee*).

cooing A prelinguistic vocal production characterized primarily by vowel-like sounds.

coreference The condition of two expressions having the same **referent** (e.g., *President of the U.S.* and *Commander-in-Chief*).

count noun One that has a plural form (e.g., *boy/boys*). Any other noun is noncount (e.g., *water*).

creole A **pidgin** that has become the native language of a group of speakers.

deceptive transparency The property of a word whose component morphemes may lead a non-native speaker to misinterpret its meaning (e.g., *outline* does not mean 'out of line').

declaration An utterance used to change the status of some entity (e.g., a resignation).

decoding Language comprehension (i.e., listening or reading).

deixis The ability of one expression to refer systematically to two or more distinct entities in the same context (e.g., *you* and *I*), depending on the speaker's point of view.

denotation The core sense of a word (e.g., *train* and *choo-choo* have the same denotation) (cf. **connotation**).

derivation A step-by-step "history" of a linguistic form, from its **underlying structure** through all the rules that apply to it, resulting in its **surface structure.**

derivational morpheme All prefixes and all noninflectional suffixes (in English); derivational suffixes typically change the **category** of the root (e.g., *-ize: critic* is a noun, but *criticize* is a verb).

determiner A syntactic **category** including articles, demonstratives (e.g., *this, that,* etc.), possessive pronouns, and perhaps quantifiers (e.g., *some, many,* etc.).

developmental process A process in second-language acquisition that is similar to one in first-language acquisition (e.g., **simplification** of consonant clusters).

dialect A systematic variety of a language specific to a particular region or social group (e.g., Australian English, African American Vernacular English).

diphthong Two adjacent vowels that form the **nucleus** of a single syllable. The diphthong phonemes in English are /aɪ, aʊ, ɔɪ/ as in *buy, cow,* and *boy.* (Note that the title of the Italian opera *Aida* /aídə/ does not begin with a diphthong because /aɪ/ represents the nuclei of two different syllables.)

direct illocutionary act One performed by an utterance whose syntactic form matches its **illocutionary force** (e.g., an imperative used to issue a **directive**). Any other illocutionary act is **indirect.**

directive An utterance used to try to get the hearer to do something (e.g., a request).

discourse analysis The study of the structure and processing of multisentence texts, both written and spoken.

distinctive features Two-valued dimensions that serve as basic building blocks of **segments** (e.g., /m/ and /n/ are both [+nasal] and [+voice]).

distributive *be* See **habitual *be*.**

dominant hemisphere The one that is primarily responsible for processing language (i.e., the left in most people).

elaborative inference One that reflects the introduction of real-world knowledge beyond **logical** or **bridging** inferences (e.g., from *John entered a room that had a chandelier,* we might infer that he was in an expensive house).

ellipsis Use of a structure with an element that is missing but can be recovered from a previous part of the discourse (e.g., *John ate but I didn't [eat]*).

embedding A **clause** found within a higher clause (e.g., *I told him [what he should do]*).

empiricism The view that we are born with relatively *little* of the unconscious knowledge we will have as adults; also known as behaviorism (cf. **nativism**).

entailment A proposition (expressed in a sentence) that follows *necessarily* from another sentence (e.g., *John murdered Bill* entails *Bill died*).

epenthesis The insertion of a **segment** into a series. Vowel epenthesis inserts a vowel between two consonants, and consonant epenthesis inserts a consonant between two vowels.

error analysis A procedure for identifying regularities in **interlanguage** forms; the learner's productions are compared to the grammar of the second language.

explicit performative An utterance containing a **performative verb** used in its performative sense (e.g., *I apologize for . . .*). Any other utterance is a non-explicit performative.

expressed locutionary act One actually expressing the propositional content for the **illocutionary act** involved (e.g., a promise must predicate a future act of the speaker, so *I promise I'll help you with your homework* is expressed). Any other locutionary act is **implied** (e.g., *I promise you won't have to do your homework alone*).

expressive An utterance used to express the emotional state of the speaker (e.g., an apology).

expressive aphasia Synonym for **Broca's aphasia.**

extension The set of all potential **referents** (if any) for a linguistic expression.

extraposition A **transformation** that moves a **relative clause** or **prepositional phrase** away from the NP it modifies to clause-final position (e.g., *A rumor <u>about you</u> just surfaced* → *A rumor just surfaced <u>about you</u>*).

factive verb A main clause verb that presupposes the truth of the proposition in the subordinate clause (e.g., *I <u>realize</u> that you are a coward* presupposes 'You are a coward').

felicity conditions Conditions that must be met for the valid performance of an **illocutionary act** (i.e., participants and circumstances must be appropriate, participants must have appropriate intentions, etc.).

field dependence A style of learning where the individual attempts to analyze all data at once.

field independence A style of learning where the individual is able to foreground specific data and analyze them.

final consonant reduction A phonological process deleting a post-vocalic, word-final **obstruent** (e.g., [dɔ] for *dog*).

final devoicing A phonological process devoicing a word-final **obstruent** (e.g., [hɛt] for *head*).

fluent aphasia Characterized by speech produced at a normal rate of speed and with normal intonation; **Wernicke's aphasia** is one type of fluent aphasia.

free morpheme One that can stand alone as a word (e.g., *not*) (cf. **bound morpheme**).

free variation Two items that can occur in the same environment without causing a change in meaning (e.g., [ǰ] and [ž] are in free variation in *garage*).

fricative A **segment** associated with restricted but uninterrupted airflow, creating turbulence (e.g., /s/).

fronting Replacing a consonant (often velar) with one articulated more forward in the mouth (e.g., [go] → [do]).

garden path sentence One to which the listener/reader initially assigns an incorrect structure due to syntactic ambiguity; this type of sentence typically causes confusion about which item is the main verb (e.g., *The young man the boats*).

gender A morphological category, usually indicated by affixation (e.g., *actor/actress*); also, the social and psychological roles, attitudes, and traits associated with biological sex.

general cognitive capacities Innate knowledge that relates to all domains of human cognition (e.g., the ability to serialize items).

generative grammar A theory of the psychological system of unconscious knowledge that underlies a speaker's ability to produce and interpret utterances in a language.

given information That which the speaker assumes is already known to the hearer; normally expressed as the subject of a sentence (cf. **new information**).

given-new contract A processing strategy that says a text is more cohesive when information that is familiar to the addressee precedes information that is being mentioned for the first time.

glide A **segment** associated with restricted air flow, but not enough to create turbulence (e.g., /y/).

gliding A phonological process changing a **liquid** into a **glide** (e.g., [kɛ́wi] for *Kelly*).

gradable antonyms Antonyms that describe opposite poles of a single dimension (e.g., *tall* and *short*).

grammatical morpheme One whose function is to modify the sense of a **lexical morpheme;** prepositions, articles, **conjunctions,** and **affixes** are grammatical.

habitual *be* A **dialect** feature, associated especially with AAVE, in which *be* refers to activities or states that occur over time or are generally true (e.g., *They be fightin'* = 'They are always fighting').

heavy NP condition A strategy that says sentences are easier to process if noun clauses or heavily modified NPs occur at the end of the sentence rather than at the beginning; e.g., *It surprised Bill that John left the party early* is easier to process than *That John left the party early surprised Bill.*

hemispherical specialization The control of separate cognitive functions by the left and right hemispheres.

hierarchical progression An AB:AC arrangement of **given** and **new information.**

high-amplitude sucking A research method that measures the increased rate at which a child sucks on a pacifier as a sign that the child has perceived a change in a stimulus.

holophrastic Describing a stage of language acquisition characterized by one-word utterances.

hyponymy The sense of one word (the superordinate) being entirely contained in the sense of another word (the hyponym) (e.g., the sense of *talk* is entirely contained within the sense of *mumble*).

iconic See **writing.**

ideograph A drawing of an object used to represent that object and related concepts (e.g., a bumper sticker depicting a heart, representing love).

idiolect The specific linguistic system of a particular speaker, with all its attendant idiosyncrasies.

idiom An expression whose meaning cannot be derived from its component words (e.g., *bought the farm,* 'died').

illocutionary act The act of *doing* something by saying something (e.g., making a request).

illocutionary force The **illocutionary act** performed by a given utterance.

I-Movement Common abbreviation for the **Inflection Movement** transformation.

implicative verb A main clause verb that presupposes a particular attitude on the part of the speaker toward the proposition in the subordinate clause (e.g., *I managed to find your keys* presupposes 'finding your keys was difficult,' vs. *I happened to find your keys* presupposes 'finding your keys was accidental').

implicature A proposition *implied* by an utterance but not part of that utterance or a necessary consequence of that utterance.

implied locutionary act See **expressed locutionary act.**

indirect illocutionary act Use of a syntactic form that does not match the **illocutionary force** of an utterance; especially common when speakers issue **directives** (e.g., *Could you close the window?* is indirect; *Close the window* is direct).

Inflection Movement A **transformation** that moves the tensed **auxiliary verb** (which is always the first verb) to the left of the subject NP (e.g., *That guy is sleeping* → *Is that guy sleeping?*).

inflectional morpheme One of eight suffixes (in English) that do not change the category of the root (e.g., {PLU}: *chair* is a noun and plural *chairs* is a noun) (cf. **derivational morpheme**).

inherent negative A sentence containing a word whose meaning includes negation (e.g., *Three students are absent*), rather than a form with an overt negative marker (e.g., *not present*) (cf. **negative sentence**).

instrument An NP representing an entity used to perform an action (e.g., *a knife* in *John cut the cake with a knife*).

instrumental motivation The desire to learn a second language for some practical purpose (e.g., conducting business).

integrative motivation The desire to learn a second language in order to make oneself part of the community or culture.

interference See **language transfer.**

interlanguage In second-language acquisition, a grammar different from both the speaker's native language and the second language.

intonation A pitch change over an entire sentence; pitch falls in declaratives and *wh*-interrogatives, but rises in *yes-no* interrogatives.

isogloss A line demarcating the area in which some linguistic feature can be found. Numerous isoglosses that coincide indicate the presence of a **dialect** boundary.

jargon aphasia See **Wernicke's aphasia.**

language-specific capacities Innate knowledge that relates only to the acquisition of language and to no other domain of cognition (e.g., the subjacency constraint).

language transfer Properties of a first language that are carried over into a second language. Positive transfer enhances second-language acquisition, and negative transfer (or **interference**) impedes it.

language universals Properties that all human languages have in common. Chomsky attributes some of these to the initial state of the human mind to account for the rapidity and uniformity of language acquisition; he calls them **universal grammar.**

left ear advantage See **right ear advantage.**

level of representation A particular point of view from which language can he described (e.g., *John kissed Mary* and *Mary was kissed by John* are the same on the semantic level of representation [they express the same proposition], but different on the syntactic level of representation [one is active and the other is passive]).

lexical ambiguity The condition of a word having more than one sense (e.g., *star* means both 'heavenly body' and 'celebrity').

lexical cohesion The repetition of a word or phrase, a synonym, a **superordinate,** or **collocation.**

lexical decomposition The representation of the sense of a word in terms of **semantic features.**

lexical morpheme One having an independent sense; most nouns, verbs, and adjectives are lexical (e.g., *man, run, tall*) (cf. **grammatical morpheme**).

linear progression An AB:BC arrangement of given and new information.

liquid Any /l/- or /r/-like **segment.**

literal locutionary act An utterance in which the words mean exactly what they say (i.e., one that is not sarcastic or exaggerated). Any other locutionary act is nonliteral.

localization of function The control of different cognitive functions by different parts of each hemisphere (e.g., the front part of the **dominant hemisphere** controls speaking, and the rear part controls comprehension).

locutionary act The act of simply *saying* something.

logical inference A connection between two propositions that is presupposed, entailed, or otherwise logically necessary (e.g., from a mention of *room,* we can logically infer the existence of walls).

main verb The right-most verb in a simple sentence (e.g., *did* is the main verb in *John did his work* but not in *John did not finish his work*).

markedness Properties consistent with **language universals** are unmarked; those inconsistent with language universals are marked.

markedness differential hypothesis Eckman's theory of second-language acquisition, which states that, of those structures *not* shared by the first and second language, difficulty increases with markedness.

mean length of utterance (MLU) A measurement of the average number of **morphemes** in a child's utterances.

metathesis Reversing two items in a series (e.g., *tig and ball* for *big and tall*).

minimal attachment A processing strategy that assigns to a sentence the simplest structure permitted by the grammar.

minimum distance principle A general rule for interpreting **bare infinitives:** The subject of a bare infinitive is assumed to be the closest NP to its left (e.g., *John told you where to go* = 'You go').

modal verb One lacking the present tense *-s* suffix with a third person singular subject (e.g., *She can go/*She cans go;* modals in English are forms of *can, will, shall, may,* and *must*).

monophthongization A process whereby speakers reduce a **diphthong** to one element, typically the first (e.g., *hide* [haɪd] → [had]).

morpheme A minimal element of meaning associated with a particular form (e.g., {pel} means 'push' as in *repel, compel,* etc.).

morphographic Describing a writing system in which each symbol represents a morpheme (e.g., 2 × 2 = 4).

morphophoneme A phonological segment representing a morpheme; typically written in capital letters within double slashes (e.g., {PLU} = //Z//).

motor aphasia Synonym for **Broca's aphasia.**

nasal A **segment** associated with a lowered velum, allowing air to escape through the nose (e.g., /n/).

nativism The view that we are born with relatively *much* of the unconscious knowledge we will have as adults; also known as mentalism (cf. **empiricism**).

negative sentence A sentence containing a negative marker such as *not* (or a contracted form of it).

neologistic jargon Nonsense words characteristic of **Wernicke's aphasia;** also known as neologisms.

neutralization Any phonological process that wipes out the contrast between two **segments** (e.g., Flapping).

new information That which the speaker assumes is not already known to the hearer; normally expressed as the predicate of a sentence (i.e., after the subject) (cf. **given information**).

node A point in a tree structure that can branch.

nonfluent aphasia Characterized by hesitant, labored speech, **Broca's aphasia** is the major type of nonfluent aphasia.

nonnutritive sucking Often used as a synonym for **high-amplitude sucking.**

nonreversible passive A **passive sentence** whose subject can logically be interpreted only as a **patient,** not as an **agent** (e.g., *The tree was struck by lightning*) (cf. **reversible passive**).

nonstandard English Any variety of English which contains **socially marked** forms.

noun clause A **clause** that functions as a noun would (e.g., the underlined clause in *I saw what you did* functions as the direct object of *saw*).

NP-movement A **transformation** that moves an NP to any other empty NP position (e.g., ____ *was-found-the key* → *the key-was-found* ____).

nucleus The vowel in a syllable.

obstruent Any member of the class of **stops, fricatives,** and **affricates.**

onset One or more consonants beginning a syllable.

operational definition Defining an entity by stipulating a procedure for producing it (e.g., the direct object of a sentence is the NP that moves to subject position when the sentence is made passive).

order of mention A general principle for interpreting the sequence of events reported in two adjacent clauses: the event in the first clause is assumed to have occurred before the event in the second clause.

overgeneralization A semantic process of using a word to refer to more things than it normally does (e.g., *car* 'any vehicle').

overlap The condition of two words having the same value for some (but not all) **semantic features** (e.g., *nun* and *niece* share [–male]).

parallel function A processing strategy that assumes that a pronoun in a particular syntactic position (e.g., subject) refers back to an **antecedent** in the same syntactic position.

passive *be* An **auxiliary verb** that always appears in a **passive sentence** and immediately precedes a **main verb** in the **past participle** form (e.g., *The Packers were beaten by the Vikings*).

passive sentence One that contains a form of *be* followed by a **past participle** (e.g., *The vehicle could have been driven by John*) (cf. **active**).

past participle The verb form following auxiliary *have* (e.g., *driven* as in *You should have driven*).

patient An NP representing an entity being acted upon (e.g., *beans* in *John ate beans*).

performance The actual physical and psychological processes that a speaker might go through in producing or interpreting an utterance (cf. **competence**).

performative verb A verb that actually names the **illocutionary act** it is used to perform (e.g., *state, order, question,* etc.).

perseveration Accessing an item that occurred earlier in a series (e.g., *big and ball* for *big and tall*).

phoneme The type of **segment** we *think* we hear when we interpret speech.

phonemic paraphasia **Anticipation, perseveration,** and **metathesis** of phonological **segments,** as a consequence of **aphasia.** Also known as literal paraphasia.

phonotactics Restrictions on the permissible sequences of **segments** in a language (e.g., if three consonants begin a word in English, the first one must be /s/ and the third one must be a liquid or a glide).

phrase structure rules Rules that specify the hierarchical arrangement and left-to-right ordering of categories (e.g., S → NP – VP).

pictograph A drawing of an object used to represent that object (e.g., a highway sign depicting a deer).

pidgin A mixture of two existing languages brought into contact by trade or colonization.

post-vocalic liquid deletion A phonological process deleting an /l/ or /r/ following a vowel (e.g., [hɛp] for *help*).

present participle The verb form following auxiliary *be* in an **active sentence** (e.g., *driving* as in *You should not be driving*).

presupposition A proposition (expressed in a sentence) that is assumed to be true in order to judge the truth of another sentence (e.g., *Hart passed the bar exam* presupposes *Hart took the bar exam*).

presupposition trigger A word or structure that presupposes the truth of a proposition or the speaker's attitude about it (e.g., *Why are you in a bad mood?* presupposes 'You are in a bad mood').

prevocalic voicing Replacement of a voiceless consonant by a voiced consonant, in front of a vowel or other voiced segment (e.g., *top* [tap] → [dap]).

pro-form substitution A test for determining whether a structural unit is a lexical, bar, or phrasal category (e.g., *one* typically substitutes for N-bar categories, as in *I studied more for the last <u>French quiz</u> than for the first <u>one</u>*).

projection problem The hypothesis that language learners acquire linguistic principles that cannot be inferred solely from the data they are exposed to.

proper noun A noun with a unique **referent;** typically cannot be pluralized (e.g., *Marilyn Monroe, New York City*) (cf. **common noun**).

prototype A typical member of the **extension** of a linguistic expression (e.g., Lassie is a prototype of *dog*).

psycholinguistics The branch of linguistics that studies the mental processes that humans employ in actual language use. Also known as psychology of language.

question An utterance used to try to get the hearer to provide information.

reaction time The amount of time a listener or reader takes in **decoding** a linguistic structure; often used as evidence of how complex the structure is to process.

readability formula A calculation designed to predict the speed and comprehension rate with which readers will process a text.

receptive aphasia Synonym for **Wernicke's aphasia.**

reduplication A process by which a morpheme or a syllable is repeated (e.g., *dada*).

reduplicative babbling A type of **babbling** in which a syllable is repeated (e.g., [ba-ba-ba]).

reference The relation between linguistic expressions (e.g., words and sentences) and objects in the real (or imagined) world. Also a method for achieving **cohesion** through the use of items such as pronouns that link parts of a text with other parts or with things in the real world.

referent The entity (if any) identified by the use of a linguistic expression (e.g., the referent of *The White House* is the building at 1600 Pennsylvania Avenue in Washington, DC).

reflexive pronoun A pronoun formed by adding *-self/selves* to a personal pronoun.

reflexive sounds Involuntary vocal productions such as burping, sneezing, and coughing.

register One of many styles of language, ranging from formal to informal.

relative clause A dependent clause that is "related" to another clause by a **relative pronoun** (e.g., *That is the man <u>who mugged me</u>*). Also known as an adjectival clause.

relative pronoun A *wh*-word (i.e., *who(m), which, that*) that functions as a noun within a **relative clause** (e.g., *That is the man who mugged me*).

representative An utterance used to describe some state of affairs (e.g., a statement).

reversible passive A **passive sentence** whose subject can logically be interpreted as either an **agent** or **patient** (e.g., *The car was hit by the truck*) (cf. **nonreversible passive**).

right ear advantage The ability to process auditory stimuli presented to the right ear to the exclusion of stimuli presented simultaneously to the left ear. Most humans, being left dominant, have a right ear advantage for linguistic stimuli and a **left ear advantage** for nonlinguistic stimuli.

scene headers Names of the typical sequences of events comprising a **script** (e.g., a "moviegoing" script might include a scene header such as Buying a Ticket).

schema (plural: schemata) A psychological framework for organizing pre-existing knowledge about the world.

script A psychological representation of the typical sequence of events in a familiar situation (e.g., a "moviegoing" script might include events such as Buying a Ticket, Buying Popcorn, Finding a Seat, etc.).

segment A psychological unit of phonology corresponding roughly to "speech sound"; **allophones, phonemes,** and **morphophonomes** are all segments. We interpret the physical speech signal in terms of segments.

selectional restrictions Semantic constraints on the NPs that a particular lexical item can take (e.g., *regret* requires a human subject).

semantic feature A dimension of sense typically having two values (e.g., [±human]).

semantic paraphasia The use of inappropriate but closely related words, as a consequence of **aphasia** (e.g., *phone* for *radio*).

sense The literal meaning of an expression, independent of situational context.

sensory aphasia Synonym for **Wernicke's aphasia.**

simplification A phonological process reducing the number of consonants in a cluster (e.g., [pɪn] for *spin*).

socially marked Any linguistic form that can cause a listener to form a negative social judgement of the speaker (e.g., *ain't*).

sonorant Any member of the class of **nasals, liquids,** and **glides.**

specifier In **X-bar syntax,** a modifier that always occurs first in a phrase, before an **adjunct, complement,** or head (e.g., the determiner *that* in the NP *that tall math student*). The term **specifier** designates a position (like **subject, direct object,** etc.), not a class of words (like **adjective, noun,** etc.).

speech act A **locutionary act** (i.e., the act of saying something) plus an **illocutionary act** (i.e., the act of doing something).

standard English Any variety of English that contains no **socially marked** forms.

stereotype A list of characteristics describing a **prototype** of a linguistic expression (e.g., barks, wags tail, has fur, etc., is a stereotype of *dog*).

stop A **segment** associated with complete closure in the vocal tract (e.g., /t/).

stopping The phonological process of a **fricative** becoming a **stop** (e.g., [dɪs] for *this*).

structural ambiguity The condition whereby an expression can be assigned more than one syntactic structure (e.g., *old men and women* = old [men and women] or [old men] and women).

structural hypercorrection The use of a form in a context where it is not normally used; usually occurs among speakers trying to affect a more formal style (e.g., *between you and I* for *between you and me*).

subcategorization restrictions Syntactic constraints on the types of **complements** that a particular lexical item can take (e.g., the verb *sleep* cannot have a direct object).

subordinating conjunction A **conjunction** that introduces a dependent clause (e.g., *although, because*).

substitution A method for establishing **cohesion** by using forms such as *one* to refer back to earlier linguistic elements (e.g., *My husband caught a cold, and now I have one*).

superordinate See **hyponymy.**

surface structure A syntactic configuration after all applicable **transformations** have applied.

syllabic Describing a writing system in which each symbol represents a syllable (e.g., *LO* = 'hello').

syllabic babbling Synonym for **reduplicative babbling.**

synonymy Two words having the same **sense** (e.g., *student* and *pupil*).

synthetic sentence One that can be judged true or false only by evaluating the state of affairs it describes (e.g., *Al Gore is President of the U.S. Senate*).

telegraphic Describing a stage of language acquisition characterized by utterances that are open-ended in length but lack most **grammatical morphemes.**

temporal conjunction A **conjunction** that establishes the order of occurrence of degree of importance among the items being conjoined (e.g., *first, second, third*).

tense In English, one of two verb inflections (present or past) that occur on the first verb form in a simple sentence (e.g., *John may/might have been eating*).

thematic progression The arrangement of given and new information in a discourse. **Linear progression** (AB:BC) makes new information in one sentence the given information in the next. **Hierarchical progression** (AB:AC) retains the same given information in successive sentences.

theory A hypothesis about the workings of a mechanism (physical or psychological) that cannot be observed directly; designed to explain observations that otherwise would remain unexplained.

tone A speaker or writer's attitude toward his or her subject matter and audience.

transformation An operation that alters syntactic structure (e.g., the I-Movement transformation changes *He-has-gone* into *Has-he-gone*).

truth conditions The conditions under which a sentence can be judged as true, false, or having no truth value.

umlaut A phonological process in Germanic languages whereby the vowel in a suffix has an effect on the vowel in the root of a word (e.g., historically, the vowel in *mice* [< *mouse*] is the result of umlaut).

underlying structure A syntactic configuration before any **transformations** have applied.

ungliding Synonym for **monophthongization.**

uninflected verb form The form following infinitival *to* (e.g., *give* as in *to give*).

universal grammar See **language universals.**

variegated babbling A type of **babbling** in which a consonant or vowel is varied (e.g., [pa-ga-ba-ga] or [pu-pi-pa-pi]).

velar fronting See **fronting.**

vowel epenthesis Insertion of a vowel (typically [ə]) to break up a series of consonants (e.g., *pastry* [pestri] → [pestəri]).

Wernicke's aphasia A type of **aphasia** characterized by **neologistic jargon;** caused by damage to **Wernicke's area.** Also known as sensory, receptive, or jargon aphasia.

Wernicke's area The area in the temporal lobe of the **dominant hemisphere,** near the primary auditory cortex (which processes sounds).

***wh*-movement** A **transformation** that moves a *wh*-item into clause-initial position (e.g., *has-John-gone-where* → *where-has-John-gone*).

writing A representational system in which the symbols no longer depict the objects they represent (i.e., one which is not **iconic**).

X-bar syntax A theory of **constituent structure** that recognizes a structural unit intermediate in size between a phrasal and a lexical category (e.g., N-bar or N' is an intermediate category between NP and N).

ANSWERS TO SELECTED EXERCISES

Chapter 2: Pragmatics

Exercise A, page 12

3. a. relation
   b. He does not know where Billy Bob is.

Exercise B, page 14

1. c. representative
   i. question

Exercise C, page 16

2. propositional content (speaker must predicate a *past* act)

Exercise D, page 18

1. c. *Won't insist* is not positive.

Exercise E, page 20

1. c. (i) *yes-no* interrogative; (ii) directive; (iii) indirect

Exercise F, page 23

1. c. implied ('Don't smoke')

Exercise G, page 24

2. a. implied
   b. nonliteral

Exercise H, page 25

1. a. (i) nonexplicit, (ii) direct, (iii) expressed, (iv) literal
   b. (i) explicit, (ii) does not apply, (iii) expressed, (iv) literal

Chapter 3: Semantics

Exercise A, page 33

1. e. [±count] Note: *table, chair,* and *pencil* each have a plural form and thus are called **count** nouns. *Water, dirt,* and *cream* don't have a plural form and consequently are called **noncount nouns.** However, what's going on when someone goes into a restaurant, orders coffee, and asks for *two creams?*

Exercise B, page 36

3. a. polygon, quadrilateral, parallelogram, rectangle, square

Exercise C, page 39

3. c. G d. C e. B

Exercise D, page 40

4. b

Exercise E, page 41

1. b. coreference

Exercise F, page 43

3. *arrived. Went* can be used only by a speaker not in New York; *came* can be used only by a speaker in New York.

Exercise G, page 44

3. analytic

Exercise H, page 47

1. (A.2) entails (A.1). Note: if *Fred is a man* is true, then *Fred is mortal* must be true; likewise, if *Fred is mortal* is false, then *Fred is a man* must be false.

   (B.1) presupposes (B.2). Note: if *Fred's wife is six feet tall* is true, then *Fred is married* must be true; likewise, if *Fred is married* is false, then *Fred's wife is six feet tall* has no truth value.

Chapter 4: Syntax

Exercise A, page 55

1. *Brick* cannot be made comparative *(*bricker)* or superlative *(*brickest),* whereas adjectives, in general, can (e.g., *older, oldest*).

Exercise B, page 57

1. b. NP, containing a Det *(the)* and AP *(red car)*

Exercise E, page 61

1. a.

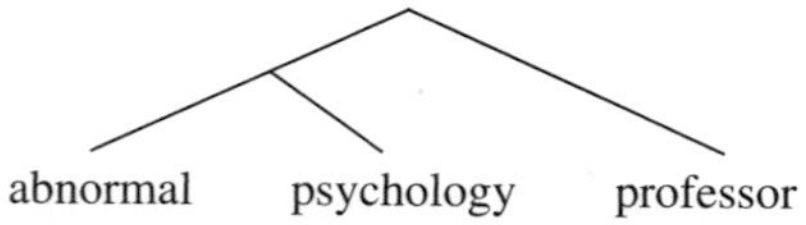

'professor of abnormal psychology'

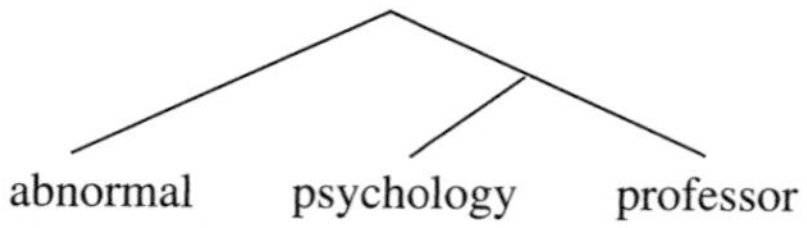

'psychology professor who is abnormal'

Exercise G, page 65

2. *Murder* requires a [+human] object.

Exercise K, page 75

1. Sentences (A–C) indicate that the verb *put* must be followed (although not immediately) by a phrase indicating location (e.g., *in the garage*). In the sentence *Where has John put the car?* there is no phrase indicating location following *put,* yet the sentence is perfectly acceptable. One way to account for the acceptability of this sentence is to assume that *where* (a phrase indicating location) originated to the right of *put* in the underlying structure (i.e., . . . *put the car where*) and was later moved into clause-initial position by the rule of *wh*-Movement.

Exercise L, page 78

1. a. Coordinate Structure Constraint

Chapter 5: Morphology

Exercise C, page 87

1. a. two
   b. one

Exercise D, page 88

1. a. restating = {re} + {state} + {PRES PART}
   {re} = grammatical, bound, prefix, derivational
   {state} = lexical, free
   {PRES PART} = grammatical, bound, suffix, inflectional

Exercise E, page 88

1. a. grammatical, bound

Exercise F, page 93

1. d. (note that *John* is a third person, singular subject)

Exercise G, page 94

1. a. present tense, future time

Exercise H, page 98

1. b. No more than one inflectional affix is allowed per syntactic category.

Exercise I, page 100

1. a. clipped form
   e. compound

Chapter 6: Phonology

Exercise A, page 110

1. a. low, front, spread, lax
   b. mid, back, round, tense

Exercise B, page 115

1. b. /ŋ/
2. a. /i/, /e/

Exercise D, page 120

2. c
4. C → [–vce] / _____#
[+stop]

Exercise G, page 127

3. a. [–nas] should be [+nas]

Chapter 7: Language Variation

Exercise B, page 139

2. False

Exercise D, page 146

2. f. both (c) and (d)

Exercise G, page 152

1. a. False. [dɪs] is.

Exercise H, pages 155–156

3. The possessive morpheme (the *-s* on *deacons'*) has been deleted.
4. e. Both (a) and (b) reflect omission of {PRES}, which occurs more frequently than omission of {POSS} or {PLU}.

Exercise I, page 160

3. I-Movement

Exercise J, page 164

3. men (since it is a direct speech act)

Exercise K, page 168

2. a. something like *Is this the person I was just speaking to?*
   b. By using overly formal forms *(the party)* and constructions *(to whom),* Tomlin characterizes Ernestine as somewhat self-important. Note that the two occurrences of the preposition *to* (one fronted and the other not fronted) suggest that Ernestine doesn't have complete mastery of the formal style "to which she aspires to."

Chapter 8: First-Language Acquisition

Exercise C, pages 183–184

1. c. /t/
7. a. gliding
   f. final consonant deletion

Exercise D, page 188

2. *feets*

Exercise G, page 193

1. b. Intonation

Exercise H, pages 198–199

2. *chair* is a basic-level term
3. a. [+round]

Exercise I, page 207

2. They support Chomsky's views at the expense of Skinner's, since none of these forms could be the result of imitation.
6. e

Chapter 9: Second-Language Acquisition

Exercise A, pages 218–219

1. French, because the front round vowels are marked.
3. c

Exercise B, page 221

1. b. consonant cluster simplification
3. Arabic apparently does not distinguish between tense and lax vowels.

Exercise C, page 223

2. The speaker analyzes *gimme* as a single morpheme meaning 'give,' rather than as a contraction of *give me.*
3. a. *Upbraid* exhibits deceptive transparency; it might be misinterpreted as meaning 'put up in a braid.'

Exercise D, page 226

2. *Regarder* is subcategorized for an NP (not a PP); this restriction is transferred to English.
5. In English, *enter* is subcategorized for an NP (not a PP); this restriction has been transferred to French.

Exercise E, page 228

2. The speaker has confused the converse pair *lent* and *borrowed.*

Chapter 10: Written Language

Exercise B, page 239

4. syllabic (standing for /kyu/)

Exercise C, page 241

4. /k/ as in *call,* /s/ as in *cell,* /č/ as in *cello* (much less frequently)

Exercise F, page 244

2. a. columnist

Exercise G, pages 245–246

1. phonemic
3. d. metathesis
   g. consonant cluster reduction
   r. This does not reflect a general process, but rather a reinterpretation of the segments represented by *x.* Normally, *x* represents /ks/; in this misspelling, *x* represents /k/.

Chapter 11: Language Processing

Exercise D, page 258

1. a. passive, nonreversible
   d. passive, reversible

Exercise E, page 259

1. a. Fill out your application form before you take it to Matthews Hall.

Exercise F, page 260

1. a. The heavy NP is *How she got a perfect score on such a difficult exam.* Revised: *What I'd like to know is how she got a perfect score on such a difficult exam.*

Exercise H, page 262

2. a. Check the cabinets and refrigerator; Make a list; Drive (or walk) to the store; Get a cart; Get groceries from the shelves; Pay for the groceries; Drive (or walk) home; Put the groceries away.

Exercise K, pages 267–268

1. a. AB:AC
5. a. Some fruits contain more oil than others. The amount of oil in a fruit determines the fruit's caloric value. Caloric value correlates with birds' fruit preferences. In other words, caloric value is one way that birds choose the foods they eat.

Chapter 12: Neurology of Language

Exercise C, page 279

2. Broca's aphasia reflects damage near the primary motor cortex, which would also control voluntary movements.

Exercise D, page 282

2. a. False (approximately 98 percent)

Exercise F, page 286

2. a. left
3. right hemisphere

Exercise G, page 287

2. c. True

Exercise I, page 291

2. a. Wernicke's aphasia
   c. semantic aphasia
   f. conduction aphasia

AUTHOR INDEX

SUBJECT INDEX